# LOTMAN AND CULTURAL STUDIES

# Lotman and Cultural Studies

*Encounters and Extensions*

Edited by

ANDREAS SCHÖNLE

THE UNIVERSITY OF WISCONSIN PRESS

The University of Wisconsin Press
1930 Monroe Street
Madison, Wisconsin 53711

www.wisc.edu/wisconsinpress/

3 Henrietta Street
London WC2E 8LU, England

1     3     5     4     2

Library of Congress Cataloging-in-Publication Data
Lotman and cultural studies : encounters and extensions /
edited by Andreas Schönle.
p.     cm.
Includes bibliographical references and index.
ISBN 0-299-22040-0 (cloth: alk. paper)
1. Lotman, IU. M. (IUrii Mikhailovich), 1922-   —Criticism and interpretation.
I. Schönle, Andreas.
P85.L68L67     2006
302.2092—dc22     2006008876

# CONTENTS

# Margins and Selfhood

# ACKNOWLEDGMENTS

This book would not have existed without the stubborn passion of Jeremy Shine, then a graduate student in political science at the University of Michigan, who came to me to propose an interdisciplinary conference on Yuri Lotman. He was planning to use Lotman in his dissertation, he said, and hoped a conference would help resolve some questions of methodology he was struggling with. Imagine what would happen if every graduate student leapt into organizing a conference when he or she hit a conceptual roadblock. The symposium took place at the University of Michigan in 1999 under the title "The Works of Yuri Lotman in an Interdisciplinary Context: Impact and Applicability." I remember distinctly vouching to myself that under no condition would I seek to publish the papers of the conference. So much for my pious intentions. Participants in the symposium, who clearly had enjoyed the whole affair, pushed hard. Chief among them was Amy Mandelker, to whom I am deeply indebted. It was in debates with her that the book project took shape and was first articulated on paper. We solicited several more articles to round out our concept, so much so that the final volume bears only a limited relationship to the original conference.

The support of several friends and colleagues was critical. In particular, David Bethea, Caryl Emerson, and William Mills Todd III offered their unfailing advice and steadfast encouragement. As is often the case, I don't know how best to express my gratitude.

It has been a treat to work with the University of Wisconsin Press. Steve Salemson provided his full backing to the volume and expertly shepherded it through its various stages. We were blessed with two exceptionally thorough reviewers, Boris Gasparov and an anonymous one, whose input greatly strengthened our contributions.

Publication of the volume was supported by the Office of the Vice-President for Research; the College of Literature, Sciences, and the

vii

Arts; the Horace H. Rackham School of Graduate Studies; and the Department of Slavic Languages and Literatures, all at the University of Michigan. These same units had also funded the original symposium.

# A NOTE ON TRANSLITERATION
## AND REFERENCING

Transliteration of names is according to the Library of Congress transliteration system, except for names that have an established spelling in English. In keeping with other publications of Lotman's works in English,
we transliterated his first name as Yuri. We refer to Lotman's translated
works whenever possible. To avoid repeating in each chapter the full reference for the same widely quoted books or articles by Lotman, we cite
only their titles. Full references can be found in the bibliography.

# LOTMAN AND CULTURAL STUDIES

# Introduction

ANDREAS SCHÖNLE and JEREMY SHINE

## I

Yuri Lotman (1922–93) is arguably one of the most prominent and influential Russian scholars of the twentieth century. A cofounder of the Tartu-Moscow school of semiotics, he applied his mind to a wide array of disciplines, from aesthetics to literary and cultural history, narrative theory to intellectual history, cinema to mythology. He advanced highly sustained theories on structural poetics, culture and artificial intelligence, and the relationship between semiotics and neurology; he proposed sweeping typological generalizations, such as his opposition between Russian and Western cultures; and he excavated layer after layer of Russian literary, cultural, and intellectual history. His interests ranged from causal connections in a semiotic series to the role of dolls in the system of culture. He touched on Freud, Charlie Chaplin, and Lenin. His semiotic analyses of Russian culture included studies of dueling, card playing, and the theatricality of polite society. Considered groundbreaking in the context of Soviet disdain for the nobility, his thick description of aristocratic culture devoted appreciable attention to the

3

situation of women and their contributions to culture ("Zhenskii mir,"
"Zhenskoe obrazovanie"). Along with numerous studies of Russian high
literature from the Middle Ages to the twentieth century, he investigated
the semiotics of St. Petersburg, the role of architecture in culture, and
the symbolic construction of space. In a path-breaking interdisciplinary
vein, he was adept at studying the interrelationship among various kinds
of art, be it the impact of theater on painting or of landscape design on
poetry. Perhaps his most influential ideas concerned the interpenetration of the arts and everyday life: his biography of A. S. Pushkin, which
demonstrates how the poet designed his social behavior as a work of art
*(Aleksandr Sergeevich Pushkin)*, and his article on the ways in which the Decembrists plotted their lives according to codes derived from drama
("Decembrist in Daily Life"), along with several other articles, spawned
a series of studies on various instances of theatricality and *zhiznetvorchestvo*
(life creation) by Russian and American scholars of all stripes.[1] This conception took hold not least because it resonated with Russian culture's
perennial valorization of art as an existential project.

Lotman was both a theorist and a historian. His uncanny command
of Russian print culture not only enabled him to introduce substantial
revisions to Russia's historiographic paradigms, transforming the ways
in which his readers thought of Russia's identity, but also stoked one of
his most endearing talents — his knack for adducing unexpected, poorly
known facts of Russian and sometimes world culture in support of a
theoretical position. Indeed, perhaps his greatest asset was the ability to
enliven history with theory and substantiate theory with history, casting
a new light on everything he touched. He was a daring and imaginative
thinker. He did not shy away from speculation and sometimes was
prone to confusing his erudition with a license to conjecture. His skill at
finding patterns and subtexts, honed on the practice of literary analysis,
served him less well when applied to social behavior: some of his last
historiographic ventures (for example, his richly contextual biography of
Nikolai Karamzin) smack of overreading. Yet, to his credit, his theoretical investigation of the role of chance and unpredictability in history and
culture, which he presented in his last theoretical book, *Culture and Explosion (Kul'tura i vzryv)*, tempered this penchant for overdetermination. He
died before he could consider how this new premise would transform his
interpretations of distinct episodes of Russian literature and culture.

In many ways his career offers a palimpsest of his times. After
serving six years in the army, including four in combat during World

War II, Lotman came back a decorated soldier, one of an estimated 5 percent of the enlisted men born in 1922 to survive the war.[2] He enrolled in Leningrad State University to finish his undergraduate studies, but despite his brilliant performance and glowing recommendation from the army, he could not be admitted to graduate school on account of his Jewish background.[3] For the same reason, he experienced difficulties finding a job, until he landed a position as teacher of Russian literature in a two-year pedagogical institute in Tartu, Estonia. The fifteenth Soviet republic, annexed in 1940, needed Russification, and local authorities did not deem Lotman's ethnicity a liability. Becoming a resident of Estonia proved to be a blessing in disguise. Lotman quickly began to teach classes in the Department of Russian Literature at Tartu University. In 1952 he finally managed to defend his dissertation at Leningrad University. By 1954 he was a regular faculty member at Tartu University. While ostensibly marginalized by this displacement from the two capitals, Lotman took advantage of the comparatively more relaxed atmosphere of Estonian intellectual life and progressively built the Department of Russian Literature into a pioneering theoretical and historical powerhouse.

In the 1950s Lotman was engaged in a reconceptualization of late-eighteenth- and early-nineteenth-century intellectual and literary history. Having been inspired by the emergence of structuralism in Moscow, he began publishing on theoretical issues in 1962 and the following year made contacts with Muscovite colleagues.[4] The institution of biannual summer schools on "secondary modeling systems" near Tartu helped establish intellectual and personal links with Muscovite scholars, which enabled the so-called Tartu-Moscow school of semiotics to coalesce.[5] In the 1950s and 1960s Lotman's scholarship was first published in scientific journals at Tartu University, although he was never completely barred from mainstream publication in Moscow or St. Petersburg. Despite small runs and poor distribution, his articles on semiotics attracted the attention of elite intellectual circles in Moscow and St. Petersburg and subsequently abroad. Starting in 1964 translations of his articles began to appear in Western European countries, the United States, and Japan.[6] His reputation steadily grew over the years, and by 1988 he had become a TV star, presenting his study of nobility culture in a series of televised lectures. When he died on October 28, 1993, Estonian president Lennart Meri interrupted his state visit to Germany to deliver an oration after the funeral—the Jewish scholar who had been hired to assist in Russifying the republic had become a pillar of Estonian national pride.[7] Since then Russian academic circles have engaged in a lively and spirited reevaluation of his legacy, one that "culminated" in 1998, when somewhat scabrous anecdotes about Lotman's everyday behavior at Tartu reached the pages of an elitist glossy magazine.[8] The history of the Tartu-Moscow school became a contested site, with various participants making contradictory claims about its emergence and development.[9]

During the 1970s and 1980s, Lotman's works and those of other Soviet semioticians were broadly influential in American and West European academia; next to Mikhail Bakhtin, Lotman was the most widely read and translated theorist of the former Soviet Union.[10] He spoke to an astonishing range of disciplines and authors: philosopher Paul Ricoeur, New Historicist Stephen Greenblatt, semiotician Umberto Eco, reception theorist Wolfgang Iser, feminist critic Julia Kristeva, and Marxist critic Frederic Jameson, to name a few, have productively used Lotman's concepts. Nonetheless, his brand of semiotics never became as prominent in the English-speaking world as did French structuralism, and Lotman received his most intense hearing in Germany and Italy rather than in the United States. There are many reasons for this state of affairs, ranging from the fact that mainstream, book-length translations of his works appeared after the structuralist wave had already swept over the United State to his unique blending of theory with (Russian) history, which rendered access to his scholarship more difficult and less vital to the non-Russianist.[11]

In the 1980s Lotman began to develop a theory of culture based no longer on the distinction between code and utterance but rather on how messages are embedded in a fluid semiotic environment from which they draw their meaning. Yet internationally the reputation of Lotman was wedded to that of structuralist semiotics, and as a result his later works have not yet found the audience they deserve. Most scholars continue to reference primarily his earlier pieces. Out of the 1,919 references to Lotman cited on the *ISI Web of Science Citation Index,* only sixty-six refer to *Universe of the Mind,* the first major summation of his views on culture after his theoretical turn away from structuralism, and only thirty-eight refer to *Culture and Explosion,* his last theoretical work.[12]

*Universe of the Mind* presents a theory of cultural dynamics that results from interactions between nonhomologous languages within a contentious field of discourses aspiring to move from the periphery to

the center. Lotman's notion of the semiosphere, the semiotic environment in which communication occurs and from which it derives its
codes, holds great interdisciplinary appeal. It tends to supersede the binary categories left over from structuralism (and sometimes retained in
deconstruction) and to provide an underlying foundation for the local investigations undertaken by cultural studies. It emphasizes shifting boundaries and hierarchies, permutations between the center and the periphery, mediations and translations, isomorphic relations between events
on the micro and macro levels, and unity through diversity. The organicist metaphor of the semiosphere serves not to essentialize discourse but
to restore to it a sense of unceasing life, of the continuous metabolic exchanges discourses undergo when they are thrown into the world.[13]

One of the attractive and unique dimensions of Lotman's theory is
that it offers a way to conceptualize change and innovation, both on the
individual and the historical scale, but without lapsing into antiquated
humanist or Romantic assumptions. *Culture and Explosion* explores two
different types of change: continuous evolution and abrupt, unpredictable transformation (i.e., explosion) that turns a culture, especially a binary one, upside down. The existence of explosive changes throws an
element of creativity and chance into history, thus calling into question
metanarratives that presume to encapsulate history.

This volume engages and extends the ideas contained in Lotman's last books. It partly draws on a symposium organized by Andreas
Schönle and Jeremy Shine at the University of Michigan on October
29, 1999.[14] The premise of the conference was to bring together scholars
from a variety of disciplines who have used Lotman in their work and
who could reflect on the ways in which Lotman enriches (or sometimes
fails to enrich) their discipline as currently practiced in the United
States. The conference organizers deliberately sought to invite scholars
who had no personal contact with Lotman, be it as colleagues or as students. They focused on the late works of Lotman, which attempt to go
beyond the Saussurean foundations of his earlier semiotics. The implicit
agenda of the conference, ultimately, was to highlight those parts of Lotman's theories slighted in American academia that could contribute to
a "mapping" of the field of poststructuralist cultural studies and its various subbranches.

As it proposes extensions and stages encounters, this volume advances a particular view of the current significance of Lotman's works.
We insert Lotman into a context he was largely unaware of, and as a

result, we mount a particular interpretation of his works. We do so
unabashedly but not unreflectively. The most visible sign of our intervention resides in our language. Most contributors to this volume use a
key concept that Lotman never used, that of *discourse*. Lotman wrote of
codes, messages, texts, and languages, but not of discourse. How does
that matter? In both *Universe of the Mind* and *Culture and Explosion*, Lotman undertakes a critique of Saussurean linguistics. The Saussurean
notion of a code that predates and determines any message that speakers convey to their addressees obscures the historical being of languages,
turning natural languages into artificial codes. Lotman clearly implies
that the concept of code should be discarded: "In fact, substituting the
notion of *code* for that of *language* is much more dangerous than it seems"
(*Kul'tura i vzryv*, 15). Such a substitution implies the primacy of the code
over the message, its inalienability over time, and its identity across a
linguistic community. Yet in fact, Lotman asserts, if our codes overlap,
they are hardly identical, for we constitute them on the basis of our linguistic experience and filter them through our memory (*Universe of the
Mind*, 12–13). Thus, the message—actual communicative exchanges—
has primacy over the code. The semiosphere "has a prior existence and
is in constant interaction with languages," which explains why codes
undergo "constant renewal" (123–24). Lotman goes so far as to admit
that any message can become a code if it is treated as such: "[T]he addressee who receives a verbal text has to decide whether the text is code
or message. This will depend largely on the addressee's inclination since
one and the same text may play the role of text and code, or by oscillat-
ing between these poles, of both at the same time" (30). The Saussurean
distinction between code and message is almost nullified here. These
concepts shed their intrinsic properties, designating instead specific uses
that language is put to. Now, in the wake of Foucault's works, the term
used to designate the ways in which language serves not only to denote
but also to construct reality is *discourse*. The term *discourse* captures the
normative function of language, the ways in which language exercises
power over our modeling of reality. We believe that *discourse* most aptly
renders Lotman's sensitivity to the ambivalent function of language, to
its ability to convey at once referential and normative representations.[15]

　　All contributors in this volume abide by what could be called a con-
structivist understanding of culture. They think of culture as a bundle of
discourses that at once enable and constrict particular kinds of meaning, identity, and behavior, rather than as a way of life informed by

a particular national spirit. Culture includes high culture but is not restricted to it. Nor is culture simply derived from a particular social order, for cultural production determines how a reality is experienced and reproduced, contributing to the very constitution of social reality.[16] This definition is congruent with Lotman's view of culture as a more or less organized set of codes.[17] Thus, when some of our contributors write of political culture, they attend to the ways in which political actors deploy discourse to strengthen and legitimize their claims to power or to reinforce the cohesion of political groups whose interests they articulate. Political culture, in this context, does not mean, say, the intrinsic propensity of a particular nation for democracy.

Yet in some of our case studies in this volume, we deal with discourses that seek to enshrine an essentialist notion of culture and use overriding binary oppositions to do so. As we analyze such configurations, for example, the entanglement of Shi'ite religious culture with Zoroastrian Manichean representations, which Kathryn Babayan describes, we remain alert to the constructedness of such discourse: even though we cannot but speak in the binary terms this culture has adopted for itself, we seek to tease out the rhetorical operations a culture undertook to enforce its dichotomous articulations. The binary nature of some of the cultural productions we investigate explains why despite our interest in the poststructuralist, postbinary Lotman, we still at times employ oppositions that smack of structuralism. Lotman never fully and explicitly renounced his structuralist framework because, we think, he deemed that it can work with regard to some types of culture. Yet an awareness of the rhetorical nature of binary oppositions prompts scholars to displace the emphasis from the content of the opposition — its essentialist claims — to its functioning as an ideological construct that exists in a particular context and pursues particular goals. As Lotman sternly asserts at the end of *Culture and Explosion,* "self-conception is not identical to reality" (*Kul'tura i vzryv*, 146). We claim that Lotman had himself executed such a transition in his late works, and we wish to extend it.[18]

## II

Lotman's concept of power is one of the central themes of this volume. Understandably, the Soviet semiotician could not theorize power explicitly, yet one can recover a particular notion of power from his works as well as fruitfully apply his concepts to an analysis of various kinds of power struggles. Both Michael Urban in "Post-Soviet Political Discourse and the Creation of Political Communities" and Marek Steedman in "State Power, Hegemony, and Memory: Lotman and Gramsci" focus on Lotman's concept of autocommunication, a circular form of communication with oneself through which a message is enhanced by recoding, thus helping to redefine the identity and to raise the status of its sender. Autocommunication captures the ways in which we tell stories to ourselves, using established metanarratives, which become filled with our own data, to develop a pregnant and distinct sense of who we are. Applying this concept to the political sphere, Urban and Steedman analyze the ways political groups disseminate discourses aimed primarily at their own members and reconfigure the ingredients of their own selves, laying down specific boundaries that demarcate "us" from "them." Steedman, for instance, shows how in 1904, Louisiana governor Newton C. Blanchard promoted the doctrine of white supremacy in a series of speeches that foregrounded a narrative of Louisiana's history in which only two actors participated: the "white people," defined as "the intelligent and property-holding classes," and the "negro," that is, the agricultural or industrial laborer, who was in a relationship of subordination to and dependence on the "white." This narrative thus specifically excluded poor whites and African Americans who had made social gains and left the plantations. Through this historical narrative Blanchard redefined the identity of Louisiana. He strove to enshrine a hierarchically inflected binary opposition that collapsed racial and social parameters and blocked off the existence of a kind of social diversity that could complicate his simple notion of Louisiana's identity as a white supremacist state. The rough contours of Blanchard's idea of history would have been familiar to his listeners, yet his restrictive definition of the cast of characters and the ways in which these discursive limitations gestured at an idealized (and distressing) vision of racial and social relations — in other words, his recoding of Louisiana's "self" — transformed its identity and, ultimately, its practices.

Politically autocommunication constitutes a way to recycle old stories while displacing the accents and reconfiguring the self-understanding, cohesion, and resolve of the group from which it emerges and to which it is addressed. Autocommunication contributes significantly to the establishment of political groups. To be effective it relies on fabricated or genuine memories shared by group members. Kathryn Babayan's contribution, "The Ever-Tempting Return to an Iranian Past in the Islamic Present: Does Lotman's Binarism Help?," develops this theme of memory and its uses at various political junctures. In her survey of the history of Iran, she discusses how the memory of binary Zoroastrian identity has endured in the centuries after the implantation of Islam, up to the contemporary period. She shows how political and religious leaders drew on the repository of Manichean cosmic symbols, numerological discourse, and philosophies of time to buttress their hold on the country or to mount resistance to the established rule. In this context of binary opposition between Zoroastrian and Islamic culture, the present is inscribed with meanings derived from the past, while the past is rewritten into the present. This imbrication of old and new leads at times to a near fusion between Zoroastrian and Muslim tenets, while at other times the boundaries between the two types of spirituality are made to harden, leading to clashes. While this binary opposition endures over the course of history and accounts for the conservative course of Iranian history, its meaning at various historical junctures nonetheless changes in response to contemporary problems. In charting the permutations between the two systems of belief, including paradoxical occurrences whereby what was once perceived to be "Iranian" becomes an intrinsic component of Shi'ite identity, Babayan relies on Lotman and Boris Uspenskii's work on cultural typologies and the role of binary oppositions in Russian culture. The underlying binary structure of Iranian culture enables her to explain the surprising endurance of a memory of the Zoroastrian past despite centuries of Islamic influence. But she complicates this framework with references to Lotman's later notion of the heterogeneity of the semiosphere. Indeed, she emphasizes the fluidity of cultural memory, which various groups actualize in various ways, and the layering of meanings that occur when texts preserve the memories of their different past readings. As a result the old is never totally superseded but endures on the margins of the semiosphere, where it continually seeks to reconfigure the new in its own image. Babayan's case study, Iranian identity over the centuries, exemplifies the active role of memory — a contested and multilayered site — in the functioning of autocommunication.

Partisan autocommunication and the "us versus them" dichotomy that underpins it harden and eviscerate political discourse, for they force political actors to produce logical incongruities in their attempt to solidify their party identity. In his analysis of the political process in

Russia in 1998–2000, Urban focuses on rhetorical appeals to concepts such as "democracy," "Western reforms," "the people," and "the Communists," which exemplify a practice of nonreferential signification: discourse is used here not to designate a concrete political reality but to articulate the binary opposition inherent to autocommunication. This system of nonreferential discourse, which political analysis misconstrues by taking these concepts at their face value, exerts a profoundly deleterious effect: it constrains the terms of political debate; fails to provide an idiom for the discussion of actual political practice; creates or invokes group identities that are largely fictive (in the sense that they lack a social reality behind them or that they are insulated from the course of world events and therefore remain stubbornly static) yet define who is to be considered a political actor; and creates rigid boundaries between group "selves," where one could imagine much more fluid membership circulation. Thus binary oppositions, autocommunication, and the nonreferentiality of political discourse reinforce one another, radicalizing political debate and creating conditions that may lead to such dramatic political clashes as the confrontation between two presidents, two constitutions, two political assemblies, and two prosecutorial teams in Russia in October 1993. Urban thus highlights the gap between political discourse and political practice and the pernicious effect of binaries. He is sensitive to the specific function of political discourse, which is not to convey information but to preach to the converted and strengthen their allegiance. But he also demonstrates how this very gap becomes in itself a condition that creates political realities. Thus the concept of autocommunication enables Urban not only to decode political discourse but also to reconnect it with actual practice. Discourse determines practice.

The alternative view, which Steedman instances, devotes attention to the factors that preexist discourse and condition its propagation. Steedman is preoccupied with the articulation between raw and discursive power. He reminds us of Gramsci's analysis of the way authorities legitimize the exercise of force by securing consent through education. In this view discourse has more of a proactive or retroactive secondary function, which is to motivate, in the semiotic sense, the use of violence. Discourse has a rationalizing, rather than a generative, function. Moreover, since it depends on institutions for its propagation, it is largely determined by the social order that it reflects. Hence, for Gramsci group identities are preshaped by social factors rather than being elaborated discursively, as Lotman or Urban would have it.

It needs to be said that Lotman and Gramsci hardly have the same kind of discourse in mind. Gramsci works with a hegemonistic model in which discourse is formulated and articulated by political authorities and addressed to subaltern groups and individuals. Lotman's semiosphere implies a much more fluid and heterogeneous environment, in which the political center's hold on public discourse is hotly contested by groups on the periphery jockeying for preeminence and in which discourse thus moves in various directions at once. Both political realities can exist to various degrees at various times and to a certain degree even simultaneously, and historical variations partly predicate the extent to which discourse affects practice.

To be sure, Lotman was not blind to the interdependence between empirical and discursive power. As Andreas Schönle discusses in "The Self, Its Bubbles, and Its Illusions: Cultivating Autonomy in Greenblatt and Lotman," Lotman has proposed a semiotic theory of social power that recognizes not only the intrinsic generativity of discourse, its propensity to affect rather than reflect social conditions, but also the ways in which the political center, that is, the hegemonic state, seeks to co-opt the emergence of competing discourses on the periphery by spreading a homogenizing metadiscourse, such as a state ideology. Lotman's idea could be extended in the direction of Gramsci's notion of consent. Indeed, this metadiscourse could be construed not only to define the identity of the state and legitimize its use of violence but also to enlist the citizen's tacit acceptance of it by preventing the rise of alternative models. The center thus foists a metanarrative on the citizenry that functions as autocommunication and asserts an identity common to the state and its constituent individuals, in turn creating a kind of unity and coherence that is then enacted in political practice. At the same time, it wards off dissent by imposing a set of discursive constraints and by disciplining its violators. In short, the center creates a system that both enables and legitimizes its actions, violent or not.

Yet what interested Lotman most were those cases when the state acts deliberately outside the parameters of its own system, that is, when its practices seem to flout its very own explanatory paradigms. In the 1960s and 1970s the exploration of this state of affairs took the form of two influential articles on Pushkin that discuss the relationship between law and mercy. In the late 1980s and early 1990s, when the pressure of censorship abated, Lotman turned to a discussion of Ivan the Terrible's behavior in the second half of his reign, when he began to spread terror by acting without apparent logic or purpose. Whether mercy or terror, in both cases one deals with a suspension, on the ruler's part, of his or her normal course of action as prefigured in the metadiscourse elaborated by the center and often inscribed in laws. Whether Lotman's attribution of Aesopian virtues to this discussion was really meant as a comment on the relationship between official ideology and actual practice in the Soviet Union is fortunately no longer relevant. What matters is Lotman's focus on the semiotic opposition between system and event or, in his later conceptual framework, between system and explosion. What interested him were the moments when power infringes on the limitations established by its own discourse, thus risking the appearance of arbitrariness.

The relationship between an individual and a figure of authority, whether political or religious, and the ways in which cultural typologies prefigure the nature of this relationship represent a second prominent theme in this collection. In "Pushkin's 'Andzhelo,' Lotman's Insight into It, and the Proper Measure of Politics and Grace," Caryl Emerson focuses on Lotman's reading of Pushkin's "Andzhelo," a verse adaptation of Shakespeare's *Measure for Measure*. This 1973 article reflects the heyday of Lotman's structuralist semiotics, a decade or so before his move toward a poststructural framework. In it Lotman identifies three layers of meaning, which neatly overlap. As a result the theme of unmerited mercy is absorbed into a mythological metanarrative, in which an unjust ruler "dies," only to return to earth seeking reconciliation with his subjects by dispensing pardons. Emerson undertakes a thought experiment that consists of imagining how Lotman's reading of the narrative poem would have changed had it rested on his later poststructuralist premises. According to Emerson, in a poststructuralist Lotmanian reading, the three layers would jostle rather than dovetail, generating what Lotman calls an explosion, a moment in which the intersection between unhomologous systems tears the fabric of meaning and generates unpredictable change and innovation. In the context of "Andzhelo," the respective logics of divine law, secular power, and worldly desire would thus collide. Or for the characters of this narrative, two models of the relation between individual and power would clash: in the first model—the contractual paradigm—individual and ruler (or god) are engaged in a system of reciprocal and compulsory relations, so that each party can expect to receive a proportionate reward for fulfilling its obligations; and in the second model—the paradigm of self-giving—the subject turns himself or herself over totally and unconditionally to the ruler, expecting nothing in return, while the ruler may similarly dispense unmotivated acts of mercy. A new model of relationship must emerge out of this confrontation, and Emerson explores how the poem interpolates a new concept beyond justice and mercy (i.e., system and explosion), namely, charity. Charity offers an alternative to relations based on contract or self-giving, for it stems neither from parity, nor from inconsistency, but from dialogue, from an openness to the changing needs of the other and from a willingness to be changed by this recognition of the other. Thus the characters' conflict is now mediated thanks to the possibility of intercession and repentance that grows out of the transformative force of dialogue and charity, thereby preparing the ground for a form of mercy that is no longer unmotivated or unjust.

In "Lotman's Other: Estrangement and Ethics in *Culture and Explosion*," Amy Mandelker reaches similar conclusions about the potentials inscribed in Lotman's late works, albeit from a different perspective. Her reading of *Culture and Explosion* centers on what she calls the metaphysics of estrangement, an ethical stance that requires one to adopt a double vision, contemplating the world simultaneously from an intrinsic and an extrinsic perspective, thus actualizing in oneself the potential for explosion. Her essay focuses on Lotman's cultural typology. Indeed, she returns to Lotman's assertion that self-giving is a mode of relationship inherent in a binary culture such as Russia's, while contract is a paradigm characteristic of Western ternary cultures. She detects not only historical inaccuracies in this conception but also signs of a Russian chauvinistic disparagement of Western negotiated modes of exchange, especially in relations with God, which Russian culture, and Lotman in its wake, demonizes. At the same time, she notes Lotman's critique of binary cultures: binary cultures fail to generate innovation, trapped as they are in a dialectic where change can only appear as an eschatological reversal of the old.

Not all contributors to this volume share Mandelker's charge of chauvinism. In "Dante, Florenskii, Lotman: Journeying Then and Now through Medieval Space," an interpretation of Lotman's reading of Dante, David Bethea traces Lotman's polemic with Russian Orthodox philosopher and mathematician Pavel Florenskii. Where Florenskii asks readers to collapse antinomial structures and to adopt concurrently two antithetical points of view, Lotman emphasizes transitional positions on a sliding scale, rather than the telescoping of a dichotomy.[19] Both

Florenskii and Lotman seek to make sense of Dante's depiction of the descent into the earth's center as an ascent toward God on the absolute axis of perfection. Florenskii posits a non-Euclidean geometry and dramatizes a moment of crossover in which descent becomes paradoxically ascent yet still leads the travelers back to their initial point of departure. This crossover then becomes a geometric metaphor for salvation, that is, for the moment of self-giving, and for the telescoping of differences that underpins Florenskii's daring assimilations between dissimilar things and his repudiation of narrative as a form of cognition. In contrast to Florenskii's geometrical mysticism, Lotman uses Dante to explicate his notion of an axiological middle space in which a progressive transition from one state to another takes place. Thus Lotman seeks to resolve semiotically the paradox of Dante's journey by positing that the opposition between conventional sign (the language of the sinful, who manipulate signs to their advantage) and holy motivated symbol (absolute language) becomes a spectrum along which the travelers advance and from which they learn, recognizing better and better the divine light that shines dimly through conventional signs. Salvation thus is a process rather than an event—a position consistent with Emerson's conclusions about the transformations of self that emerge from a commitment to dialogue. The Lotman that emerges from Bethea's article is a staunch opponent of Orthodox mysticism and eschatologism, an Enlightenment scholar who proceeds from a Western embrace of middle space, neutral or transitional axiology, and process.

Be that as it may, Mandelker proceeds to develop a third paradigm besides contract and self-giving, one that she sees inscribed in twentieth-century Jewish philosophy, which directly or indirectly may have influenced Lotman. She calls this model the covenant, a relationship with another or with God that one enters into freely but that then commits one over time, leading to a blending of one into the other, that is, to the pursuit of a unity that subsumes individual distinctiveness. Allegorized as marriage, this relationship promotes a nonsacrificial mode of commitment to the other. It gestures toward a new relation between individual and power: instead of a one-to-one interface, it establishes a symmetry or interplay between human-to-human and human-to-divine relations, thus making one a metaphor or medium for the other. Emerson, Bethea, and Mandelker agree that Lotman actively thought of ways to overcome binary oppositions, and all three seek to extend this process by thinking through the unrealized potentials of his latest works.

Several contributors to this volume are concerned with mapping the relationship between an individual and the social sphere. In "Post-ing the Soviet Body as Tabula Phrasa and Spectacle," Helena Goscilo reads Lotman's discourse on the body as a sign that betrays the degree to which an individual is embedded in a public code. She praises Lotman for recognizing the complex interplay of nature and culture in the signifying potential of the body, the ways in which the body can both denote and defy its social construction. She underscores the pertinence of the body in Lotman's semiotic analysis of nobility culture in the early nineteenth century and draws parallels between this period and the Stalinist and post-Soviet periods that concern her. The body is a unique medium for self-fashioning for it presupposes what she calls the exteriority or visibility of meaning. One could invoke here Lotman's concept of iconism, the quality of a sign that denotes its meaning in a nondiscrete, nonconventional fashion. An iconic sign precludes the dismemberment of meaning into constituent syntagms, or sentences, and instead conveys a kind of unitary signification that lends itself to symbolic extension. The body is a privileged iconic sign, and Goscilo shows how Stalinism wielded it to naturalize state ideology. Thus against the background of generalized bodily uniformity and the erasure of individual distinguishing marks, the body of Stalin was foregrounded as a mythologized sublime entity that bespoke the invincibility of the regime and the cosubstantiality of leader and people. Stalin's real body—stocky and pockmarked—became detached from its representation, and even then the featured body signified no longer Stalin's personality but the greatness of the regime. Thus the iconic sign becomes a kind of simulacrum, a signifier untethered from its signified (as Jean Baudrillard defines it) and available for strategic manipulation.

In "Bipolar Asymmetry, Indeterminacy, and Creativity in Cinema," Herbert Eagle draws attention to the importance of the concept of iconism in Lotman's works. For Lotman art derives its richness from the fact that it telescopes conventional and iconic modes of signification. In fact, Eagle shows the ways in which this asymmetry between two different semiotic systems, which Lotman first developed in reference to poetry and cinema, became the key notion in his idea of culture during his later period. Analyzing, among other things, Andrzej Wajda's *Ashes and Diamonds,* Eagle demonstrates how an iconic code is superimposed on the narrative sequence of the movie and undercuts its ostensible meaning as a glowing depiction of the Communist Poles allied with the Red

Army. Although the movie superficially adheres to socialist realist aesthetics, a web of iconic images interjects a Christian theme about Poland's martyrdom and its longing for redemption, which unhinges the movie's invocation of the binary opposition between Communist and anti-Communist Poles. The interaction between the two asymmetric codes, which allows for two mutually exclusive interpretations, remains ultimately unresolved. Through its doubleness the movie not only confounds ideological readings but eludes the grasp of the censor, who overlooked its iconic layer. Thus this movie provides a case study of how art positions itself with regard to power: instead of mounting a frontal assault, it offers an idiosyncratic language that drives a dent into the official, dominant code. Eagle firmly aligns iconic language with the periphery of the semiosphere. Indeed, the unexplicitness of iconic signs enables their circulation even in an environment of tight controls and stimulates the creativity of receivers, who must translate the semiotic potential of iconic signs into their own codes. As Goscilo demonstrates in her discussion of Stalin's body, however, iconic signs may also be appropriated by the state in its elaboration of a visual language that embodies its ideology.

In the post-Soviet period the body became a medium for individual self-presentation, for attempts to demarcate oneself from collective anonymity. The body would seem to be an ideal site for the inscription and expression of a sense of individuality: its iconic potential, its connection with nature, and its genuine physical uniqueness are all conducive to suggesting a sense of intrinsicality. Yet Goscilo shows that this aspiration to behavioral distinctiveness quickly lapsed into a new kind of conformity: the imitation of Western modes of deportment and the commodification of the body created an illusion of diversity and freedom that led to a loss of semiotic value, that is, to a decorativeness and ultimately to a new blending in the social fabric. Here Goscilo employs Lotman's concept of theatricality, of which she pursues the ultimate implications. The ubiquitous theatricality of the early post-Soviet years ultimately denotes nothing but itself, that is, it no longer serves the project of affirming a particular identity but rather emphasizes the emptiness of the self and its protean adaptability, in short, a loss of intrinsic selfhood. Goscilo's essay fittingly ends with a return to a collective body, but one that no longer bears a particular state ideology and instead bespeaks a vacuous identity, an indecisiveness born of excessive mimicry. Putin's public image as a trim, nimble man of action (the judo player) whose politics seem so inconsistent that they elude classification incarnates this new bodily identity.

By way of extending Lotman's cultural history of nineteenth-century Russian culture, especially his preoccupation with the interplay between social behavior and art, Julie Buckler analyzes a paradigm of the relationship between individual and society in her "Eccentricity and Cultural Semiotics in Imperial Russia." An eccentric is someone who seeks to dodge social determination by adopting an unpredictable, whimsical mode of behavior, one that affirms the aesthetic component of public conduct. Unlike theatricality, which rests on a comprehensible norm, eccentricity resists deciphering. It defies social codes by affirming its opacity to reading. In a word, it strives to behave in a way that does not make sense. Yet to achieve his goals, the eccentric is doomed to combine elements of social reality in an anomalous, haphazard fashion, producing the equivalent of what one could call unreflected eclecticism in the arts and exemplifying the inchoate nature of communication on the periphery. Thus, in a paradoxical way eccentricity comes to embody the social sphere it seeks to elude, to the point that it becomes a frequent trope for Russia's identity in the nineteenth century. In keeping with Lotman's spatial modeling of semiotic relations—his notion of trajectories, boundaries, and peripheries—Buckler introduces the concept of orbit to encapsulate the paradoxical movement of eccentricity, a departure from the center that winds back circling around it, thus remaining trapped in a continuous relation to it.

Buckler's essay illustrates both the pervasiveness of eccentric behavior in particular social environments and the ultimate fruitlessness of a stance that seeks to affirm meaninglessness. In contrast, in "Writing in a Polluted Semiosphere: Everyday Life in Lotman, Foucault, and de Certeau," Jonathan Bolton explores the creative dimensions of a different relationship to the center, a mode that Lotman calls translation. The site in which individuals undertake translations and recodings of social discourses is everyday life. Bolton analyzes Lotman's implicit concept of everyday life as a boundary zone where we elaborate a sphere of practical functions and semiotic codes we deem our own. Everyday life stands in a conflicting relationship to dominant codes, which we incorporate by way of translation, that is, by recoding them in light of our own semiotic systems. Lotman's vision of everyday life differs from Foucault's, which posits the center's ability to extend its signifying grids over all aspects of life and dismisses the potential for creative accommodation on the part of individuals. Lotman's notion of the everyday differs also from de Certeau's, whereby individuals mount tactical assaults against dominant codes without, however, embedding their response in any signifying coherence and without leaving any traces, a stealthy mode of behavior that echoes Buckler's eccentricity in its foregrounding of a disjoined, amorphous self. Lotman's concept of translation captures the transformations that social codes undergo when they abut against the messy sphere of practical functions and the creative impact individuals exert in superimposing their individual codes on the dominant system. Individuals are constantly experimenting with new models of behavior, which they do not entirely own but which sustain an illusion of selfhood because they feel more or less inherent. Individuals, therefore, thrive on a gray zone, on a sphere of gradations, rather than on a binary opposition between dominant code and private life. Bolton's case study, Czech writer Jan Zábrana's difficult attempts to negotiate an everyday life that lapses into neither collaboration nor dissidence, illustrates both the potential for circulation between public and individual codes and its restrictions (or pollution).

Of the four strategies of resistance to the influence of social codes that this volume discusses—bodily iconism, theatricality, eccentricity, and translation—only the last, and potentially the first, are conducive to sustaining a sense of selfhood. Theatricality and eccentricity are shown not only to succumb to social determination but also to jeopardize the relative unity and coherence of the self. And even translation points to the limits placed on an individual's self-fashioning, however promising its apparent potential. What, then, is Lotman's implied discourse about the self? Schönle discusses Lotman's semiotic model of the self, which posits an ontological similarity between self and society (both are systems of codes) and ascribes individuation strictly to a process of drawing boundaries that define the purview of what is "own." But boundaries need to be negotiated by both parties, and instead of analyzing the implications of this state of affairs, Lotman makes selfhood a function of the adopted perspective: I may invest my sense of individuality in a particular norm I call my own, even though from a broader social perspective that very norm may appear as a mass phenomenon. In other words, selfhood is the illusion of intrinsicality, a position reminiscent of Stephen Greenblatt's emphasis on the importance of cultivating the illusion of autonomous agency. Alongside this semiotic view of the self, Lotman also advances a moral one, which emerges in reference to Kant's definition of enlightenment and consists of adopting a stoic stance of disengagement from the public sphere. This view, which Schönle allegorizes as the underground, relegates autonomy to the private sphere and fosters ruthless self-examination, that is, it punctures the illusions of selfhood underpinning one's social involvement.

In "Lotman's Karamzin and the Late Soviet Liberal Intelligentsia," an analysis of Lotman's contribution to the elaboration of a political stance for the liberal intelligentsia, Andrei Zorin evokes similar themes. Lotman is a representative of the older generation of the liberal intelligentsia, one that abided by a faith in scientific progress and a teleological concept of history. For this generation the Brezhnev period of stagnation created profound disillusionment and prompted a retreat into the half-private realm of "scientific" research. Renouncing participation in political life, whether as reformer or dissident, became a trope for stoic fidelity to core moral values. At the same time, this generation also gave credence to a longstanding stereotype of Russian political culture, the myth of a one-to-one conversation with the ruler, in which a private individual can articulate his views and attempt to sway the leader. Lotman inscribed this ideal into his reading of N. M. Karamzin's career. According to Lotman the early nineteenth-century writer and historiographer (officially appointed as such by the tsar) had renounced public activity, retreated into a tightly orchestrated and modest private sphere, and devoted his life to a pursuit of historical truth, while presenting his views in unvarnished words to Alexander I. For Lotman, Karamzin implicitly serves as a model of moral integrity and commitment to truth under adverse political circumstances, a model that accounts for Karamzin's surge in popularity during the waning years of the Soviet empire. Yet Lotman projected this ideal on Karamzin's figure despite well-known facts indicating Karamzin's participation in public intrigues, so strong was Lotman's drive to inscribe his own moral stance into his scholarship.

The underlying presence of moral reasoning in Lotman's works is one of the surprising findings of this collection. Both Mandelker and Schönle invoke the underground as a primary site of moral identification, a place on the periphery from which the scholar hones his discourse in relative autonomy. This presumption of withdrawal from social involvement is conducive to reflexiveness, to a "laying bare" of the illusions of selfhood that sustain our enactment of social roles. Yet one should not absolutize this stance, for Lotman hardly fetishizes the Cartesian notion of disengaged reason.[20] Indeed, if for him selfhood necessitates the drawing of a boundary, closing the trap that leads into the underground, that boundary is more illusory than essential, since, as we have seen, the individual self functions in ways identical to the social sphere and is similarly dependent on the circulation of languages. Boundaries, as Lotman insists, are always porous (*Universe of the Mind*, 136–37). Hence, one could say the ultimate illusion, the one that reflexiveness nurtures, is the existence of a punctual self capable of disengagement from itself, which we can uncover by peeling away layers of illusions.[21] Thus reflexiveness and illusion stand in a complementary, rather than contradictory, relationship. On the moral plane this state of affairs invites the recognition that the proper attitude would involve maintaining two perspectives at once so as to estrange oneself, as Mandelker demonstrates; cultivating the transformative moment that results from the interlacing of dominant and personal discourses in everyday life, which Bolton evokes; or ultimately embracing dialogue with the other, openness to change, and predisposition toward charity, as Emerson discusses.

## III

Lotman addresses many concerns that have also preoccupied cultural studies, conceived both narrowly and broadly. Cultural studies emerged partly in response to a single-minded focus on high literature in English departments, and it rests on a definition of culture as the totality of cultural production, including mass culture in all its variety. Cultural studies has an integrative ambition: it seeks to articulate the mutual determinations and interrelations among the various facets of life—political, economic, social, erotic, and ideological—that make up culture as a whole.[22] To do so, it not only analyzes an extravagant variety of texts, from fashion and advertising to rock music and graffiti, but also approaches cultural production with an interdisciplinary, contextualizing method. As this volume illustrates, Lotman shares such an extensive purview, albeit in a different cultural and historical context: his work on dueling culture, on the semiotics of dress, on aristocratic banquet and food culture, and so on testify to a principled broadening of the traditional notion of culture.[23] Admittedly, he limits himself primarily to the study of nobility culture. Yet he addresses the relationship between high and mass culture theoretically ("O soderzhanii i strukture," 209–15), and he exhibits profound interest in folk and traditional culture—he values the specific act of reception presupposed by premodern texts and the creative recoding they invite ("Kanonicheskoe iskusstvo").[24]

Cultural studies resists grand theories and metadiscourses that purport to explain everything across historical boundaries. It is contextually specific and strives to be descriptive, although at times it borrows generously from the theories of various contiguous disciplines such as psychoanalysis, sociology, or literary theory.[25] Lotman's work ranges from the highly specific to the typological and has alternated between theoretical and historically contextual periods, but even his broad cultural typologies serve to undercut the applicability of such master narratives as Marxism. In his latest pieces Lotman repeatedly maintains that crucial binary oppositions need to be approached historically rather than a priori and, as several contributors to this volume discuss, that there is much to gain from focusing on the gradation between opposites rather than on a mere logical dichotomy.

The second defining trait of cultural studies is its concern with power. As Tony Bennett observes, cultural studies is "a term of convenience for a fairly dispersed array of theoretical and political positions, which . . . share a commitment to examining cultural practices from the point of view of their intrication with, and within, relations of power."[26] Although Lotman is perhaps not as single-minded in his analysis of the nexus between cultural production and power, this volume discusses his conceptualization of the semiotic expression of power. His analysis of the relations between center and periphery echoes the infatuation with the margins of culture in cultural studies. Lotman is acutely aware that ownership of information confers power, and he discusses the ways in which groups fight for monopoly over information and develop special languages to keep other groups at bay (*Stat'i po tipologii kul'tury*, 395). Even more pointedly he underscores the intrinsic power (or energy) of signs, their ability to effect changes in their surroundings, so that the deployment of a particular discourse is in itself a form of power ("Liudi i znaki," 9).

Two competing paradigms of culture underpin the project of cultural studies: a humanist "culturalist" concept of culture as a way of life that can be described empirically and a "(post) structuralist" perspective that posits a web of discourses that determine identity and meaning and that must be analyzed semiotically or rhetorically. The former view focuses on the experience of subjects who generate their own meanings and adapt social institutions to their own needs. The latter view conceives of the autonomous human subject as an ideological notion peddled by discourse to obfuscate the real identity of the subject as an effect of text.[27] This debate, fundamental to cultural studies, has played itself out in various forms, affecting the ways one conceives of hegemony, identity, and resistance. In the United States cultural studies has tilted heavily toward a "(post) structuralist," that is, textualist approach, which has diminished its attractiveness to the social sciences. Yet communication studies has urged that cultural studies be reoriented toward a critique of American positivism, of the grip of science on social policy, and of the idea of freedom as "our capacity to choose our ends for ourselves" (a kind of individualism that ultimately destroys the public sphere). Such critique would emphasize not the role of texts in determining identity but that of rituals and institutions in constructing forms of social relations and groupings based on a common search for identity, thereby funneling particular "ends" into a "taste, style and form of life" consistent with the development of citizenship.[28]

Lotman's definition of culture as a "bundle" of semiotic systems that may but need not be organized hierarchically (*Stat'i po tipologii kul'tury*, 397) shares the (post) structuralist premise of the primary role of discourse in founding reality. For example, Lotman considers participants in communicative exchanges full-fledged subjects only when they accept a set of restrictions imposed on them by culture ("Kul'tura kak kollektivnyi intellekt," 562). Yet at the same time, Lotman's emphasis on the natural striving of culture toward diversity (564), indeed, on the obligatory presence of diversity for a semiotic environment to function properly, mitigates the subject's dependence on discourse.[29] Thus subjects act on their impulse to autonomy by playing discourses against one another, recoding them in an act of autocommunication that generates novelty in the process. Therefore, Lotman grants individuals the capacity to intervene in semiotic systems and thereby affect their cultural environment. In a way this conception bridges the two paradigms intrinsic to cultural studies. It maintains the discursive nature of reality but empowers the subject to manipulate codes and wrest some measure of autonomy.

The approaches of cultural studies to power have depended on their primary allegiance to either the "culturalist" or the "(post) structuralist" paradigms. Early approaches tended to glamorize resistance to the hegemonic political center mounted by various social subcultures. The main framework here was the interface between a single political center and oppressed social classes that secured autonomy by elaborating their own countercultures. Following the influx of French sociological and poststructuralist thought, cultural studies ceased to vest the political center with power and instead affirmed its decentered nature as a system or grid cast over the entirety of social life and embodied in sociological organization or, even more abstractly, in the discursive underpinnings of reality. Power became so diffuse and surreptitious that the valorization of counterhegemony collapsed. The interface between state and counterculture yielded to a much more splintered view of communities organized around a shared identity based on sexuality, gender, or ethnicity. These groups were perceived as striving to develop their own values and ethics and interact with one another on the basis of a multiculturalist respect for the "other." This embrace of alterity accommodated the valorization of difference, but its tendency to reify identity prevented meaningful exchange across communities and often impeded the pursuit of a common political agenda.[30]

Even though it denies a grand narrative, cultural studies emphasizes class, gender, and race differences and cannot help but operate with binary oppositions, despite its stated goal of undercutting dichotomies. Lotman's concept of the semiosphere emphasizes the ad hoc foundation of group identities, their emergence out of an intrinsic recoding of extrinsic codes, and the circulation of texts and values among groups. Lotman does not privilege group identity and therefore offers a flexible framework applicable to a broader range of groups. In this sense he not only offers an alternative to Gramsci's notion of the rootedness of groups in class realities (which underlies early cultural studies) but also provides an answer to the dilemma between unity and decenteredness in the ways one conceives of the field of culture. For Lotman culture is essentially both, for it evidences both centrifugal and centripetal forces, which play themselves out on various, coexisting layers.[31] Boundaries that cultural agents erect should not lead to a fetishization of what is one's own *(svoi)* and what is alien *(chuzhoi)*. Lotman also conceives of identity and alterity, that is, of multiculturalism, as a sphere of engagement rather than of awed respect. His notion of dialogue is one that leads to change and hence to cultural flux, rather than to social fragmentation.

Autocommunication, as Lotman describes it, resembles what cultural studies calls hybridization, the process by which individuals or communities appropriate external cultural products by investing them with their own functions and meanings.[32] At the same time, there are

differences of emphasis in the two concepts. In an essay on popular culture, John Fiske theorizes the concept of distance—distance between an
individual and the cultural production he consumes—as a key marker
of difference between high and low culture.[33] High culture promotes de-
contextualized, depoliticized readings of cultural objects because it constructs culture as a sphere of disinterested beauty insulated from social
processes. Popular culture, in contrast, is "concretely contextual."[34] It
makes cultural objects its own by embedding them in concrete uses, in
its practices of living, identifying with them or deriving sensual pleasure
from them without any consideration of appropriate "distance." In
short, cultural objects are transposed from the realm of discourse into
the sphere of practice. To support his view of the use of culture in everyday life, Fiske quotes ethnographers who write of a "sacred inarticulate-
ness" on the part of respondents who are unable to explain discursively
the meaning they invest in particular objects or practices. Thus the
meanings that result from hybridization remain opaque to the outside
observer, who needs to develop to the greatest extent possible an ability
to experience other people's ways of living from the inside.[35] As Bolton
reminds us in this volume, this conceptualization of counterhegemony
as a nonverbal sphere of practice would be alien to Lotman, who conceives of autocommunication and translation as discursive phenomena
and who would endow resisting subjects with much more semiotic creativity than is implicit in such a theory of the everyday.[36]

Autocommunication also offers an alternative to the ways in which
cultural studies sought to incorporate Marxist ideas. The relationship
between cultural studies and Marxism is too rich and complex to lend
itself to a quick overview.[37] Yet Stuart Hall's 1983 essay "The Problem
of Ideology: Marxism without Guarantees"—one of his latest statements on the topic of Marxism—speaks to the core of the issue. In a
close reading of specific passages from Marx, Hall calls into question the
traditional understanding of some of Marx's most seminal concepts.
Thus ideology is no longer a "distortion" of social reality but a partial
view thereof; the link between economic relations and their ideological
representations can no longer be fixed, for language is multireferential
(here Hall quotes Voloshinov); the idea of class determination is refined;
and the direct correspondence between "ruling ideas" and "ruling
classes" is replaced with the notion of "tendential alignment."[38] Hall
seeks to relax the rigid links Marx establishes between ideas and economic relations, but without lapsing into a poststructuralist notion of

ideology as a free-floating representation divorced from underlying economic and social realities.[39] He therefore discusses not so much the structural determination of ideas by the socioeconomic base as the internalization of ideas, the reasons for which certain ideas catch on while others are consigned to the dustbin of history. And here Hall invokes Gramsci to suggest that "ideas only become effective if they do, in the end, *connect* with a particular constellation of social forces," that is, if their "coupling" with the ruling classes is secured.[40] Although the nature of this connection is not entirely clear, it seems safe to assume that for Hall ideologies are successful, that is, become dominant, when they represent the ruling class's view of social relations. Underpinning his discussion is the assumption that ideology has referential value, albeit, perhaps, a contested, plural, or ambiguous one.[41]

In his treatment of autocommunication, Lotman shows that when a subject internalizes an extrinsic discourse, the process of recoding weakens, if not entirely suspends, the referential force of language, as Urban discusses in his application of autocommunication to political realities in contemporary Russia. As a result ideology's relation to social reality need not be as pertinent or direct as Hall presupposes, and it may therefore serve a more disparate set of groups, not solely social classes. Ideologies become successful, that is, they articulate the identity of a group, because they connect with and reinforce a group's metadiscourses, its discursive memory, although they may come from outside. Ideology, then, has neither a partial, nor distorted, but rather an imagined relation to social reality, one that reflects a group's field of discourses more than its social experience.

The third defining trait of cultural studies is its stance of political engagement. Practitioners of cultural studies believe that their discourse matters or should matter, and they continuously reflect on their own institutional location, on the ways their discourse is embedded in institutional reality and contributes to the empowerment of disenfranchised minorities.[42] Obviously Lotman could not agitate for his values as explicitly as cultural studies does. Yet, as this collection argues, his work rests on an ethical imperative of moral resistance to the Soviet regime despite outward tactical accommodation with it. More specifically it promotes casting a double perspective on an object (intrinsic and extrinsic) and openness to the estrangement and transformation of the self that ensue. Thus reflexiveness and imaginary identification with the object of study occur concurrently.

Fundamentally Lotman shares the faith cultural studies has placed in the possibility of affecting its environment through its discursive practice. But the lack of militant rhetoric in Lotman stems not only from tactical prudence but also from a more principled position as to the function of semiotic metadiscourse and, more broadly, from a faith in the emancipating potential of language. Indeed, the starkest difference between cultural studies and Lotman lies precisely in their respective conceptualization of the relationship between language and power. Cultural studies believes that language participates, wittingly or not, in power imbalances and thus contributes to social oppression, unless the speaker actively calls into question his or her position in a social or cultural field. As a result cultural studies continuously strives to expose the nexus between power and language, illuminating this collusion even when language seems not to bear on issues of power. Thus cultural studies has developed a "hermeneutics of suspicion" that is embodied in its rhetoric. In contrast, as Emerson discusses in this volume, Lotman believes that language and art in particular add a level of reality to the existing world and thus free us from our entanglement in it. The same can be said of the semiotic metadiscourse, which provides a vantage point that enables us to exert some leverage on the reality in which we feel trapped. Accordingly, the goal of a semiotician, especially one working under totalitarian conditions and the homogenizing pull of the regime, is to expand the ranges of available discourses to empower people to develop more differentiated identities, to enhance their "polyglotism" (*Stat'i po tipologii kul'tury*, 397). Lotman's "hermeneutics of recovery of meaning" derives therefore from a commitment to linguistic diversity that requires no militant rhetoric.[43] The past is a storehouse of discourses that in themselves can serve a liberating function when reinserted in the present. Likewise, the abstract discourse of the semiotician can help wrest us from reality. This conceptual difference between Lotman and cultural studies explains the most obvious disparity between the two: cultural studies seems wedded to the synchronic analysis of contemporary society (partly, to be sure, because of its desire for its discourse to matter politically), but Lotman is committed to the restoration of the past and increasingly interested in historical change, both conceptually and contextually.

And it is here that Lotman opens up a perspective that cultural studies seems overly quick to obstruct. Like an obedient Hamlet heeding the injunction of his father's ghost ("Remember me"), Lotman commits himself to remembrance rather than vengeance or, to adopt Stephen Greenblatt's terms, to "corrosive inwardness."[44] Faced with the choice between practice and discourse, Lotman clearly chooses the latter, the cult of the dead, whose voices he lets return to life. His responsiveness to the generative powers of literary imagination makes him indifferent to the "hermeneutics of suspicion," for he wants to heed the generative powers of literary imagination. In this regard he espouses a position that cultural studies may well rejoin, once it explores the process of self-reflexive suspicion. Problematic as it may be to turn Greenblatt into a figurehead of cultural studies, the recent qualms he voices in *Hamlet in Purgatory* about a profession "so oddly diffident and even phobic about literary power" and his self-conscious exercise in "a cult of the dead that [he] and the readers of [his] book have been serving" may herald a new willingness to take seriously literary ghosts from the past.[45]

Doing so unquestionably made sense for Lotman. After all, he had to contend with a regime that was so fanatically committed to a Communist version of the Enlightenment paradigm of progress that it actively destroyed traces of other models of being. Lotman, in contrast, fought to contain the self-negating dynamics of binary cultures. There is a good reason that he made purgatory the linchpin of his paradigm of Western culture, despite its marginality in much of the West, particularly in Protestant rituals and even in many parts of post–Vatican II Catholic practice. For Lotman purgatory is a trope for a place where voices that have ostensibly died continue to live and to resonate, withholding their final word; above all it constitutes a discursive locus that Lotman wants to engage to redeem the power intrinsic in these voices.

That form of engagement, of course, is not ritualistic in the strong sense of the word. Lotman's efforts at discursive continuity resemble Shakespeare's recourse to purgatory. According to Greenblatt, the ghost visiting Hamlet has a theatrical, rather than theological, reality. Its call for vengeance hardly fits Catholic doctrine, and yet its presence calls forth the emotions that purgatory evokes in its believers. As a theatrical being the ghost draws its power precisely from the fact that it collapses competing discourses, that it elicits seemingly incompatible responses to the unspeakable experience of death. This theatrical exploitation of profound existential anxiety may seem to imply a secularization of the cult of the dead, but the relationship between theater and ritual also works the other way round, accentuating "a sense of the weirdness of the theater, its proximity to certain experiences that [have] been organized and exploited by religious institutions and rituals."[46] Purgatory, to put it in Lotman's terms, is a place where incompatible discourses abut; where clashes or explosions can be staged. It is a site of creative experimentation, a space that forces us to confront our cultural baggage, the memory of our past, and that therefore invokes all our longings and fears. As Shakespeare secularizes purgatory and ritualizes the stage, Lotman simultaneously estranges and redeems discourses in a double vision that is "magnificently . . . cannibalistic"—a corrosive inwardness, indeed.[47]

## Notes

We would like to express our gratitude to Helena Goscilo for her generous and invaluable feedback on matters of substance and style and to Ewa Wampuszyc for her expert and patient editorial work.

1. William Mills Todd III, *Fiction and Society in the Age of Pushkin* (Cambridge, Mass.: Harvard University Press, 1986); Irina Paperno, *Chernyshevskii and the Age of Realism: A Study in the Semiotics of Behavior* (Stanford, Calif.: Stanford University Press, 1988); Irina Paperno and Joan Grossman, eds., *Creating Life: The Aesthetic Utopia of Russian Modernism* (Stanford, Calif.: Stanford University Press, 1994); Svetlana Boym, *Death in Quotation Marks: Cultural Myths of Modern Poets* (Cambridge: Cambridge University Press, 1991); Svetlana Boym, *Common Places: Mythologies of Everyday Life in Russia* (Cambridge, Mass.: Harvard University Press, 1994); Monika Greenleaf, *Pushkin and Romantic Fashion: Fragment, Elegy, Orient, Irony* (Stanford, Calif.: Stanford University Press, 1994). For a helpful discussion of the two modes of life emplotment that Lotman differentiates and of the creative role of codes, see Bethea, "Bakhtinian Prosaics versus Lotmanian 'Poetic Thinking.'"

2. Egorov, *Zhizn' i tvorchestvo Iu. M. Lotmana*, 31.

3. Ibid., 46–48.

4. Ibid., 103–9.

5. The phrase "secondary modeling systems," which Lotman used throughout the 1960s and 1970s, was proposed in 1964 by B. A. Uspenskii as a euphemism for semiotics, a discipline that Soviet authorities considered undesirable, even though they tolerated structuralism. See "Tekst i poliglotism kul'tury," 142; and Egorov, *Zhizn' i tvorchestvo Iu. M. Lotmana*, 119. "Primary modeling systems" are natural languages, which classify, evaluate, and articulate reality for a given linguistic community. "Secondary modeling systems" are semiotic structures superimposed on the primary system, such as culture or the arts. Semiotics as metalanguage and music as art form would both fall under

the rubric of secondary modeling systems, which illustrates the elasticity but also the haziness of the concept. For a history of the early years of the Tartu-Moscow school, see Seyffert, *Soviet Literary Structuralism;* and Shukman, *Literature and Semiotics.* For a useful introduction to the school's subsequent work on the semiotics of culture, see B. Gasparov's introduction to Lotman, Ginsburg, and Uspenskii, *Semiotics of Russian Cultural History,* 13–29. For an excellent, short critical overview of its history and doctrine, see Todd, "Moscow-Tartu School."

6. For a bibliography of Lotman's works, see Kiseleva, "Spisok trudov Iu. M. Lotmana." This bibliography features 813 entries.

7. Egorov, *Zhizn' i tvorchestvo Iu. M. Lotmana,* 224.

8. Aleksei Plutser-Sarno, "Sedoi shalun: Shtrikhi k portretu Iu. M. Lotmana," *Na postu: Kul'tura/iskusstvo* 2 (July 1998): 18–23.

9. See B. A. Uspenskii, "K probleme genezisa tartusko-moskovskoi semioticheskoi shkoly," *Trudy po znakovym sistemam,* 20, *Uchenye zapiski Tartuskogo gos. universiteta,* 746 (Tartu: Tartuskii gos. universitet, 1987), 18–29; B. M. Gasparov, "Tartuskaia shkola 60-kh godov kak semioticheskii fenomen," *Wiener Slawistischer Almanach* 23 (1989): 7–21; and the series of articles published in *Novoe literaturnoe obozrenie* 3 (1994) and 8 (1994). See also Egorov, *Zhizn' i tvorchestvo Iu. M. Lotmana,* 117–25. Most of these pieces (with a few additions) were republished in Nekliudov, *Moskovsko-tartuskaia semioticheskaia shkola.*

10. Lotman absorbed some of Bakhtin's ideas, which helped loosen up his semiotic model, though he never fully accepted Bakhtin's phenomenological premises. See Bethea, "Bakhtinian Prosaics versus Lotmanian 'Poetic Thinking,'" as well as Reid, "Who Is Lotman and Why Is Bakhtin Saying Those Nasty Things about Him"; P. Grzybek, "Bakhtinskaia semiotika i moskovsko-tartuskaia shkola"; as well as Kvan, *Osnovnye aspekty tvorcheskoi evoliutsii Iu. M. Lotmana,* 119–30; and Shukman, "Semiotics of Culture and the Influence of M. M. Bakhtin."

11. For a competent discussion of Lotman's reception in the English-speaking world and a comprehensive bibliography of works on the Tartu-Moscow school, see Baran, "Retseptsiia moskovsko-tartuskoi shkoly v SShA i Velikobritanii." Baran shows how the influence of Lotman and the Tartu-Moscow school of semiotics has been confined primarily to Slavicist circles, despite attempts, for example, to build bridges to cultural anthropology in the 1970s and 1980s. Baran's survey de-emphasizes the latest works of Lotman and their reception. See also Blaim, "Lotman in the West." For signs of renewed interest in Lotman outside Slavicist publications, see Zylko, "Culture and Semiotics."

12. *ISI Web of Science Citation Index,* http://webofscience.com/. Strangely enough (or perhaps characteristically enough), even some Russianists have taken a dim view of Lotman's last theoretical move. See Alexandrov, "Biology, Semiosis, and Cultural Difference in Lotman's Semiosphere."

13. *Universe of the Mind* is strictly speaking not a monograph but an authorized compilation and amalgamation of articles dating back to various periods. Although the general thrust of the volume belongs to Lotman's poststructuralist phase, it incorporates inconsistent terminology and includes sections that cannot but suggest an essentializing anthropological structuralism. Clearly this conceptual inconsistency could not have helped its reception.

14. For a review of this conference, see Andreas Schönle, "Lotman in an Interdisciplinary Context: A Symposium Held at the University of Michigan," *Sign Systems Studies* 29, no. 2 (2001): 745–48.

15. Lotman's revisions to Saussurean semiotics were partly inspired by Bakhtin, as is indicated by the use of phrases such as "the unfinalized determinacy of [the text's] structure" (*Universe of the Mind*, 18). To designate his notion of language as an ideology-inflected universe, Bakhtin used the concept of *slovo*, which means the "word" but is much more capacious than the English term. Bakhtin's English translators wisely used the concept of *discourse* to render this idea. See M. M. Bakhtin, *The Dialogic Imagination: Four Essays*, trans. Caryl Emerson and Michael Holquist (Austin: University of Texas, Press, 1981), 427. Thus our terminology, we could say, emphasizes the Bakhtinian affiliation of Lotman's late ideas.

16. These distinctions have been famously explicated by Raymond Williams in his *Sociology of Culture* (New York: Schocken Books, 1982), 9–16.

17. See section III of this introduction for a discussion of the differences between Lotman's understanding of culture and the one underpinning cultural studies. Lotman's earlier works were often less consistent in their operative notion of culture. As Amy Mandelker discusses in her contribution to this volume, Lotman also used rhetoric that suggested an essentialist understanding of culture.

18. In their earlier, widely influential article "Binary Models in the Dynamics of Russian Culture," Lotman and Uspenskii grant the self-description of a culture such power that it brings about "the unity of Russian culture at the various stages of its history." In their urge to reveal the "invariants" of Russian culture, they lose all sense of its heterogeneity. Thus, despite their initial definition of culture as the "non-hereditary memory of a group, expressed in a certain system of prohibitions and commandments," their understanding of the "binary model" of Russian culture seems to legitimize essentialism, even though, strictly speaking, it claims only to describe a "non-hereditary memory," i.e., a cultural construct that is perpetuated discursively (Lotman and Uspenskii, "Binary Models in the Dynamics of Russian Culture," 30–33). V. M. Zhivov faults them with injecting a "psychological intentionality" into elements that may have functioned purely as a social code devoid of religious implications. Thus the sphere of "anti-behavior," to which Lotman and Uspenskii attribute a religious intensity, could be nothing more than secularized social behavior not unlike carnivalesque rituals in Western European countries. According to Zhivov,

the religious interpretation of such behavior belongs to high culture, i.e., to a culture's self-description. See V. M. Zhivov, "Dvoeverie i osobyi kharakter russkoi kul'turnoi istorii," in *Razyskaniia v oblasti istorii i predystorii russkoi kul'tury* (Moscow: Iazyki russkoi kul'tury, 2002), 310–15. This reading exposes the ideological nature of the alleged fundamental difference between Western and Russian culture, one that Lotman and Uspenskii's notion of "binary model" may have unwittingly perpetuated.

19. One could draw parallels between Florenskii's notion, Lotman's concept of explosion, and Mandelker's derivation of estrangement.

20. For a discussion of Descartes's ideas of rational disengagement, see Charles Taylor, *Sources of the Self: The Making of the Modern Identity* (Cambridge, Mass.: Harvard University Press, 1989), 143–58.

21. On the punctual self, a figure of modernity that finds its origins in Locke, see Taylor, *Sources of the Self,* 159–76.

22. Cary Nelson, Paula A. Treichler, and Lawrence Grossberg, "Cultural Studies: An Introduction," in *Cultural Studies,* ed. Lawrence Grossberg, Cary Nelson, and Paula A. Treichler (New York: Routledge, 1992), 14.

23. For reasons that will become clear later, cultural studies is primarily devoted to a study of contemporary culture.

24. Cultural studies and Lotman have both called into question the binary opposition between mass and elite culture. In cultural studies this recognition emerged from the turn to a model of culture as a patchwork of separate communities, each articulating its own differences. See Simon During, introduction to *The Cultural Studies Reader,* ed. Simon During, 2nd ed. (New York: Routledge, 1993), 19. Lotman presents mass literature as purely a matter of sociological appreciation rather than of semiotic structure and notes the ways in which particular writers have moved in and out of mass literature at various historical junctures. Mass literature is a paradoxical product of a culture that wants to see itself as high ("O soderzhanii i strukture," 211–12).

25. Nelson, Treichler, and Grossberg, "Cultural Studies," 7–8.

26. Tony Bennett, "Putting Policy into Cultural Studies," in *Cultural Studies,* ed. Lawrence Grossberg, Cary Nelson, and Paula A. Treichler (New York: Routledge, 1992), 23.

27. See Stuart Hall, "Cultural Studies: Two Paradigms," *Media, Culture and Society,* vol. 2 (London: Academic Press, 1980), 57–72.

28. James W. Carey, "Reflections on the Project of (American) Cultural Studies," in *Cultural Studies in Question,* ed. Marjorie Ferguson and Peter Golding (London: Sage, 1997), 1–24; quotation on 8, 12.

29. Diversity is meant here not in the sense given to this term in American cultural studies and academia as more or less equitable representation of various racial, ethnic, gender, and sexual groups but as a plurality of codes, i.e., of voices that interact richly with one another and thereby enable semiotic creativity.

30. On this turning point in cultural studies and its political underpinnings, see During, introduction, 11-14.

31. This notion derives from Bakhtin's ideas of the contest between "heteroglossia" and the "unitary language" any given culture features. See M. M. Bakhtin, "Discourse in the Novel," in *The Dialogic Imagination*, ed. Michael Holquist (Austin: University of Texas Press, 1981), 269-73.

32. During, introduction, 6.

33. John Fiske, "Cultural Studies and the Culture of Everyday life," in *Cultural Studies*, ed. Lawrence Grossberg, Cary Nelson, and Paula A. Treichler (New York: Routledge, 1992), 154-65.

34. Ibid., 158.

35. Ibid., 158-59.

36. Cultural studies has gone through several swings of the pendulum in the way it conceives of the semiotic creativity of the subjects of culture. Both communication studies and ethnography have moved away from a Foucaultian presumption of total passiveness in the face of cultural grids. Communication studies has coalesced on an "active audience theory" premised on the idea that media texts are necessarily polysemous and that the audience always deflects dominant ideology to its own uses. Ethnography has emphasized microanalyses and dialogic forms of writing to render the uniqueness of an informant's discourse and the inflections of his or her voice in a form unmediated by the analyst's conceptualization. For a critique of the impasse such positions have created, see David Morley, "Theoretical Orthodoxies: Textualism, Constructivism and the 'New Ethnography' in Cultural Studies," in *Cultural Studies in Question*, ed. Marjorie Ferguson and Peter Golding (London: Sage, 1997), 121-37. Lotman's notion of double vision, the combination of an intrinsic and an extrinsic perspective, as discussed by Mandelker, is consistent with Morley's prescription that it is, in fact, the responsibility of the analyst to propose an account of cultural behavior in terms different from those of his or her informants (130-31). In Lotman's terms it is by translating or recoding cultural discourse that scholarship drives culture forward.

37. See Jorge Larrain, "Stuart Hall and the Marxist Concept of Ideology," and Colin Sparks, "Stuart Hall, Cultural Studies and Marxism," in *Stuart Hall: Critical Dialogues in Cultural Studies*, ed. David Morley and Kuan-Hsing Chen (London: Routledge, 1996), 47-70 and 71-101, respectively.

38. Stuart Hall, "The Problem of Ideology: Marxism without Guarantees," in *Stuart Hall: Critical Dialogues in Cultural Studies*, ed. David Morley and Kuan-Hsing Chen (London: Routledge, 1996), 42.

39. For a retrospective discussion of Marxism, which voices concern with the nearly exclusive turn toward the textuality of power in American cultural studies, see Stuart Hall, "Cultural Studies and Its Theoretical Legacies," in *Cultural Studies*, ed. Lawrence Grossberg, Cary Nelson, and Paula A. Treichler (New York: Routledge, 1992), 277-94.

40. Ibid., 43–44. For a critique of cultural studies' lineage in Gramsci's notion of class, see Bennett, "Putting Policy into Cultural Studies," 23–37. Bennett calls into question the kind of politics Gramsci's framework promotes when it ignores institutional or group specificities and operates with a notion of "the people" as a unified agent.

41. Beginning in the 1980s cultural studies abandoned its interest in Marxism and, in particular, the notion of the determination of ideas through social relations—a move called for in part by the need to address issues of gender and ethnicity in its analysis of contemporary societies. Yet, as a result cultural studies "is regressing . . . to an essentially textualist account of culture," which differs from literary studies only in the range of texts it considers (Sparks, "Stuart Hall, Cultural Studies and Marxism," 98).

42. Regarding the belief of cultural studies practitioners that their discourse matters, see Nelson, Treichler, and Grossberg, "Cultural Studies," 5–7. For a useful discussion of the ethical commitment of cultural studies and its difference from postmodernism, which "undermines the elaboration of an ethic," see Jennifer Daryl Slack and Laurie Anne Whitt, "Ethics and Cultural Studies," in *Cultural Studies*, ed. Lawrence Grossberg, Cary Nelson, and Paula A. Treichler (New York: Routledge, 1992), 571–92.

43. Caryl Emerson introduces the opposition between the "hermeneutics of suspicion" (a phrase coined by Paul Ricoeur) and the "hermeneutics of recovery of meaning" in her essay on the self as conceived by four important Russian thinkers (including Lotman). She discusses the fact that all four thinkers invest the word with an ability to change the environment. See "Bakhtin, Lotman, Vygotsky, and Lydia Ginzburg on Types of Selves: A Tribute," in *Self and Story in Russian History*, ed. Laura Engelstein and Stephanie Sandler (Ithaca, N.Y.: Cornell University Press, 2000), 40.

44. Stephen Greenblatt, *Hamlet in Purgatory* (Princeton, N.J.: Princeton University Press, 2001), 208.

45. Ibid., 4, 257.

46. Ibid., 253.

47. Ibid., 254.

# Power

# SEMIOTIC COLLISIONS
# AND THE ETHICS
# OF ESTRANGEMENT

# Dante, Florenskii, Lotman

## Journeying Then and Now through Medieval Space

### DAVID BETHEA

Given his interest in complex semiotic structures and in a "semiosphere" whose ever ramifying interactions model the vast physical cosmos, it is not surprising that Yuri Lotman paused in his writings to discuss the most elaborate of all texts, the worlds within worlds of Dante's *La Divina Commedia*. Indeed, these two authors seem almost made for each other, for their passion for meaning (and meaning making) against a moving backdrop of epistemology and geo- and astrophysics are uncannily similar. In *Universe of the Mind* Lotman juxtaposes the vertical journey of Dante the pilgrim and the horizontal journey of the curious, courageous, yet "morally indifferent" Ulysses as symbolic of the seam separating the medieval and the Renaissance worldview. Homer's "wily king of Ithaca," argues Lotman, "becomes in Dante the man of the Renaissance, the first discoverer and the traveller. This image appeals to Dante by its integrity and its strength, but repels him by its moral indifference. But in this image of the heroic adventurer of his time . . . Dante discerned something else, not just the features of the immediate future, the scientific mind and cultural attitudes of the modern age; he saw the coming separation of knowledge from morality, of discovery from its results, of science from the human personality" (*Universe of the Mind,* 184). Lotman's key point is that Ulysses' journey—in Dante, if not in Homer—is only over *space* per se (however new and mysterious), that is, it embraces the notion of pure contiguity, whereas Dante the pilgrim's journey is down and up *symbolic space,* which is to say, space that is perceived as attached to meaning every step of the way and that is embodied textually through the logic of metaphor and transference. Thus Ulysses and his crew can see what eventually becomes Mount Purgatory before their shipwreck in the Southern Hemisphere but have no idea what it is (what it *means*—i.e., this place where there is supposedly no landfall) and will be unable to make their way to it. Hence, Dante the pilgrim and Ulysses the pagan traveler are "doubles" and "antipodes," just as their respective journeys are, in Lotman's reading, symmetrical yet antithetical (183–85).

Curiously, however, Lotman does not come alone to his analysis of these two quintessential journeys in the *Commedia.* He too has a double and an antipode, as it were: the priest, philosopher, and mathematician Pavel Florenskii, whose remarks in *Imaginary Spaces in Geometry* Lotman takes as his point of departure.[1] Of all the possible commentators on Dante's work, Lotman singles out Florenskii and his unique way of incorporating issues of faith and spatial poetics in a post-Einsteinian world as his initial and, as it turns out, only interlocutor in this section of *Universe of the Mind* (177–85). After citing at length a crucial passage from *Imaginary Spaces* in which Dante and Virgil are described as experiencing something like the "bending" of space as they climb the bulge of Lucifer's haunch in the *Inferno,* Lotman concludes that "Florensky in his eagerness to show how much closer to the twentieth century is the medieval mind than the mechanistic ideology of the Renaissance gets somewhat carried away (for instance the return of Dante to earth [*Paradiso,* I, 5–6] is only hinted at and there are no grounds for assuming that he travelled in a straight line); but the problem of the contradiction in the *Commedia* between real-everyday space and cosmic-transcendental space, which he highlights, is a crucial one, although the solution to this contradiction has to be sought in another direction" (179). In other words, Florenskii appears to have the correct conceptual instincts but has lost his bearings, so to speak, with the result that the "solution . . . has to be sought in another direction." We might say then, if we agree with Lotman, that the philosopher-priest is, despite his piety and heroic life, a kind of Ulysses (but ironically, a *faith-based, Christian* one) of Dante

studies—a bold but misguided traveler.[2] In this essay I expand on this dialogue between Lotman and Florenskii about the meaning of spatial
poetics in the *Commedia* and try to ascertain how Lotman's and Florenskii's different readings of the Dantesque *viaggio* provide insights into their
respective views of Russian culture. I will suggest that Lotman, with his
Enlightenment orientation, saw himself commenting on Florenskii (i.e.,
on Florenskii reading Dante) in a manner analogous (but in a *reversely*
symmetrical way) to Dante's own "correcting" of Ulysses' "amoral" nav-
igation of pre-Christian space-time. Put simply, Dante the pilgrim is to
the ultimately shipwrecked Ulysses of the *Inferno* (canto 26) as the Lotman
of the *Universe of the Mind* passage is to the "over-reaching" Florenskii of
*Imaginary Spaces.*

First, some additional background on Florenskii. As recent studies
have made abundantly clear, every crucial question of ontology had for
Florenskii an antinomial structure.[3] Whether he was speaking about
icons, language, dreams, the creative process, non-Euclidean geometry,
the interior of a cathedral, or even St. Sophia, he *visualized* two separate
and seemingly self-canceling categories and then showed, against logic
*(rassudok)*, how these categories could suddenly occupy the same space in
a privileged "crossover zone," what Steven Cassedy has termed, following Heidegger and Roman Ingarden, the "ontically transitional."[4] Thus
we have the board, glue, gesso, and gold leaf of an icon, on the one
hand, and the unmediated "Mother of God," on the other; or the composition (that which the artist, with the concrete materials at hand, *conceives* from his or her vantage) of a work of art, on the one hand, and its
construction (that which the viewer *perceives* from his or her vantage), on
the other, and so on. Florenskii constantly asks the reader/viewer of his
spatially arranged formulations to see two or more points of view *simultaneously*, to, as it were, look back from the far side and forward from the
near. The icon is a sacred object because the viewer sees the boards qua
boards *and* the Mother of God qua Mother of God; this is achieved by
*stepping through the window of belief* where separation equals identification.

Pivotal to Florenskii's antinomial thinking-cum-faith system is the
notion of "sanctuarial barrier," the limen without which the philosopher cannot envision his crossover zone.[5] The iconostasis is an ideal expression of this precisely because of its flat surface and its function as a
threshold separating sacred from nonsacred space. As Cassedy sum-
marizes, "Florensky's method was always to start with a duality . . . and
demonstrate the metaphysical inadequacy of that duality. The two

members of a duality simply reflect each other and offer no chance for movement to a higher state. A third member is always needed to transcend this aporia, and the result is the completeness of trinity. . . . What is remarkable, though, is how deeply entrenched in the pretrinitarian stage of his thinking Florensky's mind seems to be. It is as though he knew in good conscience that a Christian worldview required trinity for completeness, but put the third member of the trinity in its place almost by a kind of intellectual artifice."[6] Even Florenskii's definition of a symbol partakes of the visually constructed figure of the crossover zone (here a "window") and reveals its author to be a true child of the Symbolist epoch: "A symbol is larger than itself. . . . A metaphysical symbol is that essence whose energy bears within itself the energy of another, higher essence, and is dissolved in it; its joining with it and through it manifestly reveals that higher essence. A symbol is a window to another, not immediately given essence."[7] The symbol is neither "itself" (presumably the phenomenal reality of its "essence") nor the energy that is "larger than itself" (presumably the noumenal reality of the "higher essence"), but precisely both brought together through the image/iconic surface of the window.

This is where Dante and Florenskii's discussion of the *Commedia* enter the picture. In 1921, on the six hundredth anniversary of the death of Dante, Florenskii wrote a short but remarkably dense and provocative pamphlet in which he tried to prove that the latest theoretical discoveries in math and physics actually confirm what Christian mystics had for centuries been calling revelation—namely, that infinity could be knowable. His term for this was *aktual'naia beskonechnost'* (actual infinity). The booklet, which has since become a bibliographical rarity, was called *Imaginary Spaces in Geometry: The Expansion of the Domain of Two-Dimensional Images in Geometry* (*Mnimosti v geometrii: Rasshirenie oblasti dvukhmernykh obrazov geometrii*) and was published in 1922 by the Moscow publishing house Pomor'e. Several of the names that Florenskii cites as sources for his ideas are well known in modern accounts of the geometry of space and anticipate in interesting ways Einstein's general theory of relativity: Carl Friedrich Gauss, Bernhard Riemann, and A. F. Moebius. In essence, what Florenskii contends, contra Euclidean geometry and contra its variations in Leibniz, Newton, and Kant, is that the universe can and should be imagined as (in contemporary terminology) "a finite homogeneous galactic system."[8] That is to say, we can conceive of a universe that is both finite, in that it is bounded, *and* homogeneous, in that it has no fixed center. To put it another way, there is no other space beyond space, and yet space is not infinite. How can this be so? By seeing space as *curved*, as non-Euclidean, as having no properties *extrinsic* to itself by which to fix its dimensions, by imagining the intrinsic *relativity* of any position one is able to take in space. Those visual prompts, including Klein bottles, Moebius strips, and Escher drawings, that fascinate us because we cannot isolate their boundaries do so precisely by playing with or "bending" our perspective. From our three-dimensional space we look on their two-dimensional surfaces as optical illusions, for their bending does not pierce our space (i.e., it is not measurable outside itself) just as the Einsteinian 3-sphere cannot be *empirically* charted.

These are some of the ideas Florenskii engages in his booklet. Intriguingly, the print by Favorskii decorating the cover of *Imaginary Spaces* is itself a kind of non-Euclidean geometrician's Moebius strip: it presents *two* sides of a plane—the left side, which is visible, and the right side, which is imaginary. Florenskii asserts the integrity of the plane that can be seen from *both sides simultaneously*. Certain details from the visible side (the letter *O*) show up on the imaginary side, but fragmented, reversed in perspective, and, most important, bent or distorted. Here the author is suggesting, as on a chart, the essential curvature of space. Whereas the basic distinction in the Gauss-Riemann-Einstein model is a universe that is *finite and homogeneous*, that is, it has no fixed center (all galactic units being bounded equally by all other units) and thus no outer limit to be crossed over or pierced, the Orthodox and otherworldly Florenskii still telescopes these antinomies in perhaps his most audacious crossover zone: "A shred of the real side, while located on the border of imaginary [space] . . . conveys the fluctuation of the geometrical figure at the point where it collapses through the plane, when it has not yet been fixed in place [or "determined," *opredelilas'*], being at once both real and imaginary."[9] If the modern scientist must conclude that "it is hopeless [that is, in the absence of extrinsic criteria] to imagine curved space as being mysteriously bent through a fourth dimension," no such doubts assail Florenskii, for that is exactly what he is asserting—that the intrinsic becomes extrinsic at this "crossover zone."[10] In short, Florenskii, with the aid of Favorskii, has constructed what might be termed a *mathematical icon*: rather than the antinomies of boards versus Mother of God, we have the antinomies of three-dimensional versus four-dimensional space. When Florenskii says of the cover sketch that it "does not merely decorate the book, but *enters* as a constitutive element into its *spiritual* make-up," he is asking his reader to step through that same limen of faith we have witnessed elsewhere.[11]

Florenskii concludes *Imaginary Spaces* with an ingenious discussion of how Dante's work, in its presentation of the other world, was not only "ahead of contemporary science" but in fact startlingly prescient about notions such as the bending or breaking of space at conditions—*imaginary yet no less real*—beyond the speed of light.[12] As we recall, this is the same passage that Lotman cites as his point of departure (both into Dante and *from* Florenskii) in *Universe of the Mind*. Thus, the Russian scientist-priest anticipates by almost sixty years the work of such physicists and mathematicians as J. J. Callahan and Mark A. Peterson, who have argued in their publications that Dante's vision in the *Paradiso* of the harmonious interrelation between the heavenly spheres (which increase in size and turn more rapidly the higher the pilgrim goes) and the Empyrean (whose nine concentric circles decrease in size but, paradoxically, *increase* in rotating speed the closer they come to the blinding point of light at their center) is in fact a rather accurate replica of Einstein's "finite and homogeneous" galactic system known as the 3-sphere.[13] The reader is left with "the almost inescapable impression that [Dante] conceives of these nine angelic spheres [of the Empyrean] as forming one hemisphere of the entire universe and the usual Aristotelian universe up to the Primum Mobile as the other hemisphere, while he is standing more or less on the equator between them. . . . Taken all together, then, his universe is a 3-sphere."[14] Or as Florenskii himself formulates the paradox of relativity in his own strikingly similar terms, "Dantesque space is precisely like elliptical space. This [realization] sheds a sudden bundle of light on the medieval notion of the finite character of the world. But these ideas concerning geometry in general have recently received an unexpected concrete interpretation through the principle of relativity, and from the point of view of modern physics, universal space should be conceivable precisely as elliptical space and is acknowledged to be finite, just as time is finite, enclosed in itself. . . . The realm of imaginary space is real, comprehensible, and in the language of Dante is called the Empyrean."[15]

Thus far we have been setting the stage for Lotman and his view of Dante's journey by focusing on Florenskii as interlocutor, in particular the latter's antinomial thinking and his unique way of reading a non-Euclidean curvature in the space-time continuum into the "geometry of salvation" in the *Commedia*. Now I would like to bring into play Lotman's argument in *Universe of the Mind* by showing how it foregrounds, without explicitly saying so, the profound and irreconcilable differences between Dante's medieval Catholic worldview and Florenskii's Symbolist-tinged Orthodoxy. Along the way I shall also demonstrate, with Lotman's help, how these competing faith systems implicate very different histories and—this is the central point—different ways of negotiating a "middle space" on earth.

I will begin by introducing two additional works by Lotman to support my argument. First, his well-known study of binary models of culture (coauthored with Boris Uspenskii), from which the following passage is taken:

> In Western Catholicism, the world beyond the grave is divided into three spaces: heaven, purgatory, and hell. Earthly life is correspondingly conceived of as admitting three types of behavior: the unconditionally sinful, the unconditionally holy, and the neutral, which permits eternal salvation after some sort of purgative trial. In the real life of the medieval West a wide area of neutral behavior thus became possible, as did neutral societal institutions, which were neither "holy" nor "sinful," neither "pro-state" nor "anti-state," neither good nor bad. The neutral sphere became a structural reserve, out of which the succeeding system developed. . . .
>
> The Russian medieval system was constructed on an accentuated duality. To continue our example, one of its attributes was the division of the other world into heaven and hell. Intermediate neutral spheres were not envisaged. Behavior in earthly life could be either sinful or holy. This situation spread into extra-ecclesiastical conceptions: thus secular power could be interpreted as divine or diabolical, but never as neutral. ("Binary Models," 31–32)

This absence of a neutral space, not only purgatory itself but any middle ground over which one makes one's way to the destination of salvation/revelation, has direct application, as we shall see, to Florenskii's reading of Dante.

The second is an article in which Lotman advances the thesis that for Orthodox Slavs in general and for Russians in particular "a religious act has as its basis an unconditional act of self-giving" ("'Agreement' and 'Self-Giving,'" 125). This idea of religiously inspired behavior as being one-sided and noncompulsory, that is, as bearing no signs of an implied quid pro quo, will again be implicated in the possibility or impossibility of imagining an axiological middle space: "In the West the sense of agreement, though having its remote origin in magic, had the authority of the Roman secular tradition and held a position equal to the authority of religion; in Russia, on the other hand, it was felt to be pagan in character. . . . It is significant that in the Western tradition an agreement as such was ethically neutral. It could be drawn up with the Devil . . . but one might also make agreements with the forces of holiness and goodness. . . . [In the Russian context, however,] an agreement may only be made with a Satanic power or its pagan counterpart" (126–27). Space opens up for interpretation/negotiation when one's acts, according to a rule or "agreement," can affect the response of the interlocutor, even when that interlocutor is God.

With these two works in mind, let us now turn to the relevant passages in *Universe of the Mind*. Lotman begins with the assertion that he will be "dwelling on the meaning of the spatial axis 'top/bottom' in Dante's created world" (*Universe of the Mind*, 177). That may be so, in that Dante's world is traditionally visualized along a vertical axis, yet it is also clear that Lotman's semiotic approach owes much to an appreciation of a neutral axiological or "middle" space (one that is not inherently "right" or "wrong" but simply informative), and that its geometry is more Euclidean than non-Euclidean, more "filled in" and three-dimensional than "mind-bending" and "out of this world." That there *is* something to negotiate (i.e., space itself) is precisely what generates meaning in Dante and Lotman:

> So when Dante and Virgil move down the relative scale of the earthly "top/bottom" axis, that is, when they go deeper from the surface of the Earth towards its centre, they are at the same time in relation to the absolute axis rising up. The solution to this paradox is to be found in Dante's semiotics. In Dante's belief-system space has meaning, and each spatial category has its own meaning. But the relationship of expression and content is not an arbitrary one, unlike semiotic systems based on social conventions. . . . The content, the meaning of the symbol is not bound to its expression by convention (as happens with allegory) but shines through it. The closer the text is placed in the hierarchy to the heavenly light which is the true content of medieval symbolics the brighter the meaning shines through it and the more direct and less conventionalized is its expression. The further the text is from the source of truth, then the more dimly will it be reflected and the more arbitrary will be the relationship of content to expression. Thus on the

highest step truth is accessible to direct contemplation through the eye of the spirit, while on the lowest step truth is glimpsed through conventional signs. Because sinners and demons of different degrees use purely conventional signs they can lie, commit perfidy, treachery and deceit—all ways to separate content from expression. The righteous also converse with each other in signs but they do not put convention to ill use, and with recourse to the highest sources of truth they can penetrate into the conventionless symbolic world of meanings. (179)

This is a fascinating series of formulations when placed alongside the turning-point scene (Lucifer's bulge at the hip, discussed later) in Florenskii. Basically Lotman is saying that, viewed semiotically, Dante the pilgrim's journey through the three realms of the afterlife is one continuous and uninterrupted force field, where the geo- and astrophysics of movement (first downward, then) upward against the gravitas of sin equals theodicy, or the morally responsible making of meaning in the universe created by God. Despite the claims of "symbolic space," this movement is not about right-angled visions and singular turning points. Choices in the path do not result in wholesale movements "in" or "out." Each step is equally meaningful in the amount of information it imparts. Wherever one is located along this journey's route, one's position vis-à-vis the "truth" as told (or shown) by the forever-fallen sinners, the purgatorial "works-in-progress," and the now-risen righteous is relative (but never amoral). The pilgrim moves along this axis as along a slide rule, and with the help of his various guides, he stops to experience/interpret the meaning of what he sees, understanding that that meaning is always dependent on the interlocutor's or actor's own orientation to the truth of his or her life as refracted through the spectrum of "conventional signs-holy symbols." By operating in a world where conventional signs can be manipulated out of selfish motives and no sign is inherently holy (i.e., reflective of a higher symbolics), the sinner shows himself or herself to be faraway from the truth. Semiotics becomes the orienting tool or slide rule that shows the truth, good or bad, of each scene en route: "The solution to this paradox [how an axis can be both relative and absolute] is to be found in Dante's semiotics." Interestingly enough, however, the point in Lotman's narrative where we feel the greatest need for something akin to Florenskian mathematics—specifically, the statement that "when Dante and Virgil move down the relative scale of the earthly 'top/bottom' axis, that is, when they go deeper from the surface of the Earth towards its centre, they are at the same time in relation to the absolute axis rising up"—is also the point where space and mean-ing are the most problematic. For how can Dante and Virgil be moving up one axis (the absolute one) and down another (the literal, physical one) at the same time, without those axes in some way bending into each other? How can a journey be both straightforward and circular without a perspective on it that is simultaneously "inside" and "out-side"? To be fair to Florenskii and his iconism then, this is the moment when Lotmanian semiotics seems to appear "flattest" and most in need of the priest's mathematical mysticism.

Now, to return to Florenskii and his Dante. What we find at the end of *Imaginary Spaces* is a different sort of journey entirely, and not only be-cause Florenskii is, in Lotman's words, "getting carried away." Some-thing else is going on here, something having to do with the very nature of symbolic space:

> And so let us recall the path taken by Dante and Virgil. It begins in Italy. Both poets descend along the steep slopes of the funnel-shaped Inferno. The funnel culminates at the last, narrowest circle of the Lord of the Nether Regions [*Vladyka preispodnei*]. What is more, all the while during the descent down, a vertical position is maintained by both poets—their heads are turned in the direction of the point of departure, that is, toward Italy, and their feet toward the center of the earth. But when the poets reach approximately Lucifer's waist [*poiasnitsa*], they both suddenly *turn over* [*perevorachivaiutsia*], proceeding now with their feet toward the surface of the earth, whence they entered the subterra-nean kingdom, and with their heads in the opposite direction (*Inferno*, canto 34).[16] Having crossed the border . . . that is, having completed the path [down] and crossed the center of the world, the poets find them-selves beneath the hemisphere, whose counterpart is the place "where Christ was crucified": they [now] rise up along the crater-shaped way [*po zherloobraznomu khodu*]. . . . Mounts Purgatory and Zion, diametri-cally opposed to each other, arose as the result of that fall [namely, Lucifer's], which means that the path to heaven is directed along the line of Lucifer's fall but has an opposing meaning. In this way Dante constantly moves along a straight line and [comes to] stand in heaven, turned with his feet in the direction of his descent. But having looked out from there, from the Empyrean, at God's glory, in the end he finds himself, without any particular movement of turning back, in Florence. His journey has been a reality, but if anyone would deny the latter, then the least that can be said is that this journey must be acknowledged as a poetic reality, that is, as something conceivable and possible to imagine,

which means it contains in itself the givens for an elucidation of its geo-metrical premises. And so, moving constantly ahead in a straight line and turning over once en route, the poet comes to his prior place in the same position in which he left it.[17]

Note that whereas the physicists who speak of Dante's anticipation of the Einsteinian 3-sphere invariably single out the *Commedia*'s last book and the pilgrim's transit from the earthly to the heavenly spheres, Flo-renskii fixes on a radically different "crossover zone": the end of the *In-ferno* and Lucifer's waist or, more precisely, the seam where the thigh/loin meets the bulge of the hip/haunch.[18] Why, one wonders, does Flo-renskii the priest focus on this particular turning point to make his case about non-Euclidean optical illusion qua revelation? It has been sug-gested by at least one memoirist that Florenskii "was possessed rather by the spirit of cognition on a grand scale than by that of kindness and charity; Lucifer was closer to him than Christ."[19] But whether this inter-est in the depths of the *Inferno* (rather than the heights of the *Paradiso*) is a matter of will or of temperament ("Luciferian" pride) is an impon-derable and need not concern us here. My own hypothesis is that the vividness, the sheer graphic element of sin, coupled with its idolatry of three-dimensional form and movement, was perceived by Florenskii to be—precisely because it was fallen—more readily available to the world of the *Inferno*.[20] Thus, Florenskii telescopes all the drama of the *Inferno* into this one point in space and time where opposites can be identities—where the pilgrim and the guide can turn upside down and still walk up-right, where their heads and feet can turn in a diametrically different di-rection, and yet they can still make forward progress in their journey, where Lucifer as the very symbol for the way down can suddenly pro-vide an exit to the way up, and so on. One imagines Florenskii taking a mathematician's pure delight (is this Luciferian pride?) in the elegant posing of these paradoxical movements. Somehow Dante makes his way ever forward, turns a somersault at one juncture en route, and ar-rives back at the original point of departure in the same position in which he left. Salvation becomes a Moebius strip, and the place where the outer surface joins the inner surface is the Prince of Darkness's "nether region."

Looking at this from the Lotmanian perspective, the fact that Flo-renskii makes no mention of the tremendous learning process Dante ex-periences to reach Lucifer's hip is characteristic, as is the fact that he does not seem to notice that the underworld grows denser and, as it were, "fatter" (i.e., all the various pouches in the Eighth Circle and the rings in the Ninth Circle) the closer the two travelers get to the center of the earth (just as things will move more slowly the closer we get to the Earthly Paradise and the Empyrean later on).[21] According to medieval tradition, one's soul has two feet, the *affectus* (will, carnal appetite) on the left, which clings to the things of the earth, and the *apprehensivus* (intellect) on the right, which tries to perceive the good in a postlapsarian world. The pilgrim's steps as *homo claudus* have been measured out to the ethical centimeter by the Catholic notion of sin and retribution, that very specific adherence to the rightness of the *contrapasso*—the fitting of the punishment in hell to the unrepented sin on earth.[22] Thus, to cite the first few examples, those who refused to take sides in the battle between good and evil are, like the neutral angels, punished just beyond the Gates of Hell by chasing after banners that lead nowhere (they had no telos in life) and by being bitten by horseflies and wasps (they were themselves parasites of sorts) (canto 3); or the lustful, including the Symbolists' beloved Paolo and Francesca, are blown about like birds (just as their passions tossed them about in life) because they have forfeited their right to choose (canto 5, Second Circle); or Ciacco and the other gluttons, who gorged themselves and indulged in Florentine life, must now lie in the filthy and evil-smelling pigsty of the Third Circle and be flayed by the big-bellied Cerberus (canto 6), and so on. The number of circles in Minos the judge's tail tell each sinful soul his or her precise destination below.

But all these measurements and portionings out are, for the reasons outlined by Lotman, anathema to the spirit of Orthodoxy. To be punished in a way that fits one's misdeeds, just as to be rewarded in a way that fits one's spiritual *podvigi* (acts of heroism), is to engage in the quid pro quo that the Slavic world associates with magic (the domain of the devil), Roman law, and the Catholic Church. Here Florenskii very much follows Dostoevsky and the Slavophiles. As he writes in "Gehenna," his eighth letter in *The Pillar*:

> I want to point out the decisive difference between the view expressed here . . . and the Catholic teaching about purgatory, where the person is saved *not* in spite of, but *thanks to, as a result of* the torments of purification. It is for this reason that, for the apostle Paul, what is saved is not the person in his entire makeup, but only "he himself" [*sam*], his God-given "about oneself" [*o sebe*], while according to Catholic teaching it is

the whole person who is saved, but only having bethought himself and changed for the better under [the influence of] the disciplined retribution of purgatory. The profoundly mysterious and suprarational metaphysical act of the separation of the two moments of being ("about oneself" and "for oneself" [*dlia sebia*]) is transformed, in the vulgar conception of Catholic purgatory, into something psychological, thoroughly understandable—into justification through suffering and education through punishment.[23]

One should not be surprised, having read such statements, to find Florenskii not dwelling on the steps leading up to the way out of the Inferno—these latter would have smacked of the "false discipline," the "justification through torment," and the "edification through punishment" of Catholicism. It is not simply that these various mediating measures are too easily associated with the corruption of the historical church, with simony and the securing of one's place in the other world through negotiations in this one. Equally offensive to Florenskii's mentality is the very notion that *there is or can be something in between,* that the "crossover zone" can be stretched out, arranged with signposts, made long or steep in its own right. Salvation is not a process but a freely given act that penetrates across a threshold and pulls one (*bends* one) from "here" to "there." In this Florenskii joins hands with the Dostoevsky of *The Idiot,* whose hero tells the tale of the peasant who murders his friend for a silver watch at the same time that he genuinely asks God's forgiveness *radi Khrista* (for Christ's sake).

In another letter of *The Pillar,* Florenskii explains the phenomenon of Sophia's wisdom by first describing taxonomically the three primary categories of Sophia icons (typified by the Novgorod, Iaroslavl', and Kiev "Sophias," respectively) and then explaining what the symbolism in these icons means. In this telling there is no plot, no storyline. Instead there are one-to-one correspondences (phrasal icons, as it were) on the order of "Sophia's wings = closeness to a higher world," or "the caduceus = theurgic power," or "the crown in the form of a city wall = earth-mother/civitas."[24] One can only assume that a plot such as we have in the *Commedia,* where the salvation of one pilgrim soul is achieved through grace, to be sure, but also through the intricately calibrated blend of poetic footsteps in terza rima and physical footsteps through three massive realms of the afterlife, is already by definition too human centered, too "secular," for Florenskii's tradition. Beatrice, as the *Vita Nuova* tells us, is the ninth most beautiful woman in Florence—certainly the kind of hair-splitting in the aesthetic/potentially erotic realm that Florenskii would have absolutely no interest in. Likewise, whereas Dante is very careful about the various female intercessors, their precise positions vis-à-vis the Godhead, and even their individual qualities—recall that it is Mary who sends Lucia, who sends Beatrice—Florenskii is apt to collapse the different incarnations of Sophia. To the poet who could not speak of feminine beauty, whether physical or spiritual, without remembering the lessons of *dolce stil nuovo* and the love poetry of Guinizelli and Cavalcanti, the following telescoping of Sophia would seem very strange indeed: "If Sophia is all Creatures[/Creation], then the soul and conscience of Creation, Humankind, is chiefly Sophia. If Sophia is all Humankind, then the soul and conscience of Humankind, the Church, is chiefly Sophia. If Sophia is the Church, then the soul and conscience of the Church, the Church of Saints, is chiefly Sophia. If Sophia is the Church of Saints, then the soul and conscience of the Church of Saints, the Intercessor and Defender for all creatures before the Word of God . . . [that is,] the Mother of God . . . is once again chiefly Sophia. But the true sign of the Blessed Mary is Her Virginity, the beauty of Her Soul. It is this that is Sophia."[25]

This is a striking passage when juxtaposed with the notion of Christian beatitude in feminine form in the *Commedia*. As Zen'kovskii first noted, how can Florenskii's version of Sophia be at one and the same time "the pre-existent nature of creation," "the Church in its earthly aspect," and "creation that has been deified by the Holy Spirit"?[26] How can Sophia be both the "ideal personality of the world," that is, unfallen, and that world's Guardian Angel, a concept that presupposes there is some evil to guard against?[27] She cannot be, if any Christian plot or extended notion of theodicy is involved. The main point to keep in mind as we conclude this discussion of Catholic middle distance and Orthodox two-dimensionality (or apocalypticism) is that the former stresses *the analogous that is different* (Mary is like Lucia, who is like Beatrice, but still *they are different*), and the latter stresses the *different that is identical* (Sophia = Humankind = Church = Church of the Saints = Mother of God = Virginity). The former cannot help but create space, especially over time as the Church fathers continued to weigh and measure the subtle differences on the path from secular to divine knowledge. The latter cannot help but consume and eliminate the potential for middle space.

I do not mean to suggest that Florenskii's understanding of Dante is essentially flawed (not terribly useful information in the final analysis) but that it is to a significant degree culturally and historically determined and that it says as much about its author and his tradition as it does about its subject. How Florenskii processes not only the idea of an axiological middle space (what is visually prompted in the *Commedia* by the quid pro quo activities of those doing penance on Mount Purgatory) but more centrally the multitude of steps down to the bulge at Lucifer's hip is what is interesting. In a word, he doesn't go "there." There simply is no way or path from secular to sacred love in Florenskii. By the same token, Lotman's formulations have been especially useful and apposite in our discussion, if not without their own inbred "aporias" (e.g., they rigorously reject anything mystical or "mind-bending," surely an aspect of Dante's text that at some level needs to be reckoned with). Upon reflection one realizes that Dante is already, even in the early fourteenth century, deeply humanist (or at least on the way to becoming so: i.e., he unmistakably and personally eroticizes, even as he spiritualizes, his text), while Florenskii, writing after the revolution and fully aware of how secular powers wield apocalyptic models, is deeply antihumanist. Even as Florenskii is clearly intrigued, as a mathematician, by Dante's non-Euclidean vision, he would appear to have little patience with the sensuous, concrete, quirky, almost palpable quality of Dante's imagery. As he writes in *The Pillar:* "If the Protestant destroys Christ, then the Catholic wishes to dress himself in the likeness [*lichina*] of Christ. Whence the sensuous [*chuvstvennyi*] quality of the church service, its drama, its open altar (the altar a stage, the priest an actor), the plasticity, the sensuous music, the mysticism that is not of the mind but of the imagination/fantasy [*voobrazhatel'naia*], leading to a fixation on the stigmata (it is noteworthy that in the East there has been no such fixation . . .), the eroticism, the sense of hysterics, and so on. Whence too the Catholic mysteries, the processions, everything that operates on the imagination—the action, the shameful display, but not contemplation, not *thoughtful* [*umnaia*] prayer."[28] Hence despite his connections to the tradition of St. John of Damascus and the eighth-century theologian's assertions that the material world is sacred and spirit bearing, Florenskii leaves little room in his thinking for "matter," if by matter we mean a traditional love object in this world (i.e., "Beatrice" cannot cross over into "Sophia").[29] What he identifies as damning in the Catholic service are precisely those elements that gave Dante's poem its middle space and its love plot-cum-Christian history: its sensuous images, its potential eroticism, its drama and incipient orientation toward a three-dimensional realism, its openness (n.b. the lack of the iconostasis and the "ontically transitional"), its mysticism tinged with elements of a dark imagination.

But at the same time it would be remiss not to acknowledge the compelling, even poignant quality of Florenskii's voyage, however wayward or Ulysses-like it might seem to our postmodern understanding, into uncharted territory. Unsatisfied with any logic that finds truth in three-dimensional space, Florenskii pushes relentlessly backward into two-dimensionality (iconism) and forward into four-dimensionality (the Moebius strip, or "bendable" space). Unlike Dante's Ulysses, he is clearly not "morally indifferent," and like the pilgrim struggling upward against the weight of his own and others' fallen humanity, he fears a future "separation of knowledge from morality, of discovery from its results, of science from the human personality." He may have appeared to contemporaries as twentieth-century Russia's quintessential Renaissance man. But in reality his turn away from secularism and human-centeredness made him, as Lotman divined, the perfect medieval mind (and soul) for modern science and for the idea that movement beyond the speed of light is not only imaginable but meaningful. By the same token, Lotman's reading of Florenskii's reading of Dante is itself incredibly revealing. In it we see *homo semioticus* clearly turning away from Florenskii's neomedievalism and toward a neohumanism and neopersonalism quite new and heuristically useful for its own space-time. It is as though Dante's anxiety about the shift from the medieval to the Renaissance worldview is repeated in reverse perspective in Lotman's fear that Russian cultural space will never manage to shed its own obsessively binary, relentlessly "iconic" tradition—that is, will never make the transition to a fully embodied "trinitarian" universe.[30] Thus, if the brilliant and fascinating Florenskii might be dubbed the Ulysses of twentieth-century Russian spiritual culture, a figure whose oratorical flair inspired the sailors on board with the promise of landfall in the Southern Hemisphere (or in post-Einsteinian terms, existence beyond the speed of light), then Lotman is his total antipode—the prodigiously erudite yet modest teacher-exile whose "rage for order" is as humane as it is larger than life. Not Catholic (or Orthodox), not even Christian, he is the closest thing Russian culture has to Dante—the Dante of twentieth-century semiotics.

## Notes

Sections of this essay have been adapted from my chapter "Florensky and Dante: Revelation, Orthodoxy, and Non-Euclidean Space," in *Russian Religious*

*Thought,* ed. Judith Deutsch Kornblatt and Richard F. Gustafson (Madison: University of Wisconsin Press, 1996), 112–31.

1. *Mnimosti v geometrii,* literally "Imaginaries in geometry." See discussion later in the essay.

2. According to reports Florenskii died a latter-day martyr's death in a Stalinist labor camp, where he had selflessly tended his fellow prisoners to the end.

3. As Robert Slesinski has noted, an antinomy is, for Florenskii, "an opposition whose terms remain incompatible in the logical order, but which find their resolution and, indeed, essential complementarity in the metalogical order." *Pavel Florenskii: A Metaphysics of Love* (Crestview: St. Vladimir's Seminary Press, 1984), 145.

4. Steven Cassedy, "P. A. Florensky and the Celebration of Matter," in *Russian Religious Thought,* ed. Judith Deutsch Kornblatt and Richard F. Gustafson (Madison: University of Wisconsin Press, 1996), 101.

5. Ibid., 100–101.

6. Ibid., 108. To be fair to Florenskii, he might respond, contra Cassedy, that the third member of the trinity appears not through "intellectual artifice" but through the mediating presence of the icon as it produces the "transcending vision" that draws the viewer across the threshold into its sacred space. Still, this aspect of the optical illusion and space-bending "crossover zone" (*perekhodnaia zona*) is crucial to many of Florenskii's arguments and does seem to have a strong cognitive/mathematical quality to it. For relevant passages on Florenskii's understanding of iconic space, see his "Ikonostas," in *Bogoslovskie trudy* 9 (1972): 91–92, 96–99, 101–3.

7. Cited O. I. Genisaretskii, "Konstruktsiia i kompozitsiia v ikonologii P. A. Florenskogo," *Trudy VNIITE* (Seriia "Tekhnicheskaia estetika") 59 (1989): 47. Unless otherwise noted, the translations are mine.

8. Cf. the "antinomy of space" in Kant's *Critique of Pure Reason.* Quotation from J. J. Callahan, "The Curvature of Space in a Finite Universe," *Scientific American* 235 (August 1976): 93.

9. Pavel Florenskii, *Mnimosti v geometrii: Rasshirenie oblasti dvukhmernykh obrazov geometrii* (Moscow: Pomor'e, 1922), 63–64; cited in Lena Szilard, "Andrei Belyi i P. Florenskii," *Studia Slavica Hung* 33 (1987): 233.

10. Callahan, "Curvature of Space," 94.

11. My emphasis; Florenskii, *Mnimosti,* 58; cited in Szilard, "Andrei Belyi i P. Florenskii," 232.

12. Florenskii, *Mnimosti,* 53.

13. Callahan, "Curvature of Space," 99.

14. Mark A. Peterson, "Dante and the 3-Sphere," *American Journal of Physics* 47 (1979): 1033.

15. Florenskii, *Mnimosti,* 48, 53.

16. There is an apparent error in Florenskii's text at this point: this scene takes place in canto 34, not 23, as indicated in *Imaginary Spaces* (46). I have made the change in the cited passage.

17. Florenskii, *Mnimosti*, 45–47.

18. In the Italian: "Quando noi fummo là dove la coscia / si volge, a punto in sul grosso de l'anche" (34.76–77); and in Lozinskii's translation: "Kogda my probiralis' tam, gde bok, / Zagnuv k bedru, daet uklon pologii." Florenskii himself uses another translation (that of D. I. Min?), which foregrounds even more the notion of turning and crossing: "Kogda zhe my dostigli tochki toi, / Gde tolshcha chresl vrashchaet bedr gromadu."

19. Leonid Sabaneeff, "Pavel Florensky—Priest, Scientist, and Mystic," *Russian Review* 20 (October 1961): 316–17.

20. Florenskii had ambivalent feelings about such vividness. See the discussion later in this essay.

21. Here Florenskii is by no means alone or eccentric in his analysis. Considerable emphasis has been placed in the Russian tradition on Dante's so-called verticality, on the one moment of his transcendence rather than on the multitude of moments between any ultimate stepping across or over. See, e.g., M. M. Bakhtin, "Forms of Time and of the Chronotope in the Novel," in *The Dialogic Imagination,* ed. Michael Holquist, trans. Caryl Emerson and Michael Holquist (Austin: University of Texas Press, 1981), 156–57.

22. Cf. "All sins, which Dante arranges in a strict hierarchy, have spatial attachment so that the weight of the sin corresponds to the depth of the sinner's position" (Lotman, *Universe of the Mind*, 180).

23. Florenskii, *Stolp i utverzhdenie istiny. Opyt pravoslavnoi feodotsei* (Berlin: Rossica, 1929), 233.

24. Ibid., 374–75.

25. Ibid., 350–51.

26. See Florenskii, *Stolp*, 350.

27. V. V. Zenkovsky, *A History of Russian Philosophy*, trans. George L. Kline, 2 vols. (London: Routledge & Kegan Paul, 1953), 2:889.

28. Florenskii, *Stolp*, 723n400.

29. See Cassedy, "P. A. and the Celebration of Matter," 98–99.

30. See Lotman's very last sentences in *Culture and Explosion*, in which he asserts that it would be a "historical catastrophe" if Russia failed to adopt the "all-European ternary system and to renounce the ideal of destroying 'the old world to its foundation and then' building a new one on its ruins" (*Kul'tura i vzryv*, 148).

# 2

# Lotman's Other

## *Estrangement and Ethics in* Culture and Explosion

AMY MANDELKER

*In memoriam* Thomas G. Winner

With the republication over the last few years of Yuri Lotman's main works and letters, attempting a synoptic evaluation of Lotman's general thought has become an appealing project. We are free to allocate the semiotic enterprise to the classical Aristotelian categories: a "poetics," a "physics," and an "ethics." The first two categories, which predominated in the structuralist and poststructuralist theorizing of the Moscow-Tartu school, imply an emphasis on Lotman's "mechanics," that is, the dynamic modeling involved in the spatialization of meaning. Elsewhere I have critiqued the "mechanics" somewhat deconstructively, focusing on how we might read Lotman's metaphors of significance and his erection of models, maps, graphs, and graphemes.[1] I have argued that Lotman's discourse falls prey to certain linguistic habits of philosophical and scientific discourse that have been the target of a general feminist critique, which has exposed the engendering of the philosophical categories of space: topos, place, structure.[2] These latter categories are inherent within the discourse of aesthetics as it concerns the field of vision and its dynamics. As shaped within Lotman's thought, these spatial notions are developed with reference to concepts of the mirror and the frame: boundary, asymmetry, specularity, the *mise en abîme*.[3] These deeper demarcations trouble the deceptively quiescent surface of Lotman's theories of culture and meaning, culminating in his own revisionist essay, "The Over-turned Image," which appears in *Culture and Explosion*, his last collection of essays published in 1992 (*Kul'tura i vzryv*, 73–101), a work described as "the crowning achievement of Lotman's research on culture."[4] This culmination of Lotman's semiotic theory—a characterization of history and the ethical imperatives for the catastrophic moment—may be considered his ethics. This essay suggests that Lotman's ideas on ethics bear an affinity with a neo-Kantian philosophical tradition that views the estranged, marginalized Jewish perspective as the alternative historical path of an alien or other, as elaborated by Walter Benjamin, Emmanuel Levinas, Gershom Scholem, and Franz Rosenzweig.

Reading Lotman backward, or overturning Lotman, is a strategic approach to a less well-documented dimension of Lotman's other thought: his thought about the other. This approach is neither irrelevant nor capricious; the concept of the other is vital to Lotman's semiotic theory, in which the basic condition of existence is characterized by "a need for the *other* (the other person, the other discourse, the other culture)" (*Kul'tura i vzryv*, 13). Reading "the image on the other side" of Lotman's cultural typology reveals that where the positivist, scientistic formation erodes, an idealist, transcendental move, his last, is accomplished. This final knight's move may best be understood in relationship to what I term "the metaphysics of estrangement."[5] I introduce the term to evoke its origins in Russian formalism and to address its subsequent avatars, by placing "estrangement" in dialogue with concepts of self-identification and the other as these relate to nationalism, religion, and cultural identity. For Lotman the ability to achieve an estranged perspective represents the possibility for an unpredictable, innovative, and, most importantly, free action that enables and empowers the individual.

Lotman articulates his ideas in part by offering a gloss on contemporary Western theory. The philosophical tendency of *Culture and Explosion* is toward transcendental idealism, but in the Kantian rather than the Husserlian sense. Although the tenor of much of Lotman's thinking about otherness or difference, especially within a dialogic relationship, may be attributed to the prevalent influence of Mikhail Bakhtin on Soviet semiotics, Bakhtin himself is indebted to the neo-Kantian philosophical tradition as exemplified by Hermann Cohen and as modified in the dialogic thought of Martin Buber and other Jewish philosophers.[6] We can recognize an affinity or confluence of ideas; in particular, notions of covenant and explosive historical process as developed by Jewish philosophers Franz Rosenzweig, Gershom Scholem, Walter Benjamin, and Emmanuel Levinas resonate with Lotman's theory of culture and explosion and in his assertion that the role of the semiotician is to turn the culture upside down.[7]

Like these thinkers, Lotman begins his study of culture and catastrophe with a critique of Hegelian historiography and a revisionist study of Kant. To distinguish his explosive historical model from the Hegelian system, Lotman proposes the strategy of adopting an estranged perspective and persistently seeing double, rather than accepting a synthetic resolution of difference. This approach could be interpreted as a semiotically advanced version of the formalist idea of estrangement, refined and figured spatially by reference to the ideas of the scientist-theologian Pavel Florenskii.[8] As a problem in aesthetics, the idea of estrangement suggests a stumble, the moment of distortion or difficulty that awakens sensation. Estrangement figures in Lotman's earlier writings in his attention to the mirror, the text within the text, and the *mise en abîme*, notions that also compare to Bakhtin's ideas of double-voiced, appropriated, and inflected discourses: the other's words within the author's words. The vocal reflection is an echo that repeats yet alters the original. The dissimilar similar constitutes the figure of asymmetry. In his final treatment of the estranged perspective, Lotman mines the concept of estrangement phenomenologically, as a cognitive strategy whereby the estranged perspective clarifies the phenomenal world, rendering the familiar unfamiliar in order for perception to apprehend itself. This encounter of radically estranged cultures or semiospheres detonates the cultural explosion.

In his articles of the 1980s, Lotman had taken up the idea of asymmetry as a principle of denotation and generativity in explorations of neurology and biology, a sort of cracking of the "code" of life, cognition, and culture.[9] In the Tartu "Theses on the Semiotic Study of Culture," first published in the 1970s, Lotman describes the determination of cultural identity spatially as the imposition of a demarcating line: the operative oppositions at this time are inner/outer, us/not us, *svoi/chuzhoi*. The terms of "culture" are understood to be generated according to either an interior or an exterior position of membership and self-affiliation.

The "inner" perspective of culture is defined as the organizing force for social order and harmony; from the inner perspective anything outside the cultural order is the absence or negation of culture, or worse, chaos, disorder (Lotman and Uspenskii, "Binary Models," 30). The "internal point of view, a culture's own self-consciousness" is the proper object of investigation for the semiotician of culture.[10]

In a reversal Lotman now argues that the outsider's point of view, the marginalized perspective, is the correct perspective for the semiotician of the cultural forms of daily life. To make this case, he invokes the formalist concept of estrangement explicitly: "The natural must be presented as strange, the familiar as unknown. One's own must become alien, what is near must become far. . . . [One must] establish one's point of view from somewhere behind the margins of the usual forms of life—a situation analogous to describing one's native language, which naturally requires that position of estrangement indicated by the formalists" (*Kul'tura i vzryv*, 45). To obtain this perspective, one must cross over or delve under—traverse an intersection and complete the figure of chiasmus.

To be more precise, an explosive reshuffling is required. The insider must move to the outside, the outsider to the inside, there and back again. Lotman critiques the Hegelian philosophy of history as the failure to achieve this movement necessary for analysis; the Hegelian misreads history according to a unidirectional backward glance. Instead, the historian's gaze must take in history's course as demarcated points of "rotation on the axis of time," taking in the "lost roads" of potentiality and unpredictability (*Kul'tura i vzryv*, 57). This approach advocates a continuous pro-, retro-, and analepsis, exploring the "other" histories that meander around the linear historical path.

> Hegelian consciousness, which has imperceptibly penetrated into the very pores of our thought, nurtured in us a piety toward realized facts and a disdainful dismissal of those things that might have occurred. . . . Thinking about these lost roads in the Hegelian tradition is derided as Romanticism. . . . However, we can adopt the view that it is precisely these "lost" paths that present one of the most agitating problems for the philosophy of history. However, we should make a distinction between the two types of historical movement. One consists of processes that have arisen from an unexploded, gradual evolution. These processes are particularly predictable. An entirely different character belongs to those processes which arise in the wake of an explosion. Here every event is concluded within a smoking cloud of incomplete

potentialities. The detours which might have departed from that location are lost forever. Movement is realized not only as a new event but
as a new direction. (*Kul'tura i vzryv*, 58)

Lotman's vision of explosive change and a semiotics of estrangement
emerged from his idea of the semiosphere. First, he had to depart from
the salient feature of structuralist semiotics: the idea of language as the
primary modeling system for culture. In a tacit rejection of Claude Lévi-
Strauss's anthropology, where ritualized binarisms organize cultural
space and the space between cultures—"cooked" or "raw"—Lotman
makes the transcendental move to separate words and things, characterizing reality as a formation, in two different manifestations, phenomenal and noumenal.[11] Lotman appears to be staking his own spatial
model for semiotics on the Kantian antinomy of space in the *Critique of
Pure Reason:* "Space is nothing but the form of all appearances of outer
sense."[12] The repercussions of this move for cultural semiotics are tremendous, realized in part in Lotman's meditation on sex and death,
where he explores the intersection of physiology and culture: "Culture
is not a metaphor for sex, as Freud asserted, but sex is a metaphor for
culture" (*Kul'tura i vzryv*, 141).[13]

Second, Lotman rejects the Sapir-Whorf hypothesis on which the
structuralist enterprise may still be said to rest—the notion that language determines consciousness. Instead, Lotman posits abrasively: the
absence of a term in a language does not imply the absence of the concept. The absent concept exists—as another concept, as a rupture, or as
the very space of its own absence (*Kul'tura i vzryv*, 103).[14] Finally, Lotman
makes the multicultural move to break down Culture into cultures, by
overturning Russian culture, exploring its occulted "overturned image"
from marginalized, reversed, subverted, or estranged perspectives; in
particular, he takes on the study of gender, cross-dressing, sexualities,
and role changes in the theatricalization of daily life.

The point at which Lotman's theory begins to evolve so that he may
be seen to "part company with Uspenskii" is in his historical model,
originally built on the binary opposition between Russia and the
West.[15] When writing *Culture and Explosion*, Lotman figured the historical moment of *perestroika* as the explosion or rupture necessary for the
transition in Russian culture from a binary to a ternary cultural formation (*Kul'tura i vzryv*, 145–46). The full implication of this analysis depends
on a recollection of Lotman's earlier characterizations of Russian and

Western culture. In the famous essay coauthored with Uspenskii, "Binary Models in the Dynamics of Russian Culture," the two cultures are contrasted, according to their metaphysical and theological dispositions. The contrast between the two cultures is established to highlight the impeded quality of Russia's history in contrast to the freer possibilities for the West. Therefore, the opposition of Russia versus the West rests on the semioticians' effort to model the ways in which a culture transcribes its own history and applies an ethical evaluation to its past and future. Lotman and Uspenskii characterize this ethical procedure with reference to the concepts of linguistic truth and national identity, which unintentionally essentializes and perpetuates a messianic view of Russian culture and history.

The vexed opposition "Russia versus the West" as expounded in Lotman's earlier essays rests on two critical principles: the nature of historical process and the relationship of self to the other, characterized by reference to the theological and ecclesiastical schism between the Eastern Orthodox Church in Russia and the Roman Catholic Church in the West. In "Binary Models," Lotman and Uspenskii argue that Russian culture is based on a metaphysical binary structure of heaven and hell, good and evil, holy and sinful, future and past, "without an axiologically neutral zone" (31). In contrast, Western culture, according to Lotman and Uspenskii, has a ternary structure: heaven-hell-purgatory, the latter category permitting for "salvation after some sort of . . . trial" (25). This posited ternary structure of Western cosmology opens up a "neutral sphere of life" with the "greatly semioticized high and low spheres" (25) deferred or reified into anomalous and distant ideals. The experience of history within the ternary system would be understood as ongoing change, occurring within the neutral chronotope of ambiguous action—the final event of redemptive salvation is understood to occur retrospectively and always "later." For binary Russian culture, however, historical change could only be understood eschatologically, as a moment of conversion. Lotman and Uspenskii suggest that the essential binarism of Russia's cultural system is responsible for the reactionary character of Russia's historical evolution: the dichotomies of old versus new, native versus foreign, Russian versus Western are mapped evaluatively onto their foundation: Orthodox Christian versus pagan/Latin.

It may be too obvious to observe that Lotman and Uspenskii are themselves guilty of demonizing—while exalting—the Western, non-Orthodox other. The theological categories of heaven-hell-purgatory

utilized in this way are more an expression of residual Orthodox prejudices against Roman Catholicism than an accurate or even adequate
rendering of axiological space in either culture. To problematize this
paradigm momentarily: although the Eastern Orthodox Church has
over time articulated a rejection of the doctrine of purgatory as defined
by the magisterium of the Roman Catholic Church, iconographic evidence suggests that purgatory was an active category in the early Slavic
Christian imagination. Briefly, the Orthodox concepts of the bosom of
Abraham, limbo, and the "harrowing of hell" of the Nicene Creed are
sufficient evidence of some understanding of an intermediate space
between condemnation and redemption.[16] Furthermore, even a cursory
exploration of Christian soteriology and the doctrines of heaven, hell,
and purgatory reveals an essentially binary structure: from the "insider's" perspective, an individual is either redeemed or condemned.
Purgatory and heaven occupy the same space in the fundamental binary distinction of the historic, Latin Christian faith: eternal life or eternal damnation. At the risk of reopening the debates of the Reformation,
however one views the doctrine of purgatory, Lotman and Uspenskii
have mischaracterized purgatory as a space within which one earns
one's salvation; rather, the correct theological understanding of purgatory is as the experience of cleansing or purgation that can take place
only after redemption has occurred.[17]

Furthermore, one has only to think as far as Grushenka's onion to
note that the idea of just recompense for earthly actions serving to provide a second chance for redemption even after death was very much a
part of the Russian cultural imagination. Yet, taking note of the separate theological traditions—even within traditional Christian art of the
Eastern and the Western church, and especially with reference to concepts of rhetoric—is certainly reasonable. Adopting Lotman's own
strategy of overlaying multiple distorting lenses on the object under investigation, we might fold together on the hinge of "mere" Christian
theology the two poles of the ecclesiological divide—Latin Christianity
and Eastern Orthodoxy—to juxtapose those two discourses (the minimal pair required in semiotic analysis) against a third, non-Christian redemptive theology. Doing so allows us to explore an alternative, axiologically neutral, cultural history, that of the Jew.[18] Twentieth-century
Jewish philosophers such as Rosenzweig, Benjamin, Scholem, and Levinas consider the history of the Jews to be that "other history" "where
there is freedom of judgment" (Levinas), a "counterhistory" (Scholem),

which, as first articulated by Rosenzweig, is "beyond history," occurring in "another time" or in a parallel time underlying or weaving around the history of Christendom.[19] Jewish historical process is endless deferral or messianic delay. In Christian eschatology history unfolds in the *parousia* (the absence of the presence), but for Jews, as Scholem states, "life is lived in deferment in which nothing can be done definitively, nothing can be irrevocably accomplished. . . . The Messianic idea is the real existentialist idea."[20] Thus, Benjamin, in his *Theological-Political Fragment,* states that Jewish history "has no concrete ethical imperatives for the present."[21] Benjamin's Angel of History, therefore, completes a composite gesture of both backward and forward movement so that "progress is a kind of abrupt inversion, a being forced forward by going backwards."[22] The result is a cataclysmic upheaval, an explosion, which, in Benjamin's view of "explosive messianic time," is necessary to the historical process: "The concept of progress should be grounded on the idea of catastrophe."[23] What happens if we read Lotman's idea of cultural explosion as a response to Benjamin's challenge or as an extension of it?[24]

The implications of the foregoing theological challenge become clearer through an examination of Lotman's reading of the actual topography of heaven, hell, and purgatory—what he called a "fusion of geographical and ethical space" (*Universe of the Mind,* 175)—in Dante's *Divine Comedy.* Significantly, an earlier reading of Dante by theologian and philosopher of science Pavel Florenskii is (as David Bethea makes clear in his essay in this volume) Lotman's "initial and . . . only interlocutor" for the discussion of the *Commedia.* As a major influence in semiotic theory, Florenskii exported his notoriously deprecatory characterization of Roman Catholicism in contrast to Eastern Orthodoxy along with his philosophical teachings. This deeply entrenched cultural prejudice seems to have been unconsciously imported into Lotman and Uspenskii's formulation.[25]

In Lotman's account of the peculiar configuration of Dante's cosmography, the axis top-bottom (ascent-descent) is relative in that the "bottom" is identified with the center of earth's gravity, while the "top" indicates any radius directed away from the center; the significant and absolute axis of Dante's universe traverses the separate but clearly vertical path of Lucifer's fall from heaven to hell.[26] The apparent contradiction between the two axes—the relative and the absolute—is resolved semiotically by Lotman. Rejecting Florenskii's use of non-Euclidean geometry to resolve this problem, Lotman suggests that Dante was influenced by Aristotle's view that the "northern hemisphere, being less perfect, occupies the lower position and the southern hemisphere the upper position of the globe. So when Dante and Virgil move down the relative scale of the earthly top/bottom axis, that is, when they go deeper from the surface of the Earth towards its center they are simultaneously ascending the absolute axis" (*Universe of the Mind,* 179). What is significant for Dante, Lotman asserts, is the mapping of signification according to this absolute hierarchy: "The closer the text is placed in the hierarchy to the heavenly light which is the true content of all medieval symbolic systems, the brighter is the meaning shining through and the more direct and the less conventionalized is its expression. The further the text is from the source of truth, the more . . . arbitrary is the relationship of content to expression" (179). Thus conventional signification and the snares of arbitration are linked to the region of evil, ruled by Satan, the liar and the "father of lies." Lotman suggests a further ethical model of space in Dante as the circular movement of sorcery, magic, and the demonic is countered by the linear trajectory, the *recta linea* of Renaissance thought associated with the Christian, Augustinian conception of the redemption of time and history. This same view underlies the esoteric understanding of the logos within Christian doctrine as interpretable primarily by means of divine revelation rather than through the exercise of logical reasoning.[27]

Lotman's quest for semiotic freedom beyond the binary opposition of Christian/pagan, true/false appears in an earlier—and possibly fragmentary—study of the social and semiotic contract: "'Agreement' and 'Self-Giving' as Archetypal Models of Culture."[28] In this essay the type of social compact designated as an "agreement" *(dogovor)* is characterized as a contractual transaction whose ethical character is associated with Western European culture. An agreement is contrasted to the idea of an unconditional act of self-giving *(vruchenie sebia)*, which we may immediately recognize as the sine qua non of the Christian ethos, a type of *imitatio Christi* exalted in Russian art and culture. Lotman makes use of this essential contrast between "transaction" and "self-giving" to map the semiotic dimensions of convention and iconicity, lies and truth. This model may underlie Lotman's later ideas about ethics. To trace this movement in his thought adequately, we will need to scrutinize his earlier formulation closely.

The first distinction Lotman makes is between magical and religious intentions. The practice of magic or ritual implies enforcing one's own will, wresting the desired outcome from the metaphysical dimension by means of a significatory activity—incantation, ritual—inducing a compulsory causality. This causality must be understood as conventionally determined through the agreement or compact made or implied through the arbitration of signs. Lotman is quick to observe that "the existence of an agreement . . . implies that it may be broken, just as within the conventional, semiotic nature of the exchange there lies the possibility for deception and misinformation" ("'Agreement' and 'Self-Giving,'" 125). The agreement is transactional only; words can be twisted, intentions violated, and the beneficiary of the contract is the one who succeeds in escaping through a legal loophole while stringing the other up in his own words. Lotman explicitly designates this idea of an axiologically neutral contract as the foundation for the ethical morality of the religious institutions of the Christian West. "In the Western European tradition an agreement is neutral—it may be good or bad; however, in its specifically chivalric form, with its cult of the sign, keeping one's word becomes a matter of honor" (129). Whether the contract is good or bad (a relevant example might be the bizarre promise exacted from Sir Gawain by the Green Knight), the culture insists on its ratification and the fulfillment of the exchange as a point of honor. Just as the idea of purgatory is developed, according to Lotman and Uspenskii, to ensure that a person pays an eye for an eye and a tooth for a tooth, so one's "word" is given in Western culture with the understanding that one will get something in return for it. Thus Lotman's characterization of the chivalric code—self-sacrifice, death in battle—was considered to be an "act of exchange of life for glory."

The conventionality of discourse replicates this contractual or transactional idea, which, Lotman argues, lies at the foundation of Western culture. Thus the sign is sold out in the marketplace of ideas among the Baconian idols of the mind, so that all cultural manifestations became ritualized and conventionalized: the language of courtly love, of flowers, of clothes emphasize their essential arbitrary character in their interchangeability. For example, Lotman cites a French lexicon of love, translated into Russian, that construes beauty spots according to their placement and appearance: "A velvet beauty spot . . . on the temple indicates ill-health, a taffeta one on the left side of the forehead stands for pride, etc. . . . The key to this code, as to the code of a diplomat in foreign service, is not fixed; words are arbitrarily selected and changed for security reasons."[29] The entirely arbitrary quality of Western cultural manifestations, Lotman suggests, is apparent in the subsequent history of styles, with a complete collapse of binary signification and the crossover of opposites in cross-dressing and the theatricalization of daily life. The sordid and opportunistic character of arbitrary signification emanates from its source in the originary satanic compact.

By contrast Lotman characterizes the purely religious contract as an unconditional act of self-giving that seeks no return or recompense, an endowment, a donation, the investiture of trust. We might do well to translate *vruchenie* with the theological term *dispensation.* Such an action—which has all the appearance of arbitrariness in that there is no causal compulsion or guarantee of return—nonetheless is more truly nonarbitrary in its signifying capacity, according to Lotman: "[T]here can be no thought of any conditionality or conventionality as regards the basic values. And so in this case, the means of communication are not signs but symbols whose nature precludes the possibility of expression being alienated from content, and consequently also the possibility of deception or interpretation. Consequently relationships of this type take the form of an unconditional gift rather than an agreement" ("'Agreement' and 'Self-Giving,'" 126). In theological terms such an unconditional, self-sacrificing gift is characterized as the dispensation of "grace," the religious act of self-giving as the *imitatio Christi* referred to earlier. In Lotman's reading, therefore, Russian culture is—perpetuating the stereotype—the truly Christian culture, while Western culture, its soul sold to the devil, is debased, dishonest, and corrupt. "Service 'by contract' is suspect, but service 'as to God' is genuine" (130).

Characterizing Russian culture as enslaved to self-giving perpetuates the messianic vision of Russian society. The suggestion that the Russian ideal is expressed in this habitual posture of lordosis, the complete surrender of the self in blind allegiance and service to an ideal, whether of religion or of the state—indeed, Lotman's whole point is that the two became blended—is a notion that has recently been thoroughly ventilated in Daniel Rancour-Laferriere's study of the "slave soul of Russia," a case of institutionalized moral masochism.[30] Yet serious study of Christian theology—Catholic, Protestant, Orthodox, and every denominational divide in between—suggests that the idea of grace as the unmerited gift of God and the model for human action in selfless commitment to charity is as central to the doctrine of the

Western church, and therefore relevant to its artistic and socio-cultural traditions, as to the Eastern.[31]

In their critique Lotman and Uspenskii seem to manifest an ambivalent chauvinism; yet if they momentarily appear to valorize the Russian soul's capacity for self-abnegation, they certainly do not fail to castigate the resultant reactionary passivity. It is fairly clear that for Lotman at least, the semiotic modalities of conventionality and iconicity—the unmotivated as opposed to the motivated sign—carry heavy moral significance. What is at stake in these discriminations? If Lotman is indeed a Kantian or, more properly, a neo-Kantian, the argument in the article on "agreement" and "self-giving" should be read in relation to the categorical imperative. An ethical action for Kant is not the result of an innate, natural altruistic impulse—if it were, then that action would fulfill and hence gratify a desire, thus participating in the region of exchange or transaction brought into question by Lotman. Instead, an ethical action, Kant suggests, must occur as the result of exercising a criterial action of practical judgment that such an action is morally demanded of one.[32] Similarly, the aesthetic response to beauty does not derive from pleasure or prurience, but is the formulation of a "disinterested" judgment. The operation of judgment occurs with malaise in the case of the sublime, indexed as the painful sensation of the limits of understanding. The moral imperative is experienced as the pressure of ethical duty over natural self-interest. We are back in the realm of Christian self-sacrifice, not surprisingly, inhabiting German transcendental idealism.

The best strategy for tracing Lotman's pursuit of a free alternative in signification might be to utilize his own tactical analytic procedures. In his Foucauldian essay "The Madman and the Idiot" (*Kul'tura i vzryv*, 41–62), Lotman illustrates his ideas about unpredictability and freedom by unpacking the dichotomy of "madman/idiot" to obtain two pairs of hinged oppositions: "madman/clever man" and "clever man/idiot," thereby achieving the desirable third dimension.[33] Both the madman and the idiot are behaviorally constrained: the idiot has less freedom than normal and the madman has more freedom than normal, but only the clever man is capable of originality and unpredictability in his words and actions (the example given is Ulysses in the Cyclops episode). The clever man achieves heroic status by engineering an unexpected feat of intellectual ingenuity through freedom of choice.

If, tapping Lotman's categories of freedom and unpredictability, we were to interpolate a third term—one that opens up a region of freedom and unpredictability—into the opposition of "agreement" and "self-giving" or "contract" and "dispensation," that term would clearly have to be *covenant*. Like the "madman" and the "idiot," both "agreement" and "self-giving" are constrained. Freedom is not to be obtained within this early paradigm. Although Lotman states that the contract is axiologically neutral, that is, that it can be made with either God or Satan, he could not have been ignorant of the fact that, within the Judeo-Christian tradition, a contract between a human being and God must be designated differently—as a covenant *(zavet)*.[34]

The human-divine argument cannot be contractual, because the nature of the exchange can never be equal. What God receives from humanity is supernumerary, while what humanity receives from God is always unmerited and therefore appears as the unmotivated dispensation of grace. The covenantal idea is essential to the Christian traditions of the Roman and of the Byzantine churches. It is characterized by Vladimir Lossky as a cosmic union or "alliance" between God and humanity; in other words, the divine-human covenant is neither an agreement, an exchange, nor a one-sided offering, but an election (a "strange election" according to Levinas)—an election to an ongoing dialogue and commitment to a love relationship, allegorized as marriage in both the Old and the New Testament.[35]

The potential for neutral, unpredetermined action exists at both the moment of initiating and that of extending the covenantal relationship. Bound only to the salient commandment of love, the enactment of the covenant is always referred back to the radical exercise of free will. Further, entering into the covenant relationship creates the necessary threefold model for ongoing human activity that is correlated both to the vertical axis of divine-human relations and to the horizontal axis of human-human relationships, that is, the realm of ethics enacted across human history. The covenantal relationship, bridging the vast divides between God and humankind, self and other, chosen peoples and the nations, does so by insisting on the relational terms *I-thou*.

The appearance of an I-thou relationship in Lotman might refer us to a source in Bakhtin, who, in his earlier neo-Kantian essay "The Philosophy of the Act," negotiates the difficult terrain of the self-other dichotomy when he asks whether the "I-for-the-other" necessarily implies some loss in the region of the "I-for-self."[36] Bakhtin asks, what is the nature of the compromise between inner speech and outer directed discourse, between the private and the public or official language, deeply troubling categories for Soviet society? In her article "Bakhtin and Buber," Nina Perlina illustrates the ways in which Bakhtin's thought parallels Martin Buber's notion of the I-thou relationship, attributing the similarities to their common source in Hermann Cohen. Whether Bakhtin is the sole mediator of Jewish philosophy for Lotman or part of a wider, direct reading of what Levinas calls the Jewish "philosophy of dialogue" does not alter the conclusions that may be drawn.[37]

At the very least, returning to a Judaic understanding of a covenantal "I-thou" relationship allows us to propose an alternative to both the unfree notions of the legal contract, with its self-serving greediness, and the kenotic, Christian ideal of unconditional self-giving, with its self-destructive extravagance.[38] We then arrive at the idea of an indeterminate and unpredictable relationship that neither spares the self nor wastes it. Such an idea is uniquely resonant with Jewish philosophical and theological ideas, constructed on the notions of separateness and estrangement yet insistent on overriding the demarcation of self and other, Israelite and gentile, in the constant exhortation to be hospitable and to love the stranger.

The Judaic or rabbinic paradigm based in covenantal theology sidesteps the scholastic logical law of the excluded middle and the post-Cartesian constraint on philosophical ideation that violently negates one term of the binary opposition in favor of the other: A is not B; A and not-A. In Talmudic wisdom and the rabbinical hermeneutic tradition, "it is accepted that opposed positions can be equally reasonable; one of them does not have to be right." As Rabbi Akir resolved the famous disputes between Rabbi Hillel and Shammai, "both are the living words of God," A *and* B.[39]

In the insinuation of Judaic thought into Western philosophy and in particular poststructuralist literary theory (resulting in the characterization of "Reb Derrida" and a midrashic literary criticism), this approach has been construed as the liberation of aesthetics via rhetoric from the repressive philosophical logos.[40] However, the major monuments of Jewish philosophical thought in the twentieth century, Rosenzweig, Benjamin, Scholem, and Levinas, have had to contend with metaphysical issues within a lived context of the Holocaust, returning us to the persistent problem of the nature of the divine-human covenant as it plays out in history. The third, purgatorial space—it is said—insists on correct reward and punishment, yet the world is notoriously and radically unfair, as the book of Job evidences. The God of adult faith, writes Levinas, appears in the emptiness of a child's heaven.[41]

Bakhtin's thinking developed against the historical backdrop of world wars and Stalinist terror; the ideas of Jewish thinkers such as Rosenzweig, writing from the trenches of World War I, or Benjamin and Levinas, contending with the onset of the Nazi Holocaust and its aftermath, share that cloud of catastrophe. The Moscow-Tartu school stands in the same historical path.

For Levinas, inheritor of the Jewish problem of the redemption of the material world, the endlessly deferred messianic solution (Rosenzweig's "star of redemption," Benjamin's "explosive messianic time") was bracketed as a "magically" receding horizon in the literal face *(visage)* of the other's suffering. "To be free," writes Levinas, "is only to do what no other person can do in my place" (the Bakhtinian non-alibi in being), and what no other person can do is to respond to the face of the other before me.[42] Thus Levinas uses the response to an other—the ethics of "being other-wise"—as a wedge to unseat ontology, asserting the primacy of metaphysics. His metaphysical model, emphasizing the perceptual and the phenomenological, has strong affinities with Lotman's estranged perspective and reversed semiotics. For Levinas the vitally important orientation toward the other is the prerequisite for dialogue: "Face to face is the situation of dialogue."[43] In his gloss on Buber, Levinas expands on Buber's idea of the Meeting (the locus of the I-thou relationship) by seeking the movement that initiates the dialogue. He suggests this movement involves a crossing over to the other, attaining the chiastic, "hither side" or the "reverse side," the "exteriority" of the position "outside the subject."[44] The encounter with the face of the other encompasses the vision of a stranger as the mirror image of an estranged self—here Levinas quotes Merleau-Ponty: "[M]y right hand touches his left hand."[45] To truly see the face of the other requires turning away from the horizon of expectations (against which the face of the other appears only as a silhouette, "a profile against a luminous horizon") and reorienting oneself toward the other's face, the Hebrew word for which, Susan Handelman reminds us, is etymologically connected to the idea of turning *(panim, panah).*[46]

To see the face of the other, for Levinas, is to witness another's suffering, to know "the position of victim in a world in chaos, that is, a world where goodness does not triumph."[47] The necessity to respond is "the paradox of responsibility," but not necessarily through doing violence to the narcissistic ego, making us, in Julia Kristeva's words, "strangers to ourselves."[48] Rather, the "I" of Levinas' philosophy is the "here I am, Lord" *(hineni)* of the Old Testament hero: "The word *I* means *here I am (me voici)* answering for everything and everyone."[49] In Rosenzweig's philosophy, the *hineni* is the articulation of the covenantal relationship, or "love as command." Clearly the responsive, loving "here I am" reorients but does not inevitably immolate the self. Neither does it exact the contractual payoff; so the law of God is understood to be tempered by mercy: "I will have mercy and not sacrifice" (Matthew 9:13, KJV).

In Lotman's theory of cultural explosion and historical transition, there are only two options for the imposition of law within a binary system: the first results in tyranny (as he discusses the classical tag *Fiat justitia—pereat mundus*) (*Kul'tura i vzryv*, 143). The alternative is blood sacrifice: to avoid fulfillment of the contract through the exercise of the law, the substitutive atonement of the self-sacrificing scapegoat becomes necessary (145). Thus the critical moment of transition from a binary to a ternary system, the exact context for the penning of Lotman's *Culture and Explosion*, is potentially a fatal one. The danger, Lotman explains, is that the explosion and its aftermath may be recuperated within the very binary structures that detonated the blast. An exploding ternary structure simply reshuffles itself, "displacing [its former values] from the periphery to the center of the system" (142). In contrast, when a binary culture is completely "polarized" and has achieved "ethical maximalism"—as Lotman considers the former Soviet Union to have done at the moment of being burst by a "wedge of wedges, an explosion of explosions"— the tendency is to think in prior terms, failing to find something new. It would be a catastrophe, Lotman observes trenchantly, "if the nascent order were simply to be a copy of the West. History does not know repetitions. It loves new, unpredictable paths" (146). His position, theorizing while crossing the abyss, demands creating a space for other ways of thinking. Otherwise, Lotman cautions, "[t]he miraculous fulfillment of a utopia for humanity that is theoretically predicated on propitiatory blood sacrifice is destined, in practice, to drown in a bloodbath" (145).

In encountering the opposition of law and mercy in Lotman's writings, we must address an urgent problem: Can mercy extended toward the other be achieved without the violent, self-immolation apparently demanded by the *imitatio Christi?* Or, in Old Testament terms, taking on the Isaian role of the "suffering servant"? In her essay in this volume, Caryl Emerson suggests that Lotman retreated at the last from the link between mercy and the arbitrary. Her conclusion can be extended here by distinguishing between the ideas of self-sacrifice and mercy within Jewish thought.

Certainly, the idea of "suffering unto death" conflicts with traditional Judaic prohibitions against seeking martyrdom. Similarly, the idea that the concept of grace can be accommodated within Jewish theology is heavily contested. However, if mercy is understood as the ongoing reinvention and reinterpretation of the covenantal command to love, the concept of mercy becomes not merely "unstrained" but indeterminate and unpredictable, perilous, even painfully difficult, but not bloodthirsty or terroristic.

For both Lotman and Levinas the idea of unpredictable, free action is of signal importance. For Levinas this is a "difficult liberty" — the freedom to respond to the other.[50] Readers of Levinas such as Handelman and Andrius Valevicius have suggested that this aspect of his philosophy is a direct result of his formation in Russian culture, the influence of the Russian Christian authors Tolstoy and Dostoevsky, a kind of philosophical Rothschild's fiddle.[51] Similarly, Rosenzweig was a Jew who was enthralled by the image of Christ and who stopped just short of a complete conversion; his Judaism has been described as "churchlike." Are we looking at a Jewish ideal rewritten into Christian terms or at a Christian ideal restored to its Jewish foundations? Worse, in conceptualizing this way, do we not perpetuate yet another reductive binarism? Yet secularizing what are essentially questions of theology and theodicy into a neutral ethics is also a form of metaphysical violence, an enforced assimilation. So Derrida reprises the old question, "What has Athens to do with Jerusalem?" "Are we Jews? Are we Greeks? We live in the difference between the Jew and the Greek, which is perhaps the unity of what is called history. . . . Jewgreek is greekjew. Extremes meet." And explode.[52]

In this confrontation of cultural identities within Lotman's work, the metaphysical violence of both agreement and self-sacrifice can be juxtaposed to a proactive sphere of difficulty, unpredictability, and assay: the culture based on the ternary system is never presumptive but only "strives to make its ideal a reality" (*Kul'tura i vzryv*, 142). The capacity to sustain both an interior and an exterior view of culture simultaneously is advanced as the result of operating from the privileged site of the margin or the underground, a geographical location that might have new resonance when considered according to Dantean topography. In his last published exploration of historical cataclysms during the years of the dismantling of Soviet culture, Lotman seeks the estranged perspective of his own culture's overturned image in the pursuit of new directions. As his final signature, he sketches a semiotics of the other that permits its articulation as an ethical ideal on the other side of freedom.

## Notes

1. Mandelker, "Semiotizing the Sphere." Earlier versions of this essay were delivered as "Ethics in Lotman and Levinas" at the symposium on "The Works of Yuri Lotman in an Interdisciplinary Context: Impact and Applicability," University of Michigan, October 29, 1999; as "Yuri Lotman and Cultural Studies: Recent Developments," Princeton University, April 25, 2000; as "Jewish Philosophy and Soviet Semiotics," at "Borderlines: A Conference on Russian and Jewish Culture," Syracuse University, April 7, 2002; the Columbia University Seminar on Slavic History and Culture, November 1, 2002; and Reed College, November 18, 2002. I owe a great deal to ongoing discussions of Lotman's ideas with Andreas Schönle and have benefited from his insightful and helpful editorial direction. I am more than thankful for the collegial support, intellectual generosity, and inspiration provided by Caryl Emerson, without whom this essay could not have been written. Any errors or infelicities are entirely my own responsibility. This essay is dedicated to the memory of my teacher and mentor, Thomas G. Winner, with gratitude for his endless capacity for self-giving to his students from his vast wealth of knowledge, wisdom, and hope.

All translations from *Culture and Explosion* are my own. Other translations have been silently amended when necessary.

2. See for example, Susan Bordo, "The Cartesian Masculinization of Thought," *Signs* 11, no. 3 (1986): 439–56; Sandra Harding and M. B. Hintikka, eds., *Discovering Reality: Feminist Perspectives on Epistemology, Methodology, and the Philosophy of Science* (Dordrecht: Reidel, 1983).

3. Areas of investigation for the Moscow-Tartu school in general; see, for example, the special issue on specularity of *Trudy po znakovym sistemam* 22 (1988), *Zerkalo: Semiotika zerkal'nosti;* Boris Uspenskii's consideration of the frame in *The Poetics of Composition: The Structure of the Artistic Text and Typology of a Compositional Form,* trans. Valentina Zavarin and Susan Wittig (Berkeley: University of California Press, 1973); and V. Ivanov's *Even and Odd: Asymmetry of the Brain and Sign Systems [Chet i nechet: Asymmetriia mozga i znakovykh system]* (Moscow: Soviet Radio, 1978).

4. Zylko, "Culture and Semiotics," 406.

5. My book in progress, "The Metaphysics of Estrangement," a comparative study of Russia and the West, explores the philosophical and theological sources for the Russian formalist idea of *ostranenie* (estrangement) and traces subsequent theories of the strange or the other, noting the phenomenological dimensions of the idea and its ethical ramifications.

6. That Bakhtin's thought has parallels in Jewish dialogic philosophy has been well documented by Nina Perlina: "Martin Buber (1875-1965) and Mikhail Bakhtin (1895-1975) were both followers of Hermann Cohen and his Neo-Kantian philosophy." "Bakhtin and Buber: The Concept of Dialogic Discourse," *Studies in Twentieth-Century Literature* 9 (Fall 1984): 15. The interested reader is referred to Hermann Cohen's *Religion of Reason: Out of the Sources of Judaism*, trans. Simon Kaplan (New York: Ungar, 1972). We must acknowledge the validity of Michael Holquist's claim that the "Torah and Jewish midrashic tradition" on which Cohen and Buber relied "makes for a number of inevitable differences between their philosophy and Bakhtin's essentially Russian Orthodox frame of reference." Introduction to Mikhail Bakhtin's *Art and Answerability: Early Philosophical Essays*, ed. Michael Holquist and Vadim Liapunov (Austin: University of Texas Press, 1990), xxxv. The point in emphasizing these affinities here is to create precisely a double vision or hybrid philosophical tradition that compounds both Jewish and Christian thought (of various ecclesiological denominations), without negating or excluding any aspects of either.

7. The term "Jewish philosophy" here describes a philosophical and intellectual tradition, not a religious outlook. Lotman's personal religious views or practices as well as his sense of cultural ethnicity are not at issue in this discussion. The philosophers designated here as Jewish also participate in a particular school of thought, deftly and synoptically characterized by Susan Handelman, *Fragments of Redemption: Jewish Thought and Literary Theory in Benjamin, Scholem, and Levinas* (Bloomington: Indiana University Press, 1991). The particular works that convey ideas of otherness, historical process, and explosion are Walter Benjamin, *Illuminations*, ed. Hannah Arendt (New York: Schocken, 1969); Emmanuel Levinas, *Basic Philosophical Writings*, ed. Adrian Perperak, Simon Critchley, and Robert Bernasconi (Bloomington: Indiana University Press, 1996); Emmanuel Levinas, *Otherwise than Being, or Beyond Essence*, ed. Alphonso Lingis (The Hague: Martinus Nijhoff, 1981); Franz Rosenzweig, *The Star of Redemption*, trans. William Hallo (Notre Dame, Ind.: Notre Dame University Press, 1985); Gershom Scholem, *The Messianic Idea in Judaism and Other Essays on Jewish Spirituality* (New York: Schocken, 1971).

8. Indeed, the formalists may have been directly inspired by Florenskii's ideas; A. Hansen-Love has claimed that an essay by Florenskii on perspective in art was known to the formalists. *Der russische Formalismus*, 83n, cited in Stephen Cassedy, *Flight from Eden: The Origins of Modern Literary Criticism and Theory*

(Berkeley: University of California Press, 1990), 119. In "The Metaphysics of Estrangement," I speculate that this work was in all probability the essay "Reverse Perspective" ("Obratnaia perspektiva"), which was written in 1919 for a governmental commission but actually presented to a wider audience in 1920 at a meeting of the Byzantine section of the Moscow Institute for Research in Art History, where it apparently generated considerable discussion. "Obratnaia perspektiva," in *Sobranie sochinenii I: Stati po iskusstvu* (1985: Paris: YMCA Press): 117–92.

9. Lotman, "Asimmetriia i dialog," 590–602; "Kul'tura i organizm"; "Mozg—tekst—iskusstvennyi intellekt," 580–89; "The Semiosphere," in *Universe of the Mind*, 123–214.

10. Despite the revisionist anthropology of Clifford Geertz and others, the late-twentieth-century attempt to achieve an interior perspective remained the focus of anthropological investigation, even as it acknowledged its own inadequacy in a theoretical capitulation to the inescapable position of a perpetually estranged outsidedness, issued as a lament in Claude Lévi-Strauss's *Tristes tropiques*, trans. John and Doreen Weightman (New York: Longitude, 1974).

11. Claude Lévi-Strauss, *The Raw and the Cooked*, Mythologiques, vol. 1 (Chicago: University of Chicago Press, 1969). Regarding Lotman's separation of words and things: "Semiotic space presents itself to us as the multilayered intersection of different texts, compressed into a specific formation with complex internal correspondences, exhibiting to various degrees, translatability and untranslatability. Beneath this formation is distributed the formation of 'reality.' . . . The word 'reality' itself encompasses two different manifestations. On the one hand, this reality is phenomenal according to the Kantian definition; and then there is that reality which corresponds to the cultural, noumenal thought (according to Kant's terminology)" (*Kul'tura i vzryv*, 30).

12. Immanuel Kant, *Critique of Pure Reason*, trans. F. Max Muller (New York: Doubleday, 1966), 26. According to Lotman's son, Mikhail Iurevich, his father was always a Kantian, and the entire Moscow-Tartu school had a Kantian foundation that was expediently concealed until the final years of his father's life. "Za tekstom: Zametki o filosofskom fone tartuskoi semiotiki (Stat'ia pervaia)," in *Lotmanovskii sbornik* 1 (Moscow: Garant, 1995): 214–22. Iu. M. Lotman rests his claim on the characterization of the text *("osobennost'iu tartuskoi struktural'no-semioticheskoi shkoly")* as immanent *(veshch' v sebe)*, which he compares to the Kantian *Ding an sich*. According to this biographical-historical view, Lotman's final works were a culminating stage in a consistent evolution, rather than the more explosive volte-face I suggest here.

13. See also T. D. Kuzovkina, "Tema smerti v poslednykh stat'iakh Iu. M. Lotman," in Egorov, *Zhizn' i tvorchestvo Iu M. Lotmana*, 259–70.

14. Implicit throughout *Culture and Explosion* is the discussion of the unpredictable, the untranslatable, the incommunicable, and the incomprehensible as precisely the most valuable site for semiotic generativity and freedom.

15. Svetlana Boym, personal communication, 1999.

16. This assertion might be challenged by many Orthodox theologians. However, folklore and legend support the idea of a less rigidly divided metaphysical realm: to cite one example, Mary's descent into hell to obtain relief for sinners (*Journey of the Mother of God into Torments,* an apocryphal text of the Eastern Orthodox Church). Also, to the extent that the early church fathers acknowledged the existence of purgatory, and to the degree that the Roman Catholic and the Orthodox Church shared this patrimony until the schism, the concept of purgatory may be said to have existed in some sense in the Orthodox Church. Further, the Orthodox Church does not absolutely reject the possibility of the existence of purgatory as an "intermediate state," asserting only that "whatever the 'intermediate state' might or might not be, the church on earth does not have the right to claim jurisdiction over it." Jaroslav Pelikan, *The Christian Tradition: A History of the Development of Doctrine,* vol. 2, *The Spirit of Eastern Christendom (600–1700)* (Chicago: University of Chicago Press, 1974), 279–80.

17. See the preconciliar Baltimore Catechism dictionary, which defines purgatory as "the place of temporary punishment where the souls of those who die *in the state of grace* must be cleansed before entrance into heaven, if their love for God is not yet perfect." *Baltimore Catechism* (New York: Catholic Book Publishing, 1962), 105, emphasis added. It should be clear that the operative binary division concerns whether a soul is in or out of the state of grace at the time of death. Purgatory is not a means of working one's way out of hell into heaven.

18. This proposition may be disturbing to those of us who understand "Western culture" in Lotman and Uspenskii's model to represent a secular and free alternative to the faith-based dogmatic institutions of religion and state. This interpolation of Jewish history as a counter-history accompanying Christian and secular history without participating directly in its imperatives is intended not to capture Lotman's thought within a religious worldview but rather to follow his own semiotic directives in investigating pluralities of discourses within cultures. The fact that both Lotman and Uspenskii are Jewish by descent merely strengthens the possibility of their sensitivity to the estranged experience of the Jew in Christian or Soviet culture. I am not proposing a secret commitment to Jewish faith or a chauvinistic allegiance to Jewish identity. However, as Vladimir Alexandrov has recently observed, "Lotman's philosophical preferences and habits clearly reflect his own cultural background and lived experience." Alexandrov, "Biology, Semiosis, and Cultural Difference," 358–59.

19. "The articulation of liberty in real life." Emmanuel Levinas, *Difficile liberté: Essais sur le judaisme* (Paris: Editions Albin Michel, 1963), 153. The counterhistorical idea in Scholem is treated in detail in David Biale, *Gershom Scholem: Kabbalah and Counter-History* (Cambridge, Mass.: Harvard University Press, 1979). Harold Bloom has connected Scholem's historiography with the Nietzschean idea of counterhistory in his essay "The Masks of the Normative," *Orim: A Jewish Journal at Yale* 1 (1985): 9–25. Regarding Rosenzweig's notion of

"beyond history," see his *Star of Redemption*. The idea of the Jews enacting an alternative history to that of the Christian world is a significant tradition in Christian thought, beginning with Augustine. For a history, see Jeremy Cohen, *Living Letters of the Law: Ideas of the Jew in Medieval Christianity* (Berkeley: University of California Press, 1999). Figuratively the Jews create a diasporic textual narrative of eternal exile, gap, abyss, wandering, homelessness. For a discussion of the idea of homelessness in Soviet culture, see Svetlana Boym, *Mythologies of Everyday Life in Russia* (Cambridge, Mass.: Harvard University Press, 1992).

20. Scholem, *Messianic Idea*, 35.

21. Benjamin, cited in Handelman, *Fragments of Redemption*, 160.

22. Benjamin, *Illuminations*, 257–58.

23. Benjamin, cited in Handelman, *Fragments of Redemption*, 8. Geoffrey Hartman's gloss on Benjamin's Angel of History links historical catastrophe with redemption: "Catastrophe, instead of remaining fixed in the past, and hope, instead of being an eschatological or future-directed principle, reverse places." Geoffrey Hartman, *Criticism in the Wilderness: The Study of Literature Today* (New Haven, Conn.: Yale University Press, 1980), 78–79.

24. It is not unreasonable to assume Lotman's familiarity with Benjamin's work, both through direct reading and refractory influence. This essay is not intended to be an influence study, however, but rather is a comparative reading.

25. In "The Metaphysics of Estrangement," I suggest that Florenskii's idea of "reverse perspective" *(obratnaia perspektiva)*, which is as essential to his reading of Dante as to his aesthetics and theology of the icon, influenced Lotman's concepts of the "overturned image" (the image on the other side: *perevernutyi obraz*) and "intersection" *(peresechenie)*. Similarly, as Bethea makes clear in his contribution to this volume, Florenskii's idea of a crossover zone *(perekhodnaia zona)* is analogous to Lotman and Uspenskii's idea of the neutral zone within a ternary culture. The idea of crossing over is developed extensively in *Kul'tura i vzryv*.

26. My discussion of Lotman's reading of Dante is greatly indebted to David Bethea's discussion in this volume: "Dante, Florenskii, Lotman: Journeying Then and Now through Medieval Space."

27. In other words, anything material—human, earthly—is, in its postlapsarian condition, under satanic domination. These ideas may be linked in Lotman's thought via the Heraclitian or Johannine notion of Logos. Mikhail Yurevich Lotman attests his father was working on or had planned an essay on the "self-arising word" in which this idea, implicit in the discussion of Dante, may have received fuller explication.

28. There is some indication that the article as we have it is part of a larger lecture or essay that was never published. Andrei Zorin, personal communication, 1999.

29. Dreux du Radier, *Lexicon of Love*, trans. A. V. Khrapovitsky, cited in Lotman, "'Agreement' and 'Self-Giving,'" 137.

30. Daniel Rancour-Laferriere, *The Slave Soul of Russia: Moral Masochism and the Cult of Suffering* (New York: New York University Press, 1996).

31. The idealization of "self-giving" may be compared to what Julia Kristeva calls "abjection": the impulse toward self-mutilation and self-sacrifice occurs with the Christian internalization of the need for propitiatory atonement. In other words, the sacrifice of a scapegoat as a means of expiation is no longer expedient when the source of evil and contamination is located within the individual. To explore the philosophical and theological foundations of abjection, Kristeva notes the analogy of the effect of the art work to the purgatorial function, both in the Aristotelian notion of catharsis and in the Platonic version of "poetic purification." Kristeva suggests that Kant's *Metaphysical Principles of Virtue* govern the modern code of ethics and aesthetics, whereby self-imposed limitation, the practice of an "ethical gymnastics" (compare to *askesis*) transforms "catharsis, where transcendental idealism is concerned, into philosophy." Julia Kristeva, *The Powers of Horror: An Essay on Abjection* (New York: Columbia University Press, 1982), 28.

32. Thus, infamously, in his *Observations on the Feeling of the Beautiful and Sublime,* trans. John T. Goldthwait (Berkeley: University of California Press, 1960), Kant notes that women cannot be moral, since their impulse to charitable action is based on a "strong inborn feeling for all that is beautiful" (77): "Women will avoid the wicked not because it is unright, but because it is ugly; and virtuous actions mean to them such as are morally beautiful. Nothing of duty, nothing of compulsion, nothing of obligation! . . . I hardly believe that the fair sex is capable of principles" (81).

33. The actual terms are difficult to translate adequately. While *madman* and *idiot* convey the meaning of *sumasshedshii* and *durak,* the term *umnyi* suggests one who is in full possession of intellect, reason, wisdom, sense, and wit. If this term is translated as "sage" or "wise man," Lotman's discourse in this particular essay acquires the tone of much rabbinical writing about the *haham,* or wise man. See "Ethics of the Fathers," in *The Prayer Book,* trans. Ben Zion Bokser (New York: Behrman House, 1983), 231–57. The categories "wisdom, folly, and madness" are juxtaposed originally by Solomon in Ecclesiastes 3:12.

34. That covenant was a part of Lotman's thinking is clear in his discussion of the function of propitiatory blood sacrifice as the index or seal of the birth of a nation (*Kul'tura i vzryv,* 144–45), relying on the covenant in blood of the Old and New Testaments.

35. Vladimir Lossky, *In the Image and Likeness of God,* trans. John Erickson and Thomas Bird (Crestwood, N.Y.: St. Vladimir's Seminary Press, 1985), 86–87. Emmanuel Levinas, "Nameless," in *Proper Names,* trans. Michael B. Smith (Stanford, Calif.: Stanford University Press, 1996), 122.

36. Mikhail Bakhtin, *Toward a Philosophy of the Act,* ed. Vadim Liapunov and Michael Holquist (Austin: University of Texas Press, 1993), 54.

37. Emmanuel Levinas, "Dialogue: Self-Consciousness and Proximity of the Neighbor," in *Of God Who Comes to Mind,* trans. Bettina Bergo (Stanford, Calif.: Stanford University Press, 1998), 137–51, here 137.

38. For a fuller treatment of the idea of "covenant," see David Hartman, *The Living Covenant: The Innovative Spirit in Traditional Judaism* (New York: Free Press, 1985).

39. As cited in Handelman, *Fragments of Redemption,* 242. A spatial illustration of rabbinical dialogue is the case of the debate over the alignment of the mezuzah (prayer box) posted on the door post according to scriptural injunction. The dispute over whether the mezuzah should be displayed vertically or horizontally was resolved by posting it diagonally.

40. Susan Handelman, *The Slayers of Moses: The Emergence of Rabbinic Interpretation in Modern Literary Theory* (Albany: State University of New York Press, 1982).

41. My paraphrase. Emmanuel Levinas, "To Love the Torah More than God," *Judaism* 28 (1979): 217–22, here 218. "An adult God manifests himself through the emptiness of a childish heaven."

42. "To be in relation with the other (*autrui*) face to face is to be unable to kill. It is also the situation of discourse" (Levinas, *Basic Philosophical Writings,* 9). A similar characterization of ethical action is found in Bakhtin, *Toward a Philosophy of the Act,* 51. Elsewhere Bakhtin strikingly anticipates Levinas in his discussion of the other in the mirror, whose image is an incitement to violence as it is simultaneously the prohibition against violence. See M. M. Bakhtin, "Chelovek u zerkala" [A person in front of the mirror], *Sobranie sochinenii,* vol. 5, *Raboty 1940kh–nachala 1960kh godov* (1944; Moscow: Russkie slovari, 1996), 71. For a recent discussion of alterity in Bakhtin, see Konstantin Isupov, "The Death of the 'Other,'" in *Critical Essays on Mikhail Bakhtin,* ed. Caryl Emerson (New York: G. K. Hall, 1999), 153–70.

43. Levinas, *Basic Philosophical Writings,* 9.

44. Levinas, *Basic Philosophical Writings,* 10; Emmanuel Levinas, *Outside the Subject,* trans. Michael Smith (Stanford, Calif.: Stanford University Press, 1996).

45. These ideas are characterized by Julia Kristeva in psychoanalytic terms, where the idea of strangeness or otherness is understood according to the Freudian notion of the uncanny: "Strange indeed is the encounter with the other—whom we perceive by means of sight, hearing, smell, but do not 'frame' within our consciousness." Instead, Kristeva suggests, we become strangers to ourselves. *Strangers to Ourselves,* trans. Leon S. Roudiez (New York: Columbia University Press, 1991), 187. Quotation from Levinas, *Outside the Subject,* 100.

46. Levinas's idea is that as long as the other (*autrui*) occupies a position in "the world where I stand" "on the horizon," where the profile only has significance "in virtue of its presence within this horizon," "I have not looked at him in the face, I have not encountered his face. . . . The face *signifies* otherwise" (*Basic Philosophical Writings,* 9–10). Regarding the connection with Hebrew terms, see Handelman, *Fragments,* 268.

47. Levinas, "To Love the Torah," 218.

48. See note 45.

49. Levinas, *Otherwise than Being*, 11.

50. Levinas, *Difficile liberté*, 187.

51. Andrius Valevicius, *From the Other to the Totally Other: The Religious Philosophy of Emmanuel Levinas* (New York: Peter Lang, 1988).

52. Jacques Derrida, "Violence and Metaphysics: An Essay on the Thought of Emmanuel Levinas," *Writing and Difference*, trans. Alan Bass (Chicago: University of Chicago Press, 1978), 153.

# 3

# Pushkin's "Andzhelo," Lotman's Insight into It, and the Proper Measure of Politics and Grace

CARYL EMERSON

In 1998 Sergei Bocharov published a bicentennial essay titled "From the History of Understanding Pushkin."[1] In it he notes that Pushkin criticism has long oscillated between two poles: worshipful subjective attempts to grasp the whole of the poet followed by "scholarly secularization" of specific technical problems. The result has been a beneficial hermeneutic circle: tributes by creative artists (Dostoevsky, Siniavskii, Bitov) are periodically sobered up by more formalist studies, just as the latter are routinely saved from lifelessness by fresh holistic speculation. Yuri Lotman is not among Bocharov's critics. Lotman's distinguished contribution to Pushkin scholarship fits well under this rubric, however, for he is that unusual "strong critic" who feeds both sides of the circle. Throughout his fertile career, Lotman not only produced a mass of new critical readings but also created new genres of criticism. His work on Pushkin participates both in rapturous synthesis (for example, his 1982 biography of the poet) and at other times in more formalist or structuralist correctives to that rapture.

The present essay is a case study ending on a thought experiment. Its focus is Lotman's 1973 article on "Andzhelo," the adaptation of

Shakespeare's *Measure for Measure* that Pushkin composed in 1833 during his second Boldino autumn.[2] Lotman's study, path-breaking at the time, has not become authoritative. That it was considered by some to be flawed and incomplete is hardly surprising, for the two primary texts are also highly controversial. Shakespeare's play is among the most ethically disturbing in the canon, and the *poema* that Pushkin built off it has been denigrated since the day of its publication. Belinskii invoked the work as proof that the Pushkin who had reigned supreme for ten years was now dead; and one of the very few responses to "Andzhelo" to appear in print during the poet's life, an anonymous 1834 review in *Molva*, declared it to be Pushkin's worst work. The present essay discusses Pushkin's transposition of this troubling story, Lotman's set of codes for reading it, and three alternative readings by prominent Russian scholars. I then close with a speculation: how might Lotman have interpreted "Andzhelo" differently had he turned to a serious analysis of it later in his career, applying the insights of his final period, such as those collected in the 1992 volume *Kul'tura i vzryv* (Culture and explosion)?

This thought experiment is all the more intriguing because Lotman does touch briefly on Pushkin's "Andzhelo" in the penultimate chapter of that final book. But he does so almost as a reflex, nostalgically, without exploiting the energy provided by his new paradigms. Such inertia in the work of a great scholar-critic is itself of theoretical interest. For a degree of arbitrariness (or creative accident) must obtain in any critic's selection of a compelling text to engage; that text is subject to the preferences and methodological priorities of the moment, and its richness is inevitably reduced while being filtered through the lens currently to hand. The explicated text bonds tightly to the critical method applied to it—for a successful methodology, like Lucio in *Measure for Measure,* is a burr: it will stick. For that reason one service, or tribute, we can render strong, prolific, and complexly evolving critics like Lotman is to loosen up such fused units, allowing the critic's own later ideas to renourish canonized earlier work. The "Andzhelo" affair is especially illuminating with regard to the Lotman-Bakhtin connection. For all the root differences between semiotics and dialogism, nevertheless, when compared with the hard-wired structuralism of Lotman at midcareer, many key concepts in *Culture and Explosion* have the open-ended, untidy feel of Bakhtin about them. In this final volume, Lotman displays a heightened respect for asymmetry, untranslatability, unexpected intersections, the interruptability of messages, and the mutability of codes. It is significant that the best post-Lotman "Andzhelo" critic, the Shakespeare scholar and genre theorist Igor Shaitanov, is a serious student of Bakhtin and has been occupied with the mysteries of *Measure for Measure* for decades.

## The *Measure for Measure* Controversy (Shakespeare and Pushkin)

"Andzhelo" is the last of Pushkin's several experiments in a mixed-genre mode. A work of 535 freely rhyming iambic hexameter lines, its central portions cast in dramatic dialogue and framed loosely by narrative, it is divided into three parts with stanzas of varying length. In its formal verse structure, "Andzhelo" resembles none of Pushkin's other long narrative poems, nor does it recall Shakespearean drama. Indeed, so little remains of the texture and suspense of drama that Russian Shakespeare specialists such as Iurii Levin have classified Pushkin's text somewhere between a "verse novella, parable, and fairy tale."[3] Not only the form but also the content of this plot has struck many as strange. *Measure for Measure* was not among the Shakespearean bestsellers of Pushkin's era. In the 1820s and 1830s, the Russian public was most enthusiastic about the festive comedies and romances (crowd pleasers such as *A Midsummer Night's Dream, As You Like It,* and *The Tempest*).[4] Pushkin, however, was always more attracted to the tragedies and the histories. In the manuscript drafts for "Andzhelo," he refers to his new work as a "tale [*povest'*] taken from the Shakespearean tragedy *Measure for measure.*" There is evidence in his correspondence that he considered *The Merchant of Venice* a tragedy as well.[5]

Pushkin was not alone, of course, in finding those two grim "problem comedies" very far from comic. In each, injustice piles on injustice, deception on deception, and the death of innocent parties is avoided only at the last minute by stage-managed coincidence or administrative fiat. Confronted by such capricious moral logic, evaluations of the play fall into two basic schools. Mainstream Shakespeare scholarship has tended to read the play as bleakly cynical, opportunistic, even nihilistic; Coleridge, for example, calls it a "hateful work" in his 1827 "Table Talk." But there has always been a more charitable, pious undercurrent to the criticism. In the mid-twentieth century a wave of vigorous restitutive studies argued on behalf of the play as Christian allegory, in which justice-seeking (if overly rigid) secular law is supplanted by the miracle of undeserved grace.[6] Either way, the issues raised—political, civic, sexual, legal, theological, dramatic—are so complex and so unsatisfyingly resolved that, in the words of one critic, "there is probably no other play by Shakespeare . . . which has aroused such violent, eccentric, and mutually opposed responses."[7]

It is uncertain how much of this reception history Pushkin knew. Indeed, there is still no scholarly consensus on how much his adaptation was guided by Shakespeare's play itself and how much by available French prose translations and English prose paraphrase. However, since large patches of "Andzhelo" parallel Shakespeare and at times approach a translation of it, it will help to recall briefly the plot of that play, emphasizing those episodes that Pushkin retained in his compressed version.

The reigning duke of Vienna decides to abandon his city, which has grown corrupt under his lax rule. He appoints as his deputy one Angelo, a man strict in morals, who will not "make a scarecrow of the law." This deputy restores a long-forgotten statute against fornication—and immediately condemns to death one Claudio, who has gotten his fiancée, Juliet, with child. Claudio has a sister, Isabella, soon to take vows as a nun, who goes to plead for her brother's life. Pushkin preserves these two interviews—legalistic facedowns between a righteous intercessor and a righteous law enforcer—as dramatic dialogues, and he constructs his "Andzhelo" around them. Isabella and Angelo reveal a dangerous symmetry more profound than any local dissimilarity of female and male, petitioner and judge. The sister abhors her brother's sin; Angelo would punish it according to the law. But Isabella is appalled at the presumption of mortals to pass ultimate judgment, an indignation that gives rise to her immortal lines on

> man, proud man,
> Dressed in a little brief authority,
> Most ignorant of what he's most assured—
> His glassy essence—like an angry ape
> Plays such fantastic tricks before high heaven
> As makes the angels weep.
>
> (2.2.117–22)

Isabella's eloquence and fierce virtue act disastrously on Angelo. By the second interview, he is so obsessed that he offers to spare Claudio's life if Isabella will surrender herself to him. Shocked, she threatens to expose his lecherous hypocrisy to the world. But Angelo ridicules the very idea of such exposure, assuring her that no one would take the word of a hysterical maiden against the authority of the duke's chaste deputy.

By the second half of the story, all the tricks at comedy's disposal must be marshaled to keep deflowering and death at bay. The duke, it turns out, has been in Vienna all along, disguised as a friar. He has over-heard everything—and, as he has been the cause of all this mortal con-fusion, so now will he be its resolution. He finds a substitute for Isabella at the midnight tryst that will buy back Claudio's life in the person of another virgin, Mariana, Angelo's jilted but still faithful fiancée. So vil-lainous is Angelo, however, that even after this tryst he orders Claudio's beheading. That head remains intact only thanks to several comic (but secret) substitutions at the executioner's block—ultimately of a head from someone already deceased.

In the final scene, with the bed trick and the head trick successfully deployed, the duke removes his disguise and reestablishes justice in an-other series of fearful symmetries. Isabella, coached by the friar to per-jure herself, accuses Angelo publicly of his vile deed against her person. Angelo is condemned to death for his lechery, a verdict that duplicates the sentence he has passed on Claudio for the identical crime: "'An An-gelo for Claudio, death for death!'" Mariana is married to Angelo and informed that her new husband will be executed forthwith; Isabella, publicly slandered and disbelieved by the duke, is induced by Mariana to plead for Angelo's life. In this humiliated state, believing her brother beheaded on Angelo's orders, she falls on her knees and pleads:

> Let him not die. My brother had but justice
> In that he did the thing for which he died.
> For Angelo,
> His act did not o'ertake his bad intent
> And must be buried but as an intent
> That perished by the way. Thoughts are no subjects,
> Intents but merely thoughts.
>
> (5.1.445–51)

The duke is not persuaded by her suit and proceeds to tie up the play in his own way. He produces Claudio alive, pardons Angelo (since the economy of "a death for a death" no longer applies), and proposes marriage to Isabella, the novice whose vows were so cruelly interrupted by the caprice of her brother's arrest. This final gesture has caused audiences considerable distress. Isabella never answers the inappropriate proposal, nor is a word heard from Claudio. Although scholars have long realized that this play is about substitution and exchange—in both the Old Testament "eye for an eye" sense as well as in more loverly exchanges involving disguise, bed tricks, and other comedic devices to avoid catastrophe—nevertheless, peculiar to *Measure for Measure* is the extent to which dialogic exchange dies out at the end. All utterances end up in the mouth of the returned duke, while everyone else is silent.[8]

It is a baffling silence. In Russian repertory, neither the frozen moment at the final curtain of Gogol's *Inspector General* nor the stage direction closing down Pushkin's published version of *Boris Godunov*, "Narod bezmolvstvuet" (the people are silent), prepares us for it. *Measure for Measure* ends not on the silenced shock of bad news but on the shocked, silent reception of joyous pardons, rescues, and wedding announcements. How can one play it? The very mode of participatory comedy seems contaminated. Confronted with this final scene, one outraged Hungarian reading of *Measure for Measure* from 1990 insists that the trickster duke is simply mad, a sadomasochist who stages a "political pornoshow" for the humiliation of others while destroying natural, healthy love (always the redemptive capital of comedies).[9] Others take the hard line, insisting that mutual love or marital bliss is simply not relevant to the play's message. This is a play, they say, about civic reformation made possible through the exercise of pardons, with or without divine grace.[10]

Much in this plot about politics and mercy would have attracted Pushkin's attention. There is, first, the arbitrariness of absolute power meddling in public acts and private lives, its ability to pardon and condemn at will, activate or deactivate laws, all so utterly familiar to the poet from his experience with two emperors. Then there is Isabella, a gifted, articulate, unyielding woman who confronts an equally articulate and unyielding man—a situation that thrilled Pushkin in art, even as he fled such women in life. (Critics have noted parallels between the male-female "duels" waged by the righteous Isabella and the tough-minded Marina Mniszech of *Boris Godunov*).[11] Possibly the poet was also drawn to Mariana, who loved her rascal of a fiancé despite his spotted past and thoughtless cruelty. In 1833 Pushkin was already three years married to a dangerously beautiful woman whose affections he had never in his own mind secured, and understandably he was enraptured by scenes of husbands getting love they do not deserve. Another factor might have been the mature Pushkin's increased concern with official rank and with self-respecting forms of government service.[12]

We know that Pushkin admired Angelo. In his "Table-talk" from 1836, Pushkin singles out this conflicted figure, whose dramatic portrayal he considered far superior to the heroes of French neoclassical drama. "Characters created by Shakespeare are not, as are Molière's, exemplifying some passion or some vice, but [are] living beings," Pushkin wrote. Whereas Molière provides a Hypocrite who does everything hypocritically, "Shakespeare's hypocrite pronounces judgment with proud severity but with equity; he justifies his cruelty with the thoughtful arguments of a statesman. . . . Angelo is a hypocrite — because his public actions contradict his secret passions! And what depth there is in this character!"[13]

This complex "hypocrite" provides the title to Pushkin's version of the play. When biblical epithet gives way to proper name, we might expect a shift from a comedy of situation to a tragedy of character (Hamlet, Lear, Macbeth, Othello). But "Andzhelo" is dotted with contrary genre markers. Corrupt Vienna is changed to sunny Italy, thus restoring the nation of Shakespeare's sixteenth-century source, Giraldi Cinthio. Episodes of amoral "comic relief" (boisterous street scenes, droll hangmen blaspheming the resurrection, and bawds being sent to prison) are excised altogether. The duke is made benevolent, wise, and — most importantly — old, a veteran of life like Pimen in *Boris Godunov*, a man beyond the reach and pull of love for himself. In the spirit of the folktales that Pushkin was writing in 1833 ("The Fisherman and the Fish" and "The Dead Tsarevna and the Seven Bogatyrs"), the opening lines of "Andzhelo" ring in like a fairy tale: "In one of the cities of happy Italy / there once reigned a very kind, old duke." This folktale invocation is our cue that the ending of the play will also be abrupt, didactic, magical, which, against all reasonable expectations for this gruesome plot, it turns out to be.

After the duke's departure, the action cuts quickly to Isabella and Angelo. In Pushkin both characters are softened and made more vulnerable. Isabella becomes so pure, so saintlike, that even her rage feels somewhat flat and abstract (we see her most often on her knees or being urged to her knees). Her stirring reproach against "man, proud man," that "angry ape" most ignorant when most assured, finds no place in Pushkin's dialogue; it is not Isabella's spiritual reprimand that undoes the deputy but her submission. Angelo too is elevated and sanitized.

There is little in him of Shakespeare's unfathomably dark perversity; when we first meet him, as Levin points out, he is no hypocrite at all but only a "fanatic toward duty."[14] He *becomes* a hypocrite in the course of Pushkin's narrative, much as Othello (according to Pushkin's keen observation) *becomes* jealous precisely because he begins and remains such a wholly trusting man.[15] In "Andzhelo," too, it is virtue that sets up the fall. The deputy is honorably fulfilling his duty ("Punishing one, I save many"), and to oppose the logic of this responsible statecraft, the aspiring novice Isabella, herself no stranger to the strictest law, can offer only the irrationality of mercy. Once seized by a passion for Isabella, however, Pushkin's Angelo loses his bearings and his political will. "Subdued and embarrassed" by her chaste innocence, he falls morally and literally faints from love; "governing becomes unbearable for him." In that confused state he makes his base proposal.

Their confrontation occurs at the very epicenter of the *poema*, crystallized in the opposition of *volia* (free will, license) to *pokornost'* (the submission or obedience of subjects). In this primitive and somewhat Oriental model, many have seen the political core of Pushkin's poem. But in fact an integrated politics is difficult to extract from "Andzhelo." Pushkin is careful to separate the worldly and the spiritual realm, allotting each its own responsibilities. For all the exchange of bodies that goes on in this story, Pushkin appears less concerned with equivalencies than with *in*commensurate goods, with levels of value that cannot be made equivalent or reduced to a single devotion.[16] Readings of Pushkin's *poema*, even in the officially atheist Soviet period, refrain from ridiculing Isabella's sanctity and vows of chastity—a restraint due to more than the prudishness of Russian critical tradition. This denigrating move is routine in Western discussions of Shakespeare's drama, even from scholars as sober as Northrop Frye.[17]

After these stressful scenes—Isabella and the hypocritical deputy, Isabella and her condemned brother—Pushkin brings his tale swiftly to a close. Suspense is neatly undone by a narrative device at the beginning of part 3: "It's time for me to tell you that this old monk is / None other than the duke, in other dress." Mariana is redefined from jilted bride to Angelo's neglected wife, thus destroying the symmetry of Shakespeare's plot (and destroying whatever verisimilitude such deceits can have, since the bed trick works only if the substitute is also a virgin). Since Angelo has lain with his wife and not with his fiancée, he is technically not guilty of Claudio's capital offense; thus Pushkin can omit Isabella's lines about "intents not being deeds" and thoughts not being subjects. But Pushkin's reworking of the end is part of a larger, more beneficent vision that the poet imposes on this Shakespearean torso. Pushkin highlights the fact that Angelo repents of his lust almost as soon as he succumbs to it. Since his swinishness is more transitory and so quickly regretted, Mariana on her knees begging for his life does not have the abject coyness of Shakespeare's original. In both, however, it is Isabella's response that brings on the culminating act of mercy:

> "Pomilui, gosudar' — skazala. — Za menya
> Ne osuzhdai ego. On (skol'ko mne izvestno,
> I kak ya dumaiu) zhil pravedno i chestno
> Pokamest' na menya ochei ne ustremil.
> Prosti zhe ty ego!"
> > I Duk ego prostil.

> ["Have mercy, my Lord," she said. "Because of me
> Do not condemn him. He's lived (as far as I can tell,
> and so I think) a just and honest life,
> Until he cast his eyes on me.
> Forgive him!"
> > And the duke forgave him.]

That's the end. No punitive cat-and-mouse games with others' fates, no "away with him to prison" or to death, no wrap-up marriages. There is only the plea by a forgiving woman that an undeserving man be granted mercy. Pushkin does not include Isabella's famous lines about acts not committed being buried as mere intents (most likely, Lotman notes, for censorship reasons — the Decembrist subtext), but clearly, evil intents that "perish by the way," whether by accident, ignorance, or trickery, should be allowed to fade away.

What guided Pushkin in his handling of this venerable plot? Since this question bears on Lotman's mytho-structuralist reading and its subsequent fate, a few words are in order on sources. Apparently the poet drew on sixteenth-century Italian versions and on the philosophical tales of Voltaire as well as on Shakespeare.[18] But ultimately how scholars reconstruct the genesis of "Andzhelo" must rest on their assessment of Pushkin's English. A most sensible guide here is Alexander Dolinin. He argues that Pushkin, while, of course, consulting and contemplating the original, worked primarily with the Guizot-Pichot French prose translation (its errors left their trace on the Russian text of "Andzhelo") and with Charles Lamb's plot summaries for children. Even in 1833, Shakespeare raw was simply too difficult for Pushkin's self-taught English, the Bard's richly elaborate style too alien. And this, Dolinin insists, was a good thing, Shielded from the full impact of Shakespeare's verbal genius, Pushkin could recast the story as an intense but selective translation embedded in a "fast-moving tale . . . at times colored with a light irony toward its own plot"—precisely his own stylistic signature.[19]

Without a doubt the most influential intermediary in the compressing process was Charles Lamb's *Tales from Shakspeare: designed for the use of young persons* (Pushkin's library contained the fifth edition, 1831).[20] This debt, although routinely noted, deserves closer attention. Not only do the major encounters translated by Pushkin as dramatic dialogue in his "Andzhelo" coincide in almost every instance with the paraphrased, simplified insertions of dialogue in Lamb's prose account of "Measure for Measure," but crucial adjustments to the plot coincide as well. Lamb's task, we recall, was a Karamzinian one, a laundering of racy texts for polite female society. He was tailoring these stories for "very young children," especially young girls not given access (as were their brothers) to their fathers' libraries (iv–v); his hope was that, thus introduced, the "true Plays of Shakspeare may prove to you in older years . . . strengtheners of virtue" (vi). Appropriately for young girls' ears, the bawdy underside of Vienna's brothel life is omitted altogether (Pushkin follows suit); no explicit mention is made of Juliet's pregnancy or betrothal, only of her seduction away from her parents' house (233–34). Pushkin downplays Juliet as well, remarking only on the unfortunate consequences of extramarital love becoming visible; Mariana becomes Angelo's abandoned wife, not his fiancée (244–45)—Pushkin adopts this detail too, for all that it destroys the bed trick and the symmetry of crimes. Throughout Lamb's account, both Angelo and Claudio contemplate their lust—in thought and in deed—with more guilt, "remorse and horror" (240).

Most un-Shakespearean in Lamb, however, is his final paragraph (252). There the mythical subtext of his sanitized and morally explicit tale is revealed: a celebration of matrimony in the lap of corruption and seduction. In an optimistic if unwarranted coda to Shakespeare's multiple silences at final curtain, Lamb remarks that Isabel, "not having taken the veil, was free to marry"; that she accepted the honor of the duke's offer "with grateful joy," and "when she became Duchess of Vienna the excellent example of the virtuous Isabel worked such a complete reformation among the young ladies of that city" that she and her "mercy-loving duke," the "happiest of husbands and of princes," witnessed no more instances of the "transgression of Juliet." Again we glimpse Tatiana as an exemplar to the sinful salon; again the anxious poet desiring his glorious wife to shine, but not to shameful purpose. How could this idealization of marriage fail to appeal to Pushkin in 1833? Ending his "Andzhelo" abruptly on the all-powerful duke's act of pardon, Pushkin might well have assumed, as its logical aftermath, the aura of this festive-comedic ending supplied by Lamb. In so doing he could link his fairy-tale opening with a mythical encomium to marriage, both of which have no place in Shakespeare's more brutally political play. Among the strengths of Lotman's 1973 reading of "Andzhelo" is its sensitivity to this stratum of myth. As we shall see, however, the myth Lotman isolates in the 1970s might not have been the most potent mythic candidate for Pushkin himself.

## Lotman's Reading and Its Mixed Reception

When Lotman produced his essay on "Andzhelo" in 1973, his semiotically inflected structuralism was at its peak. *The Structure of the Artistic Text* had appeared in 1970; its ambitious definition of art as a "form of cognition" and a "magnificently organized generator of languages" summed up a decade of work on applied aesthetics (*Structure of the Artistic Text*, 2, 4). The time of crude binaries was past. It had been replaced by a faith in multidimensional, layered structures, infinitely flexible and cunning, in which all facets of a message could be stored, inventoried, and made competent to model other realities. "The idea-content of a work is its structure," Lotman wrote in the 1970 book; "An idea in art is always a model, for it reconstructs an image of reality. Consequently, an artistic idea is inconceivable outside a structure" (12). Successful literary art possessed a number of these "idea-structures," units of fused form and content, which the careful researcher could tease out. Lotman examined Pushkin's "Captain's Daughter" under this rubric as early as 1962 and "Andzhelo" eleven years later. Throughout his Pushkin writings of the 1970s and 1980s, Lotman would group those two works (plus the poem "Pir Petra Pervogo" [The feast of Peter the Great]) in a cluster whose core values were charity, unexpected mercy, and a "saving [or salvation-bearing] inconsistency" vis-à-vis existing legal norms in absolutist states.

As Lotman reads Pushkin's intent, these unexpected moments of imperial mercy are pure gain, absolute virtues.[21] Echoes of this authoritarian mercy-and-charity cluster survive into *Culture and Explosion* of 1992, anxiously adjusted to Russia's ongoing perestroika. By that time, however, the absolutist model, corroded and humiliated beyond repair, had been forced to compete with other political paradigms on Russian soil—and understandably Lotman was more skeptical of it.

Lotman opens his 1973 essay "The Idea-Structure of Pushkin's Poem 'Angelo'" by noting the utter bafflement, among friends and critics alike, when this Shakespearean torso was published in 1833, "a strange and enigmatic thing" ("Ideinaia struktura poemy Pushkina 'Andzhelo,'" 237; quoted phrase by A. V. Druzhinin). A duplicitous ruler returns to rescue his realm from disorder that he himself had encouraged earlier in his reign: in the post–Decembrist era, the historical parallels to such a plot were both naked and dangerous. Lotman suggests, however, that an overtly dissident reading cannot do justice to the full "idea structure" of Pushkin, for whom political questions were being spiritualized during these years and probed for their transfigurative value. Although idea structures are complex, they are not paradoxes; if they resemble riddles, it is because they can be solved. And part of the riddle here, Lotman discerns, is the Shakespearean tension between mercy and law. As with Pugachev's off-the-cuff intuitive justice and the imperial pardon later granted to Grinev, the irrationality of absolutism can be a humane corrective when laws prove vicious or capricious. But Lotman does not stress this aspect of Enlightenment legal philosophy reflected in Pushkin's *poema*. Rather, he turns to the semiotics of myth, which at the time was becoming an area of intense interest to the Tartu scholars. In his reading Pushkin's adaptation of the *Measure for Measure* plot must be seen first as cosmic myth, then as political allegory. This mythological core is eschatological (247–48). A good world becomes evil with age, and as it nears its end, there is a "spoiling" (239). The agent or cause of this spoiling must depart the realm, returning to it later as a savior; in the interim his surrogate, a pseudo-savior, is unmasked as a sinner. As Lotman interprets Pushkin's message, the Russian "autocracy myth" is being interrogated here across several reigns. Given the censorship, Pushkin was obliged to construct this idea system with the utmost delicacy. Later readers must extract it from between the lines—or rather from the lines in Shakespeare that Pushkin left out. Unlike Dolinin's later explanation of omissions for linguistic reasons, Lotman—in the spirit of a politicized

Pushkin so congenial to those years—selects a myth in which power, not marital vows or marital bliss, is central.

That myth had clear real-life coordinates. Tsar Alexander I (r. 1801–25) had been a liberalizing monarch, much like Shakespeare's duke. After his mysterious death (distant from the capital) in 1825, his laxness was rewarded by the excess license of the Decembrist uprising, put down with unexpected severity by his successor, Nicholas I. The executions and exiles of 1825–26 created a climate in which any literate Russian would have seen an allusion to the Decembrist folly in Isabella's plea to spare Angelo. However foolish and in error the deputy was, intents were "merely thoughts" and his intent had "perished by the way." Or as Lotman recasts this point, "the juridical liability of unrealized intentions was widely discussed by [Pushkin's] contemporaries" ("Ideinaia struktura poemy," 244). Would it not be a sublime act on the part of the newly crowned Christian monarch to pardon the Decembrists, since their attempt at tsaricide had failed? Pushkin could not, of course, translate this more inflammatory portion of Isabella's appeal, which follows immediately on her personal (and in principle nonpolitical) confession that perhaps a due sincerity had governed Angelo's deeds "till he did look on me." Any further philosophizing on unrealized bad intents would have been criminally foolhardy. So Pushkin cut off his "Angelo" narrative at precisely midpoint in Isabella's plea, replacing her tentative recommendation ("Since it is so, / Let him not die") with the more categorical "Forgive thou him!" *(Prosti zhe ty ego!)*. "And," Pushkin concludes, realizing the potential of the fairy tale, "the duke forgave him." The power of the state stoops to embrace a human being.

Much in Lotman's reading, of course, deviates from the reality of Pushkin's life. Pushkin despised Alexander I, who had never been lax or permissive in regard to him, and rather liked (or at least had high hopes for) his successor, Nicholas I. Lotman is careful to respect the impersonality of myth, which invites analogy with biography and history while releasing critics from too strict a responsibility toward either. To conclude his essay, he recapitulates the idea structure of "Andzhelo." There are, he claims, three layers, each with its own logic and worldview: the novella, the popular folk myth, and the political concept of "mercy versus power" ("Ideinaia struktura poemy," 244). As coexistent layers they can be peeled back and examined one by one. The "unity of the *poema* lies in the *coordination* of all those structural layers," which together constitute an "ideological polylogue" (251). Lotman intimates that dialogue among these layers is possible and remarks (in a footnote) that "it would not be a stretch" to bring in the name of M. M. Bakhtin. Of that potential, more in a moment. But in the given essay he presents these three stylistic subsystems as relatively fixed worlds. Or to anticipate the terms of Lotman's late work, if these layers interact at all, they do so largely in the mind of the critic rather than among themselves in the world of the text—and in neither place do they explode. If "Andzhelo" was an enigmatic thing to its earliest readers, an analysis of its idea structure can solve the riddle by assigning stable meaning to its discrete parts.

When the "Andzhelo" article was reprinted in 1992 and again in 1995, an updated footnote informed readers that Georgii Makogonenko had published "polemical opinions apropos of the ideas expressed" there ("Ideinaia struktura poemy," 250). Indeed, in his *Tvorchestvo A. S. Pushkina v 1830-e gody (1833–1836)*, Makogonenko devotes a dozen pages to a rebuttal of Lotman's essay.[22] In his view Lotman's mythological framework and his notion of mercy as a humanizer of state power are— if not altogether wrong—at least inadequate to Pushkin's concept. The relevant myth, if there is one, is not that of a dying and then resurrected or returning god. Angelo is not a "false ruler" but an appointed deputy. There is no evidence that the duke's merciful resolutions are lawful, beneficial, or welcome. Most importantly Lotman's various layers do not mesh. Lotman seeks integration elsewhere, by tracing thematic invariants through a given author's works. Makogonenko, a traditional Soviet-era Pushkinist and no friend to theory-driven interpretation, is suspicious of this methodology, with its roots in late formalism of the Tynianov school.

Makogonenko then offers his own reading of "Andzhelo." Although also political, it pursues its politics on a level more abstract and philosophical than a roman à clef. An allusion-based strategy such as Lotman's risks limiting the reader's task to mere decoding, Makogonenko argues, and this method is all the more hazardous with Pushkin, who disapproved of historical allusions in works of dramatic art. Nor was the poet in the habit of justifying an ugly present reality by confirming its reflection in some timeless myth. When the duke's realm is moved from gritty Vienna to sunny Renaissance Italy, putting us in the mood for a golden age, we are meant to focus on the healthy laws of nature that Angelo criminalizes and betrays (*Tvorchestvo A. S. Pushkina*, 114). In Pushkin's variant there are no crimes at all except for the ones Angelo commits; there is only the cruelty of the law and the despotism of state power *(vlast')* (111). Against the grain of Lotman's mytho-personalistic reading, then, Makogonenko argues that Pushkin is not testing persons by means of *vlast'* but testing *vlast'* itself (and the myth of *vlast'*) in both its long- and short-term effects. When the first type abdicates (the duke), the second type (Angelo) must inherit; *pravlenie* (governance) inevitably degenerates into *proizvol* (arbitrary or capricious rule).

Thus Makogonenko has a darker reading of Pushkin's reluctance to indulge in a "parade of happy couples" at the end of the work (*Tvorchestvo A. S. Pushkina*, 116), one closer in spirit to cynical Western readings of Shakespeare's play. The duke might be personally kind, but as a ruler he is perverse. His acts of mercy (especially pardoning a state criminal in the final scene) are evil bearing. "In the given instance, mercy as an act of the monarch is *proizvol*, devoid of humaneness" (120). Precisely such "kindnesses" and indifference to justice had caused the law to drowse in the first place. Pushkin's "Andzhelo" is structured cyclically, like the didactic and hopelessly nonprogressive fairy tales of 1833: the fisherman's greedy wife sits by the sea with a broken washtub at the beginning, and the golden fish restores that tub to her at the end. The mechanisms in "Andzhelo," being less magical, are more ominous. The law still sleeps. Lotman correctly puts mercy at the center of his reading, but his three tiers are without explanatory force. Pushkin, foe of the autocracy and friend of the people, had long been reconciled to the real workings of power and was writing a cautionary tale.

For all their differences, Makogonenko and Lotman both remain firmly in the tradition of Aesopian, politically driven readings of "Andzhelo" that were the norm for the Soviet era. After Lotman's death and increasingly throughout the 1990s, Pushkin was opened up to religious interpretation. Critics sought to identify that moment in the 1830s when the poet's concern with natural and civil law—a constant if minor theme in his writings—was superseded by "Christian-moral" law.[23] An example of "Andzhelo" scholarship from this new, more liberal period is the 1999 study by Gennadii Krasukhin.[24]

Krasukhin too finds fault with Lotman. He questions the overall validity of the political dominant. In its place he argues that Pushkin, in calling "Andzhelo" a *povest'* (tale), directs us to the psychological evolution of its heroes. Lamenting the excessive attention given to the duke (a surrogate for the tsar) and to Isabella (a surrogate for the Divine Virgin-Intercessor), he would examine the title character, the deputy himself. In an ingenious attempt to account for the Charles Lamb factor, Krasukhin argues that Pushkin presents his Angelo as an inexperienced child.[25] The grandfatherly duke makes him "tsar for a day," and he loses his way; his chastity too is more youthful idealism than seasoned wisdom. And thus Angelo's fall is as much a shock to him as to his intended victim, Isabella. For this reason he repents immediately, and for this reason also is his pardon—as well as Isabella's remark implicating her own charms as key to his temptation—appropriate. The moral message of Pushkin's tale, Krasukhin suggests, is not so much political as pan-human: Angelo had thought he was different from everyone else, but he turns out to be the same. His transgression is not the magnificent biblical one but much more modest, embarrassing, recurrent, and precious to Pushkin, who was ever alert to biological process and to the optimal timing of events in a person's life (*Doverimsia Pushkinu*, 344–46). As we know from Pushkin's jotting in "Table-talk," it was not the corruption of Angelo that interested the poet as much as evidence of his complexity and development from child to man.

One mytho-political, the other psychological-maturational: ultimately, these pre- and post-Soviet correctives to Lotman still measure Pushkin's poem by a pragmatic real-world standard, "what we know to be true." Neither can be said to offer a fresh holistic view; neither engages the "impact of shortness" and severe compression on this luxuriant plot.[26] For this we must turn to Igor Shaitanov, whose two essays on the *Measure for Measure* plot in its Russian context (1997, 2003) improve on their predecessors both theoretically and aesthetically. Shaitanov not only brings in Mikhail Bakhtin but also prepares us for a reading of "Andzhelo" that Lotman himself might have produced, had he been allotted world and time enough to benefit from his own final reflections.

In 1997 in a Vitebsk Bakhtin quarterly, Shaitanov published "Shakespeare in a Bakhtinian Light: 'Measure for Measure' and the 'Crisis of Symbolization.'"[27] Its argument is as follows. The Bakhtinian light shed on this play is neither overtly political, a riddle with real-life referents, nor is it the enlightenment of psychological realism, appropriate to a *povest'* or novel. It is, rather, "topographical." The term is taken from ten pages on Shakespeare (dated 1944, first published 1992) that were originally part of Bakhtin's dissertation on Rabelais, in which Bakhtin, while not addressing *Measure for Measure* directly, identifies three levels of interpretation adequate to all Shakespearean drama.[28] They bear some resemblance to Lotman's triad for "Andzhelo" in 1973. Images in Shakespeare, according to Bakhtin, can be actualized as prototypical workings-out in Time of the problem of crime, legality, and political power. Or they can be particularized in the cross section of a given "historical present" (Bakhtin, "Dolpolneniia i izmeneniia k 'Rable,'" 87)—roughly equivalent to Lotman's pursuit of meaning through allusion (James I of England and the Puritans, Nicholas I of Russia and the Decembrists). But prior to both those levels, Bakhtin insists, is a deeper originary layer, the topographical. This is a prenarrative evaluative stratum that precedes even the ancient folk myth discussed by Lotman and that knows only the crudest, most indisputable parameters of a physical body: "up, down, back, forward, face, inner seam, core, externality" (84). In this carnival space of elemental gestures and orientations, a fusion takes place of praise and blame, success and failure, high and low. Compression and incompatible overlap (one fact defined by its opposite) are such that narrative has not yet broken through to a linear path. Shaitanov takes seriously Bakhtin's claim that "everything essential in Shakespeare can be made to mean fully only on the first (topographical) plane" (Bakhtin, "Dolpolneniia," 87; Shaitanov, "Shekspir v bakhtinskom svete," 62). In his view the pathos of the "comedy" *Measure for Measure* lies in its heroic last stand for these fused mythic units. They are not capable of building tragedy or satire, but are "the final peal of carnival exuberance." In this late play "Shakespeare subjected carnival values to an unprecedented test in the face of historical space and Time" ("Shekspir v bakhtinskom svete," 67). These values are not so much the carnival antics of Vienna's bawds (which Pushkin will excise from his version) as the deeper carnival truth of inseparable polar extremes. Where Lotman identified three discrete levels of narrative meaning in this riddle-laden Shakespearean plot, Shaitanov sees these meanings struggling one with the other over the same tiny spot.

In 2003 Shaitanov turns again to the play and brings in Pushkin. His essay "Two 'Failures': 'Measure for Measure' and 'Angelo'" reviews the quest for codes in these two works, beginning with Lotman.[29] The stumbling block in them all is genre. Neither Shakespeare's play nor Pushkin's variant on it can be satisfactorily classified, for neither assumes a stable attitude toward the problem of power—its benefits, harms, and the risks of its transfer ("Dve 'neudachi,'" 135). Following Bakhtin, Shaitanov defines genre as a certain way of gazing at the world, taken together with the storyteller's voice attached to that visual perspective. In Pushkin's "Andzhelo," he notes, no single voice is sustained. The initial epic voice of legend and folk tale, given in stately iambic hexameter, is gradually fed bits of other diction, inappropriately modernized and personalized. This "genre heteroglossia" (146) is the final truth of the play. Although Lotman's "eschatological myth" of disappearance/substitution/return (147), is indeed present, more profound, in Shaitanov's view, is a Christian moral posed in the form of a static question rather than the deep meaning of power is forgotten, justice is handed over to law, law is handed over to humans, and humans are devoid of mercy (148).

Such nested sequences, we might add, fall into Bakhtin's oppressive category of official seriousness discussed in his notes on Shakespeare. The only antidote Bakhtin offers is to restore the rapidly spinning, ambivalent carnival image, where praise and abuse are the inner and outer surfaces of every object. One is reminded of Pushkin's refusal to call Angelo a hypocrite in any simple way, just because "his public actions contradict his secret passions." The praiseworthy and blameworthy are fused. No ordinary story logic can encompass them both or resolve their contradictions. Structural change must await intersections, explosions. "And what depth there is in this character!"

## Intersections, Explosions, and the Function of Art as Depth and Grace

Here begins our thought experiment. Before launching it, however, we should recall a path-breaking essay of Lotman's from 1981, "'Agreement' and 'Self-Giving' as Archetypal Models of Culture," in which he draws a highly provocative (although not uncontested) binary distinction between two types of culture.[30] The first type is based on pagan magic, and it makes contracts. Indispensable to its proper functioning are three types of transactions: reciprocity (each side has obligations and rights); compulsion (both sides must follow the agreed-on formula); and equivalence (an exchange of conventional signs leads to a formal agreement or a legal guarantee). Lotman suggests that Russians have long tended to consider the Western tradition of Roman and feudal law, with its emphasis on civil rights, to be of this self-centered, self-serving, "magical," and thus potentially demonic sort, obsessed with contracts and due process. The second type of culture, not pagan-magical but radically Christian and thus closer to Russia's idealized image of itself as the non-West, is based on acts of unrestricted self-giving. Interactions here are characterized by one-sidedness (one party has all the power); a lack of compulsion (one party gives everything, but the other may or may not give); and nonequivalence (acts take place that are not answered). Instead of interpersonally binding contracts, the representative gesture on this side of the binary is the "unconditional gift."

A rich set of associations immediately arises between this famous essay in binary classification and the issues of justice, pardon, forgiveness, and mercy in Pushkin's "Andzhelo." When, for example, the attempt by Shakespeare's Isabella to justify a pardon for Angelo logically, pragmatically, and contractually ("his act did not o'ertake his bad intent") becomes, in Pushkin, a blunt plea for the ruler to show mercy regardless of an offender's just deserts, it is clear that the heroine has been recast in the direction of "self-giving" and sacrifice. Pushkin incorporates a more "Russian" solution into the plot. But the dynamics of "self-giving" is ambiguous, and here we might begin pushing Lotman beyond his own mid-career critical envelope toward his later work. "Self-giving" is indeed pure, committed, uncontaminated by compromise, in its own way selfless—but it is not, of course, necessarily dialogic or suffused with charity; its very purity can render it deaf to the other and to that other's needs and worldview. *Measure for Measure* has been judged a successful "comedy of forgiveness" to the extent that it makes compatible the conflicting claims of justice, charity, and mercy in a sinful world.[31] Every major character is tested for the presence of all three of these indispensable (and incompatible) virtues. Isabella, the Shakespearean character least altered in Pushkin's version, is so generously endowed with purity and a sense of justice that the lesson she must learn is charity. Her intersection with the demonic Angelo moves her unexpectedly beyond her earlier self-contained rhetoric of condemnation and spiritual ecstasy. Somewhere amid the shocks, ruptures, and betrayals she suffers during the two days and one night of the drama, she has learned the new language of charity and is now using it. Thus to understand her evolution in Shakespeare's plot as well as in Pushkin's, we must leave the insulated binary worlds of self-giving and contracts and enter a world enriched by interruption, untranslatability, and explosion.

Would Lotman have endorsed this shift? The final stage of his thought has been variously understood. Some critics see a continuity between his early work and the essays in *Culture and Explosion*. Others, like Amy Mandelker, are more radical, seeing in Lotman's turn toward images of intersection and rupture a growing distrust of conventional representation through signs, even a distrust of language itself as the universal modeling system for semiotics. In her essay for this volume, Mandelker makes a strong case for Lotman's demonization of the contract-ridden West, doomed to reproduce itself and its prejudices, in favor of the more sacrificial Eastern Orthodox model. In her view his later moves oblige us to reconfigure the Russia-versus-the-West paradigm that the younger Lotman had imposed, at times grossly, on complex material. But Lotman's message is mixed. He makes a passionately topical plea at the end of *Culture and Explosion* for post-Communist Russian culture to "rekey" itself in a ternary mode—because binary structures, he suggests, are too intolerant, too fragile, too impatient, and thus liable to collapse altogether when the local explosion occurs. As Lotman notes in the book's final phrase, "to miss this opportunity would be a historical catastrophe" (*Kul'tura i vzryv*, 148). In the spirit of these final pages, it would seem that Lotman should no longer be content to derive unexpected mercy for his heroes from the old binary model. In a ternary model a different and perhaps less arbitrary sort of charity should become possible: one growing out of polylogue, blank unreadable areas, multiple and as yet undecoded languages, newly available perspectives, and an ability to change oneself radically while remaining alert to the other's changing needs and views.[32] Might these latter-day Lotman insights be applied to a fresh reading of "Andzhelo"?

No single work of Pushkin's is analyzed in detail in Lotman's last book. But the presence of the poet is powerfully felt, especially in one recurring benchmark, Pushkin's definition of poetic inspiration *(vdokhnovenie)*.[33] Lotman values in this definition its cognitive richness, its fast pace and reliance on *un*predictability as the primary resource of any creative act. Explosions of inspiration continually create ruptures in the semiotic fabric. The duty of art is to rescue the newly released potentials from the realm of the abstract, to pin them down and thus, in Pushkin's phrase, "facilitate their explaining" (*Kul'tura i vzryv*, 27). All artistic activity oscillates between two types of creativity, "that which works within a given language, and that which awaits an unpredictable explosion" (29). And each type of creativity, we learn at the end of the book, has its own image of God: gradual, internally consistent processes know "God as the great Pedagogue"; explosion knows God as the "Creator-Experimenter" (136).

Pushkin is mentioned again briefly in the penultimate chapter, titled "Perspectives" (*Kul'tura i vzryv*, 141–46). Here Lotman contrasts the effect of an explosion within a binary as opposed to a ternary structure. Strike a ternary structure and it might be rocked hard but not blown off its foundation; in some of its corners people will hardly be aware that an explosion has occurred. A binary structure, with its more limited vocabulary and balance points, will be penetrated throughout by shock waves. When characters begin to beg for mercy rather than demand justice — and here the examples Lotman provides are Masha Mironova's plea for Grinev before Catherine II in "The Captain's Daughter" and Isabella's plea for Angelo before the duke — this is an indication that the collapsing structure was a binary and has been rent by explosion.

Like self-giving, explosion is a complex and ambiguous value. Although alert to the dangers it poses to binary cultural contexts, Lotman nevertheless loves the explosive moment. Only at such junctures can there be an immediate, abundant proliferation of potentials: these potentials are not yet organized, but neither have they become soberly pragmatic, the predictable outgrowth of gradual processes. Not without some national pride, Lotman admits that although binary environments are indeed brittle and catastrophic, the "profound crises" to which they are prone make them liable to "fundamental renewals" (*Kul'tura i vzryv*, 144).

To demonstrate this point Lotman invokes the ending line of "Andzhelo": "I Duk ego prostil" (And the duke forgave him). "The entire meaning of the *poema* is compressed into this concluding utterance," he remarks (*Kul'tura i vzryv*, 143). Most unfortunately, he does not elaborate. Having invoked his familiar motif of mercy versus law, he backs away from deriving it afresh — and thus the old opposition is not enriched with the ideas of intersection and explosion that fill his new and final book. This will now be our task. To frame the thought experiment properly and grasp what is at stake, we must consider one more chapter in *Culture and Explosion*, "The Phenomenon of Art" (129–36).

Here Lotman re-asks one of his perennial questions, why is art necessary to life? He urges us to rethink critically the neo-Romantic idea that art is opposed to reality as freedom is opposed to necessity. What art does, rather, is to create a new *level* of reality, one that is distanced and thus available for experimentation. This process is marked by a "sharp growth in the degree of freedom vis-à-vis the reality" familiar to us on the ground (*Kul'tura i vzryv*, 129).

What is that freedom? Let us consider only one scene — in fact, only half a line from one scene, the concluding phrase of "Andzhelo," "I Duk ego prostil," which for Lotman contains the entire compressed meaning of the piece. In 1973 Lotman had decoded this final line on three levels:

as a psychological novella (an Enlightenment parable), as folk myth (the true ruler returns and justice is restored), and as an allegory on "mercy versus power" (Pushkin's plea to lighten the Decembrists' fate). These three levels were seen to coexist, work in tandem, and thus could be peeled back for leisurely examination. In an "intersection and explosion" model, of course, such passive analysis will not yield the necessary insights. In late-Lotman aesthetics, we must posit three-dimensional worlds that are *not* compatible and not willing to nest quietly one within the other. We must imagine their collision creating new values that are unrecuperable and one-way, unexpected to those who generate them and incomprehensible to the bodies that receive them. Such, I believe, is the nature of the two exchanges between Angelo and Isabella that sit at the center of Pushkin's *poema*.

In that text worldly desire and secular power intersect precipitously with divine power. The language each speaks is incommensurately different from the other. When Angelo proposes a "contract" that would trade Isabella's body for Claudio's life, she cannot tolerate the thought—not because she doesn't love her brother, and not because she is a prude or a hysteric (as secular Western readings often see it), but because in her world, from her perspective, her body is no longer hers to dispense with in that manner. It has been elsewhere consecrated. She would gladly die to save her brother, but she has no language for life at the cost of a betrayal of chastity. Thus the first intersection between novice and deputy, divine law and secular law, ends in an explosion. Unpredictable variables and new mediating values might have been generated during the catastrophe, but at this point the parties involved are in no state to understand or formalize them. Isabella and Angelo find themselves in the condition described by Lotman in an earlier section of *Culture and Explosion*, the chapter titled "A System with One Language" (a critique of the Jakobsonian communication model). There is no overlap in their languages. But precisely this potential for dialogue to grow out of a deadlock is what fascinates Lotman. At these stupefied points, he writes, whatever the estranged parties understand of one another will be trivial, and "the value of the dialogue turns out to be linked not with any intersecting part, but with the transfer of information between nonintersecting parts" (16). Communication is suddenly understood to be most necessary precisely where it is most obstructed, even "at the extreme, even where it is rendered impossible" (16). In Lotman's new model, when the languages we know break down, God the Great

Pedagogue (who governs us by causality and is at pains to "demonstrate his knowledge") becomes a risk taker, God the Experimenter.

This first catastrophic intersection releases potentials and paves the way. When Isabella and Angelo meet at the end—more truly in Pushkin's compressed, cleansed variant, less so in Shakespeare's crueler original—some new language has become available that is inconsistent with anything either has spoken before. Each party acts within a new set of competencies. She has perjured herself, speaking of Angelo's aggression against her body as if it had actually occurred. He has witnessed himself in the contemptible grip of lust, followed by breach of word. He can repent; she can intercede. And appropriately in this new atmosphere, the duke can forgive. Calculations of the rightness or justice of this scene in light of what has gone before (contractual thinking) are not to the point. What matters are the potentials of a previously unknown language, promising a huge learning curve whose shape even the author dares not predict. In terms provided by *Culture and Explosion*, mercy is no longer at the mercy of a mere recoding or an executive fiat. And where will this act of forgiveness lead? That we are not given to know. Dramatic action is focused in the explosive, unexplained moment and then cut off. Charles Lamb's radiant ending to Shakespeare's plot (doubtless attractive to Pushkin but not written into his *poema*) is only one of several options beyond that cutoff. For the fates of characters in Pushkin are governed ultimately not by deeds, which so quickly become unfree, but by attitudes, which are always free. The humbling tone and acknowledgment of human failure that stuns us in the abrupt conclusion of *Evgenii Onegin* pervades the end of "Andzhelo" as well.

Might the explosion model of "delayed revelation" help us understand Shakespeare as well as Pushkin? It is significant that after several decades of suspicious and angry readings, *Measure for Measure* scholarship is again becoming more sympathetic to spiritually elevated interpretations of Shakespeare's difficult play. Its origins in medieval morality plays and allegory again compete for attention with sociorealistic explanations. Defenders of the play note that the central device of medieval dramatic genres is teaching by example, and that audiences were expected to identify with the sinful hero, not self-righteously pass judgment on him. One recent study by Robert Bennett examines the "Erasmian spirit" of the play in Christian-humanist terms that are quite compatible with Lotman's mature understanding of the aesthetic task.[34] Two comments from Lotman's final years might serve to bring together in a final synthesis Shakespeare, Pushkin, and these theories of art.

In a talk transcribed in Tartu in 1990, Lotman addressed the nature of the aesthetic experience.[35] Art is a highly ethical thing, Lotman insists, but it is neither a "textbook nor a guide to morality" ("O prirode iskusstva," 434). Consider Shakespeare: murders, crimes, incest, the gouging out of eyes. But in art this is all somehow possible, "and no one accuses Shakespeare of immorality" (435). Or rather, those who do so accuse him are mistaken, for art is a model of life, not life itself, and "we never confuse them" (435). One purpose that this model might serve was clarified by Lotman three years later, in a newspaper interview that began with the question: "Does one's attitude toward Pushkin change in the course of one's life?" Lotman's answer shrewdly balances both of his critical priorities, subjective personality and objective methodology. We are in dialogue with Pushkin, he answers, because "the system that Pushkin created and released into the world is a dynamic structure, it accumulates meaning, it grows smarter, it forces us to grow smarter, it answers questions for us that Pushkin could not have known. This system is the poet himself" ("Pushkin pritiagivaet nas," 439). But lest this promise of system lull us into a straightforward decoding of semantic layers in our search for meaning, Lotman adds the following about genius: "A genius differs from other gifted people by a high degree of unpredictability. This trait of genius was to the greatest degree inherent in Pushkin" (440). Genius, it would appear, is the only system so robust that unpredictability and explosion can only magnify it.

## Notes

1. Sergei Bocharov, "Iz istorii ponimaniia Pushkina" (1998), in S. G. Bocharov, *Siuzhety russkoi literatury* (Moscow: Iazyki russkoi kul'tury, 1999), 227–60, esp. 227–29. All translations, unless otherwise noted, are mine.

2. Lotman, "Ideinaia struktura poemy Pushkina 'Andzhelo.'"

3. Iu. D. Levin, *Shekspir i russkaia literatura XIX veka* (Leningrad: Nauka, 1988), 58.

4. See the lucid discussion in Catherine O'Neill, *With Shakespeare's Eyes: Pushkin's Creative Appropriation of Shakespeare* (Newark, Del.: University of Delaware Press, 2003), chap. 2, "Of Monarchs and Mercy: *Measure for Measure* in Pushkin's Works."

5. A. S. Pushkin: *Polnoe sobranie sochinenii* (1948; repr., Moscow: Voskresenie, 1994), 5:425.

6. Out of the extensive literature on *Measure for Measure*, Richard Wheeler lays out the basic complaint: "Individual fulfillment, marital intimacy, and communal renewal are celebrated together in the festive endings of earlier comedies; . . . [in *Measure for Measure*, however,] Shakespeare seems not to finish quite so large and powerful a play as the one he starts, but to change the rules—excluding powerful trends of feeling already admitted into the action—so that the play can be finished at all." Richard P. Wheeler, *Shakespeare's Development and the Problem Comedies: Turn and Counter-turn* (Berkeley: University of California Press, 1981), 3, 5. Is the duke an omnipotent, godlike figure, spinning fibs, sparing lives, and dispensing pardons at will? A demonic moral scientist experimenting on helpless subjects? A symbol of the playwright, as Prospero would be in *The Tempest*, whose magical job is to pull the plot together by pulling strings? For an exemplar of "chapter and verse" Christian criticism, see Roy W. Battenhouse, "*Measure for Measure* and Christian Doctrine of the Atonement," *PMLA* 61 (1946): 1029–59.

7. Ernest Schanzer, *The Problem Plays of Shakespeare* (London: Routledge & Kegan Paul, 1963), chap. 2, 71.

8. For a good discussion of the substitution-and-exchange argument, see Zvi Jagendorf, *The Happy End of Comedy: Jonson, Molière, and Shakespeare* (Newark, Del.: University of Delaware Press, 1984), 132–34.

9. István Géher, "Morality and Madness: A Hungarian Reading of *Measure for Measure*" (1990), in *Shakespeare and His Contemporaries: Eastern and Central European Studies*, ed. Jerzy Limon and Jay L. Halio (Newark, Del.: University of Delaware Press, 1993): 142.

10. Thus Lawrence Ross argues that "marriage is the remedy for incontinence and the divinely appointed proper use of potency," and thus wives are duty bound to reform their husbands. (We recall Mariana's plea to the duke to pardon Angelo: "They say best men are moulded out of faults, / And, for the most, become much more the better / For being a little bad. So may my husband.") These duties are largely unrelated to Eros. "The hopes for spiritual reconciliation and human fulfillment in new life are most emphatically placed in the relation of the male characters to their mates in marriage." See Lawrence J. Ross, *On Measure for Measure: An Essay in Criticism of Shakespeare's Drama* (Newark, Del.: University of Delaware Press, 1997), 144.

11. See Henry Gifford, "Shakespearean Elements in Boris Godunov," *Slavonic Review* 26 (November 1945): 154–55; and George Gibian, "*Measure for Measure* and Pushkin's *Angelo*," *PMLA* 46, no. 4 (June 1951): 426–31, esp. 431.

12. For a lapidary discussion of Pushkin's quest for "the sublimity of service" during these later years, see Andreas Schönle, *Authenticity and Fiction in the Russian Literary Journey, 1790–1840* (Cambridge, Mass.: Harvard University Press, 2000), 181–202. Pushkin, Russia's greatest poet and Karamzin's successor as imperial historian laureate, languished at the undistinguished ninth

grade in the Table of Ranks. Was not the Russian government obliged to provide opportunities for its subjects to serve honorably, and if not, what degree of obedience did a noble subject owe his political superiors in keeping with his dignity? For these career ambitions, see also Chester Dunning, "Rethinking the Canonical Text of Pushkin's *Boris Godunov*," *Russian Review* 60 (October 2001): 569–91.

13. From Pushkin's "Table-talk," in *Sovremennik*, 1836, cited by Tatiana Wolff, *Pushkin on Literature* (1971; repr., Evanston, Ill.: Northwestern University Press, 1998), 464–65.

14. Levin, *Shekspir i russkaia literatura XIX veka*, 60.

15. Pushkin refers to Othello in "Table-talk," in a passage preceding the Angelo comments: "Othello is not jealous by nature—on the contrary, he is trusting." In Wolff, *Pushkin on Literature*, 464.

16. For this idea of a "separation of realms" in "Andzhelo" (and its interrogation of the proper limits to authority in each), I am indebted to Olga Peters Hasty, whose ongoing, as yet unpublished thoughts on Pushkin and Shakespeare have proved both stimulating and indispensable in the evolution of the present essay.

17. Northrop Frye sees Shakespeare's play as "broken in half": the first half is a "dismal ironic tragedy" that combines Claudio's bitterness, hilarious bawds and hangmen, and sanctimonious meetings between Angelo and Isabella, who "start maneuvering around each other like a couple of knights who are in such heavy plate armour that they can't bend a joint"; the second half is a fairy tale, in which the duke must metamorphose into a trickster figure to ensure a comedic outcome. "Measure for Measure," in *Northrop Frye on Shakespeare*, ed. Robert Sandler (New Haven, Conn.: Yale University Press, 1986), 140–53, esp. 146, 149. Also anti-Isabella is Harold Bloom, who (unsurprisingly) values only the drunken murderer Barnadine, a "sublime" Falstaffian figure who refuses to die at the convenience of his jailers. Bloom dismisses Isabella as hysterical, Angelo as sadistic, the duke as duplicitous without motivation, and the play overall as "a comedy that destroys comedy" through its desperate nihilism. "Measure for Measure," in Harold Bloom, *Shakespeare: The Invention of the Human* (New York: Riverhead Books, 1998): 358–80. Bloom's favorite among the book-length studies of the play is Marc Shell's apocalyptic *End of Kinship*, in which this most extreme pitting of law against sexuality in the duke's Vienna is said to express the larger Elizabethan fear of incest and uncontrolled breeding, a fear that Shakespeare can counter only by positing the unrealizable ideal of a "chaste incestuous marriage." Marc Shell, *The End of Kinship: "Measure for Measure," Incest, and the Ideal of Universal Siblinghood* (Stanford, Calif.: Stanford University Press, 1988), 173.

18. See Levin, *Shekspir i russkaia literatura XIX veka*, 57–60, and also, for the Voltaire connection, S. A. Fomichev, *Poeziia Pushkina: Tvorcheskaia evoliutsiia* (Leningrad: Nauka, 1986), 231–39.

19. Alexander Dolinin, "Pushkin and English Literature," in *The Pushkin Handbook,* ed. David M. Bethea, chap. 22 (Madison: University of Wisconsin Press, 2006), 433.

20. See Levin, *Shekspir i russkaia literatura XIX veka,* 58n44, for reference to the Modzalevskii catalogue to Pushkin's Library. Among the holdings of the Rare Books Division of Princeton's Firestone Library is a copy of this same 1831 fifth edition, Charles Lamb, *Tales from Shakspeare: designed for the use of young persons* (London: Printed for Baldwin & Cradock, Paternoster Row, 1831). "Measure for Measure" is retold on 233–52 (page numbers in text).

21. Lotman does not charge Pushkin with political naiveté, however. In his essay on "The Captain's Daughter," he insists that mercy for Pushkin did not imply belief in any utopian fantasy of liberalism emerging from bureaucratic despotism. Pushkin was a man of "sober political thought." He merely dreamt that state life, at select moments, could know "genuine human relations." See Lotman, "Ideinaia struktura *Kapitanskoi dochki,*" 223; the phrase "salvation-bearing inconsistency" [*spasitel'naia neposledovatel'nost'*] comes from Lotman, "Pushkin: Ocherk tvorchestva," 205.

22. G. P. Makogonenko, *Tvorchestvo A. S. Pushkina v 1830-e gody (1833–1836)* (Leningrad: Khudozhestvennaia literatura, 1982), 98–130, on "Andzhelo"; and 104–24, on Lotman's essay.

23. See, for example, V. I. Kuleshov, "Znachenie poniatiia 'zakon' v khudozhestvennom mire A. S. Pushkina," in *Pushkin i sovremennaia kul'tura,* ed. E. P. Chelyshev (Moscow: Nauka, 1996), 78–91.

24. Gennadii Krasukhin, *Doverimsia Pushkinu* (Moscow: Flinta/Nauka, 1999), 328–61. The discussion of "Angelo" occurs as section 3 of chapter 5, alongside treatment of "The Bronze Horseman" and "The Queen of Spades."

25. Krasukhin is not accurate here: Angelo is specifically identified by Pushkin as no child to politics; he is a "muzh opytnyi, ne novyi / V iskusstve vlastvovat'" (an experienced man, not new to the art of wielding power) (part 1.3.29–39).

26. The phrase is Svetlana Evdokimova's, in her editor's introduction to a volume of essays and translations of Pushkin's *Little Tragedies* (13). She discusses Pushkin's quest for the "short tragedy"—on analogy with the short story—in the poet's idiosyncratic blend of Romantic monodrama and neoclassical stylization, asking whether a compressed, intense, polyvalent utterance can in fact be performed. See Svetlana Evdokimova, *Alexander Pushkin's Little Tragedies: The Poetics of Brevity* (Madison: University of Wisconsin Press, 2003), 3–38.

27. I. O. Shaitanov, "Shekspir v bakhtinskom svete: 'Mera za meru' i 'krizis simbolizatsii,'" *Dialog: Karnaval, Khronotop,* no. 4 (1997): 55–79.

28. Shaitanov, "Shekspir v bakhtinskom svete," 62; reference is to "Dolpolneniia i izmeneniia k 'Rable,'" in *M. M. Bakhtin: Sobranie sochinenii,* ed. S. G. Bocharov et al, vol. 5 (Moscow: Russkie slovari, 1996), 80–129, esp. 84–87.

29. Igor' Shaitanov, "Dve 'neudachi': 'Mera za meru' i 'Andzhelo,'" *Voprosy literatury* (January–February 2003): 123–48.

30. The terms in the title are more accurately rendered "contract" and "handing over oneself." The premises of these two basic types of culture are summarized in the English edition on 125–26.

31. The term "comedy of forgiveness" belongs to Robert Grams Hunter, in his *Shakespeare and the Comedy of Forgiveness* (New York: Columbia University Press, 1965); see especially his chapter 9 on *Measure for Measure* (204–26). Hunter reads the play as a modernized Renaissance allegory in which sin is countered by mercy, justice, and charity; the happy end of "comedy" is achieved when each major character has been tested (and passed) on all three virtues. "As the advocate of Mercy, Isabella has spoken with the tongue of men and of angels," Hunter notes, "but in the role of Justice she has proved notably lacking in charity. She has ruthlessly condemned her brother for falling short of her own heroic ideal" (217). Her own personal heroism is manifest in her unwavering choice of death over violation—but this is courage, not charity. For "it is one thing to say, 'Death before dishonor,' and quite another to say, '*Your* death before *my* dishonor'" (216). Hunter's point (offered from a modern perspective) is that although fornication would certainly place her soul in jeopardy, were Isabella to believe fully, she too could count on God's charity under these circumstances (215).

32. For many details of this hypothesis, I am indebted to Andreas Schönle, whose intelligent monitoring of this essay through several versions is here gratefully acknowledged.

33. Pushkin's definition provides the subtext for Lotman's chapter "Semantic Intersection as an Explosion of Meaning: Inspiration" (*Kul'tura i vzryv*, 26–30): "The disposition of the soul to the most vivid perception of impressions, and thus to the rapid assimilation of ideas, which facilitates their explanation."

34. Robert B. Bennett, *Romance and Reformation: The Erasmian Spirit of Shakespeare's* Measure for Measure (Newark, Del.: University of Delaware Press, 2000). The point of humanist rhetoric, Bennett writes, was not logical, legalistic, or doctrinal; its purpose was to orient the reader toward "wonder and admiration" (56). Interpreted in this way, the end of *Measure for Measure* is not unrealistic or inconsistent. It is wonderful. The duke, as a creature of natural rather than positive law, is the mentor and mediator of wonder. Angelo is the Puritan legislator who would stamp it out. The hero of the tale, the indispensable touchstone of virtue who must work so hard to achieve charity, is Isabella, Christian humanist in action.

35. As recorded by G. Amelin.

# POLITICAL REALITIES AND
# RHETORICAL BOUNDARIES

4

# Post-Soviet Political Discourse
# and the Creation of
# Political Communities

MICHAEL URBAN

The work of Yuri Lotman has yet to make its mark among Western political scientists. In this chapter, I argue that this condition has been particularly unfortunate for those among them who are concerned with Russia. Since the fall of Communism and the lifting of restrictions on scholarly access, investigations of that country's political culture have steamed ahead. However, the standard approach to the cultural aspects of Russian politics strikes me as entirely inadequate, if not altogether misleading, unless informed by methods such as those Lotman employed and by some of the ideas he has advanced. These methods and ideas enable us to locate representations in the discursive structures from which they spring, thereby avoiding hypostatized conceptions that often clutter our thinking.

To illustrate, consider how the conventional (positivist) concept of political culture—which separates subjective states concerning one's beliefs or values about the political world from the actual meanings embedded in political conduct—has been deployed in numerous mass opinion surveys attempting to measure such things as the receptivity of Russians to democracy and to related values such as tolerance or respect for law.[1] In their own way these studies have tended to reproduce that deeply rooted binary opposition that has structured Russian politics in the post-Communist era, according to which the public is divided into democrats and antidemocrats. But these groups are constituted in Western opinion research in a manner quite different from the actual process of discursive interaction that constitutes them in Russian political society. There democrats are identified principally by two related factors: support for certain politicians associated with "reform" and opposition to those (antidemocrats) who challenge or oppose them. To be sure, democrats also articulate a certain ideology, thus distinguishing themselves symbolically from their opponents, but their formal representation of ideas and values is of secondary importance. The main consideration concerns political practice: With which power bloc, in and around the government, are political actors associated?[2] In contrast, Western opinion studies have constructed their democrats in a different fashion, based on their responses to survey questionnaires. Under these procedures marking the appropriate boxes on the survey instrument, rather than actual political practice, would set democrats apart from others. As a consequence these studies appear to be at a loss to explain why most "democrats" have endorsed manifestly undemocratic actions—say, the executive's abrogation of the country's constitution, the shelling of parliament, or the staging of unfair elections—while most Russian "democrats" have interpreted these same events as victories for democracy, inasmuch as they resulted in the defeat of their opponents. By contenting ourselves with recording surface characteristics, such as the utterances of politicians or mass responses to survey questionnaires, we miss the ways in which words function as signifiers representing and, indeed, generating conditions in the world of politics. We gather data on political culture in ways that ignore the very meanings embedded in it.

    This study makes that case. As an introduction I present the skeleton of my argument according to a simple model incorporating three of Lotman's concepts: the binary structure of Russian cultural representations, autocommunication, and the nonreferentiality of signs. These ideas should be understood not as direct representations of empirical reality but as a complex or a system, the analytical elements of which can be used to interpret the political world. This model is displayed schematically in figure 4.1. In this formulation each element in the system would be consequent on—and, in turn, sustain—the other two elements. Starting from the term appearing at the apex of the triangle, the

Figure 4.1. Three Communicative Moments in Russian Political Discourse

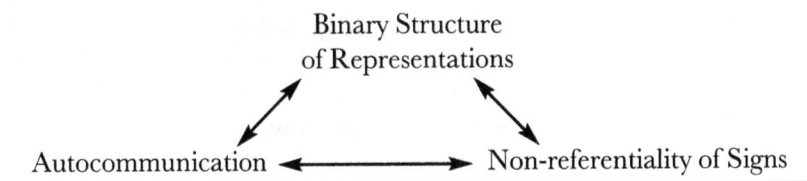

Binary Structure
of Representations

Autocommunication ←——————→ Non-referentiality of Signs

binary structure, we see that the rigid dichotomies obtaining in the cultural system of representations—at core: we (positive)/they (negative)—engender practices of autocommunication (lower left point in fig. 4.1) whereby the "we" engage in discursive practices that exclude the other. Talking only to themselves, so to speak, this "we" is able to control the content of its communication, fashioning signs in accordance with its own volition rather than in ways consonant with intersubjective communication that would actually be mediated by references to the world that it purportedly indexes. These same relations among the elements can be retraced by beginning at either of the other two points in figure 4.1. Autocommunication as a practice would reinforce the dichotomies in the binary structure; nonreferential discursive practices would do the same while also sustaining autocommunication, inasmuch as the world does not intrude to complicate the expression of volitions.

To illustrate how this complex might be applied to the political world, consider a typical instance of apparently paradoxical communication that was particularly important because of the stakes involved. At the end of this study I return to this example, offering an interpretation based on the concepts set out in figure 4.1. In 1998 the Communist Party of the Russian Federation found itself in a serious bind. As the largest party in the State Duma and with some of its members parceled off to allied factions, it controlled a majority of seats in the legislature. In March President Boris Yeltsin dismissed the government and nominated Sergei Kirienko—someone anathema to the Communists—to the post of prime minister. By May, with the Communists leading the effort, the Duma had twice rejected Kirienko. A third rejection would leave the matter to Yeltsin. Constitutionally he would have the option of either putting forward a new candidate or dissolving the legislature and (perhaps) calling new elections. Faced with the near certainty that a third rejection would result in Yeltsin taking the latter course, the Communists met on the eve of the final vote to lay strategy. Either they dropped their hitherto absolute opposition to Kirienko—and thus would be made to eat the many words that for weeks they had been uttering on this matter—or Yeltsin would send them home. Emerging from that meeting, Gennadii Seleznev, the Duma's Communist chairperson, faced the assembled press and announced, "Tomorrow, we are voting *against* Kirienko and *for* the preservation of the State Duma."

On the plane of practical communication—and, given its ostensible semiotic context, that is precisely where Seleznev's remark seemed to lie—this statement was utter nonsense. If anything Seleznev seemed to be saying that enough of their members would vote *for* Kirienko to confirm his nomination, and *against* the State Duma as an autonomous institution where society's representatives gather to vote their political consciences. Moreover, the fact that the chairperson of the Duma would be speaking such nonsense with respect to an absolutely critical political event appeared to excite no concern. His words were received with complete equanimity and apparent understanding. How might we account for this paradoxical statement and its reception in political society? We can find a solution to this puzzle by exploring the relations among the elements contained in the triangular model represented in figure 4.1.

## The Binary Structure of Representations

Lotman's work on the binary structure of Russian culture—adumbrated in his essay with B. A. Uspenskii ("Binary Models in the Dynamics of Russian Culture," 30–66) and worked out in more detail in his *Kul'tura i vzryv*—represents a particularly incisive instrument for slicing into Russian politics. Its utility is perhaps most immediately apparent in the compactness of its modeling of change at the macro level. By conceptualizing Russian cultural values as "distributed in a bipolar field divided by a sharp boundary without an axiological neutral zone" ("Binary Models," 31), Lotman has theorized those cyclical aspects of Russian political development to which numerous observers have drawn attention.[3] Stated baldly, inasmuch as the normative present is distinguished within this binary structure solely on the basis of its opposition to the culture's negative pole, change can only assume the form of normative inversion whereby the prescribed and the proscribed switch places (*Kul'tura i vzryv*, 141–48). Conceptions of the new thus appear "as a total eschatological change" (Lotman, Ginsburg, and Uspenskii, *Semiotics of Russian Cultural History*, 32). In historical perspective, a cyclical effect accompanies changes because "at each new stage, changing historical conditions and, in particular, external cultural influences, lead to a new perspective on cultural development that will activate one semantic parameter or another. As a result, the same concepts can appear at each stage furnished with a new content, depending on the point of departure. These underlying structures of development are what allow us to speak of the unity of Russian culture at the various stages of its history. It is in the transformations that invariants are revealed" ("Binary Models," 33).

The possibilities for realizing some of those values with which politics is often associated—progress, development, improvement—thus appear forfeit at the outset. Collective action aimed at accomplishing such purposes is embedded within a cultural system whose binary structure limits alternatives to the thoroughgoing negation of the prevailing totems, their would-be replacements represented by a revalued synthesis of taboos. Future change completes the cycle by again reversing "plus" and "minus."[4]

To illustrate this pattern with an example drawn from contemporary Russian politics, consider how some ten years of "reform," ostensibly conducted to secure certain Western values and institutions—democratization, rule of law, civil society, marketization, privatization, and so forth—have given way in the current period to a palpable sense of Thermidor. Vladimir Putin, the country's second president, both reflects this sentiment and, with slogans such as "dictatorship of law" and "patriotism and popular welfare," actively stimulates it. He seems not in the least bit shy or furtive about his presumed historical role, instantly responding to a journalist's question, "Which political actors are of interest to you?" with "Napoleon Bonaparte."[5] The rearrangement of the symbolic universe presently under way recalls with particular poignancy Lotman's binary model and its dynamics.

We can observe this same process on a single page of Russia's oldest and largest daily newspaper of Western orientation, *Nezavisimaia gazeta (The Independent Gazette)*. Its April 5, 2000, edition featured back-to-back essays by Gavriil Popov, one of the top leaders of the democratic movement that overthrew Communism, and Moscow's first elected mayor, and Aleksandr Iur'ev, who heads the Department of Political Psychology at St. Petersburg State University. Contrary to the idea of "all human values" and the civic notion of national identity that he had propounded eight or ten years ago, today's Popov has unabashedly gone over to the side of ethnopolitics. In an essay employing categories such as "roots" and "blood," he argues for a state policy aimed at increasing the number of ethnic Russians by a factor of two or three. And entirely reminiscent of the "there-is-no-alternative" approach characteristic of the discourse of Russia's democrats a decade ago, Popov contends that this desideratum is of overriding importance inasmuch as "no other programs are of any use for Russia if the country does not have enough (ethnic) Russians [russkikh]."[6]

In equally striking fashion Iur'ev has inverted the previous project of the democrats, whose purpose it was to liberate society from the tutelage of a state laying claim to an eschatological mission that intimately involved it in the moral upbringing and conduct of its population. Today, says Iur'ev, society has lost its moral center. Public language is dominated by terms such as "the exchange rate of the ruble" and "foreign investments" that leave no place for "higher moral values." Consequently he calls on the state to stem the rising tide of anomie by fulfilling its historic task and one of its basic obligations, namely, to assist people in the "acquisition of faith."[7]

If Popov's views represent the biological side of Thermidor, Iur'ev's speak to its spiritual component. In both cases yesterday's target of annihilation—the totalitarian state—is recommissioned to perform services that are, if anything, even more illiberal than those associated with Communism's project. The remedy for an intolerable situation is framed in both instances as the thoroughgoing negation of present circumstances and those values associated with them. And what other semantic inventory might be rummaged for the ingredients of such a remedy? According to Lotman's model, that which the country has just escaped reappears under another name on the horizon of the future as the singular hope that must be pursued.

In the field of international relations, Sergei Medvedev has recently incorporated some of Lotman's ideas on binary oppositions into a provocative essay outlining the contours and cycles of Russia's foreign policy. He has demonstrated how certain epochal events, such as the Soviet Union's unilateral termination of the Cold War, cannot be comprehended on the conventional calculus of strategic action, raison d'état, or any other notion available to (neo)realist theories of the international system. Rather, he demonstrates that they emerge predictably out of the binary structure of Russian culture as the particular way in which that culture is able to formulate a project. Accordingly, in the arena of foreign relations, the end of "the Communist empire"—as Russia's first post-Communist statesmen were likely to refer to the preceding order— led not to an evolutionary process that modified state policy but instead to a radical break that confused state policy itself and the national interests that it would pursue with the detested Communist past. Hence, in its infancy the new Russian state replaced the Iron Curtain with something like a big welcome mat, its foreign minister claiming that Russia has no national interests other than "all-human values." Recoiling from the practical impossibility of this formulation, political society set about activating opposing semantic parameters, such that by the midnineties unanimity reigned on the issue of restoring Russia's great-power status.[8] To be sure, unanimity in this respect would not imply uniformity, as the same signifier—*derzhava* (great-power state or empire)—can refer to more than one signified. However, irrespective of that interpretive question, the point remains that the discursive drift toward this signifier *(derzhava)* marks in foreign affairs the same turn in the cycle of reversing "plus" and "minus" that we noted with respect to Popov and Iur'ev.

Medvedev's work conforms closely to the style of exposition and analysis that one encounters in Lotman's writings. And like Lotman's work, its value is likely to be overlooked by Western—perhaps, especially, American—political scientists, whose professional conventions militate against the expansive, interpretive thrust of this approach. In the face of this disciplinary divide, let us consider some implications of Lotman's binary theory of culture that can be located lower on the ladder of abstraction, making them more serviceable to political science purposes, if not more suited to political scientists' tastes. To do so, we must keep in mind the nonreferentiality of signs commonly found in Russian political discourse.

## The Nonreferentiality of Signs

The scope of modern politics as a field of representations, along with the opacity that continues to surround the inner world of political processes as a field of power, creates considerable potential for uncoupling signification from practice. On the plane of public life, politics in any modern society is produced and consumed as collections of symbols, stock stories, displacements, personifications, and so on that putatively function as shorthand for the "real" proceedings that are far too complex to portray on that plane, much less to comprehend adequately. Largely untethered from actual practices, the subjectified political thus evinces an enormous amount of semiotic freedom. Utterances are not much constrained by those things or conditions to which they are purported to refer.[9] In the Russian case this situation is particularly acute, at least in part because of the binary structure of culture that Lotman has identified.

During the 1990s politics and commercial business activities in Russia became largely synonymous with concepts such as "theft" and "corruption." Following Alena Ledeneva's analysis of informal exchange relations *(blat)* during the Communist period, we can observe how this condition sprang directly from the longstanding bind that characterized social relations.[10] On one hand, in daily life the great majority of individuals were enmeshed in relations of *blat,* using the physical access provided by their official positions to appropriate state resources and trade them illegally with others. On the other hand, no public discourse was available to thematize these activities. Rather, in the public realm the state's sacral categories concerning Communist obligations to society, the selfless morality of the builders of Communism, and so on reigned supreme. As a consequence not only did these official descriptions of the prevailing order lack the practical referents celebrated in Communist discourse, but the actual practices themselves could not be named or discussed. In this case naming included a certain "misrecognition," a category developed by Pierre Bourdieu to account for phenomena such as gift giving or the culturally mandated rendering of aid to those in need. With respect to the gift, the reciprocity involved with such exchanges can be obscured from participants because the exchanges are staggered across time, each instance of giving thus appearing as an isolated act of pure kindness. Hence, the practice is sustained as such because the parties involved can deny that any exchange is occurring; part of the practice includes a misrecognition of that which is "objectively" transpiring.[11] Similarly, *blat* as a social practice bore the marks of the immoral assigned to it in public discourse by the state, but as individual activity it appeared in an entirely different form. *Blat,* as a category, was regarded as something evil and as something that only *others* did; yet the actual experience of *blat* involved the misrecognition among participants that they themselves were embedded in extended exchange networks misappropriating and redistributing state property. Rather, each phase of *blat* exchange — separated in time from reciprocal acts and usually mediated through several members in the network such that one did not receive from the same party to whom one had given — allowed for the misrecognition that it was merely selfless help rendered to deserving individuals. This misrecognition was integral to the practice, enabling participants to view their own behavior as moral even while they condemned the immorality of those who practiced *blat*.

The consequences of this nonreferential signification for a society instituting a private economy were enormous. There was no available normative code to engage the opportunities for money making newly licensed by the state. Consequently, the old polarity — what "we" do (good) versus what "they" do (bad) — reasserted itself in a new way. Some individuals took advantage of the situation — either on account of their connections to favor-dispensing associates in government positions, or because of their willingness to employ ruthless violence against competitors, or both — to amass considerable wealth. Most people suffered severe impoverishment and complained of *bespredel*, a term (literally: "without limits") bespeaking a hostile, anarchic situation from which all morality had vanished. Moreover, relying on Lotman's binary model, Nancy Ries has argued effectively that the only semiotic material available from which to fashion representations and identities under these disorienting circumstances has come from the negative pole of the old official normative order. That order, now ritually inverted, makes available for new (positive) identities "the archetypal images of American 'bad guys'" such as gangsters and prostitutes.[12] It has been against this backdrop that innumerable voices calling for state intervention, such as that of Iur'ev, have been raised.

A second illustration of nonreferential signification that can be framed by Lotman's binary model concerns the violent demise of the Russian republic that had emerged from the USSR. I have already offered an extended analysis of that event, viewing it entirely from the standpoint of its manifest discursive practices and will summarize here how the conception of that study was informed by Lotman's binary model.[13] Within two years of Communism's collapse, Russian political society had been divided into two mutually opposed camps, each aimed at extinguishing the other. Over the eight-month period leading to the bloody denouement on the streets of Moscow, capped by the shelling of the parliament building on October 4, 1993, the country had witnessed two large assemblies on "national accord"—functioning since February 1993—each of which denounced the other as illegitimate; two rival constitutions, put forward, respectively, by the president and the Supreme Soviet; two separate and much publicized prosecutorial teams, each associated with one of those institutions, rooting out corruption in the opposing camp; and as the crisis peaked, two presidents purporting to direct two national governments. These developments represented a spiral of conflict whose sources prominently include the discursive practices present in Russian political society at the onset of the post-Communist period (*Kul'tura i vzryv*, 145–46).

In a palpable sense the fall of Communism induced a crisis of identity across the political spectrum. Hitherto the many political groupings marching under the banner of democracy had secured only one mode of signification to mediate their identities publicly: anti-Communism.[14] The binary logic displayed in that struggle was remarkable in itself. Having functioned officially for some seventy years as—according to Lenin's celebrated dictum—the "mind, honor and conscience of our epoch," the Communist Party appeared in the discourse of the democrats (effectively all of whose leaders had been members of the Communist Party themselves) as the unmitigated malevolence visiting one after another atrocity on the Russian nation. This reversing of positive and negative poles was, no doubt, especially serviceable with respect to capturing political power. But when the Communist Party had been vanquished and outlawed, the moorings of democratic identity dissolved along with it. Consequently, the victorious democrats reproduced the same binary discursive practices within their own ranks.

In this context the matter of nonreferential signification assumed a new dimension: renaming. Political differences—and these usually amounted to no more than current affiliations with one of the two loci of power in the post-Communist order, the president or the Supreme Soviet—would be expressed by hyper-naming, by canceling the self-representations of the other side and tagging it "Communist."[15] Accordingly, signification in the world of politics took the form of unmasking opponents as "Communists," a practice that concomitantly valorized the speaker who had performed such a public service and validated his or her political position as something issuing from the *narod*—that is, "the people" or "the nation"—that had been victimized for so long by these (antipopular, antinational) Communists.[16] The only means available for signifying identity in Russian political society, as a speech community, were those afforded by this bifurcated world. One group emphasized—to distinguish itself from its opponents, the "Communists"—its allegedly Western credentials, claiming that its purpose was to surmount the dreadful past by ushering in a new, "civilized" future for the nation. The other—again, in distinction to its opponents, the "Communists"—promised to retrieve for the nation its authentic culture that Communism had all but extinguished. In both cases realizing the national purpose—either by instituting "reform" or by recovering "the Russian idea"—meant constructing a symbolic world in which there was no place for the other side. Each of these representations was equally nonreferential. The first invited envisaging some future Russia that resembled idealized constructs of the West; the second entertained the notion of returning to a comparably idealized past. Neither proved capable of thematizing conditions, problems, and potentials in the actual Russia wherein the speakers resided. The drastically constrained possibilities encased in this binary structure directly generated in political communication that doubling of opposing political institutions referenced earlier as well as the violence that put an end to it.

## Autocommunication

Lotman's treatment of the concept "autocommunication" would be germane to much of the foregoing. Here I would like to highlight its utility for analyzing a somewhat different problem in Russian political discourse, namely, the manner in which political identities have been sublimated onto an allegedly national identity that they claim to embody. My first encounter with this problem occurred in 1992 while I was studying newly formed political parties outwardly oriented toward democratic norms and modes of expression. My interest at this time was in discovering how these nascent political organizations were developing programmatic responses to the vexed question of Russian statehood in the context of the USSR's recent collapse.[17]

For three of the four parties in my sample—the Social Democratic Party of Russia, the Republican Party of Russia, and the Democratic Party of Russia—conventional forms of political analysis seemed quite sufficient. That is, on the basis of interviews with party leaders and by reading various party documents on the subject, it was possible to distinguish the general outlook of each party from the others and to observe how each of their orientations toward the issue of statehood was consonant with their respective interpretations of democracy. For instance, the Social Democratic Party of Russia—given its sensitivity to social factors and the importance of collective rights—placed great store on the notion of the self-determination of nations and therefore emphasized the voluntary nature of the Russian federation and the concomitant rights of its various peoples to home rule with maximum autonomy. On the other hand, the Democratic Party of Russia—whose political identity was anchored in individualism—conceived of statehood for the federation as something indivisible. It thus envisaged a strong central state capable of guaranteeing equal rights to individual citizens throughout the country, irrespective of their national affiliations or the particular federal units—Russian provinces or non-Russian national republics— in which they resided. It was even the case that in interviews, party leaders would adopt a markedly practical attitude toward their party's positions on this issue, freely admitting shortcomings and inconsistencies in their programs and defending those same programs on the basis of reasoned arguments demonstrating that while their approach might not be without problems, the extant alternatives would do even greater damage to the democratic principles they were attempting to advance.

The fourth party in my sample, however, sharply disturbed the pattern prevailing in the other three cases. Although an ally of the other parties in the larger democratic movement that overthrew the Communist order, the Russian Christian Democratic Movement had more recently engaged in discursive practices that separated its members entirely from the ranks of Russia's democrats. Evident in both texts and interviews was that which from Lotman's perspective could be viewed as a form of autocommunication in which "members of a group who use a cipher are in this instance regarded as a single 'I' . . . [constructed by] a text [that] aims to become one 'great word' with one single meaning" (*Universe of the Mind*, 27, 47). In this instance that cipher or "great word" was the Russian *narod*, whose "organic mode of life"—itself alleged to reflect the deep spirituality of a chosen people—had been all but extinguished by the nefarious forces of Communism and, more recently, Western materialism. In this discourse the *narod* functioned as a Christlike victim that the party had been summoned to protect. Accordingly, the victimizers were categorically distinguished from the victim, in part by portraying Communism not as a Russian phenomenon at all but as the doing of something called the "international lumpen regime," whose first conquest had been the Russian nation.

This was perplexing. If it were possible to interpret the positions of the first three parties on the question of statehood as logical extrapolations of their respective versions of democratic values, then what could be said about this fourth "democratic" party arguing for a restoration of empire and authoritarianism in the name of an organic construct of a suffering and victimized nation? Moreover, how could one explain the vast difference in the mode of expression separating this party from the other three? Whereas principles enacted into programs found practical referents in the first three instances (citizens, property owners, non-Russian minorities, and so on), the fourth one prominently featured mystical entities (the *narod* expressing its "organic mode of life," "the international lumpen regime") whose existence seemed to depend entirely on the imagination of those participating in the discourse. This was a very strange version of political speech if one could indeed regard it as political speech at all. Whom was it intended to persuade?

Along the lines of Lotman's insistence on locating communication within the culture in which it transpires, I began to recast the discourse of the Russian Christian Democratic Movement and to alter my own interpretative apparatus in the process. Instead of applying the conventions of Western political analysis—which, after all, had seemed to work satisfactorily for the first three parties in the sample—to the utterances and texts of the fourth, I attempted to see how the respective discourses of each party simply functioned to distinguish it from others on the political field. From this standpoint it became evident that all four parties were representing themselves not so much to a would-be public, the ostensible target of their messages, but to themselves by perfecting the political dialects that anchored their respective identities. Accordingly, I was forced to retrace my steps with respect to the first three parties, making problematic my initial assumptions. Their discursive practices now appeared not as transparent, instrumental-rational communication but—like the fourth party in this respect—as a culturally coded system of representations whose valorized elements set them invidiously apart from competitors. Certainly, the prevailing political context had everything to do with these practices. It will be recalled in this respect that Yeltsin's "reform" unfolded as a thoroughly state-centered project in which the executive had carte blanche to institute new policies. This arrangement sidelined political society, removing its influence from the actual course of events. Consequently, the practical context of the programs belonging to the parties in my sample—whether on the question of Russian statehood or any other matter—was cancelled by the executive's monopoly over public policy. With no chance of implementation, what did these programs represent? Shorn of their capacity to enter the practical world of politics, they remained statements of collective identity and nothing more. They were instruments by means of which individuals signaled their membership in collectivities. Accordingly, I began to understand Russian political expression in this context as a form of identity politics and to employ Lotman's concept of autocommunication to investigate it.[18]

Lotman's concept of autocommunication concerns those counterintuitive cases in which a subject does not transmit information to another but directs his message back to himself. Lotman expresses it as I-I communication, as opposed to the more common I-she/he variety in which information is transferred from one party to another. In I-I communication what is at stake is not the information—which is, of course, already known to the sender-receiver—but "the rank of the message [that] is raised" (*Universe of the Mind*, 21). For example, were I in a given instance to voice my dispositions—"I don't care how it makes me look to others, I'm doing right by admitting my errors"—I would be engaging in autocommunication that valorizes my actions and, by implication, myself. Alternatively, to use one of Lotman's examples, I might read this very chapter in print, transferring thereby no information to myself (for I, after all, have written it) but raising the rank of this information, which now, as a published work, connotes a greater degree of authority. Consequently, although no information is generated or transmitted in autocommunication, nonetheless "the message acquires new meaning during the communication process" (*Universe of the Mind*, 22; *Kul'tura i vzryv*, 133). This new meaning transforms the subject-object of communication, whether redoubling my resolve, in the first illustration, to admit my errors, or, in the second, appreciating the weight of my thoughts in printed form.

Lotman mentions in passing that the "I" in autocommunication can be a group, but he does not develop that idea. However, much of his discussion of rhetoric intersects with the matter of forming a collective "I" (*Universe of the Mind*, 27–53), and I reference it here in regard to the I-I communication I have encountered in a recent investigation of the efforts of various segments of Russian political society to supply the nation with a new, post-Communist identity construct.

Following his reelection as president in 1996, Boris Yeltsin created a special commission of experts charged—in clear violation of the country's constitution—with the objective of writing a new state ideology for Russia. However, their year-long effort led to nothing but a report on other formulations of a national idea produced by various individuals and groups in political society.[19] In this respect the political center much resembled its counterpart in Lotman's "semiosphere," characterized by a weak or "colorless" capacity to signify (*Universe of the Mind*, 141). Accordingly, strong representations would appear on the "periphery," in this instance among some democrats and, even more so, among the hybrid Communist-patriots of the Communist Party of the Russian Federation (KPRF).

The former have produced some texts that manifestly seek to marry the idea of democracy to putative Russian political and cultural traditions. Although relatively open to practical references in the world, these texts—proceeding from two inconsistent points of departure, Russian traditions and modern democratic principles—nonetheless arrive at nonsensical destinations. In one case Russia's new democratic idea is prefigured by the regime of former Chilean dictator Augusto Pinochet; in another public, communal, and individual spheres are collapsed into a single national "crisis" that—contrary to the stated objectives of its author—could only be resolved practically by the resurrection of a totalitarian state.[20] Moreover, both of these examples from democratic discourse share with their Communist-patriotic opponents in the KPRF one overriding feature: the tendency to construct a *national* identity that manifestly excludes vast numbers of their compatriots who do not subscribe to it.

The discourse of the KPRF on the issue of national identity represents an even more striking and detailed illustration of Lotman's rhetorical text, characterized by a "structural unity of two (or more) subtexts encoded with the help of several mutually untranslatable codes . . . [such that] the text looks like different discourses which have equal rights throughout its course" (*Universe of the Mind*, 57). In this case the discourses are, of course, Communism and patriotism, and all compromises between them occur at the expense of the former. Thus the principal category of Communist theory, class struggle, is supplanted by that of nation. In the Russian case this nation is said to possess certain "instincts" that lead it naturally to form and to support a great-power state or empire *(derzhava)* that realizes on the temporal plane a number of spiritual and religious values. This temporal-spiritual amalgam has been tested historically by all manner of satanic forces emanating from the West, from invading armies to false confessions (Catholicism, Protestantism, and atheism) to spiritually corrosive materialism. Yet the nation and its state have time and again risen to meet these threats, as Stalin did by turning the country away from the destructive path of international proletarian revolution and toward that of rebuilding the Russian *derzhava*. At present Russia is said to face its greatest challenge: its state has been captured by a "fifth column"—those possessed by the alien creed of liberal-democratic ideology—who have set about the task of extinguishing the nation and its culture on instructions from the world oligarchy resident in the West. Not only would there be no place for the ideas of their political opponents in the authentic Russia depicted in the KPRF's texts, but as the "bureaucratic party of national treason," these same opponents could personally look forward to nothing better than long prison sentences.

These texts reflect, then, a particular purpose, as Lotman might have it, encoding their messages for insiders and against others, neither creating nor transferring information but preserving it, ratcheting up its level of semioticity, and thus drawing the group together as an "I" (*Universe of the Mind*, 63–74). What is particularly striking in this respect is the nonreferentiality of the discursive practices. The rhetoric of the KPRF on the matter of national identity is a totalizing one that dissolves individuals into a national construct whose dimensions exhibit the familiar binary structure of Lotman's cultural model: good/evil; selfless sacrifice/treasonous ambition; patriots and culture bearers/satanic agents of foreign powers sowing chaos. It is worth recalling that these eschatological texts have issued not from some obscure sect but from the country's largest political party, which, at the time of their composition, had enjoyed the dominant presence in Russia's Duma, capable of marshaling majorities on most issues. Its actual political practices, as might be expected, cannot be thematized within the scope of its rhetoric, just as its rhetoric finds no practical referents in the world of politics. The KPRF would thus serve as a robust but by no means unique example of autocommunication and the nonreferentiality of signs in contemporary Russian politics. Its texts raise the semiotic level of the messages that it addresses to itself—for instance, its putative defense of the nation against an "occupation regime in the Kremlin" bent on destroying it—while presenting to other (potential) parties in communication either unintelligibility or hostility.

At the same time the KPRF's practices as a political party in large measure have been dictated by the exigencies of political life in which the messages and actions of others must be reckoned with. It was precisely these circumstances that informed the paradoxical communication we encountered at the beginning of this study: voting against the nomination of Kirienko for prime minister while (somehow) simultaneously voting to preserve the Duma. Although the KPRF must respond to conditions beyond its control—the Hobson's choice issued by the executive either to endorse a candidate that the KPRF had publicly pilloried or to be sent packing—autocommunication would displace that practical dilemma onto the plane of signification, where it can be solved in a particular way. Thus Seleznev's paradox of simultaneously voting for and against can be understood to mean: "We did not create the impossible situation that now confronts us and therefore should not be held accountable for actions that we are forced to take. Our intentions, you must know, have been and remain the best." This form of communication would succeed to the degree that the addressee has identified himself or herself with the sender of the message, thus placing himself or herself in a position to decode and to accept its subtextual content, which hinges on the nonreferential character of the KPRF's signifying practices: militantly claiming to oppose the very government that it elects to office.

These remarks lead to two concluding observations about political communication that follow from Lotman's work. The first, with respect to Russia in particular, concerns the way in which political communities cohere by means of discursive practices featuring nonreferential autocommunication structured by strong binary oppositions. The forms of this coherence result both from the severe limits placed on political practice by the executive branch, which all but monopolizes the process of governing, and from communicative practices that underscore the subjectivity of the political community, insulate its signification from events in the world, and correspondingly cancel the practical dimension of its messages. Here the implications of the model set out in figure 4.1 would be that the discursive construction of political community is predicated on the concomitant construction of an anticommunity putatively composed, in part, of fellow nationals. Paradoxically—and with reference to historical experience, self-destructively—this community is said to realize itself in the process of struggle against this "other."

The second observation concerns political language in general in an age of mass-mediated politics. If nonreferential signification indicates that a group variety of autocommunication is taking place, then that same nonreferentiality can be regarded as a marker directing our attention to a layer of semiosis in texts and utterances to which studies of political communication have too often paid scant attention. From this vantage we notice that, more than just speaking ideologically or participating in other "distorted" forms of communication, we are often enough—and assumedly for our own purposes—merely talking to ourselves.[21] In the United States the so-called war on drugs, which has been under way for decades, provides one example of what I have in mind here. Its principal signifier—the "war"—represents a misleading (nonreferential) metaphor (How does one make war on "controlled substances"?) that would qualify as a species of distorted communication. At the same time, however, the concept of autocommunication allows us to recognize in that trope another level of meaning. On the one hand, precious little information is, in fact, transmitted in this militarized discourse, but its value is constantly raised by the urgency of war, invoked by regular reports on drug seizures and arrests. These have become sufficiently routinized to indicate effectively nothing beyond the fact that the "war" goes on and that society continues to recycle information about it. On the other hand, the nonreferential character of the "war on drugs" as signifier facilitates the politics of instituting a binary structure in this discourse by depersonalizing the enemy. Were narratives framed around the idea of a war on drug users and suppliers, then the great majority of citizens (consumers or producers of tobacco, alcohol, and innumerable mood-altering pharmaceuticals) would appear as potential targets. Nor would references to legality—say, to a war on the users and suppliers of illicit drugs—help very much. This formulation would both repersonalize the enemy—The government has *declared war* on me? On my children? On my friends? *War* on terminally ill people easing their pain by smoking marijuana?—and would draw immediate attention to the laws themselves (Why has this drug been declared illegal and that one not?). A simple "war on drugs" avoids these problems while simultaneously inserting an imaginary boundary between a putative majority that it constructs as an inchoate "drug-free America" and the remainder of the citizenry to whom "zero tolerance" is to be shown. It may be, then, that the "war on drugs," as a form of distorted communication, has functioned effectively because of the presence in its rhetoric of nonreferential autocommunication predicated on the binary structure of a "drug-free America" versus some "drug-dependent" sector of the population whose very membership in the political community is thus rendered uncertain. To the degree that we engage in these practices, we are enacting a particular political community organized discursively on the unspoken basis of those things that "we all know": the war is being waged against "them," not "us." Yet, while contributing directly to sustaining political community in an immediate sense, these same practices can also involve a dumbing down of public intelligence as well as a marginalization of extant—and, perhaps, beneficial—political alternatives. From the perspective of the longer term, then, such practices represent seductions that cast a long shadow of crisis on any political community preoccupied with them.[22]

*Notes*

1. The origins of this positivist concept, employed by political scientists in a host of subsequent studies, are traceable to Gabriel Almond and Sidney Verba, *The Civic Culture: Political Attitudes and Democracy in Five Nations* (Princeton, N.J.: Princeton University Press, 1963). For a criticism of this approach that demonstrates its particular unsuitability to the Russian case, see Robert C. Tucker, *Political Culture and Leadership in Soviet Russia* (New York: Norton, 1987), esp. 3–8. An extended review of many of these opinion surveys can be found in Frederic Fleron Jr., "Post-Soviet Political Culture in Russia: An Assessment of Recent Empirical Investigations," *Europe-Asia Studies* 48 (March 1996): 225–60. An incisive critique of this same literature appears in James Alexander, "Surveying Attitudes in Russia: A Representation of Formlessness," *Communist and Post-Communist Studies* 30 (June 1997): 107–27.

2. The YABLOKO party, the smaller of the two democratic factions in the current State Duma, would represent an exception to this rule.

3. For example, Robert Tucker, *The Soviet Political Mind*, rev. ed. (London: Allen & Unwin, 1972); Alexander Yanov, *The Origins of Autocracy: Ivan the Terrible in Russian History* (Berkeley: University of California Press, 1981); Nicholas Timasheff, *The Great Retreat* (New York: E. P. Hutton, 1946).

4. Interestingly, Lotman's views on this matter appear to parallel Vladimir Propp's discussion of the dynamics of folklore. "Inherited folklore," writes Propp, "comes in conflict with the old system that created it and denies this system. But it does not deny the old system directly but rather the images created by it, transforming them into their opposites or giving them a reverse, disparaging, negative coloring. The once sacred is transformed into the hostile, the great into the harmful, evil or monstrous." See his *Theory and History of Folklore* (Minneapolis: University of Minnesota Press, 1984), 11. Although it is impossible to pursue this point within the scope of this chapter, it is worth pointing

out that Soviet political discourse has been successfully analyzed on the basis of folklore models, and that post-Soviet political discourse might then be viewed as the continuation of the transformative binary pattern posited by Propp. Studies employing the folklore approach to Soviet political discourse include Michael Urban and John McClure, "The Folklore of State Socialism: Semiotics and the Study of the Soviet State," *Soviet Studies* 35 (October 1983): 471–86; Alexandre Bourmeyster, "Utopie, idéologie et skaz," *Essais sur le discours soviétique,* no. 3 (1983): 1–53.

5. Anatolii Kucherena, "Ustalost' ot svobody?" *Nezavisimaia gazeta,* April 18, 2000, 8.

6. For an example of the earlier approach, see Michael Urban, *The Rebirth of Politics in Russia* (Cambridge: Cambridge University Press, 1997), 90–92. Quotation from Gavriil Popov, "Beregite russkikh," *Nezavisimaia gazeta,* April 5, 2000, 8.

7. Aleksandr Iur'ev, "Kogda bezzashchitnymi stanoviatsia vse," *Nezavisimaia gazeta,* April 5, 2000, 8.

8. Sergei Medvedev, "Power, Space and Russian Foreign Policy," in *Understandings of Russian Foreign Policy,* ed. Ted Hopf (University Park: Pennsylvania State University, 1999), 15–55.

9. See, for example, Murray Edelman, *Constructing the Political Spectacle* (Chicago: University of Chicago Press, 1988); George Lakoff, *Moral Politics: What Conservatives Know that Liberals Don't* (Chicago: University of Chicago Press, 1996).

10. Alena Ledeneva, *Russia's Informal Economy of Favours* (Cambridge: Cambridge University Press, 1999).

11. Pierre Bourdieu, *Outline of a Theory of Practice* (Cambridge: Cambridge University Press, 1977), 5–8; 170–73; Pierre Bourdieu, *The Logic of Practice* (Cambridge: Cambridge University Press, 1990), 105, 234.

12. Nancy Ries, *Russian Talk: Culture and Conversation during Perestroika* (Ithaca, N.Y.: Cornell University Press, 1997), 175.

13. Michael Urban, "The Politics of Identity in Russia's Postcommunist Transition: The National against Itself," *Slavic Review* 53 (Fall 1994): 733–65.

14. Urban, *Rebirth of Politics in Russia,* 201–27.

15. On the concept of hyper-naming, see Edelman, *Constructing the Political Spectacle,* 74.

16. In related contexts these practices have been analyzed by A. N. Baranov and E. G. Kazakevich, *Parlamentskie debaty: Traditsii i novatsii* (Moscow: Znanie, 1991), esp. 16–30; Nikolai Biryukov, Jeffrey Gleisner, and Viktor Sergeyev, "The Crisis of Sobornost': Parliamentary Discourse in Present-Day Russia," *Discourse and Society* 2, no. 2 (1995): 149–71.

17. Michael Urban, "Contending Conceptions of Nation and State in Russian Politics," *Demokratizatsiya* 1, no. 4 (1993): 1–13.

18. Some of the results of this effort appear in Urban, *Rebirth of Politics in Russia*, 86–92, 106–15, 152–55, 204–33, 298–302.

19. Michael Urban, "Remythologising the Russian State," *Europe-Asia Studies* 50, no. 6 (1998): 969–92.

20. For the Pinochet example, see Vitalii Naishul', "O normakh sovremennoi rossiiskoi gosudarstvennosti," *Nezavisimaia gazeta*, May 23, 1996, 4–5. For the second example, see Igor' Chubais, *Ot Russkoi idei—k idee Novoi Rossii* (Moscow: GITIS, 1996).

21. The concept of distorted communication has been developed by Jürgen Habermas in "On Systematically Distorted Communication," *Inquiry* 13 (Winter 1970): 205–18; *Legitimation Crisis* (Boston: Beacon, 1975); *Communication and the Evolution of Society* (Boston: Beacon, 1979); and *The Theory of Communicative Action*, vol. 1 (Boston: Beacon, 1984).

22. Jean Baudrillard, *Seduction* (London: Macmillan, 1990).

# 5

# State Power, Hegemony, and Memory

## Lotman and Gramsci

### MAREK STEEDMAN

> Louisiana's political renaissance began in the year 1877 when the government of the state was restored to the hands of the white people — the intelligent and property holding classes.
>
> Governor Newton C. Blanchard of Louisiana

In August 1904 Louisiana governor Newton C. Blanchard declared that September 14 of that year would be celebrated as Louisiana Day at the St. Louis World's Fair. The Louisiana Purchase Exposition, as that year's fair was titled, celebrated the centennial of the 1803 treaty with France that brought the large Louisiana Territories to the United States. More recent territorial gains were implicated in the theme. For some the Louisiana Purchase justified the imposition of U.S. rule on the Philippines, Puerto Rico, and Cuba following the 1898 Spanish-American War. As the country debated whether the United States should practice the Old World politics of empire, the celebration of the Louisiana Purchase commented on expansion into the Pacific. Manifest Destiny went forward with renewed purpose. The fair staged debates over racial biology and eugenics, while displaying members of Filipino and Native American tribes in specially built simulations of their "native" habitat. The organizers carefully intertwined imperialism, white supremacy, and voyeurism for the visiting public.[1]

The context could not have been better for a newly elected governor who had fought for white supremacy in his state. But Governor

Blanchard had very specific reasons for choosing September 14, a "day justly memorable in [Louisiana's] annals," as Louisiana Day.[2] On that day in 1874, the White League stormed and took control of the Louisiana state government buildings in New Orleans. This white supremacist paramilitary organization had links to the Democratic Party. It ousted the Republican administration, whose legitimacy the league did not concede. The outcome of the 1872 election, which had again given Republicans control of the state, had been contested by the Democrats. They continued to feel that the election had been stolen from them. The league set up its own government, controlled by Democrats.

President Grant refused to recognize these Democrats. He sent U.S. troops against them, and they surrendered before there was any fighting. Still, as the New Orleans *Daily Picayune* reminded its readers in 1904, Democrats saw the day as the "anniversary of the new birth of Louisiana from the terrible tyranny, darkness and misery imposed upon the State by the infamous Reconstruction acts of a sectional Congress."[3] What Democratic governor Blanchard wanted to commemorate in St. Louis was this truncated history, focused on the overthrow of the interracial regime of the Republican Party along with the eventual establishment of white rule and segregation. In this and other instances, Governor Blanchard sought to construct a historical narrative that would shape the political memory of white Louisianans to constitute the identity of the state and those it sought to represent.

Interpreting the resonances of Blanchard's 1904 proclamation can be relatively straightforward in light of the relevant historical background. Realists might consider this shaping of political memory to be an incidental or peripheral aspect of power. They might emphasize the violence used to gain power or the legal mechanisms that white Democrats used to maintain it. I argue instead that this case reveals symbols to be central aspects of state power. Events such as Louisiana Day play what Antonio Gramsci calls an "educative" role. They are devices that people in power use to produce a "'spontaneous' consent" of the citizenry to their rule.

Two concerns intertwine here. One is the familiar idea that the meanings of historical events become contested in political struggles. Edmund Burke and the English radicals fought over the meaning of the Glorious Revolution in England; Israelis and Palestinians sift archaeological data for ways to legitimize their claims; nationalists in the Balkans trot out famous battles of the past to the same end. The list could expand without end. A second, closely connected question is how these contests help constitute the identities of the participants. What processes occur?

It is in relation to these two concerns, and especially the second, that Yuri Lotman's theoretical interventions can be most useful to political theory. In his *Universe of the Mind,* Lotman explores the ways some forms of communication actively restructure social and personal identities. Working toward a model for the transmission and generation of meaning in cultures, Lotman specifies mechanisms for restructuring identities. I demonstrate that his concept of autocommunication allows us to see that some communication does not operate primarily to transmit information or persuade others. Instead it forms an internal dialogue that shapes the identity of the self. Combining insights from Lotman and Gramsci offers a nuanced account of how Blanchard's political shaping of history forms part of a politics of identity.

## Hegemony

Let us begin with Gramsci. Antonio Gramsci's central contribution to political theory and specifically Marxist theory was his development of the concept of hegemony. Jailed by the Fascist government in Italy in the late 1920s, Gramsci would die six days after the expiration of his prison sentence in April 1937. In prison he set himself a course of study, producing the *Prison Notebooks* that represent the bulk of his published writings. The topics covered in the *Notebooks* are extremely wide ranging, from linguistics to reflections on Machiavelli's *Prince* to considerations of Fordist production methods in America. Most influential, perhaps, are his sustained attempts to combat the reductionist "Economism" then dominant in strands of Marxism. In this context Gramsci centered his analysis on the relation between the state and civil society, especially the mechanisms by which the ruling class secures the consent of the ruled to its control of the state.

Gramsci identifies two different aspects of this task of securing consent: leadership and education. Leadership can be exercised by hegemonic groups within the broader civil society or state and among various subaltern groups. As Jeremy Lester observes, hegemony is not a negative concept for Gramsci. It is sought even by Communists and the working class.[4] Indeed, one subaltern group tends to exercise hegemony over the others, educating them to share its sense of the struggle. Thus hegemony implies the ability of some groups to lead others: to win their consent, organize them, and direct them. As the word *subaltern* suggests, military metaphors run throughout Gramsci's account. Yet the insight crucial to the concept of hegemony is that all leadership depends on the "'spontaneous' consent" of the led.[5] Hegemony is an achievement separable from the simple exercise of force.[6]

As has been recognized at least since Machiavelli, the coercive apparatus of the state is a crucial prize in political struggles. Central to the modern state is, in Max Weber's formulation, its "monopoly of legitimate physical violence."[7] For our purposes the key word is *legitimate.* Sheer control of the state's apparatus of coercion, its devices for securing "domination," is insufficient; the control must also be seen as legitimate. Gramsci's hegemony is what the ruling class achieves when it can secure popular consent for the state's use of coercion.

An episode from the life and times of Governor Blanchard illustrates the point. In the late nineteenth and early twentieth centuries, the lynching of people of African descent became endemic across the South. State authorities did little to prevent lynching and perhaps facilitated it on occasion. Still the practice undermined the state's monopoly on the legitimate means of violence, impugning the authority of the state government. Blanchard was committed to reasserting the state's prerogatives, at least symbolically. Early in 1906 in a northern parish of the state, a black man was tried for murder. The outcome appeared a foregone conclusion, and the accused was convicted and sentenced to death. The political crisis faced by Blanchard revolved around the state's need to carry out the process. Blanchard traveled to the trial to prevent the man from being lynched by local white people. His personal presence ensured that the convict was not lynched within the three days required by law to intervene between the sentencing and the execution.

At issue was not whether the man was guilty or whether he would die but whether the state would control the situation. If the death sentence had been carried out by a mob, the legitimacy of the court process and the privilege of the state in the exercise of punishment would have been diminished. Blanchard thought the matter important enough to travel the length of the state to attend proceedings in a local court. His purpose was not merely to coerce the local populace into compliance but also to show that the state would mete out "justice" as it saw fit. Above and beyond the racial politics of such trials, Blanchard's dramatic action attempted to maintain the hegemony of the constellation of forces that had assumed the mantle of white supremacy and exercised state power in its name.[8]

This example also spotlights the "educative" function of the state. For Gramsci law is a solution to the "'juridical problem,' i.e., the problem of assimilating the entire grouping to its most advanced fraction." The principal aim of law is less punishment or justice than education: "[I]t is a problem of education of the masses, of their 'adaptation' in accordance with the requirement of the goal to be achieved. This is precisely the function of law in the State and society; through 'law' the State renders the ruling group 'homogenous,' and tends to create a social conformism which is useful to the ruling group's line of development."[9]

Many laws and court cases from the 1890s into the early twentieth century in Louisiana, as well as the reframed constitution of 1898, can be seen in this light. Their express justification often was to ratify existing practices and protect the traditional, natural, God-ordained order. Of course, segregation and antimiscegenation laws helped create realities they were claiming merely to protect. White supremacists wanted such laws precisely because white and black Louisianans had been marrying each other, eating together, and, crucially, politicking together. Once stated, the point seems obvious. Yet U.S. Supreme Court decisions such as *Plessy v. Ferguson*, which held segregation to be compatible with the Fourteenth Amendment to the U.S. Constitution, rested partly on the reasoning that the South's racist order—in fact being created then—was not in the least new.[10]

Even today it is hard to shake the sense that the disenfranchising constitutions of this period were "inevitable" results of white racism.[11] But white supremacists like Blanchard had to create legal and political structures that would "educate" Louisianans to that "inevitability." Blanchard's Louisiana Day festivities should be seen in this light. In several places Gramsci makes clear that he does not limit "law" to statutes passed by legislatures. Rather the "general activity of law" is "wider than purely State and governmental activity and also includes activity involved in directing civil society, in those zones which the technicians of law call legally neutral—i.e., in morality and in custom generally."[12] Events such as Louisiana Day simultaneously presented the newly legalized subordination of African Americans in Louisiana as natural, inevitable, progressive, even "humanitarian."

Shaping political memories of past events is one way for those who control the state to achieve hegemony and secure the social conformity, or at least social acquiescence, necessary to sustain their rule. But how can this construct identities? How can shaping the political meanings of events by shaping memories constitute or reconstitute political identities? To explore these questions, let us turn to the work of Yuri Lotman.

## Lotman and Gramsci

Several scholars have noted similarities between key concepts developed by Lotman and Bakhtin, on the one hand, and Gramsci and Bakhtin, on the other.[13] This is not the place for an extended comparison of Lotman and Gramsci, yet their theories might be more similar to each other than either is to Bakhtin's. Lotman's work might not be well known to scholars of politics or rhetoric, but his intellectual trajectory will be familiar. Starting within a broadly Saussurean framework, Lotman moved in what could well be described as a "poststructuralist" direction.[14] His richly detailed, largely historical accounts of Russian culture and his more abstract elaborations of semiotic theory shift from structure to contingency, from synchrony to diachrony, and from language or (more narrowly) information processing to the interaction between linguistic and nonlinguistic aspects of social life. What Julia Kristeva calls the "subject of enunciation" plays an increasing part in Lotman's theoretical models. Like Kristeva, Lotman describes a kind of *sujet-en-procès*, whose boundaries shift continually and whose internal coherence faces chronic contestation.[15] This subject emerges from a process of engagement between "codes" that comprise the self and alternative "codes" from beyond the self's semiotic boundaries.

Lotman's work parallels Gramsci's in several important respects. They share a concern with ways that people acquire their conception of the world in relation to dominant groups. For Gramsci people always arrive at these conceptions within the context of their larger social identities: "In acquiring one's conception of the world one always belongs to a particular grouping which is that of all the social elements which share the same mode of thinking and activity."[16] Both theorists treat language as central to the reproduction of these conceptions.[17] Lotman's work can give further texture to Gramsci's views on hegemony. It can show how the shaping of political memory, as an aspect of hegemony, constitutes people's identities. To delve deeper into Lotman's theory, let us begin with its account of the role of memory in the production of cultural meaning and the self. Then we can turn to Governor Blanchard's politics as a form of what Lotman calls autocommunication.

## Memory and Autocommunication

One of the central themes of Yuri Lotman's *Universe of the Mind* is that memory is a basic function of all thought. For Lotman memory is central not only to an individual human being but also to texts and cultures, which he sees as "'thinking' semiotic structures" (*Universe of the Mind*, 2). At this basic level memory is simply "the capacity to preserve and reproduce information (texts)" (2). But the third part of this volume presents a more complicated account. In cultural terms memory is a "dialogue" between past and present, not merely a mechanism for transmitting information: "Memory is more like a generator, reproducing the past again; it is the ability, given certain impulses, to switch on the process of generating a conceptualized reality which the mind transfers into the past. . . . The interrelationship between cultural memory and its self-reflection is like a constant dialogue: texts from chronologically earlier periods are brought into culture and, interacting with contemporary mechanisms, generate an *image* of the historical past which culture transfers into the past and which, like an equal partner in a dialogue, affects the present" (272). Memory is an image of the past reproduced in the present that gives new shape to the present. Thus the commemoration of the Louisiana Purchase in 1904 explicitly placed the meaning of the purchase in dialogue with the meaning of the Spanish-American War. Both acquired new meaning through their juxtaposition and dialogue in the context of Louisiana Day.

Memory is also, then, the product of dialogue. As such it involves the translation and incorporation of texts from the past into the cultural system of the present. "Texts" from past and present transform each other through this translation. Since the texts differ enough to be mutually untranslatable in part and thus asymmetrical in Lotman's terms, any translation generates meaning that is not exactly present before the translation took place. Any text is transformed to some degree when passing into a new cultural context, just as the new text transforms that context. Insofar as culture is a set of texts, translation becomes "a primary mechanism of consciousness" and a producer of new cultural meanings and memories (*Universe of the Mind*, 126).

At its most straightforward this translation is the transmission of a message from one person (or culture) to another. One speaker transmits a coded message to another, who must "decode" it to extract the meaning. Lotman contrasts this model with autocommunication, in which the sender and the receiver are the same "person." The underlying semantic content of the message remains the same in autocommunication, but "recoding" transforms its meaning. Lotman illustrates the concept with the example of "diary jottings . . . which are made not in order to remember certain things but to elucidate the writer's inner state, something that would not be possible without the jottings" (*Universe of the Mind*, 21). In such jottings "the message is reformulated and acquires new meaning"; it is "qualitatively transformed." A parallel restructuring occurs in the identity of the diary jotter: in autocommunication, "while communicating with himself, the addresser inwardly reconstructs his essence, since the essence of a personality may be thought of as an individual set of socially significant codes, and this set changes during the act of communication" (22).

This restructuring happens by "recoding" the original message according to a "second code" that rearranges the elements in the original message. This operation endows those elements, like the message as a whole, with new and supplementary meaning. Imagine that our diary jotter is undergoing psychoanalysis. On returning to his diary after a session, he would re-present earlier jottings in light of interpretive codes provided by the therapist. The supplementary meaning would result from their restructuring as a new mechanism of interpretation rather than as a separate addition of new informational content to the message.[18]

The jottings themselves take on the quality of signs that refer not only to their own, original semantic content but also to their location within the supplementary code. These signs can be expressed in subsequent jottings by means of shorthand comprehensible only if we have access to the secondary code of the jotter. In this way texts take on meanings that are not simply reducible to their informational contents.

Autocommunication reorganizes the personality of the communicator while "raising the rank" of a message yet without erasing its previous semantic content. Like all forms of communication, it depends on memory: the diary jotter must remember the secondary code for the supplementary meaning of the text to be present. The meaning of the text, in all its complexity, depends on linguistic and nonlinguistic contexts but also on the ability to reproduce those contexts in subsequent re-presentations of the text. The resulting "dialogue" between the jotter's past and present reshapes both and therefore the jotter. Autocommuni-cation and memory combine to remake aspects of his personality.

The process occurs also beyond individual consciousness. In the con-text of Louisiana Day, the storming of government buildings by white supremacists in 1874 becomes recoded. Its meaning now relates to a larger historical narrative of white imperialism. For Lotman this, too, is an instance of autocommunication. Indeed, "culture can be treated both as the sum of the messages circulated by various addressers (for each of them the addressee is 'another,' 'she' or 'he'), and as one message trans-mitted by the collective 'I' of humanity to itself. From this point of view, human culture is a vast example of autocommunication" (*Universe of the Mind*, 33).[19] Culture thus organizes a "collective personality with a com-mon memory and a collective consciousness" (34). Below the level of all humanity, particular cultures are examples of autocommunication.[20]

Lotman's theory displays the interdependence of memory and mean-ing making. We can see how the production of new meaning entails the formation of new memories, just as memory enables the generation of meaning. Lotman identifies a form of communication, autocommu-nication, that actively involves the constitution and reconstitution of the communicator's identity. Yet according to Lotman's theory, we need not restrict the "self" to individual biological humans. Instead the "self" can be collective, up to and including humanity as a whole. What re-mains is to extend this theory to politics.

## Politics as Autocommunication

What might we learn from imputing Governor Blanchard with a politi-cal form of autocommunication?[21] For Lotman autocommunication has three characteristics: "[I]t does not add to the information we al-ready have, but . . . it transforms the self-understanding of the person who has engendered the text and . . . it transfers already existing mes-sages into a new system of meanings" (*Universe of the Mind*, 30). We can see immediately that Blanchard's pronouncement, relayed through newspaper accounts and word of mouth, added no information to what was already available to Louisianans.

In the absence of a relevant narrative of history, however, neither the remarks from Blanchard nor the warm words of the *Daily Picayune* would have conveyed much sense of the significance of the governor's choice. The connection between September 14, 1904, and September 14, 1874, occurs solely through allusion and coded references. Blanchard called the earlier day "justly memorable," and the *Picayune* termed it a "glorious day in 1874," yet neither related the actual events of the day. The newspaper came closest, but it still talked indirectly of an "immortal act" and a "new birth" from "terrible tyranny, darkness and misery." In these statements rhetorical flourish is more central than specific information.

Of course, it was unnecessary for Blanchard or the *Daily Picayune* to go into details. This was a familiar story to anyone who read about Blanchard's pronouncement. The rhetoric that cast the Democratic return to power as a "redemption" or "renaissance" of the state had been circulating since at least 1877—if not, in anticipation, earlier. "Tyranny" and "imposition by a sectional Congress" were code words deployed by Democrats and white supremacists during the previous forty years of conflict in the state and throughout the American South following the Civil War. The words conjured a "noble struggle" against tyranny and oppression, a struggle conclusively won only through the recent institution of racial segregation and the effective disfranchisement in Louisiana of people of African descent. We can see here precisely the "reduction of words" that Lotman attributed to autocommunication: a small set of words invokes common memories complete with associations built over thirty years of telling much the same historical narrative.

Lotman's analysis suggests that we should not ascribe to Blanchard the intention of imparting information, transmitting a message, or even attributing new meanings to old events. His public pronouncements and the celebration itself are better seen as forms of autocommunication. They contribute to an internal dialogue that shapes the identity of white-supremacist Louisianans, with the Democratic Party as their "leading faction." Blanchard produced three important effects: he identified white supremacy as a progressive movement; he identified the Democratic Party, as the agent of "redemption," with the cause of white supremacy; and he associated white supremacy itself with the political dominance of elite whites like himself. Thus Blanchard drew on and reshaped a set of political memories to reconstitute the "personality" of a white-supremacist Louisiana.

The celebration of Louisiana Day within the context of the Louisiana Purchase Exposition inserted the "noble struggle" of Louisiana Democrats into a broader discourse and historical narrative. The victory of white supremacy in Louisiana became part of the general westward expansion of white Americans. It fed into the decimation and subordination of nonwhites from the Appalachians to the Philippines. The exposition presented this expansion as progressive and inevitable. One rationale for including displays of Native American and Filipino tribes was precisely that anthropologists expected these peoples to die out in an "irreconcilable conflict of races."[22]

The ceremonies marking Louisiana Day reinforced these connections. The celebration reenacted the signing of the Louisiana Purchase Treaty. The State of Louisiana commissioned a replica of the Cabildo, where the treaty was signed. In this building Governor Blanchard joined representatives from Spain and France as well as ancestors of people present at the first signing to participate in a dramatic re-creation. Before the reading and signing came a military parade. David R. Francis, president of the Louisiana Purchase Exposition Company, which had organized the fair, wrote that "Brigadier General Rice conducted the procession to the Cabildo. Military features of the parade were strengthened by the addition of a detachment of the Jefferson Guard, the battalion of Philippine scouts and band, the battalion of the Philippine constabulary and band, the United States Marine Corps and a battalion of United States troops."[23] Soldiers who had fought in the Spanish-American War marched with soldiers then occupying the Philippines to hail, as Blanchard said, the "new birth" of Louisiana from the "tyranny" of racial democracy.

The exposition mixed these potent themes with technological development and scientific progress. It commemorated the centennial of the Louisiana Purchase by incorporating it into an imperialist story of growing domination of the world by the white race. Louisiana Democrats could place their recent history within these new coordinates. White supremacy would not be reactionary and conservative; it would be progressive in the broadest sense, participating in the dynamism of the new age. In this way Louisiana Day transformed the identity of white supremacists in Louisiana.

At the same time, the celebration presented white Louisiana Democrats as the central actors in Blanchard's narrative of history. What Lawrence Powell has called the "invented tradition" of "September

Fourteen" was in fact "largely the symbolic property of the silk-stocking classes" in Louisiana. The tradition affirmed not only white supremacy as such but also the assimilation of white supremacy to the domination of Louisiana politics by "the silk-stocking classes."[24] Governor Blanchard was well aware of this social subtext. His inaugural address of May 1904 had offered a related narrative with a similarly restricted cast of racial "types." The emphasis was on "self-government," that is, domination of state governance by white men from Louisiana without interference from the federal government.

Blanchard foregrounded the theme of white government. He began with the image of rebirth. "Louisiana's political renaissance began in the year 1877," he said, "when the government of the state was restored to the hands of the white people—the intelligent and property holding classes."[25] 1877 (rather than 1874) was the year when Democrats took full control of the state government. But Blanchard's theme was the same as in his later Louisiana Day pronouncement. The state had been "reborn" by replacing a Republican and racially integrated regime with white-supremacist Democrats. Yet Blanchard did not portray all white people in Louisiana as equal participants in the narrative of rebirth. He qualified the phrase "white people" by adding "the intelligent and property holding classes." These were not so much subcategories of "white people" as a delimitation for what counted fully as "white." Self-governance meant white supremacy, but the governing "self" should be these "white people—the intelligent and propertied classes."

Blanchard had identified the historic character of Louisiana with a specific type, "white people." His purpose was not to deny that people of color lived in Louisiana but to shape "the negro's" identity and relation to the state. "To close the door of hope against any child within the borders of the State, whatever be his race or condition," said Blanchard as a progressive, "is illogical, un-Christian, un-Democratic, and un-American." This might sound strange coming from the mouth of a man who resorted to violence and fraud to prevent some people from voting on account of their race. "The negro is here," Blanchard nevertheless affirmed. "He is a man and a citizen."[26]

Many northern newspapers praised Blanchard for this observation, but they paid less attention to the next sentences: "He is useful and valuable in his sphere. Within that sphere he must be guaranteed the equal protection of the law, and his education along proper lines—mainly agricultural and industrial—is at once a duty and a necessity. He must be

protected in his right to live peaceably and quietly, in his right to labor
and enjoy the fruits of his labor. He must be encouraged to industry and
taught habits of thrift."[27] Blanchard was saying that the state must educate its citizenry; and unlike some whites in the South, he meant this
to include "negroes." But who were these "negroes?" As with "white
people," Blanchard's delimitation is telling. "The negro" was definable
by his "sphere." In this sphere he was "useful and valuable," presumably to "white people." This sphere was "mainly agricultural and industrial." Ergo "the negro" was a laborer—and not "closing the door of
hope" meant educating "negroes" to be happy laborers.

To be sure that he wasn't misunderstood, Blanchard concluded with
standard fare for white supremacists: "No approach towards social
equality or social recognition will ever be tolerated in Louisiana. Separate schools, separate churches, separate cars, separate places of entertainment will be enforced. Racial distinction and integrity must be preserved. But there is room enough in this broad Southland, with proper
lines of limitation and demarcation, for the two races to live on terms
of mutual trust, mutual help, good understanding and concord. The
South asserts its ability to handle and solve the negro question on humanitarian lines."[28] "Lines of limitation and demarcation" were central
to Blanchard's purpose. In his inaugural address and his declaration of
Louisiana Day, Blanchard effectively constituted the boundary as well
as the identity of "Louisiana." For Lotman drawing boundaries is "one
of the primary mechanisms of semiotic individuation." Indeed the
boundary "can be defined as the outer limit of a first-person form" (*Universe of the Mind,* 131). As Lotman makes clear, "[t]he boundary of the
personality is a semiotic boundary. For instance, a wife, children, slaves,
vassals may in some systems be included in the personality of the master, patriarch, husband, patron, suzerain, and not possess any individual status of their own; whereas in other systems they are treated as separate individuals" (138). Blanchard's rhetoric operated within this logic.
Rather than exclude people of African descent from the personality of
Louisiana, Blanchard's rhetoric included them—in the form of "the
negroes"—as "citizens" within Louisiana. Yet their role was unmistakably subordinate: "no approach to social equality or social recognition"
was left open.

Relegated to the margins of political significance, the political and social gains of African Americans beginning in the 1870s do not surface in
Blanchard's categories. "Negroes" do not include politicians, newspaper

editors, planters, shopkeepers, or any of the other social positions that real African Americans might have occupied in the decades before Blanchard's address in 1904.[29] Instead he defined "negroes" as members of an agricultural labor force, now properly returned to positions of happy subservience.

Some people, however, were so "marginal" to Blanchard's narrative that they might as well not exist. As Lotman notes, "[W]hole layers of cultural phenomena, which from the point of view of the given metalanguage are marginal, will have no relation to the idealized portrait of that culture. They will be declared 'non-existent'" (*Universe of the Mind*, 129). "Poor whites" made no appearance in the Louisiana narrated by Blanchard. In the early twentieth century, poor whites were marginal politically as well as socially. The voting restrictions embodied in the new constitution of 1898, aimed primarily at black Louisianans, also disenfranchised poor whites. Louisiana's voting population of 206,354 in 1896 declined by 1904 to only 54,222. Roughly half of the drop was due to the virtual disappearance of blacks from the voting rolls after 1898; the rest reflected a sharp decline in registration among poor whites.[30] As voting citizens, therefore, black and lower-class white Louisianans were indeed effectively declared "non-existent."

## Center and Periphery

Lotman's semiotics of culture gives us a firmer grip on how political contestation over the meaning of past events can constitute our political identities. They help us decode Governor Blanchard's political rhetoric. Yet they do not guarantee success for strategies like Blanchard's. Lotman's account of center and periphery clarifies what is at stake.

Clearly the Blanchard narrative failed to correspond to the worldviews or identities of many Louisianans, particularly those of African descent. In *Universe of the Mind*, Lotman suggests that a culture's "self-description" is continually contested. "One part of the semiosphere," or cultural space, "in the process of self-description creates its own grammar. . . . Then it strives to extend its norms over the whole semiosphere. A partial grammar of one cultural dialect becomes the metalanguage of description for culture as such" (128). This extension is never wholly successful. Even for the "center," with norms that become the standard for the culture as a whole, this description is an "idealization."

The further in cultural terms that people are from the "center," the less its idealized description corresponds to the "semiotic reality lying 'underneath'" (*Universe of the Mind*, 129). On the "periphery" there is often a large gap between the norms or values of the dominant description of the culture and the actual practices, norms, or values of those who inhabit this cultural location.[31] For Lotman this gap is the precondition for "semiotic dynamism" (134). On the periphery new and subversive semiotic practices emerge. Ultimately the periphery bids to become the center of the semiosphere, imposing new norms on its predecessors.

In many ways the post–Civil War history of Louisiana corresponds closely to this pattern. Governor Blanchard's "intelligent and propertied classes" had successfully imposed their views of Louisiana's history and political culture on the polity as a whole. For forty years Louisianans had struggled over the meaning of freedom and citizenship and debated who should own land and benefit from cultivating it and what place people of African descent should assume in the state and its society. By 1904 white supremacists were the victors. As Blanchard's words and deeds show, the "center" tried to impose its description of the social hierarchy on the state: blacks were agricultural laborers, whites were intelligent and propertied, while whites and blacks could live in harmony and happiness if whites solved the race question "on humanitarian lines." For people murdered, assaulted, or raped by these same white supremacists, however, there was a "gap" of enormous proportions between this description and their own understandings of recent history, especially in their personal lives.

People of African descent in Louisiana had their own "semiotic practices" to subvert those of the white supremacists. The testimony of a former slave, Eliza Pinkston, can serve as an example. She was attacked in her home in north Louisiana in November 1876, when Democrats waged a campaign of terror against black and white Republicans. Her husband and child were killed in the attack; Pinkston was raped and left for dead. Escaping in late November to the relative safety of New Orleans, she brought a criminal case against two of her attackers. It was heard in a New Orleans municipal police court.

Remarkably Pinkston found herself cross-examined in the case by John McEnery, the man named governor by the Democrats during their brief coup of September 14, 1874. One of the men she accused was

Tom Lyons, a "colored Democrat," whom she located at the site of her husband's murder. McEnery asked her whether she knew where Lyons lived. Henry Pinkston, Eliza's husband, had apparently been to Lyons's house in the past, when Lyons had tried to persuade him to join the Democrats. McEnery asked sarcastically, "When colored people visit each other, do they not know where each other live, generally?" She simply responded, "I don't know, sir." But asked again "whose planta- tion" Lyons lived on, Pinkston shot back, "When colored people visit they never say they are on such and such a place, but on a place of their own, but that such and such a man has authority."[32]

This answer reveals a way black cotton workers subverted the nam- ing practices of white people. Even as they recognized the inequalities that shaped plantation life, African Americans did not follow whites in calling a plantation by the name of its white owner or occupant, as in "the McEnery Place." Black resistance to white naming practices had wide ramifications. The antebellum legal system endowed white land- owning men with authority as household heads—authority that in- cluded control over their wives, children, slaves, and employees. White men's naming practices revealed that, even after slaves had been eman- cipated, landowning white men still saw a social landscape shaped by the antebellum legal system. A white man such as John McEnery con- tinued to emphasize his control over the land, yet black sharecroppers like Eliza Pinkston had come to see their homes as "their own."

There were alternative, if not always subversive, semiotic practices on the "periphery." In 1904 these did not provide resources sufficient for a challenge to the supremacy of the dominant political discourse, but Lotman's account suggests that this is always a possibility. When Pink- ston brought her court case in 1877, ensuing years of struggle were not guaranteed to end in disfranchisement and segregation. Nevertheless, it had become clear by 1904 that black Louisianans would face radically limited opportunities for producing their own public discourse, let alone challenging that of white Democrats.[33] Lotman does not imply that every move from the periphery will succeed; indeed, his account con- nects with Gramsci's in describing a form of power where semiotic mechanisms can help the center maintain its position. Lotman's ac- count, however, indicates the structure of the semiotic space, the semi- otic gap, from which black and poor white Louisianans on the periph- ery could hope to launch incipient cultural rebellions.

## Conclusion: Hegemony and Autocommunication

Neils Helsloot has argued that "linguists study, often on too abstract a level, the way social groups are 'articulated' by language practices. Alternatively, they could take up organizing/dispersing practices, struggles for schism *and* alliance, as part of the way in which human individuals form their lives (their identities/differences) through language." Helsloot urges us to attend to the ways in which language constructs identity and difference *in one and the same move*. Linguistic or semiotic strategies aimed at consolidating a particular identity simultaneously seek to disperse alternative forms of identification. Helsloot intends his remarks to correct, through a link to Voloshinov (Bakhtin), what he regards as Gramsci's excessive emphasis on the need to achieve a "totalizing and all absorbing unity."[34] I have used Gramsci and Lotman to explain how white supremacists went about achieving unity — in part by marginalizing and dispersing alternative identities. In combination the work of Gramsci and Lotman can help us trace such dynamics — and doing so also provides ground for political theorists interested in tracing the microstructures through which hegemony is constructed as identity.

A number of striking similarities in the two theories make their combination attractive. Particularly intriguing is the resonance between Lotman's theory of center and periphery and Gramsci's dialectic of hegemonic and subaltern groups. For both Lotman and Gramsci, communication takes place in the context of structural asymmetry. Gramsci's framework ties class identities to specific positions in a system of production, but this resembles Lotman's view that people acquire and develop a cultural "grammar" within the context of a (possibly more complex) terrain of cultural identities and practices.[35] Gramsci, like Lotman, describes a process of competition among groups that seek to impose their views on others. Their struggles shape individual consciousness and the "collective consciousness" of the people involved.

For both theorists this imposition implies a gap, or at least potential for one, between the conceptions of the dominant group and that of peripheral or subaltern ones. According to Lotman the "grammar" that comes to dominate the semiosphere is an "idealization," even an "illusion" (*Universe of the Mind*, 128). As we approach the periphery, it is increasingly so, although the idealization structures real social relations. According to Lotman it is nonetheless from the periphery that new cultural productions, new meanings, arise. Similarly the Communist Party

operated for Gramsci precisely in the gap between the worldviews generated in a civil society dominated by capitalist interests and the new
forces emerging among the working classes. Success by the Communist
Party in organizing a collective will among workers would be the precondition for a general restructuring of society. The Communist Party
would be a "myth-prince," waging an ideological battle. To the extent
that it could reorganize the world in its own image, the party could also
reshape social relations.

   In Blanchard's Louisiana, as we have seen, contests to the unity
of the center were muted. Mounting an effective challenge to white supremacy in Louisiana would have entailed a solid alliance between African Americans and poor whites, but white Democrats had defeated just
such an alliance in the previous decade.

   The success of white Democrats depended on another mechanism
of dispersal identified by Lotman. The boundary is for Lotman the basic
mechanism of individuation. It is easy to think of this in terms of Hegel's
familiar claim that identities are always formed, in part, with reference
to some other, external to the self. But the boundaries that Blanchard
drew also had the effect of actively dispersing alternative ways in which
Louisianans might have thought about identity. Rather than alliances
based on class, religious, or linguistic differences (to mention three possibilities salient in Louisiana), Blanchard's semiotic practices combined
with legal, economic, and violent forms of intimidation to solidify race
as the relevant form of identification.

   As Andreas Schönle has argued, then, Lotman provides a "semiotic
theory of social power."[36] In contrast to Gramsci, Lotman focuses neither on the state nor on how ruling classes secure consent to their rule.
Nor does he attend to the relation between cultural, economic, or political forms of power. But the similarities may be more important than the
differences. The shared emphasis on asymmetrical communication, on
language or culture as a site of power, and on struggles for hegemony
within the domain of culture can sustain an approach drawing from both
theorists. While each departs from the structuralist orthodoxy of their
predecessors, both retain a robust sense of structure in their accounts of
culture, politics, and economics. Moreover, they presume some form of
underlying coherence as necessary for meaningful communication to
take place. For Gramsci this is a political achievement, the result of hegemony rather than its precondition; for Lotman, on the other hand,
such a conception of the semiosphere is susceptible to naturalization, at

times bringing to mind the image of a self-regulating biosphere rather than an arena of political contestation.[37] But, broadly, these commitments connect Gramsci and Lotman more closely to each other than to Bahktin.

In combination each theory can be used to overcome the limitations of the other. Where Lotman's semiotic theory risks presenting power as a relation among "texts," Gramsci's political theory attends to the agency of these texts and its political designs. Where Gramsci shows how some dynamics generate cohesion, Lotman explores how related dynamics disrupt it. Where Lotman's account might focus too exclusively on culture, Gramsci's can remind us of connections between culture, economy, and polity. And where Gramsci's concept of hegemony seems to imply that identities are shaped through contestation over worldviews, Lotman's semiotics can give us a more precise account of how this happens.

Drawing on this combination, we see how leaders like Blanchard deployed diverse resources—legal and political, semiotic and extrasemiotic—to reshape southern conceptions of citizenship. Blanchard and his ilk had come to control these resources largely through force and fraud. As Gramsci and Lotman suggest, however, white southerners used these resources to reconfigure the relationships between the state and its citizens, black and white. They justified their exercise of state power as the protection of an established white supremacy they were in the process of creating. And they structured the social landscape around racial identification. Leaders like Blanchard achieved each of these steps in part through semiotic state practices that reconceived the relationships between the rulers and the ruled while giving those relationships concrete forms.

## Notes

1. Robert W. Rydell, *All the World's a Fair: Visions of Empire at American International Expositions, 1876–1916* (Chicago: University of Chicago Press, 1984).

2. *Daily Picayune*, August 21, 1904.

3. Newspaper clipping from the *New Orleans Daily Picayune*, August 21, 1904, in Newton C. Blanchard, Scrapbooks, 1892–1906, vol. 3, Louisiana and Lower Mississippi Valley Collections, Louisiana State University Libraries, Baton Rouge.

4. Jeremy Lester, *The Dialogue of Negation: Debates on Hegemony in Russia and the West* (London: Pluto Press, 2000), esp. chap. 3. Lester offers an "archaeology"

of pre-Gramscian uses of the concept. The literature on Gramsci's political theory is large—some recent examples include Christine Buci-Glucksmann, *Gramsci and the State* (London: Lawrence & Wishart, 1980); Joseph V. Femia, *Gramsci's Political Thought: Hegemony, Consciousness, and the Revolutionary Process* (Oxford: Clarendon Press, 1981); Benedetto Fontana, *Hegemony and Power: On the Relation between Gramsci and Machiavelli* (Minneapolis: University of Minnesota Press, 1993).

5. Antonio Gramsci, *Selections from the Prison Notebooks,* ed. Quintin Hoare and Geoffrey Nowell Smith (London: Lawrence & Wishart, 1971), 12.

6. Ibid., 59.

7. Max Weber, "The Profession and Vocation of Politics," in *Political Writings,* ed. Peter Laswell and Donald Speirs, 309-69 (Cambridge: Cambridge University Press, 1994).

8. Newspaper clipping from the *New Orleans Daily Picayune,* February 22, 1906, in Blanchard, Scrapbooks, 1892-1906, vol. 3.

9. Gramsci, *Prison Notebooks,* 195.

10. *Plessy v. Ferguson,* 163 U.S., 1896, 537 and 559.

11. For a recent example of this argument, see Rogers Smith, *Civic Ideals: Conflicting Visions of Citizenship in U.S. History* (New Haven, Conn.: Yale University Press, 1997).

12. Gramsci, *Prison Notebooks,* 195 and 242.

13. For comparisons of Gramsci and Bakhtin, see Lester, *Dialogue of Negation,* 98-103; Craig Brandist, "Gramsci, Bakhtin, and the Semiotics of Hegemony," *New Left Review,* no. 216 (March/April 1996): 94-109; and Niels Helsloot, "Linguists of All Countries . . . ! On Gramsci's Premise of Coherence," *Journal of Pragmatics* 13 (1989): 547-66. Amy Mandelker compares Bakhtin and Lotman in "Logosphere and Semiosphere: Bakhtin, Russian Organicism, and the Semiotics of Culture," in *Bakhtin in Contexts across the Disciplines,* ed. Amy Mandelker, 177-90 (Evanston, Ill.: Northwestern University Press, 1995), as does Gunhild Agger in "Intertextuality Revisited: Dialogues and Negotiations in Media Studies," *Canadian Aesthetics Journal / Revue canadienne d'esthetique* 4 (Summer 1999), available at http://www.uqtr.uquebec.ca/AE/vol_4/gunhild.htm. Several other essays are also useful as introductions to Lotman's work, among them Julia Kristeva, "On Yury Lotman," *PMLA* 109, no. 3 (1994): 375-76; Thomas A. Sebeok, "The Estonian Connection," *Sign Systems Studies* 26 (1998): 20-41; and Umberto Eco's introduction to *Universe of the Mind.* A more technical introduction to the work of Soviet-era semioticians, along with a collection of articles by Lotman and others, can be found in Daniel P. Lucid, ed. and trans., *Soviet Semiotics: An Anthology* (Baltimore: Johns Hopkins University Press, 1977).

14. Amy Mandelker discusses this possibility in "Logosphere and Semiosphere."

15. Kelly Oliver, ed., *The Portable Kristeva* (New York: Columbia University Press, 1997).

16. Gramsci, *Prison Notebooks*, 324.

17. Lester, *Dialogue of Negation*, 70–71. Gramsci's rather scattered remarks on language are collected in "Notes on Language," translated with an introduction by Steven R. Mansfield, *Telos*, no. 59 (1984): 119–50.

18. Lotman uses examples of "rhythmical series, ranging from musical repetitions to repeated ornamentation" as ways in which poetry, for example, exhibits this autocommunication. Lotman says that these are strictly "constructed according to clearly expressed syntagmatic principles but have no semantic meaning of their own; we can treat them as external codes whose effect is to restructure verbal communication. However, for the system to work there has to be a confrontation and interaction between two different principles: a message in some semantic language and the intrusion of a purely syntagmatic, supplementary code" (*Universe of the Mind*, 25). The example of psychoanalysis is not accidental. Lotman's description of autocommunication is remarkably close to Julia Kristeva's contrast of "chora" and the "symbolic," though without her theory of drives. Like Lotman, Kristeva treats meaning as generated partly through the confrontation between two different principles, one linguistic in the narrow sense and the other not, though they are still in some way "ordered." And for Kristeva, as for Lotman, this is expressed most purely in poetic form. See selections by Julia Kristeva from her *Revolution in Poetic Language* in *The Portable Kristeva*.

19. This works on the principle of the "isomorphism" of individual and social levels of analysis. Merrell, among others, has criticized this as a failing of structuralism that Charles Peirce avoided. The concept of social or group "identity" seems to warrant a limited sense in which social entities and individuals are similarly structured, but later in the discussion I examine ways that political identities differ. See Floyd Merrell, *Sign, Textuality, Word* (Bloomington: Indiana University Press, 1992), 18.

20. More properly stated, all cultures involve both autocommunication and 'I-she' communication. Lotman suggests the possibility of categorizing specific cultures according to which of the two predominates.

21. In treating politics as autocommunication, I build on a suggestion by Michael Urban in "The Politics of Identity in Russia's Postcommunist Transition: The Nation against Itself," *Slavic Review* 53 (Fall 1994): 733–65, on 744.

22. Eric Breitbart, *A World on Display: Photographs From the St. Louis World's Fair, 1904* (Albuquerque: University of New Mexico Press, 1997). The quotation is from William T. Sherman's letter to David F. Boyd on May 20, 1867, William T. Sherman Letters, folder 1, Louisiana and Lower Mississippi Valley Collections, Louisiana State University Libraries, Baton Rouge.

23. David R. Francis, *The Universal Exposition of 1904* (St. Louis: Louisiana Purchase Exposition Co., 1913), 272–73.

24. Lawrence Powell, "Reinventing Tradition: Liberty Place, Historical Memory, and Silk-Stocking Vigilantism in New Orleans Politics," in *From*

*Slavery to Emancipation in the Atlantic World,* ed. Sylvia Frey and Betty Wood (London: Frank Cass, 1999), 128.

25. Blanchard, Scrapbooks, 1892–1906, vol. 3.

26. Ibid.

27. Ibid.

28. Ibid.

29. Women are entirely absent from the narrative as well. On the relation between gender and institutionalized white supremacy in the United States, see Glenda Gilmore, *Gender and Jim Crow: Women and the Politics of White Supremacy in North Carolina, 1896–1920* (Chapel Hill: University of North Carolina Press, 1996).

30. Joseph G. Dawson III, ed., *The Louisiana Governors: From Iberville to Edwards* (Baton Rouge: Louisiana State University Press, 1990), 201. Mark T. Carleton wrote the biographical entry for Newton Crain Blanchard. The specific mechanisms included literacy and property qualifications plus a poll tax. To ensure that at least some whites who would have been disenfranchised by these measures would still be eligible to vote, the 1898 constitution had a "grandfather clause" for those who had voted or whose father or grandfather had voted before January 1, 1867. They could continue to register but had only a four-month period to take advantage of the exception. Details on the provisions and debates over their adoption appear in Michael L. Lanza, "Little More Than a Family Meeting: The Constitution of 1898," in *In Search of Fundamental Law: Louisiana's Constitutions, 1812–1974,* ed. Warren M. Billings and Edward F. Haas, 93–109 (Lafayette: Center for Louisiana Studies at the University of Southwestern Louisiana, 1993). The classic source on effects of the disfranchisement constitutions across the American South is J. Morgan Kousser, *The Shaping of Southern Politics: Suffrage Restriction and the Establishment of the One-Party South, 1880–1910* (New Haven, Conn.: Yale University Press, 1974).

31. *Center* and *periphery* are relational terms, and the distance between them is semiotic, not necessarily geographical.

32. Testimony of Eliza Pinkston to the U.S. Senate on Denial of Elective Franchise in Louisiana at Election of November 7, 1876, 44th Congress, 2nd sess., Senate Report 701, vol. 2, pt. 2, 909–87. I explore these issues more fully in "Gender and the Politics of the Household in Reconstruction Louisiana, 1865–1879," in *Gender and Emancipation in the Transatlantic World,* ed. Diana Patton and Pamela Scully (Durham, N.C.: Duke University Press, 2005).

33. There were still many institutions within the black community itself. On the role of women, for example, see Evelyn Brooks Higginbotham, *Righteous Discontent: The Women's Movement in the Black Baptist Church, 1880–1920* (Cambridge, Mass.: Harvard University Press, 1993).

34. Helsloot, "Linguists of All Countries . . . !" 564.

35. The most prominent extension of Gramsci's concept of hegemony seeks precisely to unmoor the concept from its traditional Marxist underpinnings:

Ernesto Laclau and Chantal Mouffe, *Hegemony and Socialist Strategy: Towards a Radical Democratic Politics* (London: Verso, 1985).

36. Andreas Schönle, "The Self, Its Bubbles, and Its Illusions: Cultivating Autonomy in Greenblatt and Lotman," in this volume. Schönle identifies two "technologies of power," one for the center-periphery logic discussed here and the other centered for terror and unpredictable behavior. Lotman's example of a terrorist is Ivan the Terrible.

37. Helsloot, "Linguists of All Countries . . . !," 553–56.

# 6

# The Ever-Tempting Return
# to an Iranian Past
# in the Islamic Present

*Does Lotman's Binarism Help?*

KATHRYN BABAYAN

History thrives on the exploration of human diversity in time and space. Its seductiveness lies in the ability to recognize something that is totally different yet fully human in that we can comprehend it. History also provides the reader with a multitude of stories about past transformations, the dynamics and processes of which remain ambiguous, for texts do not spell out the mechanisms of change. These may be inferred from signs and symbols encoded in texts. And the task of the historian lies in contextualizing symbols to uncover meanings and texture, layer by layer, recreating and imagining the landscapes in and about which texts were recorded in the past.

As a cultural historian I have been influenced by the works of Clifford Geertz and his interpretations of culture as a web of meanings encoded in symbolic forms (languages, artifacts, rituals, calendars). I think Geertz and Yuri Lotman share in their understanding of semiotic systems and in the tight fit they observe between clusters of symbols and the moods, motivations, and behaviors that these symbols shape. Memory is a cultural phenomenon that speaks through signs and influences behavior.[1] Culture, however, is mutable. Geertz's methods are essentially synchronic; that is, they tend to help us understand one face of history as a temporal complex. But the other face of history as transformation, the diachronic aspect, remains untapped in his notion of culture.[2] Here is where Lotman's meditations on culture help to make sense of change in time.[3] Lotman and Uspenskii's work on the semiotics of Russian culture in the light of history focuses on sites of conflict, dialogue, and change within cultures that speak different languages. They conceptualize cultural difference at the intrasociety level. Although Geertz tends to emphasize differences between societies, writing comparatively about "the Javanese" or "the Berbers," Lotman disturbs this "single functioning whole" by proposing a "semiotic physiology" that posits a dynamic between different languages embedded in the whole (semiosphere), privileging heterogeneity within Russian culture (*Universe of the Mind*, 125–26). Lotman opens an analytical space to consider how cultural systems are transformed within complex, or, as he calls them, "collective" cultures, raising the possibilities for disjunctions or continuities.[4] The Bakhtinian trope of heteroglossia allows for a refinement of such processes of change, for an approach sensitive to the diversity of social voices uttered through language.[5] For Bakhtin language is alive; its vitality lies in the process of becoming. Its transcription is not only a product of its context but is also subject to multiple refractions and meanings that encompass a variety of worldviews, group behaviors, and fleeting tendencies. Such stratification and heteroglossia highlight a dynamic between cultural systems and the particular language of social groups. The life and development of language can thus be explored as an expressive system born of social, religious, and political milieus in perpetual dialogue and movement.

One can see both continuities and discontinuities in the fragments from the Irano-Islamic past that I study, and I am fascinated by the ways in which this Iranian past blends with the Islamic present, in different forms and shapes as well as in degrees of transmutations. The problem of trying to explain cultural continuities amid change lies at the core of this essay. To conceptualize such a dynamic process without losing a sense of multiplicity within an ever-evolving system is difficult. Lotman's binary model of change, based on his reading of medieval and early modern Russian history, is useful when examining the Iranian case, where a similar transformation from a dualist past to a monotheist present was occurring. The questions arises whether patterns of change are contextually specific, in that they pertain to similar historical moments, or whether a deeper cosmological affinity must exist for such paradigms to be pertinent. Theoretical formulations derived from one cultural system may be even more relevant when applied to another culture that possesses similar blueprints or templates. Lotman's meditations may be telling us about those cultural landscapes that tend to be rooted in a binary worldview. Russian and Iranian cultures share dualist systems that permeate the ways in which they give meaning to their universe and configure their social and political realities. Lotman suggests that we apply a binary framework to explore cultures according to their own terms of cognizance, by searching out and analyzing the symbolic forms—words, images, institutions, memories—by which people represent themselves to themselves and to one another. This may shed light on why Lotman has not become trendy in Western academia, not only because he was introduced to the Western world in an age of deconstruction but also because his theories may be telling us more about those cultural landscapes rooted in dualist mentalities. Lotman, however, nuances his structuralist schema. Although he senses a psychological need in premodern Russia to imagine and narrate history through bipolar lenses, Lotman recognizes the traffic between these two poles, particularly in the ways in which dualist idioms are subject to multiple refractions and meanings that generate dialogue and movement.

In the messianic rebellions in medieval and early modern Iran, one can discern a curious and ever-present rhetoric among some Irano-Islamic religious movements (heresies) of a return to an Iranian past, to a time before the advent of Islam. How are we to understand this rhetoric? Vivid memories of a pre-Islamic past are preserved in texts, memories that continue to be evoked through storytelling up to a millennium after the Islamic conquests of the Iranian plateau. Central to my analysis is a case study of the messianic movement of the Nuqtavis, who rose against the Safavi dynasty (1501–1722), proclaiming an end to the first thousand years of Islamic rule (1000 AH/1592 CE) with the reestablishment of Persian hegemony. The massive endurance of historical memory in Iran is striking. The historian R. G. Collingwood coined the term *encapsulated history* in his *Philosophy of History* to refer to specific European attitudes to the past whereby large tracts of history that were known and preserved were nevertheless seen as forbidden alternatives to the dominant values of the present. The problem of how the past comes to form a symbolic resource that can be brought back into the present is fascinating. The Renaissance is one example, but it is not nearly as drastic as the Iranian case. Lotman and Uspenskii's work on the role of dualist models in the dynamics of Russian cultural change depicts a total reversal more similar to the Iranian case than this gentler leverage of an encapsulated past on the present exercised by Judaism and paganism in Western culture.[6]

Lotman and Uspenskii characterize Russian cultural change as "stages that replace each other dynamically, [in which] each stage is oriented toward a decisive break with what preceded it—whether the Christianization of Russia or the reforms of Peter the Great" ("Binary Models," 31). Their description of a "Russian" bipolarizing of the pagan past in a Christian present is related, as they see it, to a deeper structural binary permeating cultural values that affect the way the Christian present is constructed and the pagan past is imagined. This initial inscription of the old into the new plays a significant role in future processes that generate a reshaping or a revival of the old. Such binary ways of experiencing history are related to religious cosmologies that shape cognitive patterns of interpretation. Basic cultural values— whether political or religious—of medieval Russia are distributed in a "bipolar field and divided by sharp boundaries without an axiologically neutral zone" (31).

Lotman and Uspenskii see cognitive dissonance between the Catholic Christian West and Orthodox Christian Russia in the distinct ways in which these confessions imagine their cosmology, each sensing the world through respective patterns of twos or threes. The Catholic West imagines three symbolic zones in the afterlife: heaven, purgatory, and hell, and it assumes three types of earthly behavior: sinful, holy, and neutral. The existence of these neutral spheres forms a structural reserve out of which succeeding systems can develop, and so the momentum for change is gradual. Catholic Western culture sees no necessity to emphasize continuity or to recreate it, because the neutral ground mediates between two poles and dissipates the dialectic effect ("Binary Models," 32). In other words, there exists a recognized sphere through which new ideas can enter without having to define themselves in relationship to a binary.

Lotman understands the Russian medieval system, on the other hand, as constructed on a duality, whereby options in the afterworld are either heaven or hell—no intermediate world is envisaged. Earthly behavior is conceived of as either sinful or holy. Such a bipolar religious construction manifests itself in secular power, which is deemed either divine or diabolical, but never neutral. The particular phenomenon of Russian value orientation generates distinct cultural systems, processes, and tempos of historical change: "[C]hange occurs as a radical negation of the preceding state. The new arises not out of a structurally 'unused' reserve, but results from a transformation of the old. . . . Thus, repeated transformations can in fact lead to the regeneration of archaic forms" ("Binary Models," 32–33).

For Lotman the initial moment of encounter—the ways in which the old is inscribed into the new—is central to future dynamics and processes of change. The concurrent creation of a new Christian (Orthodox) Russia and the consolidation of an image of the old are understood as a psychological necessity for Russia to define herself. In this process an "artificial" pagan pantheon preceding the conversion of old Russia is created. Conversion then occurs as an exchange of sacred spaces and holy men. The old has to be formed in order to define the new, so the new imbues symbols of the old even if the latter is adopted only as antibehavior. Here Lotman begins to complicate his structuralism. In the long *durée*—through successive processes of change—what is imagined as new has already been perceived as old in a prior stage of transformation. And with every process of self-description, there is a need for a unified canonization of some texts and exclusion of others. These texts (content and code) form one of the repositories for cultural memory—a pool of symbolic resources that can be brought back into the present, but only for that particular "cultural group" that can recognize and speak the code (*Universe of the Mind*, 18). Lotman sees these texts as preserving a memory of past readings of themselves, preserving a context in which a given text was read, and awarding the reader the ability to remember these past readings. Moreover, heteroglossia allows for a multitude of overlapping readings of the same text by different "language groups," a useful observation with regard to the movements I study because they read canonical sacred Muslim texts such as the Qur'an and the hadith in different ways.

The ways in which the Persianate ethos participated in the making of new Muslim (Shi'ite and Sufi) identities and cultural systems is a story of conversion, of attempts made to apply traditional patterns of thought to a novel phenomenon, of the rise of a new revelation (Islam), and the emergence of Arab rule in the Iranian world.[7] Some Persianate practices and modes of consciousness continued to exist despite prevalent Muslim (Sunni) hegemonies, breathing life into heterogeneous spaces of opposition amongst the *ghuluww*, or exaggerators. Others adapted to and survived in "legitimate" Muslim arenas, shaping new forms of religiosity (Shi'ism and Persianate Sufism). The analytical frames offered by Lotman, Geertz, and Bakhtin will help us examine the identity of one of these groups, the Nuqtavis, who revolted (1590) in early modern Iran, proclaiming the inauguration of Persian rule after a millennium of Islamic dominance. What the Nuqtavis define as Ajami (Persian), using mixed Mazdean and Muslim cultural symbols, represents a construction of themselves in relation to what they term "other" and "Arab."[8] The Nuqtavis identify their form of mysticism with those independent ascetics, the roaming *qalandars* and *rinds*.[9] As the founder of the Nuqtavi movement, Mahmud Pasikhani writes, "The turn of the final praiseworthy *rinds* [sufis] has arrived. What the Arabs taunted the Iranians with has passed."[10]

In Safavi historiography the Nuqtavis are placed within the category of heresy, *ghuluww*, literally "exaggeration." *Ghuluww* is a pejorative term coined by Muslim (Shi'ite) heresiographers, emerging in the tenth century to define and distinguish Shi'ism from a series of religious movements that had risen at the advent of Islam. Muslim heresiographers applied the concept of *ghuluww* to a particular kind of other, namely, pre-Islamic gnostics and dualists. Their definitions, of course, were ideologically motivated and intended to alienate conceptually groups thus distinguished from their own mainstream. Although these Muslims who came in time to represent the norm have historically labeled the *ghuluww* as heretics and beyond the pale of Islam, *ghuluww* exemplifies an interpretation, a particular fusing of Muslim tenets with dualist traditions stemming from the gnostic cultures of Asia Minor, the Fertile Crescent, Mesopotamia, and the Iranian plateau—those core lands in which Islam came to spread its visionary seeds and articulate its divine mission.

These so-called exaggerators symbolize an old worldview against which Islam originally came to define itself as well as one among many interpretations and adaptations (languages) of Islam; dynamics similar to what Lotman delineates in his theory of change are at play here. The conversion of those lands that had been under Persian cultural and political hegemony played a pivotal role in the evolution of Shi'ite Muslim identity in Anatolia, Iraq, and Iran. *Ghuluww* should be understood in relation to Abrahamic monotheisms, more particularly the monotheism of Muhammad as embedded in the Qur'an. *Ghuluww* entails a sense of time and being distinct from monotheisms in its cyclical imagination, its idea of successive prophetic unveilings, and its belief in reincarnation, especially the incarnation of the divine in humans. Some denizens of Asia Minor and Iran, in their binary imagination of the supernatural, had the freedom of selecting their demons and angels on earth. Muhammad's vision, which must have represented a current in late antique Arabia, defined itself, in part, against a more prevalent and older mode that sensed time cyclically and saw supernatural power represented on earth through human agents who were either good or evil. The Qur'an insists that Muhammad is human, that there is an end to time, and that the day of judgment looms near. A gnostic sense that an enlightened elite had access through special knowledge (gnosis) to universal secrets impinged on the essence of monotheistic prophecy and revelation. This esotericism would continue to animate the spiritual landscapes of some exaggerators, Shi'ites and Sufis, and to polarize Muslims down to our modern age. In this process of labeling *ghuluww* as other, some Muslims continued to imagine themselves in relation to it. In time they came to absorb aspects of this other, unwittingly internalizing *ghuluww*. This distinct cultural system *(ghuluww)* within Islam held on firmly to its "old" worldview and way of being and understood Muhammad and his revelation as one among many that have and shall come forth in ever-unfolding cycles of prophetic emergences.

In my work on the Nuqtavis, I have isolated three memory hooks on which a Persian past fastened itself: the Persian language (its alphabet, poetry, and epic romances), the solar calendar, and the physical ruins of pre-Islamic Iran. For the Nuqtavis the four distinct letters of the Persian alphabet acted as visual and sonic reminders to every Persian speaker and reader that they are different from the Arabs, that they speak a different language although expressed through a shared alphabet. Persian and Arab Muslims both began their calendar with the migration of Muhammad from Mecca to Medina (622 CE), marking the advent of Islam. But the Persian solar reckoning of time distinguished Persians from Arabs, who measured time according to the lunar calendar. Vast monuments from the pre-Islamic past—physical ruins reflected upon in Persian poetry—are associated with a lost Iranian glory and with a hope of regaining it.

Images of the messiah in Nuqtavi writings evoke an early modern sense of "Iranianess" a thousand years after the victory of the Arabs and Islam. The founder of the Nuqtavis, Mahmud, called himself the "millennial king," using the Persian regal title of kingship, playing on millenarian expectations associated with Zoroastrian prophecy. But Mahmud also named himself the awaited Muslim messiah (Mahdi), to draw on the similarity between these two loci of divinity in Persian and Arab cultures. Mahmud was trying to legitimize his views by drawing on traditional Muslim proof texts, for he uses the Qu'ran and dictums of the prophet (hadith) throughout his writings, claiming that Muhammad had anticipated his manifestation. Moreover, Mahmud constructs a binary opposition, not only in his choice of Persian and Muslim messianic titles but also in his reference to the solar versus the lunar calendars and to an alchemical versus a creationist theory of the universe. Mahmud explains: "In Ajami [Persian] I am water, fire, air, earth; in Arabic I am the soul creator."[11] Mahmud is constantly translating for the Muslim imagination that which is Ajami and is similar to yet distinct from Islam. In this process of defining one in relation to the other, Mahmud is distinguishing a Persianate cultural system within Islam, one that is different from its Arab context.

The sun and the king appear as Iranian twin symbols in Nuqtavi thought, evoking both spiritual and temporal sovereignty. Kings enjoyed a divine status in Iranian tradition (see *Shahname,* or the *Epic of Kings*), and Persianate movements that rose against Muslim subjugation rejected Muslim prescriptions to face Mecca during prayer. Instead, Persians held onto the rising sun as their direction of prayer, for the sun was the point that centered and situated Mazdeans within their cosmos. The symbol of the sun and the king also appear in Muslim astronomy: the zodiacal sign of Leo that came to be associated with kingship was often represented as the sun emerging from behind the lion's torso. But the sun of the Nuqtavis reveals another layer of meaning. The sun is juxtaposed to the moon. Here the calendrical association between the Muslim choice of a lunar reckoning of time and the Persian solar calendar informs the Nuqtavi binary worldview. Muhammad is believed to be the moon and Mahmud the sun, so Persians are associated with the day and Arabs with the night. In this process of translating elements of Iranian cosmology onto a Muslim context, the Nuqtavis seem to have transferred notions of aggressive moon kings onto the Arab conquerors, who had adopted the lunar calendar, delegating the role of the peaceful sun king to an awaited Iranian king-messiah.

Nuqtavi associations between the moon-Arabs (Muhammad) and sun-Persians (Mahmud) are based on the particular calendars of the two groups, on the different ways in which they measured time. Arabs computed time according to the phases of the moon, and Persians according to the houses of the sun. A remembrance of the solar calendar as Persian and of the lunar calendar as an Arab innovation is preserved in Nuqtavi thought. That denizens of Safavi Iran, including Persians and Turks, continued to follow the seasonal rhythms of the solar calendar may have contributed to the vitality of a system of myths and lore associated with the sun in Mazdean cosmology. And that both Persians and Turks participated in this way of being and sensing time explains in part the ethnically mixed composition of Nuqtavi devotees. The multidimensional meanings (in numerology, astronomy, alchemy, and psychology) that the Nuqtavis attached to the solar and lunar calendars illuminate the Nuqtavi ethos: "So whatever is the sun is old and whatever is the moon is new."[12]

The moon was understood to represent Muhammad, not only in the astrological sense that the moon presides over the horoscope of Muhammad but also in an ontological sense, in an affinity of being that Muhammad and the moon share. In the Nuqtavi cosmic sense of history, occurrences in Muhammad's life were believed to be synchronic with lunar phases; thus Muhammad's rise occurred on the fourteenth of the lunar month, which corresponds to the full moon. According to Mahmud, this is why Muhammad did not claim to be the circular sun.[13] There is a web of significations in Nuqtavi writings on the sun and the moon that reflect their understanding of change and of human psychology. A mathematical dimension lies at the core of these ideas, for there is a Pythagorean effort to measure physical phenomena numerically and to comprehend patterns established by numbers metaphysically. Everything is seen as rooted in mathematics. Mathematics illuminates the corresponding place of each form within the structure of the universe. There seems to have been a sense that the complexity of the universe was a result of simple rules, models, or algorithms (recipes), termed in Nuqtavi vocabulary the "pure compound," embodied in the first living organism that was similar to Adam. Only when the individual came to comprehend the mechanisms behind the generation of life could he or she feel and experience it. And so the craft of an artist and that of a mathematician were deemed analogous in that they exercised creativity in depicting the invisible forms of generation with the precision of a brush stroke or a mathematical equation.

Mahmud is questioned by one of his followers regarding the reasons he considered Persian months old. He responds that the western sun, which he equates with the last person, is eternal and unchanging: "The sun has not come like the moon, moody."[14] What makes the sun singular and superior in the eyes of the Nuqtavis is its consistency, its ever-presence at the leavening of Adam as well as at the end time of the last person. The particular position, role, and function of the sun in the universe affirm its superior rank. For Mahmud the number twelve is the mathematical description of the unique sun as well as of those forms that correspond to it. Mahmud names the twelve Persian months to draw on the connection between the sun and the twelvefold Persian structuring of time. He links the twenty-eight-day lunar month with the Arabs, whose alphabet is comprised of twenty-eight letters.

The number twelve is deemed to have been even more deeply rooted in Persian culture, not only in the way Persians calculated time but also in the way they expressed themselves through language. The Persian language itself, particularly the four singular letters of the Persian alphabet, are key to this cosmic similarity to the sun. The twelve-month Persian solar calendar is associated with four extra letters differentiating Persian from Arabic. Indeed, the number twelve is embodied in the three dots *(nuqta)* that distinguish the four singular Persian letters *p, ch, zh, geh.* The first three letters are all written in the Arabic alphabet literally with three dots. The fourth letter, *geh,* however, is written with a line, equivalent to three dots. Four singular Persian letters, comprised of three dots each, if multiplied, give the numerical value of twelve. And here lies the basic mechanism, the mathematical equation, behind the Nuqtavi science of dots, for which they received their epithet, Nuqtavi (pointillists). What is peculiar to their system is that dots are associated with particular Persian letters, visual and sonic reminders to every Persian speaker and reader that the Persians are culturally different from the Arabs, that they speak a different language, although it is expressed through a shared alphabet. This consciousness of a Persian past symbolized in language and calendar has had reverberations into the modern period, whether in the pan-Iranist endeavors of intellectuals such as Ahmad Kasravi to purify the Persian language or in the attempts of the last king of Iran (Muhammad Reza Pahlavi) to revive a pre-Islamic Persian glory as he reformed the Iranian solar calendar that reckoned time from the rise of Islam to a solar calendar that begins its history a millennium earlier with the rise of the Achaemenid dynasty.

Mahmud associates Mazdean apocalyptics with Muslim eschatology: "When in Ajami we say twelve thousand, this is the right of the Ajami sun, who is the last master of the auspicious conjunction [of Saturn and

Jupiter] and the seal of manifestation and laws. . . . [He] is the complete manifestation."[15] Mazdean cosmology envisioned a "world year" of twelve millennia corresponding with the twelve-month calendar. It divided human history into three millennia "ushered in successively by Zarathustra and the first two World Saviors."[16] The Mazdean Third Savior, Saoshynat, is here equated with the Muslim apocalyptic world conqueror, who would emerge with the auspicious conjunction of Saturn and Jupiter (associated in early modern Islam with Alexander and Timur) as well as the Mahdi (Hidden Imam) and the Persian sun. Alid, Turco-Mongol, and Mazdean apocalyptic symbols and cosmological views exist in symbiosis within Nuqtavi discourse. Mahmud is cast as the twelver (Shi'), for his soul is manifest in the twelve Imams.[17] The twelve solar months, twelve Persian dots, and twelve imams are all identical; "they are the Persian soul, the manifestation of which is the sun, and the manifestation of twelve is from the sun."[18] There is a circularity in Nuqtavi logic, for Nuqtavis claim that "the sun has twelve houses and the twelfth imam implies him (Mahmud), who is the manifestation of $p$, $ch$, $zh$, $g$."[19]

A conception of a relationship between anthropology, astronomy, ethics, politics, and psychology permeates Nuqtavi thought. Stars are designated as friends of God; they are the imams and the caliphs, just as Muhammad is the moon. They travel and work together and rise and set together, as the sun rises and sets; they all turn black and become hidden along with the sun's soul. All the major Muslim historical figures are believed to have had astral and planetary counterparts. Ali holds a prominent role as the propitious planet Jupiter as well as the morning star, "who is the loyal announcer and precursor of the sun."[20] The other planets are seen to symbolize the successors of Muhammad (i.e., caliphs) as well as the first generation of the founding fathers of Muslim schools of law.[21] The superiority of the Persian solar calendar to the Arab lunar one is expressed in Nuqtavi writings, not in terms of precise calculations of time but in terms of human qualities. The Nuqtavis deem valuable the permanence of the sun, the fact that it is unchangeable and indestructible. The moon, in contradistinction, is constantly altering its shape, waxing and waning. Consistency and stability, both in terms of form and ability, mark the sun's superiority as a model. In a cyclical imagination of repetitive patterns, the element that is deemed eternal and invariable is the sun, rising every morning, setting every evening, only to be encountered the next day in the same way. Immutability in

the midst of predictable patterns of change lies at the conceptual core of
the Nuqtavi cosmos.[22] The peerless and unique sun is associated with a
warm spirit, with pleasantness and sweetness.[23] Once again, it is
contrasted to the characteristics of the moon, which is seen as cool,
weeping, weary, and sad. Moods are ascribed to the moon and to the
sun and by association to Persians and to Arabs.[24]

Although the language used to express the Nuqtavi ethos and worldview incorporates Muslim cultural symbols, it conjures different meanings and memories that reveal a complex process of shared histories and
experiences. At certain apocalyptic junctures, differences seem to create
ruptures within the Muslim semiosphere. Then the boundaries between
these languages harden, and clashes between languages occur, leading
to attempts to negate each other (*Universe of the Mind*, 131–34). Abbas I
(r. 1587–1629), the Safavi king who suppressed the Nuqtavi revolt, orchestrated his own mock abdication and reenthronement to mark the
end of an "old" era and the beginning of a new millennium in which
the ways of metempsychosis were proclaimed extinct. Abbas I evoked
the same symbols of the sun, the king, and the millennial messiah, albeit
transformed within a new semantic field of meaning, even though past
readings of these symbols remained inscribed in Safavi texts.

In metahistorical terms, though the advent of modernity came to
further complicate the processes of binary oppositional change, identification with a Persian past and the will to return to it resurfaced, taking
on a very different incarnation in the form of Iranian nationalism with
the chauvinistic flair characteristic of nationalist visions. Binary tensions
between what was officially identified as Mazdean and Alid continued
to mark the history of Iran. The Safavis as agents of official culture had
produced a dominant discourse that crystallized this dual image, shaping a sense of "Iranianess" for the future denizens of modern Iran. The
ebb and flow of Iranian history gravitated toward imaginative visions in
which both Shi'ite and Iranian symbols were used to construct narrative
memories. How governments manipulated these two symbolic repositories and which aspects were appropriated, redefined, and branded as
excess shaped the trajectory of the history of modern Iran.

The Persian language (its alphabet, poetry, and epic romances), the
solar calendar, and the physical ruins of pre-Islamic Iran were symbolic
resources that would be mobilized and reanimated during the three centuries following Safavi rule. Both the successor dynasties of the Qajars
(1785–1925) and the Pahlavis (1925–79) began to rewrite Iranian history

with different degrees of emphasis on pre-Islamic Iran, supplanting or writing out Shi'ism in the process. Safavi representations of the Maz-dean sun, a symbol of sacral kingship, and the Shi'ite lion, evoking Ali's chivalric struggles for truth, were fused together, serving as twin symbols of monarchy.[25] Qajar imagery added a crown that enshrined the lion-and-sun symbol as though visually asserting the power of kingship over civil and religious domains. A process was set in motion that formalized the lion-and-sun symbol into a national emblem of Iran written into the first Iranian constitution of 1906. Afsaneh Najmabadi has unraveled this fascinating trajectory, exposing the layers of meaning and the iconic shifts embedded in this single sign, which continues to enjoy multiple associations of "Iranianess."[26] Her readings illuminate the gendered and sexual impulses behind the evolution of this icon, relating it to the project of modernity that introduced ideals such as romantic marriage and heterosexual love under the gaze of the West. Her standardization of this symbol delineates the ground required for competing and contesting meanings of "Iranianess" to emerge in time. Just as the sun came to shine its feminine face and the masculine lion became her partner, the lion-and-sun symbol came to be associated with early Qajar kingship. Gradually, as the sun began losing her feminine features toward the end of Qajar rule, she was transformed into an abstract circle, finally to be desexualized by Reza Shah Pahlavi. In Irano-Muslim culture, in which male bisexuality was the norm, it would not be embarrassing for a monarch to be associated with a bigendered imperial logo. But as the Western perception of sodomy as "unnatural" became internalized by an elite of Iranians exposed to the West, the female figure had to be veiled in a male-dominated national iconography.[27]

With the Pahlavis, the lion-and-sun symbol became so associated with an oppressive westernizing monarchy that the Islamic Revolution that toppled it replaced it with Arabic calligraphy inscribing the monotheism of the new regime. With the victory of a rationalist interpretation of the word of God, a single language of Shi'ism was imposed by a Shi'ite clergy that, as the agents of God, had now established a theocracy, allegedly at the behest of the Messiah (Mahdi) himself, embodied by Imam Khomeini in the popular imagination. The Persian past was now being erased. As Najmabadi notes, although the lion had a definite iconic association with Ali in Safavi and Qajar visual culture, it was eliminated in the era of Islamic rule as a national symbol. Returned to its previous religious domain, it was displayed in banners hoisted during Muharram commemorations marking the martyrdom of Husayn. Although in 1979 Ali and his progeny had in reality appropriated the authority of monarchs and messiahs, and religion and politics had merged once again, the lion had been contaminated by Pahlavi kingship with its re-introduction into the Persian symbolic field. In summary, the lion, which had been a symbol of Rustam's heroism in the *Shahname* and an Irano-Semitic icon of kingship in medieval Iran, was marked with the figure of Ali and would be fused during the Safavi episode with Shi'ism. The lion was then returned to its old domain of identification with the Qa-jars and the Pahlavis, but their opponents, the rulers of the Islamic re-public, redefined it as a sign of the historically corrupt regimes of Per-sian shahs. What was deemed as old was in fact a synthesis of the old and the new.

Ironically, it is the West, with its interest in archaeology and its re-introduction of Greek histories, that preserved an interpretation of the Iranian past beyond what had been commemorated in Ferdowsi's *Shah-name:* the ruins of Persepolis and the Sasani palace of Ctesiphon would provide the legitimacy for a new form of Persian revival. French archae-ologists, who had a monopoly over Iranian antiquities under the late Qajars, began to provide scientific backing to a mythical history of Per-sian glory.[28] In a step to reclaim Iran's integrity as a nascent nation-state, Reza Shah revoked the French concessions of 1895 and 1900 through an act of parliament in 1927 and came to personally protect the material remains of an Iranian past for his program of nation building. With his establishment of the Museum of Iran Bastan (1937), inspired architecturally by the Sasani palace at Ctesiphon, Reza Shah began to codify a singular meaning for these ruins. No longer were they signs of Persian glory that alerted Arab or Iranian Muslims to the success of Islam and the mutability of Persian kingship, but rather they were to be read and felt as sites of ancient pride recalled into the present sense of "Iranianess."

Reza Shah officially recast his nation as Iran, a term used locally, rather than the Western appellation Persia, which had entered Euro-pean discourse through the Greek designation of their enemy, the Per-sians who ruled from Fars. He also chose a new name for his family, adopting the term *Pahlavi,* which designated the ancient language of Ira-nians before the Arab conquest, before Arabic words colonized the Per-sian alphabet. Although Reza Shah had supposedly forgotten his own Iranian past, prompting him to ask an American Orientalist, Donald

Wilber, the meaning of the word *Pahlavi*, Reza Shah was not only responding to an Iranian inferiority complex vis-à-vis the West.[29] A current of Iranian nationalism was active among scholars such as Sadegh Kia and Ibrahim Pourdavus, the first professors to teach in the Department of Archaeology established in 1937 at the Tehran University by Reza Shah. Sadiq Kia published his research on the Nuqtavis in a journal he had established with like-minded colleagues titled *Iran Kudeh*, "The Land of Iran." Such Persian impulses had been voiced earlier in Qajar Iran by intellectuals and politicians such as Akhunzadeh and Mirza Aqa Khan Kirmani. These men relied on Ferdowsi's narrative poem, the *Epics of Kings*, as a *lieu de mémoire*, seeing it as a pivotal text for the continuity of Persian culture and its resilience against Arab dominance.[30] Thanks to Ferdowsi, they believed that the fate of Iranians did not resemble that of the Egyptians.[31] The Persian language became the privileged site to mine for nationalism and anti-Arab sentiment. And we must not forget that these voices spoke at a time when Iran's Muslim neighbors were formulating their own versions of Arab and Turkish nationalism. The rejection of Arabs and, by association, of Islam prompted an Iranian identification with Europe. Already Orientalism had marked Islam as backward, despotic, and carnal. The Persian linguistic kinship with French or English through its Indo-European roots served as a bridge to the West that could save Iran's face from its Islamic taint. A movement to purge the Persian language of Arabic words produced a genre of writing in pure Persian *(parsigari)* that had a previous incarnation in Safavi Iran.[32] A genealogy can be traced from the Nuqtavis who fled to India—Azar Kayvanis—to a nascent nationalism voiced in the form of Zoroastrian revivalism and the preservation of the Persian language. Dictionaries codifying a version of Persian unfettered by Arabic were the most fashionable vehicle for self-expression. But such movements underscored Persian superiority, deemphasizing the universalist dimension of Nuqtavi thought.

Both Pahlavi monarchs, father and son, manipulated these tendencies and exaggerated the identification of Iran with its pre-Islamic past. Structurally they uprooted the clerical establishment, depriving it of its legal and educational functions. The clergy retreated into their mosques, from which a new revolution remembering a Shi'ite past would emerge. Alongside such institutional changes that had cultural and political reverberations, Muhammad Reza Shah broke with the Islamic calendar and instead inaugurated a new era that would reckon time through solar

calculations beginning with the reign of the Achaemenid monarch
Cyrus. His twenty-five-hundred-year commemoration of Persian monarchy at the site of Persepolis was the most extreme of the many manifestations of Pahlavi revival and was the brainchild of another Orientalist,
Arthur Pope, who surveyed Iranian art and architecture.

The new Western factor would complicate the complex dynamics of
Iranian identity formation, whether in the territory of Iran or among an
Iranian diaspora living in the West since the Islamic Revolution. Persian xenophobia under the Pahlavis generated various kinds of oppositions, both secular and religious. Among the clergy Khomeini was the
most vocal. Breaking the silence of contemporary accommodating clerics, Khomeini blamed the Pahlavis for Iran's enslavement by the West.
He argued for the incompatibility of monarchy and Islam, citing Muhammad as his source. Even intellectuals like Al-e Ahmad and Ali Sha-
riati, who had toyed with Marxism, spoke in the common language of
Shi'ite Islam represented by Khomeini. Each, of course, placed a different emphasis on the centrality of Shi'ism. For these men who voiced a
diffuse Iranian malaise, the Persian revival and its concomitant obsession with the West were deemed foreign to the Iranian people at large.
Iranians not only knew nothing of this Persian past, but a consumerism
was infesting Iran and eating at the soul of every citizen; even villagers
were struck by it. Al-i Ahmad diagnosed this "spiritual enslavement of
Iranians to the alien God that Europe had injected into Iranian imagination" as the height of Iran's confusion.[33] He coined a word for this
disease—*gharbzadegi,* Euromania—and likened it to "locusts in fields of
wheat, who infest the wheat from within, leaving behind only skin."[34]
Despite Al-i Ahmad's break with his own clerical heritage and his can-
did critique of the rigidity, hypocrisy, and superstition of clerics, his ensuing struggles to find a home for himself in Iranian political life left him
with an emotional longing that was filled by those Shi'ite memories and
rituals that made him an Iranian—something that became clear to him
during his pilgrimage to Mecca. The Iranian revolution of 1979 spoke in
this very language of cultural resistance. As Al-i Ahmad had anticipated, it would be a revolution of the "word," for only if the word were
uttered from within its religious domain (Shi'ite) could it have the power
to succeed. But although the Islamic Republic eliminated the sun-and-
lion symbol and attempted to eradicate Persian New Year celebrations,
the discipline of archaeology, and Pahlavi textbooks on pre-Islamic
(Achaemenid and Sasani) history, these sites remained rooted in Iranian

cultural imagination. Today they are sites of resistance both inside the boundaries of Iran and among exiled Iranians in the West. Whether nostalgia or kitsch, the lion-and-sun emblem on coffee mugs and the revival of Zoroastrian studies in Iran as well as among amateur scholars in exile represent a Persian past that functions as a living and organic *milieu de mémoire*. The Islamic Republic somewhat reluctantly reengaged these sites as the war with Iraq necessitated a revival of nationalism. Shi'ism as a universal ideology has not freed itself of the referent that is Iran, at least in this historical cycle.

During the millennium-and-a-half history of conversion of former Sasani dominions to Islam, Mazdean and Alid idioms have been the most vocal styles of expression. Mystics, monarchs, messiahs, and, more recently, mullahs have been endowed with the authority to privilege particular memories and historical narratives, either merging the two languages, as Shah Isma'il did, rejecting Shi'ism, as did the Pahlavis, or asserting the hegemony of Shi'ism, as Khomeini did. Such binary dynamics exhibit diametric responses, influencing the cyclical processes of change—moving to and from an Arab (Islamic) present to a Persian past. What is constantly shifting is what continues to be constructed at every turn of history as "Iranian" and "Shi'ite." Despite attempts from the rise of Islam up to the Islamic Revolution in Iran to reject one for the other, the duo has resisted separation. Continuities are not linear; they do not necessarily live on in their distinct domains, for in every (re)invention of "Iranian" or "Shi'ite," both elements have already been merged. Rather, they have experienced previous incarnations in each other's fields of representation. What is seen as Shi'ite in one cycle of history is actually imagined as Iranian in another age.

In this essay I have traced the trajectories of change and continuity in the Persianate world through a binary framework embedded in the cosmology of pre-Islamic Iranian cultural systems (Mazdean dualism). Lotman's binarism allowed me to analyze this genealogy, revealing the complex ways in which Persian and Muslim languages interacted with each other. A picture of the multifaceted impact of the Persianate ethos on the making of Islamic identities emerged—whether in the construction of heresy and antibehavior or of Iranian nationalism. As Lotman and Uspenskii have posited: "Given such a consistent and cyclically repeated negation of negation, the possibility of forward development is determined by the appearance of a new perspective. At each new stage, changing historical conditions and, in particular, external cultural influence lead to a new perspective on cultural development that will activate one semantic parameter or another. As a result the same conceptions can appear at each stage furnished with a new content, depending on the point of departure" ("Binary Models," 33). Change, even when functioning through binary processes, generates different cultural systems where continuities are recreated masquerading as "archaic" forms.

## Notes

Sections of this essay have been published in my book *Mystics, Monarchs, and Messiahs: Cultural Landscapes of Early Modern Iran* (Cambridge, Mass.: Harvard Middle East Monographs, 2002). I would like to thank Boris Gasparov and the anonymous reader of the volume for their incisive comments on my chapter, which I have attempted to address here.

1. See Lotman, *Universe of the Mind*, 217–20; Mieke Bal, Jonathan Crewe, and Leo Spitzer, introduction to *Acts of Memory: Cultural Recall in the Present* (Hanover, N.H.: Dartmouth College Press, 1999).

2. William Sewell makes this point in his chapter "Geertz, Cultural Systems, and History: From Synchrony to Transformation," in *The Fate of "Culture": Geertz and Beyond,* ed. Sherry Ortner (Berkeley: University of California Press, 1999). This issue had already been raised by Natalie Zemon Davis in "Anthropology and History in the 1980s: The Possibilities of the Past," *Journal of Interdisciplinary History* 11 (1981): 267–76; and discussed by Suzanne Desan in *The New Cultural History,* ed. Lynn Hunt (Berkeley: University of California Press, 1989), 52–53.

3. I would like to thank Peter Brown for introducing me to Yuri M. Lotman and B. A. Uspenskii, "Binary Models in the Dynamics of Russian Culture."

4. See Sewell, "Geertz, Cultural Systems, and History," 46, for his discussion of the paucity of social theory dealing with the problem of historical change. "The overriding problem posed by most social theory has been accounting for social order or structure. This is true, for example, not only of Geertz's work but of nearly all anthropology before 1980. And even those theorists who have made the explanation of change a central problematic— principally, Karl Marx, Max Weber, and such successors as Louis Althusser, Jürgen Habermas, or Immanuel Wallerstein—have usually employed such teleological notions of temporality that their concepts must be extensively revised to be useful to historians."

5. M. Bakhtin, "Discourse in the Novel," *The Dialogic Imagination* (Austin: University of Texas Press, 1981).

6. Once again, I am grateful to Peter Brown for bringing Collingwood's *Essays in the Philosophy of History* (Austin: University of Texas Press, 1965) to my attention and for his generous comments, which I have used here, on the differences between European attitudes to the past and the "massiveness" of memory in the Iranian world.

7. For the coining of the term Persianate, see Marshall Hodgson, *The Venture of Islam*, vol. 2 (Chicago: University of Chicago Press, 1978), 293–94. Hodgson uses the term to signify a cultural orientation within Islamdom that was inspired by Persian traditions and used the Persian language as a vehicle of expression. Unlike Hodgson, I do not limit the Persianate ethos to the spheres of "high" literate culture. See my recent book on this subject, *Mystics, Monarchs, and Messiahs*.

8. I use the term Mazdean to refer to the interpretations of Zoroaster's visions that place Ahura Mazda (Lord Wisdom) at the center of their cosmology.

9. The following sixteenth- and seventeenth-century Persian sources have been used to understand the Nuqtavis: Iskandar Bek Munshi, *Tarikh-i Alam Ara-yi Abbasi* (Tehran: Kitabfurushi-yi Islamiy ye, 1971); Afushtah-yi Natanzi, *Naqavat al-Asrar* (Tehran: Intisharat-i Ilmi va Farhangi 1971); Jalal al-din Munajjim Yazdi, *Tarikh-i Abbasi* (Tehran: Intisharat-i vahid1987); Mobed Shah, *Dabistan-i Mazahib* (Tehran: Kitab khanah-i Tahuri 1983); Sadiq Kiya, "Nuqtaviyan ya Pasikhaniyan," *Iran Kudeh* 13 (Tehran, 1941).

10. Mobed Shah, *Dabistan-i Mazahib*, 1:276. Unless otherwise indicated, the translations are mine.

11. Kiya, "Nuqtaviyan ya Pasikhaniyan," 276.

12. Kiya, "Nuqtaviyan ya Pasikhaniyan," citing an untitled Nuqtavi text, 77.

13. Ibid., 81.

14. Ibid., 84.

15. Ibid., 77.

16. Mary Boyce, *Textual Sources for the Study of Zoroastrianism* (Chicago: University of Chicago Press, 1984), 20.

17. Kiya, "Nuqtaviyan ya Pasikhaniyan," citing untitled Nuqtavi text, 77.

18. Kiya, "Nuqtaviyan ya Pasikhaniyan," 77.

19. Ibid., 81.

20. Ibid., 83.

21. Ibid., 86. Venus, for example is associated with the first caliph, Abu Bakr (d. 634), as well as with the jurist Shafi'i (d. 820). Mars is associated with the second caliph, 'Umar (d. 644), as well as with the jurist Abu Hanifa (d. 767).

22. Ibid., 84.

23. Ibid., 85.

24. Beyond Nuqtavi circles, there seems to have been a more general construction of such temperamental differences between Arabs and Persians. The Arab polymath al-Suyuti (d. 1505), writing in Mamluk Egypt, compares the

Persian language with Arabic, and says that revelation is articulated with softness in Persian and with harshness in Arabic. Cited in Shaul Shaked, "Some Iranian Themes in Islamic Literature," in *From Zoroastrian Iran to Islam* (London: Variorum Reprints, 1995), 149.

25. Ali was the paternal cousin and son-in-law of Muhammad. He holds a central position for the Shi'ites as the appointed successor of Muhammad and the first Imam.

26. Afsaneh Najmabadi, *Women with Mustaches and Men without Beards: Gender and Sexual Anxieties of Iranian Modernity* (Berkeley: University of California Press, 2005). My discussion of the lion and sun icon is based on Najmabadi's innovative reading of Iranian modernity.

27. See Najmabadi, *Women without Mustaches*, for this argument and for another layer of the eclipse of the sun, the advent of modern Iranian women in the public domain. My narrative here draws on her arguments.

28. See Kamyar Abdi's article "Nationalism, Politics, and the Development of Archaeology in Iran," *American Journal of Archaeology* 105 (2001): 51–76, for an insightful survey of the uses and abuses of archaeology in the nationalist project of Iran.

29. Ibid., 63. Abdi cites this quote from Donald Wilber's *Riza Shah Pahlavi: The Resurrection and Reconstruction of Iran* (Hicksville, N.Y.: Exposition Press, 1975), 163.

30. Pierre Nora, *Realms of Memory: Rethinking the French Past*, vol. 1, *Conflicts and Divisions* (New York: Columbia University Press, 1996).

31. Muhammad Tavakoli-Targhi, "Refashioning Iran: Language and Culture during the Constitutional Revolution," *Iranian Studies* 23 (1990): 81.

32. Tavakoli-Targhi speaks of this Persian purification movement in the context of modernity in Iran. And in his article "Contested Memories: Narrative Structures and Allegorical Meanings of Iran's Pre-Islamic History," *Iranian Studies* 29 (1996): 165, he hints at a connection between Azar Kayvan, who emigrated from Safavi Iran to Patna, and what he terms a neo-Mazdean revival through the production of texts such as the Dasatir and the Dabistan-i Mazahib. However, he does not extend this lineage to nationalist discourses of the twentieth century.

33. I quote from Roy Mottahedeh's *Mantle of the Prophet* (New York: Pantheon Books, 1985), 298, which captures the vicissitudes of Persian political culture through key figures of Iranian history. His perceptive reading of Al-i Ahmad has influenced my understanding of modern Iran. His book is a gift to Iranian historiography not only because of its methodological innovations (the mixing of history, allusion, and fiction), but also because of Mottahedeh's clarity of thought and the ease with which his prose flows.

34. Ibid., 296. Mottahedeh has played with this metaphor used by Al-i Ahmad in his gharbzadegi.

# Margins and Selfhood

# SELF-REFLECTION AND
# THE UNDERGROUND

# 7

# The Self, Its Bubbles, and Its Illusions

*Cultivating Autonomy in Greenblatt and Lotman*

ANDREAS SCHÖNLE

Yuri Lotman, one of the founders of Soviet semiotics, and Stephen Greenblatt, the unwitting progenitor of New Historicism, have both been intensely preoccupied with mapping the sphere of culture and defining the coordinates of the individual self. Even though both scholars claim the mantle of cultural poetics, they are rooted in different critical traditions, belong to different cultures and generations, and work on different material. We have no reason to believe that Lotman ever read Greenblatt, and Greenblatt quotes Lotman only once, in an article in which he acknowledges that he borrows the concept of "poetics of culture" from Lotman.[1] And yet they share surprisingly much, from the mundane to the conceptual. Both are powerful and influential theoretical thinkers who are at the same time committed to meticulous library and archival work. Both have not only proposed new theoretical paradigms but also enriched our knowledge of particular periods and cultures through their exploration of the breadth of culture and their flair for recognizing the significance of seemingly marginal cultural artifacts. In fact, they share a certain distrust for the totalizing nature of theoretical discourse, attempting to incorporate into their studies a sense for the contingencies of cultural processes (*Kul'tura i vzryv,* 23–24, 63; *Universe of the Mind,* 232).[2]

Both Lotman and Greenblatt set their discourse in opposition to a prevailing ideology. For Lotman this means the vulgar sociological interpretation of Marxism, while for Greenblatt it is the liberal, humanistic celebration of Renaissance culture and its great artists.[3] Both occupy a position on the margins of their respective societies. An ethnic Jew who could find employment only on the outskirts of the Soviet Empire, in the comparatively more relaxed atmosphere of Estonian academic life, Lotman embodies in many respects the ethos of the Russian intelligentsia, with its outward accommodation of Soviet behavior norms and inner striving toward personal freedom and moral ideals.[4] Greenblatt's work derives from the youth culture of the 1960s and its opposition to the Vietnam War. He views his Renaissance studies as a form of engagement with the present era.[5] And if his situation as an assistant professor at Berkeley in 1969 seems somewhat less precarious than that of a Jewish semiotician working in the Brezhnev years, his background nonetheless inspired him to write out of what he calls an insurrectional mind-set.[6]

Yet the political stance of each scholar remains largely implicit in his writing. Scholarship does not collapse into militancy, and not simply because of tactical concerns for self-preservation. Indeed, both writers programmatically assert the value of self-distancing and self-estrangement, which they conceive not as a pursuit of value-free judgment but rather as the result of a dialogue with the past that unfolds as a genuine give-and-take exchange. As Amy Mandelker discusses in the early pages of her essay in this volume, Lotman explores the notion of double vision, or "seeing double," as she calls it—an elaboration of the formalist notion of estrangement. Indeed, this hermeneutics of double vision follows logically from Lotman's ideas about communication as a field of tension, a bidirectional stretching of the partial overlap between the language of the sender and that of the receiver (*Kul'tura i vzryv,* 16).[7] Greenblatt and Gallagher use "double vision" explicitly in the context of their discussion of the aesthetic experience, in which "we never feel that we can simply put off all our historically conditioned longings, fears, doubts, and dreams, along with our accumulated knowledge of the world, and enter into another conceptual universe. But at the same time we do not experience works of art—or indeed any significant textual trace of the past—as confirmation of what we already know. In a mean-ingful encounter with a text that reaches us powerfully, we feel at once pulled out of our own world and plunged back with redoubled force into it."[8]

But what most of all legitimates my comparison is their similarity in underlying interests. Both Lotman and Greenblatt seek to conceptual-ize the relationship between the aesthetic and the social, and both do it while explicitly eschewing a totalizing model. They study the imbrica-tion of aesthetic discourse with other kinds of texts, neither collapsing the aesthetic into the social nor granting it a priori, incontestable auton-omy. Aesthetic discourse both engages and estranges the social sphere, and its boundaries are in themselves a disputed cultural artifact. More broadly we could say that both writers attempt to delineate a theory of the relationship between culture and the social sphere that does not fold the cultural into the social and that remains sensitive to the intrinsic vigor of culture.[9]

To Lotman this vigor depends largely on the asymmetry that ob-tains between various types of discourses and their resulting mutual untranslatability. Codes articulate reality in various ways, and their modeling of the world does not overlap. Out of their complex interaction arises the creation of new meanings, that is, the representation of new layers of reality that had not been encoded heretofore, creating the pos-sibility of "breakthrough into the noumenal world" (*Kul'tura i vzryv*, 30). This notion of the expedience, indeed urgency, of discursive asymmetry also underpins a programmatic move undertaken by New Historicism, the harnessing together of aesthetic and nonaesthetic texts in a quest for historical reality. Witness the following, self-consciously sentimental acknowledgment:

> The greatest challenge lay . . . in making the literary and the nonliterary seem to be each other's thick description. That both the literary work and the anthropological (or historical) anecdote are texts . . . helped make it possible to conjoin them; but their ineradicable differences—the fact that neither is purpose-built for the other, that they are incom-mensurable and virtually impossible to foveate simultaneously—made the conjunction powerful and compelling.
>
> We wanted to recover in our literary criticism a confident convic-tion of reality, without giving up the power of literature to sidestep or evade the quotidian and without giving up a minimally sophisticated

understanding that any text depends upon the absence of the bodies and voices that it represents. We wanted the touch of the real in the way that in an earlier period people wanted the touch of the transcendent.[10]

In both cases playing two dissimilar textual universes off each other is seen as a means to getting at what lies behind the text, whether that be the "real" or the "transcendent."

Both writers treat culture as a field of discourses—Lotman would call them codes—that at once enable and constrict individual behavior.[11] Both seek to conceptualize agency and creativity. Unlike hardcore Foucauldians, Lotman and Greenblatt allow for individuality and originality, yet without lapsing into the Romantic myth of inspired creativity. The self, in their account, is not entirely a product of social discourses, even though it is subject to intense pressures and faces drastic limitations in the range of its choices. Nor is the author dead.[12] The author is alive and well, even though he or she has to fight for a place in the sun in an environment of harshly competing discourses. Creation obviously is not something one does in superb equanimity of mind in the privacy of one's study. It is always a form of high-stakes social and political engagement. Many of the authors the two scholars write about have spent time in prison or exile—some have even died violent deaths, at the hands of the hangman, in a duel, or driven by inescapable social pressure to commit suicide. These dramatic life stories reflect the polarized nature of the cultural fields the two scholars strive to map out. Both the Renaissance in England and the late eighteenth and early nineteenth centuries in Russia are periods when competing parties tug and tear at the cultural fabric, in radical and often violent ways, ultimately leading to a profound shift in cultural paradigms. In short, both Lotman and Greenblatt are deeply concerned with answering a vexing, if morally unavoidable question, namely, the degree to which the self retains freedom and autonomy in an oppressive sociopolitical environment.

In light of the similarities between Lotman and Greenblatt in interests, subject matters, and basic assumptions, a detailed comparison of their methodological presuppositions, critical concepts, interpretive strategies, and conceptual models seems appropriate.[13] Emphasis will be placed here on the late works of Lotman, those written in the 1980s and early 1990s, in which he distances himself from Saussurean presuppositions and adopts a more supple notion of codes.[14]

This essay will demonstrate that both Greenblatt and Lotman see the relationship between the aesthetic sphere and the surrounding culture as a process of continuous exchange of information and energy, but they conceive of these transactions differently and use different metalanguage to describe them. Similarly, in their analysis of the relationship between culture and power, they seem to place accents differently. Lotman's semiotic approach is more attuned to the irreducible heterogeneity of the cultural sphere and seems to disregard vectors of power, whereas Greenblatt's social theory is more sensitive to the ways in which cultural discourses transmit power that originates in social practices. Yet despite these apparent dissimilarities, on closer analysis one realizes that both theorists navigate the vexed terrain of the sociopolitical power struggles inherent in semiotic discourse, and that they differ not so much in their analysis of cultural diversity as in their characterization of power. If both Lotman and Greenblatt emphasize that power seeks to impose semiotic homogeneity, the former thinks of power as a concrete, unified, albeit unpredictable agent, while the latter posits more abstract yet plural sources of authority. Ultimately the main difference between Lotman and Greenblatt is the way they conceptualize the strategies for autonomy available to the individual self. For Greenblatt the self achieves some degree of independence from social and discursive practices by cultivating the illusion of its freedom. In contrast, for Lotman the quest for autonomy entails puncturing illusions and withdrawing from the social circuit.

## The Aesthetic Sphere and the Mechanisms of Culture

For Lotman it is primarily the reader who defines a particular text as an aesthetic composition. The aesthetic effect arises when a text is read as a code and then projected onto the inner stage of the reader's consciousness, where this code informs the reader's inner dialogue with himself or herself. The aesthetic effect, then, stems from an ambivalence regarding the status of a text, as code or as message, and hence from the indeterminacy of its referent (*Universe of the Mind*, 30–32). For Lotman art is a sphere of free experiment outside the parameters of cultural norms. It often violates established values and norms, but it does so with an eye toward an audience preoccupied with ethical questions. Hence art is not immune from cultural norms, even though it appears to negate their validity. Ethics and aesthetics are as inseparable as they are opposite (*Kul'tura i vzryv*, 129–32).

Even the text is seen as a fluid entity. For Lotman a text has no intrinsic boundaries. Instead it is embedded in a cultural continuum and acquires limits only when authors and readers endow it with a particular function as text. The notion of text, that is, emerges from the intersection between the points of view of creator and receiver (*Kul'tura i vzryv*, 102–3). A text is also endowed with a structure that reveals itself only over time, that is, a text comes to light more as potential than achievement. Over time it accumulates a memory of its past significations (*Universe of the Mind*, 18–19). Texts, then, exhibit an ever-changing intersection between the past and the future. They are engaged in a process of becoming that unfolds both synchronically and diachronically.

Greenblatt also problematizes the text, rejecting the New Critical notion of organic unity and preferring to speak in terms of masses of textual traces. He does so partly to recognize contingency in the production, performance, and reception of texts, and partly in light of the historical record showing that cultural agents in the Renaissance had little stake in and care for the integrity and presumed notional totality of a literary text.[15] For Greenblatt it is especially important to understand that a text is not to be seen as the intangible and irreplaceable "container" of all of its meanings, a kind of convenient packaging for easy consumption by its readers. Instead, texts are collective productions—productions of creators as well as receivers—not only because language is a collective production but also because texts are embedded in social life, so much so that they become "signs of contingent social practices."[16] Calling into question the distinction between social life and literature is a programmatic gesture in Greenblatt. But he performs this gesture not to drive the last nail into the coffin of the aesthetic sphere but rather to draw attention to the various ways in which each culture—and within it each cultural agent—demarcates the boundaries of art that render the aesthetic autonomous.

The differences in the ways Lotman and Greenblatt conceptualize the artistic text are largely attributable to their respective frames of reference. In keeping with semiotic presuppositions, Lotman still views the text as a message transmitted with the help of one or several codes that the receiver must decode. And even if he grants the message greater complexity and fluidity than before, even if he emphasizes the creative dimension of encoding and decoding and activates the contextual embedding of a linguistic exchange, the communicative act is still primarily an exchange of codified information, however unstable and undetermined.

Greenblatt, in contrast, draws on the lexicon of social theory and emphasizes accordingly the exchange of economic and symbolic currencies between cultural agents. He avoids reductionism by operating with a broader notion of value than that of Marxist critics. For Greenblatt works of art assume an economic value, but they also offer emotional and ideological goods: they provide pleasure of various kinds and serve various interests, political and otherwise. Thus the artistic sphere and the social sphere are nonhomologous yet interdependent entities.[17] The exchanges between culturally demarcated spheres represent a "process of movement across the shifting boundaries between them."[18] Importing categories from one sphere into the other—in concepts such as "the poetics of culture" or "the social energy of works of art"—is then both apt and precarious. The metaphors capture the kinds of adjustments undertaken in the transactions between two systems, albeit in an indirect way that requires the scholar to exercise considerable care. Economics becomes the master discourse, since what Greenblatt ultimately seeks to describe is the circulation of value through negotiated exchanges.

Lotman draws his master discourse from biochemistry. As Amy Mandelker has noted, Lotman's concept of semiosphere, the semiotic environment that enables and sustains semiotic exchanges, alludes to a tradition of organicist thinking originating in the works of Russian biologist V. I. Vernadskii, who proposed the concept of the biosphere.[19] But what is striking is the high incidence of geological metaphors—witness the image of the semiosphere seething like the sun, where "centers of activity boil up in different places, in the depths and on the surface, irradiating relatively peaceful areas with its immense energy" (*Universe of the Mind*, 150). Circulation of energy, layering in strata, cataclysmic events, these are some of the qualities a geological formation shares with the semiosphere. What interests Lotman most in this geospherical framework is the idea that the earth's complex layers of mineral matter enable and support organic life. The superimposition of live and dead matter serves as an analogy to the ways in which texts that seem to have served their purpose are returned to life in a new semiotic environment (127). The boundary between the mineral and the organic is really a filter promoting constant exchanges, like the unceasing translations between various semiotic systems that characterize semiotic activity within the semiosphere.

In short, both authors resort to a metalanguage, and we may wonder what difference there is between a biochemical and an economic conceptualization of exchange. To a large degree both vocabularies are used figuratively. The former, it would seem, stresses the self-impelled, quasi-unconscious, largely unpredictable nature of semiotic interaction, while the latter points more in the direction of a conscious, calculated search for parity. The former seems also to take the broad view, focusing on the kind of processes that take place in a time span of *longue durée*, while the latter is more likely to zoom in on singular, local, and semelfactive transactions. Yet Lotman takes great care to emphasize that his notion of semiosphere is adaptable to various kinds of temporality and to various degrees of deliberateness in historical change, and it does seem that his metaphors render him a certain disservice (*Universe of the Mind*, 223–28). Ultimately what distinguishes Lotman from Greenblatt is not the metaphors they use but the way they conceive of the state of affairs these metaphors describe.

## Culture and Power

There are a number of advantages to the semiotic view, which focuses on the communicational content of an exchange and chooses to ignore the vectors of power that underpin discourse. Semiotics is more attuned to the diversity of messages, to the subtle shades of meaning expressed in them, to the genres messages seem to fall into, to the high incidence of miscommunication, and to the sheer cacophony of utterances that constitutes social life. Lotman's semiosphere is a complex, fluid, contradictory, and contentious space. It is organized by boundaries hastily put up and easily trespassed. It is constantly changing, yet its changes unfold with varying speeds at once: natural languages, say, evolve slowly, while sartorial fashions turn around much faster. All of this makes for a framework well equipped to account for the ways in which languages shape our consciousness and constitute our reality, rather than mirroring it. In short, in good cultural studies fashion, this framework tells us that discourse is power, more than that it transmits power (*Universe of the Mind*, 233). The semiotic metadiscourse, then, enables us to transcend the discursive foundations of our identity—a liberating capacity all the more important in a totalitarian society organized around a monolithic ideology that substitutes itself for reality.[20]

Yet the semiotic approach is nothing if not a method for abstracting the way discourses function in real life. Not all power is discursive in nature, and Greenblatt rightly underscores the ways in which messages express desires and articulate power, both of which partly predate the emergence of a given communicational act.[21] Greenblatt is careful to have it both ways, endowing artistic discourse with considerable agency of its own—he calls it energy—as well as connecting literature back to its institutional setting and, further, to the social practices that it depicts. Literature is all the more successful at transmitting preexisting social values and interests because within its boundaries it claims to suspend the real world. Thus it circulates all kinds of social energy in a seemingly playful manner. "Power, charisma, sexual excitement, collective dreams, wonder, desire, anxiety, religious awe" are conveyed haphazardly, without being subject to a controlling, totalizing system.[22]

If Greenblatt's theory seems to be sensitive to the diversity and heterogeneity of discourses within the cultural sphere, in practice, when he analyzes the social embedding of particular texts, Greenblatt draws a picture of contextual relations that is considerably more homogeneous than his theory would imply. One of his favorite conceptual devices is to draw analogies between disparate phenomena. The destruction of the Bower of Bliss in Edmund Spenser's *Faerie Queene*, for example, is made to stand simultaneously for the European response to the native cultures of the New World, the English colonial struggle in Ireland, and the Reformation attack on images. These homologies are projected onto an underlying analogy adumbrated by Freud, namely, that inhering between sexual repression and social exploitation. And if Greenblatt's treatment of *The Faerie Queene* is redeemed by its sheer erudition and originality, it does not fully succeed in allaying doubts as to its underlying logical articulation, which turns the text into an allegorical representation of a Freudian cultural mechanism deemed universal.[23] Similarly, the rhetorical device for which New Historicism has become famous, the focus on an extremely local event, rendered in an anecdote, which then serves as an anchoring point for the discussion of an analogous, much broader cultural phenomenon, rests on a similar assimilation of the local to the typical. This move traces its genealogy to Erich Auerbach's *Mimesis*, which extrapolates sweeping conclusions about the representational premises of a canonical work of art from the close reading

of a single fragment—Gallagher and Greenblatt call the use of the anecdote an "Auerbachian device."[24] Yet they concede that New Histori-
cists were "less inclined to share [Auerbach's] distaste for leveling . . .
less convinced that the world was tending toward the erasure of difference."[25] And they acknowledge the circularity that inheres in resorting
to a historical anecdote chosen because it sounds like the writings of a
canonical author in order to illuminate this very author.[26] In this regard
Lotman's notion of a heterogeneous semiosphere seems more able to
capture the irreducible uniqueness, novelty, and complexity of certain
artistic texts, as well as the sheer diversity, broadly speaking, of messages
uttered in a given semiotic environment. At the same time, Lotman's
approach seems to fail to account for what interests Greenblatt in the
first place, namely, the ways in which messages, including cultural and
artistic ones, convey and manipulate a power that originates in surrounding social practices.

In fact, of course, Lotman could not be oblivious to the social realities underpinning communicative acts, for under the Soviet regime
attention to social constraints on discourse was a matter of survival.
Whether Lotman chose not to give more prominence in his theory to the
articulation between social practices and semiotic exchange because of
tactical concerns or because of genuine lack of interest is ultimately irrelevant. What matters is that Lotman does, in fact, propose what we could
call a semiotic theory of social power, that is, one that is in keeping with
his overall semiotic assumptions. In *Universe of the Mind* he introduces a division between two kinds of discourse, that on the center and that on the
periphery. The center presents a kind of master plot, which seeks to absorb under its logic all incidental messages. It features a highly integrated
structure and assumes a normative function with regard to all discourses
circulating in the semiosphere. It thus serves as a metalanguage that both
enables and restricts discursive communication. Semiotic activity and
creativity are relegated to the margins of the semiosphere, where the hegemony of the center's master plot subsides. The periphery is the place
where discourses clash, where improvisation and innovation take place,
where alien discourses trickling in from contiguous semiospheres exert
an impact. Multiplicity, heterogeneity, disorder, disjunction, and chance
characterize the periphery. The periphery challenges the center, and
particular discourses in it seek to supplant the master plot the center
seeks to impose. Thus a semiosphere presents an asymmetric paradigm
of competing systems (*Universe of the Mind*, 127–30, 134–35, 162).

Lotman adopts a spatial metaphor to model the relationship between hegemonic and subjugated discourses. His theory rests on the assimilation of two parameters: center versus periphery, on the one hand, and integrated versus disjoined semiotic organization, on the other. Integration, one could say, is the semiotic expression, albeit not the cause, of what makes a particular discourse hegemonic. The cause is obviously external to the process of communication, and as such the semiotician does not need to conceptualize it. Thus the question with which this section started—a comparison of the extent to which our two cultural theorists are able to conceptualize culture without reducing its diversity and complexity—takes a new turn. Indeed, for Lotman, one could extrapolate, the degree of unity or diversity of a cultural field is itself a cultural variable, for it depends on whether a given semiosphere has undergone a stringent process of homogenization, which the center foists on it through both semiotic and nonsemiotic means.

Yet in his latest theoretical book, Lotman seems to call into question the nexus between extrinsic social power, a semiotic center, and the structural integration of the semiosphere he had adumbrated in the articles published in *Universe of the Mind*. Indeed, in *Culture and Explosion*, Lotman recognizes that even in totalitarian societies, one must recognize that not all power is predicated on the imposition of a consistent, integrated ideological master plot. Writers trying to survive in the Soviet Writers' Union in the Stalinist years knew all too well that they had to be on the lookout for minute yet consequential changes in official ideology. Unpredictability is as essential a power mechanism as discursive homogeneity. Lotman seeks to come to terms with this phenomenon by analyzing the behavior of Ivan the Terrible, whose erratic actions in the second half of his reign defied all logic. Lotman concludes that Ivan can be understood only within the parameters of the antinomy between system and explosion, which underlies culture. In choosing explosive behavior, Ivan maximizes unpredictability by stripping his policies of all apparent purpose.

To sum up this semiotic analysis of power, we could say that Lotman envisions two technologies of power: one resorting to an orderly normative master discourse, the other using asemiotic unpredictable behavior. The binary opposition between system and chaos, in other words, defines the alternatives of power. The latter is more often the resort of agents on the periphery, yet it can be coopted by the central authority. Thus the two antinomies that underpin his analysis of power—center versus periphery and integration versus disjointedness—do not overlap. In effect, it is by allowing their permutation that Lotman reaches a satisfactory semiotic theory of social power.

Greenblatt shares Lotman's sense that cultures gain stability only by foisting a master discourse on their constituent spheres. He describes a mechanism he calls blockage—"the social imposition of an imaginary order of exclusion"—by which cultures control the influx of texts and ascribe a given order to their central representations.[27] This mechanism ensured, for example, that the Christians discovering sites and traces of Aztec devotion either overlooked or repressed the obvious homologies between their own cult and that of the Aztecs.[28] Yet Greenblatt also emphasizes that airtight enclosure is impossible and that even in early modern Europe, where the rhetoric of absolute blockage was ubiquitous, the reality of semiotic circulation was more porous than one would think.[29]

Greenblatt, too, faces the vexing question of correlation between social and semiotic power, between what is external and what is intrinsic to the act of communication. Consistent with his attempt to develop a social theory that eschews reducing the cultural to the social, Greenblatt avoids positing a center of authority that seeks to draw all cultural phenomena under its homogenizing blanket. As he discusses the position of culture in a capitalist society, he rejects two opposite views: the Marxist argument that capitalism promotes culture as a private and therefore inauthentic sphere walled off from underlying economic relations as well as the poststructuralist argument that charges capitalism with leveling differences and ultimately destroying individuality. Greenblatt is convinced that both views fail, because capitalism's relationship to culture does not lend itself to a monolithic theoretical treatment. In his view capitalism can both promote and prohibit individuality. Likewise, it can both facilitate and annihilate art.

Thus, in their analysis of the relationship between social power and culture, Lotman and Greenblatt reach positions that are ultimately quite compatible, in spite of the superficial dissimilarities noted here. Both writers make a point not to erase completely the boundary between social life and the field of culture, and both focus on cultural diversity as a test case of the relationship between culture and power. Ultimately both reach the conclusion that power is likely to enforce a kind of homogeneity that the cultural field as a whole strives to resist, but that in certain cases power may also provoke diversity. In this particular respect, however, they differ in their analysis. For if Lotman's case study of power is Ivan the Terrible, that is, a uniquely ruthless example of autocratic rule, Greenblatt thinks of capitalism as a more abstract, if less unified source of power. For Lotman power is unpredictable only to the extent that its unique embodiment chooses to behave whimsically, while for Greenblatt power is unpredictable because of its plurality. Ultimately, then, the two authors differ not so much in their conceptualization of culture as in their theory of power, and they do so, obviously, because they derive their theory from the experience of their own immediate sociopolitical environment.

## A Postcolonial Agenda?

Yet Greenblatt and Lotman's underlying political agenda is similar, for both authors invest the heterogeneity, diversity, and complexity of the cultural sphere with the function of enabling some degree of freedom. Indeed, we could say that both authors share an acute sense of the potential and real threats to the individual self, which leads them to develop a slightly sentimental, even melancholy view of traditional societies: both celebrate the superior semiotic alertness of members of traditional societies, while simultaneously acknowledging that this semiotic vigor has failed to help them withstand the pressure of modernity.

Lotman's opposition between center and periphery has a wide range of applications. It can serve as an alternative to the dialectic in conceptualizing historical change—and hence help us eschew teleological master narratives—but it also addresses a range of issues now commonly treated in postcolonial theory. Obviously the emphasis on the ways in which the periphery challenges the center usefully demonstrates that the empire can "write back with a vengeance."[30] The circulation of discourse between the center and the periphery is a two-way street, despite the differences in the nature of the texts produced by the center and the periphery and despite the time lag between the periods during which the two interlocutors are semiotically productive. Lotman, indeed, proposes a schema of creolization of cultures, which emphasizes the active recoding taking place in a subordinated culture, and which, given favorable conditions, can lead to the periphery usurping the centrality of the former center (*Universe of the Mind*, 146–47).[31]

Both Lotman and Greenblatt try to conceptualize the difference between traditional and modern societies, and both do it in a somewhat contrarian fashion. For Lotman modern cultures are characterized by the predominance of a type of communication he calls I-she/he exchange, in which a given package of information is conveyed from an addresser to an addressee. The receiver of such a message is objectified and deprived of creative activity inasmuch as his or her role is confined to mere decoding. This type of communication, which facilitates the circulation of information and the development of knowledge, is characteristic of dynamic societies, yet it entails a drastic division between the producers and the recipients of information. I-I communication, in contrast, is a type of communicative exchange in which the message is actually reformulated during the communication process by way of a creative, supplementary recoding undertaken by the recipient. As a result the receiver can be the same as the sender, since the message changes along the way. And even when different from the sender, the recipient acts as a subject inasmuch as he or she coauthors the message. I-I communication is typical of traditional societies, in which receivers have to translate the standard plots of myths, rituals, or folk tales into messages relevant to their own lives. Traditional societies are thus substantially more creative in their semiotic activity than their modern counterparts, but they are also more conservative, in the sense that they evolve more slowly, because their spontaneous semiotic inventiveness is not inscribed in fixed messages and is therefore lost to a broad audience. Lotman betrays his personal preference for traditional societies when he oddly asserts that readers of a modern novel are more passive than readers of a fairy tale (*Universe of the Mind*, 34–35).

Greenblatt initially posits that Renaissance Europeans were endowed with a talent for improvisation, a faculty he defines as "the ability again and again to insinuate themselves into the preexisting political, religious, even psychic structures of the natives and to turn those structures to their advantage."[32] Yet by the time he writes *Marvelous Possessions,* his book on the conquest of the New World, Greenblatt calls into question the proposition that Europeans handily vanquished the natives because of their superior semiotic technology. The book is partly written as a polemic against Tzvetan Todorov, who had attempted to demonstrate that the Europeans' syntagmatic semiotic system, which emphasizes the uniqueness of events and the causal links between them, is better adapted to warfare than the paradigmatic semiosis favored by the Native Americans. In keeping with the latter, Native Americans had, according to Todorov, embedded the violent Spanish aggression

into a preexisting mythical master plot, badly miscalculating the historical uniqueness of the invasion and resigning themselves too quickly to a
situation they saw as foreordained.[33]

As he analyzes the writings of New World explorers, Greenblatt emphasizes their semiotic blindness. Their voyages led not to a genuine acquisition of knowledge but only to a confirmation of previously formed
expectations.[34] Far from insinuating themselves into the semiotic structures of the natives, Europeans could "only continue to entrap, kidnap,
and project vain fantasies."[35] They showed little proclivity for learning
the vernacular language and instead used interpreters picked, or rather
abducted, from among the natives, many of whom proved unreliable.[36]
Thus the Europeans failed to out-semiotize the Native Americans—the
evidence suggests that the latter certainly matched, if not surpassed, the
improvisational skills of the former.[37] And if the invaders nonetheless
won the war, it was only because the European symbolic order turned
gold into a desirable commodity and provided the conquerors with an
economic and religious rationale for recklessly killing the natives to appropriate their riches.[38]

In short, both Lotman and Greenblatt make a point of emphasizing
the superior semiotic alertness of members of traditional societies, and
they do so because they want to celebrate the heterogeneity and creativity of the periphery, a political ideal they maintain despite knowing that
historically semiotic inventiveness has not been able to resist brute
power.

## Selfhood and Autonomy

What is the fate of the self in the discursive fields described by Greenblatt
and Lotman? Greenblatt evades historical determinism and underscores
agency, though not necessarily free agency. For him individuals are enmeshed in various networks of sociocultural and discursive practices that
constrict their options and subvert their intentions.[39] Both *Renaissance
Self-Fashioning* and *Shakespearean Negotiations* exemplify the drastic limits
placed on a self's autonomy and ability to resist social forces. The linchpin of the former, the much-abused notion of self-fashioning, derives
its potency from its ambivalence. It is clear that this concept concerns
the fashioning of a self, but by whom: social forces or the individual?
Greenblatt uses the term in both senses. And yet when he writes that

self-fashioning "involves submission to an absolute power or authority situated at least partially outside the self" and that it "occurs at the point of encounter between an authority and an alien," one wonders what has happened to individual agency.[40] In a later piece Greenblatt refuses to grant this dismissal of individual agency universal validity.[41] In the conclusion to *Renaissance Self-Fashioning*, however, he does just that. Reflecting on the intellectual journey he performed writing this book, which took him from a presumption of autonomous self-fashioning to a discovery of individual submission to outside forces, he relates a personal story that brought home to him the extent to which "in our culture" one needs to cling to the fiction of autonomous self-fashioning, for to renounce it is to "abandon the craving for freedom."[42] The autonomy of the self, then, is an illusion, but it is an empowering one, for it sustains our drive to gain control over our identities, however fruitless this drive may be in the final analysis.

Lotman proposes a semiotic theory of the self that consists of two parts: one dealing with the ways the self constitutes and changes its identity for itself, and the other with interactions between this self and social codes. The self develops its subjective identity by absorbing a message coming from outside and projecting it onto a supplementary code coming from within (*Universe of the Mind*, 22). To keep it simple, suffice it to say that the self is endowed with the ability to recode messages it receives and to restructure its own identity in the process. This restructuring results from the creative intersection between two nonhomologous codes. A diary would be an example of this restructuring, in which discourses from everyday life are introjected and refashioned according to the rhythms, inflections, and nuances of first-person narration.

Now this self needs to publicize its reconfigured identity, and here matters become more complex. In keeping with his spatial modeling, Lotman views the social assertion of identity as a drawing of boundaries. "One of the primary mechanisms of semiotic individuation," he notes, "is the boundary, and the boundary can be defined as the outer limit of a first-person form" (*Universe of the Mind*, 131). Yet this boundary needs to be recognized by the social sphere. As he himself recognizes, boundaries belong to both frontier systems, the one inside and the one outside (136). Lotman never explores the implications of this state of affairs for the individual self. Indeed, for him the question is inconsequential, for the self is simultaneously an individual part of society and an isomorphic image of the whole of society, depending on the semiotic vantage point one chooses. On the micro level the self appears as distinct from the collectivity, and yet from a more distanced point of view, the self looks like a small-scale replica of the collective body it inhabits. Lotman's example is dandyism, which is a mass phenomenon to the cultural historian but a form of individualization to a dandy (226). "The actual notion of 'individuality,'" Lotman maintains, "is not primary or self-evident but depends on the means of encoding" (234).

This notion of the two "hypostases" of the person makes sense from the point of view of retrospective cultural semiotics, but for an individual self engaged in a battle for survival in the present, it is a bittersweet realization that his or her behavior can be seen at once as individual and collective. For surely this person will favor a subjective way of encoding the world and will expect the world to acknowledge his or her point of view. Does not Lotman's view cast doubt on the possibility of genuine individuality? In a passage in *Culture and Explosion*, Lotman opposes the idiot, the madman, and the intelligent man. The only unpredictable one of the three is the madman, for the idiot displays *patterns* of inappropriate behavior, while an intelligent person behaves "according to the rules and laws of social conventions" (*Kul'tura i vzryv*, 41). Is then Lotman as dismissive of individuality as Greenblatt?

One finds in Lotman traces of a longing for a different model of the self, one that explores the possibilities of genuine autonomy. In a discussion of the difference between traditional and modern societies, Lotman refers to Kant's famous definition of enlightenment as "humanity's emergence from a state of immaturity in which it is kept by its own fault. Immaturity is the inability to use one's reason without guidance from another person."[43] Upon presenting Kant's concept of rational autonomy as an ideal notion of personality, Lotman adds this strange gloss: "[A] culture oriented towards a person's capability to choose his or her own behaviour strategy requires rationality, caution, circumspection and discretion, since each event is regarded as 'happening for the first time'" (*Universe of the Mind*, 248). This passage is remarkably revealing, especially since as an example of this, Lotman refers to Victor Turner's discussion of the Ndembu society, which demonizes a man making a choice because the Ndembu associate individual choice with violating the established order. An example from a traditional society, then, serves to exemplify the predicament of the modern individual.

Why, then, does one need circumspection and discretion to make a rational choice? What kind of idea of social order underlies this confession? To discover what is at stake, let us look at the ways in which Lotman analyzes individual biographies. In his biography of Pushkin, Lotman shows how sensitive to various behavior codes the poet was. Throughout his life Pushkin excelled at enacting codes. Abrupt changes in his writing and in his behavior are attributable to switches from one behavior code to the other, say from the norms of the *honnête homme*, who acquires a repertoire of genres and styles to choose from depending on his audience, to the romantic hero, who is required to abide by one norm consistently (*Aleksandr Sergeevich Pushkin*, 57–58). Agency, that is, lies in the choice between various conventions. During the events leading to his death in a duel, Pushkin confronted a series of intrigues that aimed to ridicule him as a hapless cuckold. Lotman describes the aristocratic society that circulated gossip about his wife Natalia's affair with Georges d'Antes as a bunch of servile courtiers with little self-respect. Pushkin responded with uncompromising behavior, challenging d'Antes to a duel and thereby transforming the affair from low vaudeville into high tragedy. For Lotman, Pushkin's emphatic adherence to the aristocratic code of honor was his way of triumphing over his enemies, even though he lost his life in the process (179–84).

Lotman gives Pushkin only a binary choice: either he could resign himself to the role of the cuckold, or he could restore his honor by putting his life on the line, that is, by demonstrating his willingness to renounce everything dear to him—his life, his art, his family—to restore his honor. Pushkin, however, coined the phrase the "captive of merciless honor" in his "The Prisoner of the Caucasus," and neither of the two alternatives seems particularly liberating. Both leave the individual enmeshed in a tightly woven net of social conventions. That Pushkin takes the initiative by forcing a lethal outcome does not yet mean that he succeeds in transcending the social determination of his behavior. He simply chooses one conventional logic over the other.[44]

Stella Abramovich notes that sending anonymous letters was not considered dignified enough to warrant challenging the perpetrator to a duel and that in his fatal duel Pushkin clearly went beyond what the honor code required him to do.[45] According to this cultural historian, then, Pushkin's options were not binary: even within the parameters of the code of honor, which Pushkin chose to abide by, there was room for maneuver, and if Pushkin opted for an escalation of the conflict, it was only because of his provocatively narrow interpretation of the code of honor, which by 1837 was fast losing its normativeness.

In granting Pushkin only a binary choice between equally conventional courses of action, Lotman drastically reduces Kant's notion of rational autonomy to a mere selection between two poles of a precoded dichotomy. And yet Lotman ends his biography in a sort of rapture: "Pushkin entered Russian culture not only as a poet, but also as a genial master of life, who had received the unheard-of gift of being happy even in the most tragic circumstances" (*Pushkin*, 250). We need not recollect all the bleak specifics of Pushkin's life to realize how desperate this eulogy sounds. If, in fact, Pushkin could have restored his honor without risking his life, or if his honor was not injured to an extent requiring him to throw his life into the balance, then one wonders why Lotman chooses not to heed the implications of this state of affairs. For it appears that Pushkin's behavior was not so much driven by the lack of alternatives to a stark social dichotomy as it was impelled by a personal desire to provoke a radical outcome, a psychological motive several critics have conceived of as a drive to flirt with death.[46]

One can consider his eulogy to Pushkin in parallel with a stunning confession Lotman makes in 1985 in a private letter to his friend and colleague B. F. Egorov:

> On my side I am also getting close to my freedom. To me liberty is the freedom from illusions. When all the soap bubbles burst—what is left is freedom. And in recent years I have been bravely and definitively cleansing my soul of soap bubbles. For the last line one needs to have a clean house. Realizing that I have no disciples, that my laboratory, which I had sought to obtain so intently and which seemed so important to me, is nothing but a soap bubble, having experienced a series of disappointments, I suddenly discovered for myself a lot of vitality, rather than despondency, and even a certain feeling of beginning, rather than ending. And of freedom. Indeed, no one can deceive us, we only deceive ourselves. And this is why even in the seemingly strongest moments of passion there is always a feeling in the depth of the soul saying: "Are you not pretending?" Disappointments free us from self-deception, from the fear to tell ourselves the truth, i.e., they give us freedom. (*Pis'ma*, 341–42)

The metaphor of the soap bubble or the bubble in general has a venerable pedigree in Western literatures. Its meanings range from "figment of the imagination" as in Schiller's "mein Gehirn treibt öfters wunderbare Blasen auf die schnell, wie sie entstanden sind, zerspringen" (my mind often creates wonderful bubbles, which burst as quickly as they appear) to "vain social pursuit" as in the famous "all the world's a stage" monologue in Shakespeare's *As You Like It:* "Then a soldier, / Full of strange oaths and bearded like the pard, / Jealous in honor, sudden and quick in quarrel, / Seeking the bubble reputation / Even in the cannon's mouth" (2.7).[47] In Russian *myl'nyi puzyr'*, soap bubble, means someone or something fragile and trivial. It is used in such a way by Chekhov in *Uncle Vanya*, in which Ivan Voinitskii disparages his brother-in-law, the scholar Aleksandr Serebriakov, as someone "completely unknown, a non-entity! A soap bubble!"[48] But the connection between soapy air and calculated self-deception that underpins Lotman's letter derives, I submit, from Dostoevsky's *Notes from the Underground:* "The day after tomorrow, at the latest, you will begin to despise yourself for having wittingly cheated yourself. The result: a soap bubble and inertia," as the Underground Man puts it in his soliloquy.[49]

This connection with the *Notes from the Underground* is, of course, particularly pregnant, in that it firmly aligns Lotman's commitment to introspection and retreat with what one could call the ethics of the underground in Russian culture. The self finds its freedom not in successful social ventures but in withdrawing from social involvement or, more precisely, in renouncing the search for self-realization in the social arena. Hence the idea that circumspection and discretion are required to exercise one's freedom of choice. The autonomy of the self is clearly relegated to the private sphere. What Lotman saw in Pushkin's uncompromising stance is something similar to what he cultivated toward the end of his own life—withdrawal from investment in the social circuit, ruthless self-examination, and a stoic abidance by core moral values.

In short, if for Greenblatt it is cultivating illusions that sustains the self's quest for freedom, in Lotman it is the opposite—puncturing soap bubbles—that liberates the self. Quite possibly this polar opposition reflects the different life experiences of the two scholars: one reared in late capitalism with its production of multiple, diversified, small illusions or simulacra, as postmodernist critics like to call them, the other working in socialism with its production of one monolithic grand illusion.[50] Ultimately it is this idea about the nature of freedom that undergirds the two writers' cultural theories. If for Greenblatt cultural life is fluid and complex enough to enable the self to negotiate some degree of autonomy, if only an illusory one, for Lotman, the further withdrawn from the center of culture, the freer one is. Thus their respective analysis of power determines their idea of freedom. Under the regime of a plurality of centers of power, such as exists in capitalism, the self can negotiate some autonomy, while under the regime of a stringent centrality of power, the only possible liberating gesture lies in withdrawal. One could go so far as suggesting that the postcolonial agenda I imputed to the two theorists is linked to their analysis of the self. Perhaps the creativity of traditional societies is one of the illusions Greenblatt's self needs to nourish to retain the will to resist, and perhaps delving into the semiotic universe of traditional societies is one of the ways Lotman's self withdraws from involvement in the social circuit surrounding him. In any case, the encounter I staged here between Lotman and Greenblatt testifies to the rich intersections between a semiotic and a social theory of cultural production.

## Notes

This essay is an expanded and revised version of "Social Power and Individual Agency: The Self in Greenblatt and Lotman," *Slavic and East European Journal* 45, no. 1 (2001): 61–79.

1. Stephen Greenblatt, "Towards a Poetics of Culture," in *The New Historicism*, ed. H. Aram Veeser (New York: Routledge, 1989), 14n10. He and Catherine Gallagher also indirectly refer to Lotman in a retrospective acknowledgment of the theories that enabled the emergence of New Historicism: "We eagerly read works of 'theory' emanating principally from Paris, Konstanz, Berlin, Frankfurt, Budapest, Tartu, and Moscow." Catherine Gallagher and Stephen Greenblatt, *Practicing New Historicism* (Chicago: University of Chicago Press, 2000), 2.

2. Stephen Greenblatt, *Shakespearean Negotiations: The Circulation of Social Energy in Renaissance England* (Berkeley: University of California Press, 1988), 3.

3. On the question of Lotman's relationship to Marxism, see M. L. Gasparov, who claims somewhat facetiously that in its method, Lotman's structuralism was more genuinely Marxist than the scholarship of his Communist contemporaries. "Lotman i marksizm," *Novoe literaturnoe obozrenie* 19 (1996): 8–10. But his argument rests on a problematic extension of Marxist critical concepts and premises such as "existence determines consciousness," "dialectics," and "historicism," as well as on the collapsing of the social and cultural spheres and the conflating of Marxism and science. B. F. Egorov writes more precisely of the endurance of basic Hegelian–early Marxian premises, but accompanied by a rejection of the primacy of class consciousness and a greater sense of the complexity of cultural phenomena. *Zhizn' i tvorchestvo Iu. M. Lotmana*, 87–92.

4. Regarding Lotman's personal history, see Egorov, *Zhizn' i tvorchestvo Iu. M. Lotmana*, 46-49. Regarding Lotman's embodiment of the ethos of the Russian intelligentsia, see Andrei Zorin's contribution to this volume. See also T. D. Kuzovkina, "Tema smerti v poslednikh stat'iakh Iu. M. Lotman," in Egorov, *Zhizn' i tvorchestvo Iu. M. Lotmana*, 260-61, on Lotman's deliberate self-fashioning as a "Chelovek-intelligent."

5. Stephen Greenblatt, "Resonance and Wonder," in *Literary Theory Today*, ed. Peter Collier and Helga Geyer-Ryan (Cambridge: Polity Press, 1990), 77.

6. Stephen Greenblatt, "What Is the History of Literature?" *Critical Inquiry* 23, no. 3 (1997): 461.

7. Understanding the past on its own terms, if that were possible, would yield informational tautology. Yet understanding it on our terms would generate total misunderstanding—hence the need for a movement back and forth.

8. Gallagher and Greenblatt, *Practicing New Historicism*, 17. See also Greenblatt, "Resonance and Wonder," 77.

9. New Historicism explicitly wants to have it both ways, giving due to the "creative matrices of particular historical cultures" yet recognizing the potential independence of texts. Gallagher and Greenblatt, *Practicing New Historicism*, 16.

10. Ibid., 31.

11. Lotman's discussions of texts that can be received either as code or as message essentially erase all distinctions between code and message but the functional one (*Universe of the Mind*, 29-30), thus inviting the analogy with "discourse," which similarly denotes a text that can both convey information and exercise a normative function.

12. On the death of the author, see Michel Foucault, "What Is an Author?" in *Textual Strategies: Perspectives in Post-Structuralist Criticism*, ed. Josué V. Harari (Ithaca, N.Y.: Cornell University Press, 1979), 143-45; as well as Roland Barthes, "The Death of the Author," in *Image, Music Text*, ed. and trans. S. Heath (New York: Hill & Wang, 1977), 142-48.

13. For a comparison between Lotman and Clifford Geertz, which likewise follows the strategy of emphasizing converging ideas between the two scholars despite their divergent intellectual pedigrees, see Andrei Zorin, "Ideologiia i semiotika v interpretatsii Klifforda Girtsa," *Novoe literaturnoe obozrenie* 29 (1998): 42-46.

14. On Lotman's theory of the semiosphere as poststructuralist semiotics, or post-poststructuralism, see Amy Mandelker, "Logosphere and Semiosphere: Bakhtin, Russian Organicism, and the Semiotics of Culture," in *Bakhtin in Contexts across the Disciplines*, ed. Amy Mandelker (Evanston, Ill.: Northwestern University Press, 1995), 178-79. By the time he wrote some sections from *Universe of the Mind*, Lotman had almost erased the difference between code and utterance, since according to him a code can be refashioned in the process of communication and any text can serve as a code for the production of another text (*Universe of the Mind*, 29-30).

15. Stephen Greenblatt, introduction to *The Power of Forms in the English Renaissance* (Norman, Okla.: Pilgrim Books, 1982), 4; and Greenblatt, *Shakespearean Negotiations*, 3–4.

16. Greenblatt, *Shakespearean Negotiations*, 4–5. For a discussion of the fluidity of the text and of the difficulties of isolating units suitable for analysis, see also Gallagher and Greenblatt, *Practicing New Historicism*, 14–15.

17. Greenblatt, "Poetics of Culture," 12.

18. Greenblatt, *Shakespearean Negotiations*, 7. Greenblatt's language here recalls Lotman's definition of an event as the shifting of a character across the borders of a semantic field (*Structure of the Artistic Text*, 233).

19. Mandelker, "Logosphere and Semiosphere," 183–89.

20. O. A. Sedakova, "'Vechnye sny, kak obrazchiki krovi. . . . ' O Iurii Mikhailoviche Lotmane i strukturnoi shkole v kontekste kul'tury 70-kh gg," in *Lotmanovskii sbornik*, 263.

21. As he analyzes the discourse deployed by the Spanish to legitimate the conquest of America, Greenblatt concludes that "[w]ords in the New World seem always to be trailing after events that pursue a terrible logic quite other than the fragile meanings that they construct." And yet he is unwilling to dismiss words completely, for he sees them as components and symptoms of a larger symbolic system that motivates and enables the conquest (*Marvelous Possessions: The Wonder of the New World* [Chicago: Chicago University Press, 1991], 63–64).

22. Greenblatt, *Shakespearean Negotiations*, 18–19.

23. Stephen Greenblatt, *Renaissance Self-Fashioning from More to Shakespeare* (Chicago: University of Chicago Press, 1980), 179–92. Note that New Historicism seems to have become increasingly suspicious of the uses of theory. In *Practicing New Historicism*, Gallagher and Greenblatt trace their genealogy to Herder's rejection of universal history and his ideas on the extraordinary malleability of human identity. New Historicism, that is, firmly sides with the particular and against the universal (5–7).

24. Gallagher and Greenblatt, *Practicing New Historicism*, 35.

25. Ibid., 44.

26. Ibid., 26. In fairness one should add that within history, as opposed to literary studies, the "Auerbachian device" serves as the linchpin of "counterhistories" that undermine totalizing and discriminatory grand narratives (Ibid., 49–74).

27. Greenblatt, *Marvelous Possessions*, 121.

28. Ibid., 132–35.

29. Ibid., 121.

30. The expression "the empire writes back with a vengeance" belongs to Salman Rushdie, quoted in Srinivas Aravamudan, *Tropicopolitans: Colonialism and Agency, 1688–1804* (Durham, N.C.: Duke University Press, 1999), 5.

31. Lotman introduces the term *creolization* of semiotic systems in *Universe of the Mind*, 142. His schema is akin to the phenomenon Mary Louise Pratt

describes as "transculturation," the way "subordinated or marginal groups select and invent from materials transmitted to them by a dominant or metropolitan culture." *Imperial Eyes: Travel Writing and Transculturation* (London: Routledge, 1992), 5–6.

32. Greenblatt, *Renaissance Self-Fashioning*, 227.

33. Tzvetan Todorov, *La conquête de l'Amérique: La question de l'autre* (Paris: Seuil, 1982), 92–93.

34. Greenblatt, *Marvelous Possessions*, 88.

35. Ibid., 117.

36. Ibid., 106.

37. Ibid., 99.

38. Ibid., 63–64.

39. Greenblatt, "Resonance and Wonder," 74–75.

40. Greenblatt, *Renaissance Self-Fashioning*, 9.

41. Greenblatt, "Resonance and Wonder," 75.

42. Greenblatt, *Renaissance Self-Fashioning*, 257.

43. Egorov emphasizes the role of Lotman's article "Ideinaia struktura *Kapitanskoi dochki*" (1962) as an important milestone in his rejection of Marxist ethics (for which freedom is the awareness of one's being determined). In this article Lotman examines the ways in which the main characters of the novel transcend the morality dictated by their social position and affirm universal values such as duty and mercy. According to Egorov, Lotman followed in Pushkin's stead and "raised the universal, the good, the merciful above the categories of class consciousness" (Egorov, *Zhizn' i tvorchestvo Iu. M. Lotmana*, 89).

44. Raising similar questions, David Bethea comes to different conclusions, uncovering in Lotman what strikes me as Pushkin's idea about creativity and freedom as a playful enactment of roles. Bethea fully espouses Lotman's reading of Pushkin's death, in "Iurii Lotman v 1980-e gody: Kod i ego otnoshenie k literaturnoi biografii," *Novoe literaturnoe obozrenie* 19 (1996): 14–29. On Lotman's ideas about overcoming death through artistic creativity, see Kuzovkina, "Tema smerti v poslednikh stat'iakh Iu. M. Lotman," 268–70.

45. Stella Abramovich, *Predystoriia poslednei dueli: Ianvar' 1836–ianvar' 1837* (St. Petersburg: Rossiiskaia Akademiia Nauk, 1994), 74.

46. Natan Eidel'man, *Pushkin: Iz biografii i tvorchestva, 1826–1837* (Moscow: Khudozhestvennaia literatura, 1987), 372–73; and Abramovich, *Predystoriia poslednei dueli*, 25.

47. Schiller quoted in Jacob and Wilhelm Grimm, *Deutsches Wörterbuch*, vol. 2 (Leipzig: Verlag von S. Hirzel, 1860), 67.

48. A. P. Chekhov, *Polnoe sobranie sochinenii i pisem v tridtsati tomakh*, vol. 13 (Moscow: Nauka, 1986), 80.

49. F. M. Dostoevskii, *Polnoe sobranie sochinenii v tridtsati tomakh*, vol. 5 (Leningrad: Nauka, 1973), 109.

50. Regarding this concept of capitalism, I have in mind Fredric Jameson's idea of the gigantic expansion of culture through society in late capitalism, whereby simulacra or pseudorealities permeate all social relations. "The Cultural Logic of Late Capitalism," *Postmodernism, or, the Cultural Logic of Late Capitalism* (Durham, N.C.: Duke University Press, 1991), 1–54. The only problem with Jameson's approach is that he fails to recognize that illusions, simulacra, or pseudoevents, whatever one wishes to call them, can serve the cause of individuation or differentiation, rather than necessarily bringing about meaningless homogeneity.

# 8

# Lotman's Karamzin and the Late Soviet Liberal Intelligentsia

ANDREI ZORIN

No one who lived in Moscow during the turmoil of the late 1980s and early 1990s will ever forget December 1991. On December 8, the Soviet Union was dissolved in Belovezhskaia Pushcha; on December 25, President Gorbachev declared on TV his official resignation, and the red flag was publicly replaced over the Kremlin by the Russian tricolor. The same month witnessed the peak of food shortages, and the population of Moscow had to queue for hours in the mornings for simple items such as bread and milk. Everyone was waiting with hope and fear for the announced reforms due to start right after the New Year.

It was exactly during these days that Russian intellectuals were celebrating the 225th anniversary of N. M. Karamzin's birthday. Traditional academic conferences organized in Moscow and Petersburg attracted much public attention. The hall of the Pushkin Museum on Volkhonka Street was crowded for the three days of the Moscow conference. On December 11, three days after the signing of the treaty that dismantled the USSR and initiated the CIS, a lavish literary celebration was held in the Kolonnyi Hall of the House of Soviets, which was traditionally reserved for important official ceremonies. The celebration was greeted by President Yeltsin, who wrote in his letter to the participants:

> The life of N. M. Karamzin, the great historian, represents a heroic deed [*podvig*] of a person who gave all his strength, experience, and talent to the cause of his Motherland. Today in this critical moment for our country, we look with special feeling and understanding on our historical experience while reading the lines of the great work of historical thought that is *The History of the Russian State.*
>
> In this book our contemporary and compatriot will find the great and the tragic; here the human is harmonically united with the national. . . . *The History of the Russian State* teaches us historical optimism. In the struggle of human passions, evil sometimes prevails. But motherland lives, Russia revives, the spirit of Russians strengthens.[1]

This official letter signed by the president of the country in one of the most dramatic periods of its existence provides direct evidence of the level that the canonization of Karamzin in Russian culture acquired by the time of the collapse of the USSR. On December 11, the day of the jubilee, the semiofficial newspaper *Izvestia* published an interview with Sigurd Shmidt, one of the leading Russian historians, under the title "He Helps Us Today to Understand What Is Good and What Is Evil in History."

This canonization process was comparatively quick. Throughout the Soviet period Karamzin was traditionally viewed as a second-rate writer. The sentimental aspirations of his youth were credited with certain, though qualified approval, while his mature works, especially the historical and the political, were viewed with deep suspicion. Under Soviet censorship neither *The History of the Russian State* nor *Memoir on Ancient and Modern Russia,* Karamzin's other major political work, were republished.

However, by the time of perestroika this reputation began to change. During this period Karamzin was regarded as one of the hidden authors whose heritage had to be restored to Russian readers, along with that of authors persecuted by the Communists, such as Nikolai Gumilev, Andrei Platonov, and even Aleksandr Solzhenitsyn. Two of the most widely published Russian fiction writers, Valentin Rasputin and Sergei Zalygin, wrote a letter to Gorbachev urging him to allocate all the paper (which, like all other commodities, was at that time strictly rationed) needed to print their works to the publication of Karamzin's *History.*

This astonishing promotion of a once-forgotten historian in the national cultural hierarchy derived from the widely held belief that all contemporary questions have their answers in history and that knowing the truth about national history, which had been concealed from the country by the ill-meaning Communists, would resolve all existing problems. It was also rooted in the system of ideological beliefs and the modes of thought of the former Soviet liberal intelligentsia.

The historical consciousness of the Soviet public was shaped by the famous definition of the three stages of "revolutionary liberation struggle in Russia" described by Lenin in his essay "In Memory of Herzen." According to Lenin the struggle against tsarism extended through the noble period represented by the Decembrists, the *raznochinskii* period represented by the Narodovol'tsy (People's Will), and the proletarian period, when the Bolsheviks finally appeared on the historical stage.[2] The popularity of this schema was attributable to its quasi-Hegelian tripartite structure, to the teleological interpretation it gave to history, and, first and foremost, to the fact that every schoolchild in the Soviet Union memorized it and all historical and literary curricula in schools and universities were organized accordingly.

This Leninist triad became the substratum of the public perception of national history shared even by those whose political views were resolutely anti-Soviet. What is more, because censorship precluded the open discussion of Soviet history, nineteenth-century Russian history traditionally served as a pool for analogies. Thus the same schema became an interpretative tool for understanding the present-day situation in the Soviet Union as well. Such Aesopian allusions became especially popular in the mid 1960s, after the end of the thaw and especially after the Soviet invasion of Czechoslovakia in 1968, when the majority of the intelligentsia finally relinquished its hopes for the democratization of the Communist system.

The interplay between the historical experience of the nineteenth and twentieth centuries was viewed in a double perspective. First of all, the ruling regime claimed to be and in a way was perceived as a legitimate heir to the revolutionary tradition beginning with the Decembrists and culminating in the Bolsheviks. Accordingly, such claims strongly compromised this tradition in the eyes of liberal intellectuals, who turned their attention to prerevolutionary thinkers and politicians of conservative and sometimes outright reactionary stance, such as Konstantin

Leontiev and Vasilii Rozanov. At the same time, the Communist system was seen as the product of traditional Russian authoritarianism; thus those who had protested against the latter could be seen as the forerunners of the rebels against the former.

However, the legacy of both the Bolsheviks and the Narodovoltsy, the members of the so-called People's Will, was largely rejected by anti-Soviet protesters. Indeed, their relative closeness to the actual Communist regime and their terrorist legacy compromised them. With the Decembrists the situation was much different. They stood a century apart from the actual experience of the October Revolution; like Soviet dissidents they were "awfully far from the people," as Lenin remarked in his Herzen essay; most importantly, they were completely and, as many people then believed, willingly defeated.[3]

The poetry of the inevitable defeat constituted much of the charisma of the Decembrists. The attempted military coup d'état at Senate Square was perceived as a venture doomed in advance, dictated not so much by political calculations as by the moral impossibility of reconciling oneself to slavery and baseness. The novel of Bulat Okudzhava describing the Decembrist uprising was appropriately titled *The Gulp of Liberty*. Songs of the popular bards Aleksandr Galich and Iurii Kim linked those historic events with the demonstration in Red Square in 1968 when a handful of dissidents decided to voice their protest against the invasion of Czechoslovakia.

The Decembrists became cult figures in two mutually exclusive pantheons. In his book of interviews President Putin related how the Leningrad KGB, where he served at that time, prevented a dissident demonstration in Senate Square by organizing an official rally to commemorate the Decembrists. And paradoxically the dissident interpretation of the Decembrist movement was partially fed by an official one. However negatively the liberal intelligentsia regarded the legacy of Bolshevism, it adopted its underlying historical teleology, which seemed to promise a certain if remote future victory to the heroic, self-sacrificing struggle of the dissidents.

In "Petersburg Romance," a historical song devoted to the Decembrists, Galich wrote about the fundamental ethical test to which a human being is subjected:

И все так же, не проще
Век наш пробует нас:

Сможешь выйти на площадь?
Смеешь выйти на площадь?
Смеешь выйти на площадь?
Сможешь выйти на площадь?
В тот назначенный час.

[In the same way, not easier
Our time challenges us:
Can you come to the square?
Dare you come to the square?
Dare you come to the square?
Can you come to the square?
In that determined hour.][4]

Before singing it, the bard usually told his audience that he had first performed this song in the presence of Pavel Litvinov, who a few days later
would become one of the participants in the 1968 Red Square demonstration. According to the poet, hearing the quoted words, Litvinov
"smiled somewhat strangely."

Apart from this introduction "Petersburg Romance" had an epigraph from Karamzin's 1797 poem "Tacitus":

Он (Рим—А. з.) сам виновник всех своих злосчастных бед,
Терпя, чего терпеть без подлости не можно

[Rome is guilty in all its horrible calamities.
Enduring what can't be endured without baseness.][5]

Speaking about ancient Rome, Karamzin alluded to Russia under
Paul I, and Galich used these lines in relation to the Communist Soviet
Union. The political protest of revolutionaries and dissidents found
its correlation in the ethical protest of poets and historians—Galich,
Tacitus, and Karamzin, the last in both his incarnation as a writer and
as a historian.

Yet the Decembrists could most definitely not serve as a role model
for the majority of intellectuals, who were little inclined to come to the
square and preferred less dangerous modes of dealing with the system.
These people preferred someone who would be less revolutionary and
preferably even antirevolutionary but at the same time morally irre-
proachable and uncompromised by collaboration with the authorities.
Karamzin was an ideal figure for this type of idealization, and among

the literary historians who worked for several decades on the reassess-
ment of his legacy, Lotman's voice was by far the most influential.

Lotman studied Karamzin for more than forty years, and his main
works on the man and his ideas constitute an eight-hundred-page volume. His first publication on Karamzin appeared in 1951 *(A. N. Radishchev v bor'be s obshchestvenno-politicheskimi vozzreniami i dvorianskoi estetikoi
Karamzina)*. In this early work, submitted as his first (candidate) dissertation at the absolute nadir of Soviet humanities after the notorious campaign against the so-called *kosmopolity*, he more or less follows the traditional view of Karamzin as a reactionary, in contrast to the allegedly
more revolutionary-minded Radishchev. However, even here the depth
and the complexity of his analysis of Karamzin's ideas differs dramatically from the traditional pattern. The decisive shift occurred in his classic articles "The Evolution of Karamzin's Worldview" and "The Ways
of the Development of Russian Prose in 1800s–1810s," published during
the thaw period.[6] In these articles Lotman follows the subtle and complicated path of Karamzin's intellectual development in the period preceding the beginning of his work on *The History of the Russian State* and
during the completion of his chef d'oeuvre.

Especially important is Lotman's analysis of Karamzin's political
position. Although he describes the views of the historian as deeply conservative, he also emphasizes his moral and intellectual independence,
which totally excluded any suspicion of political servility. "Karamzin,"
writes Lotman, "repeatedly expressed his conviction that true freedom,
necessary for the human being, consists in personal independence and
self-respect" *(Karamzin, 408)*. This independence proved exceptionally
strong in the shocking description of the tyranny of Ivan the Terrible in
the ninth volume of the *History*, which became a sort of reference and inspiration for future Decembrists, who a couple of years before the appearance of the ninth volume had completely denounced the political
ideas of Karamzin as expressed in the first eight volumes (see *Karamzin,*
409–18).

Thus an official historiographer who was a staunch defender of
authoritarian rule became one of the harshest critics of its excesses. Historical truth and moral independence prevailed in him over political
loyalties and ideological convictions. Lotman was the first to note this
contradiction between public and personal in which priority was given
to personal and ethical imperatives above all other considerations. At

the apex of the thaw, such analysis could not receive much public attention. Lotman's article was published in a marginal scholarly publication known only to the specialists in the field. However, several years later a demand for the figure of an independent conservative suddenly arose, and this line of interpretation became fashionable and vibrant.

In 1968 another leading Russian literary historian, Vadim Vatsuro, published an essay titled "The Heroic Deed [*podvig*] of an Honest Man."[7] This title was a quotation from Pushkin's short essay "Excerpts from Letters, Thoughts, and Remarks," written in 1828, ten years after the publication of the first eight volumes of *The History of the Russian State* and two years after the death of the historian. Vatsuro analyzed the debates around Karamzin in 1818, when along with the future Decembrists, Pushkin severely criticized the historian and wrote a biting epigram on his work, accusing him of defending tyranny and the whip, and in 1828, when Pushkin tried to rescue the glory of the historian both from the traditional criticism of his autocratic views and the emerging official cult.

Vatsuro's goal was to explain this change. He wrote about the historical periods "when abstract debates on morality stop being only speculative [and] disclose their political meaning. Then the title of the 'honest man' grows in value; it no longer signifies only personal qualities, it is given only as a reward for public achievements. Such was the time that began after December 14, 1825."[8] The author obviously meant—or at least the reader obviously understood—that such a period also started after the thaw, when all forms of political activity were suppressed and ethical questions acquired a decisive importance. To choose the path of an honest person was first and foremost a political choice. From these pages emerged Karamzin seen through Pushkin seen through Vatsuro, a perspective that leads us from an unfree historical epoch to one relatively freer. This semantic perspective not only made the discussion easier from the point of view of censorship but also underlined the historical heritage.

Vatsuro's essay was published in the historical almanac *Prometheus,* which at the time was one of the most popular publications of the liberal intelligentsia; with a circulation of one hundred thousand, it ensured that Vatsuro's essay, unlike Lotman's earlier articles, reached a relatively large audience. This edition of the almanac was officially authorized by censorship in 1968, one month before the invasion of Czechoslovakia, after which the regime of censorship hardened dramatically.

The publication of Vatsuro's article was accompanied by a footnote announcing the upcoming publication of a book by him and M. Gillelson that would include the essay. Titled *Through Intellectual Dams* and devoted to the struggle of nineteenth-century Russian writers with censorship, this book appeared four years later, in 1972, and immediately became an intellectual bestseller.[9]

Vatsuro's article established for the first time Karamzin's image among Russian intellectuals. It is highly probable that Galich took the quotation he used as an epigraph to the "Petersburg Romance" from this article. However, the basic interpretative pattern that manifested itself in this vision of Karamzin's personality was established by Lotman's earlier article.

The same holds true for one of the first Soviet-era biographies of Karamzin, written by the famous and highly popular historian N. Ia. Eidelman. Eidelman initially intended to focus on the publication of *The History of the Russian State* and its reception, but his book evolved into a full-scale biography, albeit a brief one lacking critical apparatus.[10] Eidelman points out the "outstanding tribute in Russian culture that can be called *the personality of Karamzin*. Karamzin is a highly attractive moral personality who influenced many by direct example given in friendship and even more by the presence of his personality in poems, stories, articles, and especially in the *History*."[11]

Eidelman emphasizes the connection between the moral stance of Karamzin and his professional activity, his work as a historian. Thus, the life strategy of the Soviet scholar who chose to express his disagreement with the regime not through political protest but through independent and secluded research is legitimized and even acquires a heroic dimension. "Pushkin's definition 'a *heroic deed of an honest man*' is first of all a *moral* assessment of a scholarly work," writes Eidelman. "Behind the words of a great poet-historian lies the notion of the superhuman difficulty of heroism — to write history without betraying one's ideals, without trying to adjust to those in power or vice versa, to everyday talk, to fashion, 'the winged novelty.'"[12]

Retaining personal honesty and writing a true account of history constitute, according to Eidelman, the inner freedom that was the main value for the intellectuals of that period. "We'll dare to say," he writes of this characteristic in conclusion, "that it was a heroic deed of a *free man*. In his epoch Karamzin was one of the men most endowed with inner freedom. . . . Karamzin spoke freely both with the tsars and the Decembrists

without ever being afraid of anyone. He wrote what he thought, portrayed historical characters based on an enormous mass of new material, managed to discover old Russia as Columbus discovered America
and to pass his discovery on to as many people as possible, preserving at
the same time the dignity of history and the dignity of the historian."[13]

This formula sums up the logic underlying the canonization of
Karamzin among liberal intellectuals. Apart from his heroic struggle to
maintain his integrity and independence, the idea of history writing was
absolutely essential to his image. The ideal of a thinker who in the quiet
of his study writes a historical work to preserve historical truth for later
generations corresponded to the general perception that it was utterly
impossible to do anything useful in the present situation and that existing social practices could not be changed, but that one's duty was to discover and record the truth about the past. History became the main site
of dispute between liberal intellectuals and the authorities, whose efforts
to falsify historical knowledge were continuously laid bare. History written by solitary and selfless enthusiasts was opposed to the myth invented
by the Bolsheviks.

No doubt this perception was highly pessimistic. The mind-set of the
liberal intellectuals of the period was strongly tainted with a mixture of
pessimism, skepticism, and stoicism. In a way the ideal posture was formulated in Solzhenitsyn's commandment for prisoners of the gulag:
"Do not believe, do not be afraid, do not ask for anything." Karamzin,
as described by Lotman and other major scholars following his path,
was characterized by this distinctive blend of uncompromising pessimism. The Russian historiographer was definitely never a prisoner. On
the contrary, he spent part of his life at court in direct contact with the
emperor, but in this environment it was equally important not to be
afraid and never to ask for anything, while the art of asking was traditionally practiced by everyone around him.

In the 1980s Lotman began work on Karamzin's biography, which was
intended to synthesize decades of work in the field. The book was published in 1987, in the perestroika period, but was written and, more importantly, conceived earlier. "I give some importance to this book,"
wrote Lotman in a letters. "I started to work on Karamzin in 1947,
when this theme was not regarded as valuable. . . . With this book I want
to draw for myself some conclusions about what I have done and to finish (also for myself) this theme so that I can complete in my remaining
years other projects that I have already started" (*Pis'ma*, 338).

In one of the final chapters, titled "The Results," Lotman sum-
marizes what he has written on Karamzin and his ideas over many years:

> The role of Karamzin in the history of Russian culture cannot be mea-
> sured solely by his literary and scholarly work. Karamzin the man was
> in himself a great lesson. As the embodiment of independence, honesty,
> self-respect, and tolerance of others, not in words and preachings but in
> his whole life, which unfolded before the eyes of generations of Rus-
> sians, he taught a lesson; and if not for that lesson, the man of the Push-
> kin era would undoubtedly not have become what he was in Russian
> history. It is not by chance that the Decembrists, who sometimes radi-
> cally criticized Karamzin's *works*, always spoke with great respect about
> his *personality*.
>
> Still one cannot ignore the fact that Karamzin's life also presents a
> negative example, and when you reach the end of his deeply heroic life
> you feel sorrow rather than the joy that a man who exhibited the sub-
> lime beauty of his soul and who never turned from the path he had cho-
> sen should have inspired.
>
> Why? Why is there no feeling of victory? (*Karamzin*, 297–98)

Lotman finds the answer to this question in the complete disillusionment characteristic of Karamzin's thinking from his early years. He
quotes from one of Karamzin's early poems, in which the twenty-seven-
year-old poet aspires for life "without fear and hope." In the context of
this total hopelessness, a carefully arranged private life and regular hard
work stop being a daily routine and assume heroic dimensions:

> For the last ten years Karamzin's life outwardly appeared to be an idyll:
> a loving family, a circle of friends, work, respect, stable if modest in-
> come earned by tireless labor. And yet when you read page by page the
> remaining documents, letters, and memoirs, you begin feeling some-
> thing akin to horror. The living room is cozily lit, but beyond the win-
> dows there is darkness. Under the thin cover of everyday happiness,
> darkness is looming.
>
> Karamzin structured his own life in such a way that he could live not
> hoping for anything. Life without hope. (*Karamzin*, 298)

This passage, marked by an emotional flavor uncharacteristic of
Lotman's style, shows deep personal empathy between the author and
his hero. For most liberal intellectuals, social life under the decaying Soviet regime seemed the complete triumph of violence, deceit, and aggressive mediocrity. Rooted in the old Stalinist legacy, it held forth no expec-
tation of change in the foreseeable future, apart from changes for the

worse, when the dark forces of history would break through the deceptive image of pretended stability. In a way this level of despair legitimized and justified the complete renunciation of social activism, be it through collaboration with the regime or in outright opposition to it. In fact, with all its pathos of heroic sacrifice, dissident activity was connected with some degree of moral optimism, which was viewed by the sympathizing majority as unforgivable naiveté bordering on outright foolishness.

However, it is still unclear why in this intellectual framework a reasonable degree of professional success, financial stability, and family happiness would be regarded as total failure, if not complete tragedy. The answer to this question seems connected to the fact that despite the glorification of the values of private, individual life implicit in this worldview, it was inherently deeply political.

The thinking of this generation of liberal intellectuals was rooted in the sixties, a period determined both by de-Stalinization and by scientistic progressivism. The characteristic belief that advances in the natural sciences, especially in physics, would resolve all social problems deeply influenced Lotman's early structuralist ideas about employing a scientific approach, and in particular information theory, to assess the quality of artistic texts. This idea was strongly stated in Lotman's first theoretical book, *Lectures on Structuralist Poetics*, published in 1964.

As an older member of this generation, Lotman could add to this his personal war experience and the idealistic vision of victory over fascism as a final triumph of reason over the forces of darkness. This vision easily survived the anti-Semitic campaign of the late 1940s and early 1950s ("Vospominaniia," 308, 312) and was dramatically reinforced by the thaw, which added Stalinist deviations to the list of obstacles that had been successfully overcome in the unstoppable course of social progress and the development of human understanding.

It is evident that for this generation and its intellectual leaders the prevailing cynicism and disillusionment of the Brezhnev years were especially shocking and unbearable. And the emerging ideal of a private and independent individual bound to keep his moral integrity inevitably acquired the traits of tragic resignation, endurance, and stoicism. The ensuing resentment against political life did not lead to the disappearance of political interests, quite the contrary: intellectuals of the seventies and eighties were strongly politicized, closely following changes in the official line, scrutinizing the personnel shifts in the Politburo, listening to Western radio stations, reading both clandestine literature and official newspapers, and sympathizing with the heroic if useless struggle of the dissidents.

However, according to a deeply rooted Russian tradition, political participation in national life was never envisaged as acting in the capacity of a public intellectual. A political and intellectual environment, a public sphere, that is, where an activity of this sort would be even remotely possible, was evidently beyond even the most daring dreams. Instead, the only way one could imagine carrying out one's political ambitions was in the role of someone who speaks to the highest authorities, offering them advice and expertise.

As outspoken an enemy of the Soviet regime as Solzhenitsyn gave his political manifesto the title "A Letter to the Leaders." Later he explained that he did not address the actual leaders of the Communist Party but only the future leadership of free Russia. However, an episode related in his autobiographical work "An Oak and the Calf" casts doubt on this statement. There Solzhenitsyn recounts how after his arrest in 1974 guards brought a new suit to him in his prison cell in Lefortovo. The decision to expel him from the USSR had already been made, but Solzhenitsyn did not know about it and instead assumed that he was being taken to a meeting with the leaders of the Politburo.[14] Needless to say, Solzhenitsyn was one of the few people in Russia who never hesitated to speak to the public, and yet even he was subconsciously cherishing the hope of being able to speak to the highest authorities.

The intellectuals of the period were extremely interested in stories of direct physical contact between political leaders and popular writers, for example, in telephone conversations between Stalin and Bulgakov or Pasternak. Natan Eidelman once told me he was planning to write a book about the short conversation between Nicholas I and Pushkin on the day when Pushkin was summoned to St. Petersburg from exile.

No doubt, Karamzin could also serve as a role model here. The educated Russian public was fascinated by his long conversations with Alexander I, in which the historian was acting as private person and even as personal friend, never sparing the emperor his critical remarks. "I was always sincere," wrote Karamzin in his diary after Alexander's death. "He was always patient, kind, incredibly polite, did not ask for my advice, though he listened to it without following it. . . . I did not keep silent about the taxation in time of peace, about the weird financial system adopted by Guriev [A. D. Guriev, the finance minister], about the terrible military settlements, about the strange choice of some of the most important dignitaries, about the Ministry of Enlightenment or of endarkenment, about the necessity of reducing an army that fights only Russia, about the fictitious improvement of roads so unbearable for the nation — at last about the necessity of having strict laws, civil and administrative."[15]

Lotman quotes this and similar passionate diatribes several times in his works on Karamzin (e.g., *Karamzin,* 303, 409, 599). Most important is the role this quotation plays in one of his last articles, "Memoir on Ancient and Modern Russia," one of the most enigmatic texts ever written by Karamzin. This memoir was never meant for publication, and its publication history was extremely complicated both before the Bolshevik Revolution, because of its incredibly fierce criticism of Russia's monarchs, and after it, because of its defense of absolutism and serfdom. "Some censors were afraid because Karamzin's opinions were 'daring,' others, because they were 'reactionary,' the result was the same," writes Lotman (*Karamzin,* 588).

The text of the memoir was discovered in 1834. Pushkin tried to publish excerpts of it in his magazine but could not obtain permission to do so.[16] Later it was published abroad and in strictly academic publications specially prohibited from general circulation. In the Soviet era the censors banned it several times, most recently the censors prevented its inclusion in the two-volume edition of Karamzin's works that appeared in 1984.[17]

Thus for generations of Soviet readers, the memoir became an example of prerevolutionary samizdat, *tamizdat,* or a publication with a DSP sign (*dlia sluzhebnovo pol'zovania,* for business use only). Coincidentally, the only academic publication of the text was prepared by Richard Pipes, who was reputed to be a determined *antisovetchik* and the author of the famous "empire of evil" phrase articulated by President Reagan.[18] (Pipes later disclaimed authorship.) A text that attracted the attention of such an ideological enemy must certainly be of extraordinary merit. And the Russian public believed in the incredible force of the hidden word. The publication history of Bulgakov's *Master and Margarita* and its most famous catch phrase, "Manuscripts don't burn," was another example of the intensity of these beliefs.

Lotman's article served as a preface to the first official Soviet edition of the "Memoir" in the semipopular magazine *Literaturnaia ucheba* (no. 4, 1988), which then had an impressive print run of over fifty thousand copies. Such unbelievable figures were characteristic of late perestroika. (Soon after the reforms of 1992 they plummeted.) In his argument Lotman does not avoid addressing the most difficult and dramatic problem concerning the "Memoir," Karamzin's staunch defense of such obvious social evils of Russian life as absolutism and serfdom and his fierce opposition to the extremely cautious and halfhearted reforms of these institutions planned by the emperor and his state secretary and right-hand man, Mikhail Speransky.

However, Lotman interprets Karamzin's attitude toward reforms not so much in political as in moral terms, viewing it as a consequence of utter disillusionment on the part of the memoirist, who was convinced in advance that all plans would end in yet another bout of bureaucratic frenzy. "Karamzin evaluates the reformist activities in light of the entire tradition of government reforms in Russia after Peter I," writes Lotman. "All of them had one thing in common. Not a single one of the legislative projects was completed; not a single one became a reality in the political life of the country. For decades there were many activities in which tsars and dignitaries participated, committees and commissions were organized, careers were made and awards given, public hopes and fears emerged. *And nothing was done.* This was a starting point for the skepticism that defined Karamzin's attitude toward government reforms" (*Karamzin*, 591–92).

This statement obviously fails to give enough credit to eighteenth-century reforms, especially those of Elizabeth and Catherine II.[19] Moreover, it seems to make a totally unsubstantiated claim that, had Karamzin believed in the success of reforms, he would have probably approved of them. Lotman here is mainly interested in two possible types of positioning vis-à-vis the authorities. One is exemplified by Speransky: "Speransky had two souls: he was Marquis de Poza, who aspired to capture the will and the heart of the tyrant and to transform him into his tool; and he was a disciplined bureaucrat, skillfully translating the ideas of his boss into smooth official language. Speransky knew how to bow; he put Alexander's thoughts in paragraphs" (*Karamzin*, 593). Karamzin embodied a very different model. "In 1811 Karamzin had an exceptional opportunity: to address the tsar personally, without censorship or other limitations inevitable in publication, and to disclose his views about the activities of the monarch as the head of state in general. It is hard to find in history a person who would use such an opportunity to voice as many bitter truths" (591).

It is noteworthy that Karamzin, too, is described as a sort of Marquis de Poza, who in Schiller's tragedy *Don Carlos* risks his neck in telling the truth to the monarch. Lotman was fascinated by this character and its historical significance. In other articles he used it to explain enigmatic details in biographies of Radischev and Chaadaev, who, according to Lotman, were trying to follow the pattern delineated by Schiller ("The Decembrist in Daily Life," 115–19; and "Iz kommentariev k *Puteshestviiu*," 127–28).

But unlike Speransky, Karamzin had most definitely only one soul. And again unlike Speransky, who for all his readiness to bow before the strong was finally exiled and humiliated, Karamzin's behavior brought him personal victory: "One can wonder at Karamzin's unprecedented courage. In choosing this style of relations with the tsar, he was following his straightforward and noble nature. But it proved tactically to be the best way to gain Alexander's trust. . . . With the instinct of a great soul, Karamzin chose the only reasonable position: complete personal independence, no demands for himself, and unquestionable straightforwardness in his opinions. This often insulted the tsar . . . but he could never deny Karamzin his respect and in a way silently gave him the authority to speak not as a courtier but as the voice of history" (*Karamzin*, 599).

This interpretation seems highly biased, to say the least, if we look at it in the context of data already available to nineteenth-century historians such as M. Korf and A. Pypin. "The Memoir on Ancient and Modern Russia" was not so much a solitary and heroic gesture as part of a calculated and unscrupulous intrigue against Speransky, initiated by the small court of Alexander's younger sister, Grand Duchesse Catherine Pavlovna, in Tver.[20] Catherine urged Karamzin to write the memoir and even provided him with some unpublished projects by Speransky, given to her by her brother. At the same time the grand duchess also sent Alexander the "Memoir on Martinists" written by her close associate and Karamzin's friend F. Rostopchin, in which the author claimed to have discovered a Masonic conspiracy in Russia coordinated by Speransky and inspired by Napoleon.[21] It is highly probable that a series of memoranda written by Joseph de Maistre condemning Speransky also received tacit approval from the Tver court.[22]

Willingly or not, Karamzin became a participant in this game. Before the decisive meeting with the tsar in Tver, he wrote about Catherine Pavlovna and her family with great warmth and tenderness in his letters and even characterized his visits to Tver as "one of the greatest delights of [his] life." However, after Catherine submitted his manuscript to the emperor, he wrote with some irritation to the same correspondent that he did not want to travel to Tver again.[23] He probably realized that he had been used against his will.

It is worth noting that Lotman's article was not an academic enterprise but a preface to the publication of a text intended for a popular magazine. The genre allowed the author to become much more involved emotionally than would have been possible in a more conventional work. The opposition between Karamzin and Speransky as modeled by Lotman becomes here a mythological duel between an independent intellectual and a "liberal" bureaucrat. Lotman disliked Speransky in his capacity as court reformer in exactly the same way freethinking intellectuals of the 1960s and 1970s despised their former friends who joined the Communist Party, as they explained, to change the system from within. It was common wisdom that doing so was totally impossible and that integration into the system led only to personal moral degradation. Such rationalizations were generally considered to be a hypocritical disguise for careeristic and pecuniary aspirations. Karamzin provided a historical model for an alternative behavior:

> Why did Karamzin choose such a dangerous way?
>
> The first reason lies in his belief that the personal dignity of a man constitutes not only his personal virtue but also his duty and tribute to the history of his native country. Later when Karamzin was pressed to visit Arakcheev, he wrote to his wife that doing so would be a betrayal of his duty to his own moral dignity. Self-respect is a duty to "my heart, beloved wife, children, Russia and humanity." To say that one's own dignity is a duty to Russia and humanity was possible because in Karamzin's worldview (as in Pushkin's in the 1830s and later in Tolstoy's) personal dignity served as a main alternative to bureaucratic rule. . . .
>
> But there was another reason as well. Karamzin spoke with the tsar not only as a man who had reached complete inner freedom but also as a historian. . . . A historian speaks about contemporary events with the impartiality of future generations. . . . He is the one who makes his contemporaries hear what these later generations will say about them This is his civil duty. (*Karamzin*, 598)

Lotman had never stated his moral and political ideal more straightforwardly and completely as he did in this brief, popular article written late in his life. Constrained neither by the requirements of academic rigor nor by censorship, he could speak with his full voice. Evident contradictions between his schema and facts well known to him testify to the strength of his moral passion. In a way he spoke on behalf of an entire generation.

Lotman's article was published in late 1988, the happiest year of perestroika, during the short period of truce between party reformers and the liberal intelligentsia who aspired to give moral and intellectual directions to the course of reforms. Shortly afterward, in May 1989, Gorbachev, the ultimate embodiment of a progressively minded apparatchik who strove to reform the system from within after decades of bowing to party elders, and Sakharov, the symbol of moral resistance to the Soviet regime, clashed at the First Congress of the People's Deputies. Sakharov died later in the year, and since then the role of former dissidents and freethinking intellectuals in the process of change began to erode. The real breakthrough was achieved a couple of years later by the renegade apparatchik Yeltsin and the group of young technocratic economists surrounding him. Needless to say, these developments proved to be completely contrary to the worldview espoused by Lotman and the social strata he represented.

In Lotman's personal life these years were tragic. In 1989 he suffered a stroke and shortly after that his wife died. After a partial recovery, he spent his remaining years dictating his last theoretical and philosophical works and heroically trying to overcome physical weakness and despair.[24] He felt disengaged from the enormous political catastrophes taking place around him. In a letter written in December 1992 to one of his closest friends, he spoke about a colleague whom both of them had known since their youth: "Our fate with Iakov Semenovich [Iakov Bilinkis, a literary historian] was to switch places constantly. Now I think about eternity and he about politics. Give him my regards and tell him that politics will do without us and we without it" (*Pisma*, 359). The following year he died.

Karamzin's popularity in a way followed the same pattern. After 1991 it gradually declined. When published, both *The Memoir of Ancient and Modern Russia* and *The History of the Russian State* proved to be not revelations that could alter the course of national history but rather outdated and boring examples of political thought and historical narrative of the early nineteenth century, important and interesting for specialists but hardly so outside that narrow circle. The scholarly edition of the *History* appeared with great pomp in the late 1980s but ended with the fifth volume (out of twelve). Each volume had a smaller print run than the previous one, and many copies still remain unsold. The *Memoir,* also republished in a separate edition in 1991, does not seem to attract much scholarly or public attention. Karamzin's myth obviously faded, and nowadays it is the status that Lotman continues to enjoy in Russian culture that supports it for the most part. However, Lotman's attempt to rewrite Russian history is nonetheless fascinating as one of the most socially influential and intellectually stimulating enterprises in the history of Russian academia.

## Notes

1. B. N. Yeltsin, "Privetstvennoe pismo," in *Venok Karamzinu* (Moscow: "Academia," 1992), 8. Unless otherwise noted, translations are mine.

2. See V. I. Lenin, "Pamiati Gertsena," *Polnoe sobranie sochinenii,* vol. 21 (Moscow: Gospolitizdat, 1961), 261.

3. Ibid.

4. A. A. Galich, "Peterburgskii Romans," *Pokolenie obrechennyh* (Frankfurt am Main: Possev-Verlag, 1975), 15.

5. Ibid., 13.

6. Iu. M. Lotman, "Evoliutsiia mirovozzreniia Karamzina (1783–1803)," *Uchenye zapiski Tartuskogo gos. universiteta* 51 (1957): 122–166 [also in Lotman, *Karamzin,* 312–48]; "Puti razvitiia russkoi prozy 1800–1810-kh gg.," *Uchenye zapiski Tartuskogo gos. universiteta* 104 (1961): 3–57 [also in Lotman, *Karamzin,* 349–417].

7. V. E. Vatsuro, "Podvig chestnogo cheloveka," in *Promethei,* vol. 5 (Moscow: Molodaia Gvardia, 1968).

8. Ibid., 34.

9. V. E. Vatsuro and M. I. Gillelson, *Skvoz' umstvennye plotiny* (Moscow: Kniga, 1972). The book was republished in 1986, the first year of perestroika. On the publication history of the book, see A. E. Milchin, "Pis'mo izdateliu," *Novoe literaturnoe obozrenine* 44 (2000): 444–45.

10. N. Ia. Eidelman, *Poslednii Letopisets* (Moscow: Kniga, 1983). This biography was preceded by E. V. Osetrov, *Tri zhizni Karamzina* (Moscow: Molodaia Gvardia, 1985), but this work was originally published in a provincial magazine, *Volga* 6–7 (1982). Of little literary or scholarly merit, it did not attract significant attention.

11. Eidelman, *Poslednii Letopisets,* 160.

12. Ibid.

13. Ibid., 160.

14. A. I. Solzhenitsyn, *The Oak and the Calf* (New York: Harper & Row, 1980), 436–37.

15. N. M. Karamzin, *Neizdannye sochinenia i perepiska,* pt. 1 (St. Petersburg: V Tip. N. Tiblena, 1862), 11–12.

16. See A. G. Tartakovskii, *Russkaia memoiristika i istoricheskoe soznanie XIX veka* (Moscow: Arkheograficheskii proekt, 1997).

17. N. M. Karamzin, *Sochinenia,* vols. 1–2 (Leningrad: Khudozhestvennaia Literatura, 1984).

18. Richard Pipes, *Karamzin's Memoir on Ancient and Modern Russia: A Translation and Analysis* (Cambridge, Mass.: Harvard University Press, 1959). A Russian version also prepared by Pipes appeared the same year.

19. A. B. Kamenskii, *Ot Petra I do Pavla I. Reformy v Rossii: Opyt tselostnogo analiza* (Moscow: RGGU, 1999).

20. See M. A. Korf, *Zhizn' grafa Speranskovo,* vols. 1–2 (St. Petersburg, 1861); A. N. Pypin, *Obshchestvennoe dvizhenie v Rossii pri Alexandre I* (St. Petersburg, 1900).

21. F. V. Rostopchin, "Zapiska o martinistakh, predstavlennaia v 1811 godu grafom Rostopchinym velikoi kniagine Ekaterine Pavlovne," *Russkii Arhiv* 9 (1875): 80–81.

22. See: Alexander M. Martin, *Romantics, Reformers, Reactionaries: Russian Conservative Thought and Politics in the Reign of Alexander I* (DeKalb: Northern Illinois University Press, 1997).

23. N. M. Karamzin, *Pis'ma k I. I. Dmitrievu* (St. Petersburg, 1866), 137, 140. See Pipes, *Karamzin's Memoir,* 72–75.

24. Egorov, *Zhizn' i tvorchestvo Iu. M. Lotmana,* 213–37.

# ICONIC SELF-EXPRESSION

# 9

# Bipolar Asymmetry, Indeterminacy, and Creativity in Cinema

### HERBERT EAGLE

Two objectives have driven Yuri Lotman's work on cultural texts: (1) explaining the indeterminacy and multivalence of their meaning and (2) demonstrating their ability not only to transmit and preserve information but also to create new meaning. As early as his *Lectures on Structural Poetics* (1964), Lotman attempted, in the context of information theory, to prove that when a text uses two distinct codes (he had in mind normal verbal syntax *and* poetic correspondences based on rhythm and sound), it has increased informational capacity. But it was most clearly in his work on cinema that the notion of a *bipolar asymmetry of codes* (one conventional and the other iconic) as the crucial semiotic mechanism in art and culture emerged. The complex interaction of these codes in cinema gave Lotman insights he used to expand his analysis to all the arts and to both the synchronic and the diachronic aspects of what he came to call the *semiosphere*. Because film, in its constant interweaving of the conventional and the iconic, provides an exceptionally clear model of bipolar asymmetry, I propose to describe how Lotman's assertions with regard to indeterminacy and creativity play out in cinema, to illustrate them with respect to two extended examples, and to outline their relationship to film theory as it has developed in recent decades.

In his early works *Structure of the Artistic Text* (1970) and *Analysis of the Poetic Text* (1972), Lotman had followed his Russian formalist predecessors Iurii Tynianov and Roman Jakobson in systematically revealing the crucial role of patterning in verse (of features such as numbers of syllables, location of stresses, repetition of sounds, organization of grammatical features, and typographical layout); such patterning creates a rhythmic order based on which meanings are forced into juxtaposition and comparison, independent of their relationship in the syntax of sentences. Tynianov had stressed that the essence of verse structure lay in opposition between two systems: (1) the normal "syntactico-semantic" organization of language in which words build up larger meanings according to conventional linguistic rules; and (2) meanings implied by the segmentation into verse lines, where formal equivalences point to semantic relations. As he noted: "[B]etween words there arises a *relationship according to position*" (Tynianov's italics).[1] Lotman's restatement of this in *Analysis* drew attention to the indeterminate meaning created in poetry, genuinely new meaning because of the impossibility of capturing it in ordinary *natural* language:

> [A] *poem is a complexly constructed meaning.* This signifies that entering into the integral structure of a poem, the meaningful elements of a language are connected by a complex system of correlations, comparisons, and contrasts impossible in an ordinary language construct. This gives each element separately and the construction as a whole an absolutely unique semantic load. Words, sentences, and utterances, which in the grammatical structure are found in different positions, which are devoid of similar characteristics and, consequently, are non-comparable, prove in the artistic structure to be in positions of identity and antithesis and, consequently, comparable and contrastable. This reveals in them unexpected new semantic content impossible outside of poetry. (*Analysis*, 35, Lotman's italics)

Verse structure produces what might be called a *verbal topology* in which words are connected to one another in a rhythmic space. In this sense the poem is not only a chain of words building up into a meaning syntactically but also at the same time a *word picture* that must be apprehended as a single integral sign, a complex icon comprehensible as a web of implied similarities and/or differences. Here Lotman verges on his later stress on bipolar asymmetry; in *Structure* he says: "Verbal art begins with an attempt to overcome the fundamental property of the word as a linguistic sign—the arbitrariness of the connection between the planes of expression and content; it constructs a verbal artistic model according to the iconic principle, as in the fine arts. This is not accidental, but organically linked to the use of signs in human culture" (55).

In approaching cinema as an art, Lotman faced a problem opposite to that encountered in his analysis of verse. That poetry was made up of natural language was self-evident; its iconicity had to be explored. Cinema, on the other hand, was widely regarded as iconic. Indeed, not only did a filmed action, as a visual signifier, resemble what it signified (thus making the sign an icon), but such a signifier was also an index (a signifier that is existentially connected to what it signifies), inasmuch as it could be considered an automatic recording, linked to the event itself via optics and chemistry. Showing that film also conveyed meaning through conventional signs was a more demanding task, as was demonstrating that in cinema meaning was not simply denotative, not univalent, but just as complexly multivalent, indeterminate, and creative as in poetry. Cinema's iconicity had been traditionally thought of in terms of its realism, its ability to capture authentic life by reproducing it in a very direct way; this property was not regarded as a feature that promoted ambiguity, since photographic reproduction, seemingly automatic, appeared to be limited in its capacity to create new meaning. In *Semiotics of Cinema* (1973) and in *Dialog s ekranom* (1994), the latter coauthored with the film historian and semiotician Yuri Tsivian, Lotman stresses the opposite, cinema's escape from mere depiction.

Here again, as in the case of poetry, the prior work of Russian formalists proved useful to Lotman: "When Iu. N. Tynianov in his works on the theory of poetic language advanced the idea of the 'compactness of the poetic line'—whose essence was that in the poetic verse the sense of a word goes beyond its typographic boundaries and spreads over the verse, 'infecting' surrounding words—this was that very same montage of words which in cinema was expressed as the montage of shots" (*Dialog s ekranom*, 23, my translation). Shots in a montage sequence are thus "deformed" and take on new meaning because of the relative nature of visual properties of each shot in comparison to adjacent shots. *Differentiation* between shots is the key concept in Tynianov's theory of cinema.[2] Sergei Eisenstein would, a few years later, term this the *collision* of shots.

Lotman expands this argument, emphasizing the conflict between the iconic and the conventional dimensions of the film medium's semiotic system. The shot brings measurability and discreteness into cinematic language; it interrupts normal spatial and temporal continuity and replaces it with a conventional cinematic syntax with its own developing rules for how the spaces and times of a series of shots are to be understood. "The shot acquires the kind of freedom inherent in the word. It can be isolated, combined with other shots according to semantic, rather than natural affinities and groupings, or it can be used in a figurative—metaphoric and metonymic—sense" (*Semiotics of Cinema*, 23). Paradigmatic potentialities exist in cinema in two distinct ways: according to the semantic level (the same referent is repeated, but in different stylistic modalities—size, camera angle, lighting, for example) and according to stylistic modality (the same distinctive feature of style occurs in the visual treatment of a series of different referents). Lotman perceptively argues that any stylistic feature of cinema can become meaningful: "Thus, everything that can be done in a minimum of two ways can become an element of cinema language, everything that gives the director the freedom to choose one solution or another and the viewer the ability to understand why a particular choice was made" (*Dialog s ekranom*, 26, my translation). There will be a most common variant of a stylistic feature, which Lotman terms *unmarked*, and other variants that are *marked* (the close-up instead of an unmarked medium shot; a skewed camera angle; slow motion or fast motion instead of normal motion; somewhat blurred, so-called soft focus instead of the usual sharp focus; the presence of black-and-white shots in a color film, or the reverse). Such oppositions become the basis of conventional signs with repeated use within a corpus of films, even when the earliest manifestations have an iconic basis. Thus, the close-up indicates importance and frequently metaphoric or metonymic meaning (no longer literal closeness or careful attention of an observer to an object); black-and-white in a color film signals a memory, dream, hallucination, or simply a temporal flashback; soft focus evokes tender emotions, and so on (*Semiotics of Cinema*, 32–33; *Dialog s ekranom*, 21). Thus, most film images are not exclusively iconic but carry conventional meanings as well. "A network of meaning is superimposed on what we see. Knowing that we are watching . . . a string of signs, we necessarily disassemble the flow of visual impressions into meaningful elements" (*Semiotics of Cinema*, 25).

Not only are the semantic and stylistic features of shots material for the construction of conventional signs, but they also can be used to create tropes: "The image automatically becomes a carrier of *cinematic information* precisely because of the montage of two internally conflicting visual images which together become an iconic sign of some third concept which is not merely the sum of the first two. *Cinematic meaning is meaning expressed by the resources of cinematic language, and it is impossible outside that language"* (*Semiotics of Cinema*, 42, Lotman's italics). As in poetry the visual text is decomposed into "a collection of structurally assembled differential features which easily lend themselves to comparison and contrast" (43). On the basis of juxtaposition of two different images, a new icon is formed, one whose meaning is generally multivalent and ambiguous. And, of course, in a film many more than two images are juxtaposed because of visual comparisons and contrasts on many levels: "Every time an element of film—a gesture, a pose, an event, an entire shot, a group of shots—enters into a semantic relationship with another such element, we are dealing with montage. . . . The second montage element must vividly recall to our memory the image of the first and enter with it into complex semantic relationships" (*Dialog s ekranom*, 24, my translation). Hence the meaning of the resulting integral sign, the film, is quite complex.

Lotman's model is an elaboration of Eisenstein's notion of collision montage. Eisenstein likened the juxtaposition of two shots to the superimposition of two ideograms in Chinese or Japanese writing; the resultant meaning is a metaphorical interpretation of the combination (one of Eisenstein's examples is the combination of the ideograms for "heart" and "knife" to yield the ideogram for "sorrow").[3] But whereas Eisenstein in the 1920s believed that such montage collisions could be calculated and planned to produce a desired effect, Lotman stresses their openness to a variety of interpretations (depending on the codes within the receiver of the message). Here he is closer to some of Eisenstein's later formulations, which pointed toward certain meanings as incapable of adequate translation, with cinema constituting a combination of "verbal-logical" and "image-sensual" thinking. Eisenstein's description of his montage sketches as a form of inner speech captures his notion: "Like thought, they would sometimes proceed with visual images. With sound. Synchronized or non-synchronized. Then as sounds. Formless. Or with sound-images, with objectively representational sounds. . . . Then suddenly, definite intellectually formulated words."[4] In Lotman's more analytical language: "The worlds of iconic and conventional signs do not simply coexist, they are in constant interaction, in continual material crossover and repulsion. The process of their mutual transfer is one of the essential aspects of cultural comprehension of the world by humans employing signs" (*Semiotics of Cinema*, 7).

Iconism in cinema, as in poetry, is not limited to the communication of individual images. Much more important is the *correlation* of images with one another and their interaction with meanings provided through conventional sign systems. The complex correlation of images in a film through formal stylistic means implies semantic homologies between the correlated signs, but it does not specify (as in a conventional sign system) what exactly these homologies mean. We have a network of implied metaphors subject to different possible interpretations. This network constitutes a composite icon, a unitary sign whose meaning cannot be translated into a syntactic chain of well-defined signs in a conventional language. Nonetheless, conventional sign systems within the text have an effect on the interpretation of the iconic sign, which constitutes the text as a whole. They may encourage certain implications of the iconic sign, or they may contradict them. In the latter case the cinematic text is as paradoxical in its meaning as it is multivalent.

Lotman's views on the mutual interpenetration of the iconic and the conventional provide important insights with respect to the semiotics of cinema elaborated in the West in the late 1960s and early 1970s by theoreticians such as Christian Metz, Umberto Eco, and Peter Wollen.[5] These theoreticians sought to apply to the cinema the Saussurean model of a semiotic system. In Saussure's projected discipline of semiology, sign systems in culture were to be explored by analogy to the way that structural linguistics approached natural language; this led to attempts to understand film language in terms of conventional signs. For example, Eco attempted to reveal the conventional underpinnings of film's apparent iconism, whereas Metz bracketed off cinema's iconic signs as indecomposable and then turned to elaborating the conventions at work in the construction of larger syntactic units. Metz noted that cinematic signs lacked the *double articulation* of natural languages: the presence of minimal formal units, such as *phonemes* (differentiable but possessing no fixed meaning), out of whose combinations minimal units of meaning, *morphemes,* are created. Even the smallest compositional units, such as individual film frames or objects within those frames, always already have some iconic meaning. Indeed, the decomposition of shots into smaller units of which they consist (objects, relative distances, movements, and so on) seems to fly in the face of spectators' apprehension of the shot as an iconic representation of an event taken as a whole. Wollen stressed cinema's indexicality and iconicity as essential qualities but claimed that all three aspects of the sign identified by the philosopher-semiotician C. S. Peirce (index, icon, conventional symbol) played a role in cinema's complex sign system. But Wollen proposed no comprehensive system to explain the mutual interaction of these three kinds of semiotic processes.

The tendency to champion either conventional or iconic language was sometimes discussed as a conflict between the film theory and practice of Sergei Eisenstein and the critical preferences of André Bazin.[6] As we have noted, Eisenstein at times treated the shot as a minimal unit, akin to a word or even a morpheme, which could be collided with the next shot to yield, metaphorically, a new, more abstract meaning. Bazin, on the other hand, claimed that montage (film editing) went against the grain of the medium's true potential to convey extensive episodes of life in an authentic way; instead, Bazin favored film styles that used shots of long duration and shots that captured space in its depth. For the theoreticians of the 1960s and 1970s, this controversy pointed both to the presence of conventional sign structures and to a seemingly undeniable iconicity. But how to combine the two in a systematic treatment of cinema as a language? And how to take account of the artistic (that is, creative) nature of this language? Metz concluded that film was not a language in the Saussurean sense, because the shot appeared to be an indecomposable unit, one that was already analogous to a sentence rather than to a word. Cinema did possess certain syntactic conventions for linking its sentencelike semantic units (the shots) into more extended units; Metz attempted to create a taxonomy of such larger units, which he termed the "Grand Syntagmatique." But Metz's influential analysis left out the important role of stylistic variables such as camera distance, camera angle, lighting, colors, soundtrack music, and the like.

Lotman's approach suggests a more comprehensive way out of the dilemma by describing the coexistence of iconic and conventional sign processes at different levels of integration of meaning within the filmic text. Iconicity is the primary means for conveying actions and the environments in which they occur, but the combination of such actions to form a narrative that has coherence spatially, temporally, and causally is accomplished through editing strategies that have come to be governed by conventional norms. Cinema does not possess units analogous to phonemes, but it does possess binary oppositions in the form of stylistic choices with respect to various features. *Marked* variants with respect to particular stylistic choices can, over time, develop conventional meanings. But this by no means exhausts the meaning-creating potential of the cinematic text. The images in its shots and the accompanying stylistic modalities, as distinctive features, make possible nonsyntactic correlations across the entire film, thus conveying ambiguous meanings through a *second* kind of iconicity comparable to that which functions in poetry.

In his discussion of the use of verbal texts within films, Lotman briefly mentions Andrzej Wajda's *Ashes and Diamonds* (1958) as a film in which an emblematic verbal text (from which the film takes its title) is seen as a faded inscription on a tombstone and then is recited, partly from memory, by the main character. To illustrate Lotman's concepts of conventionality and iconicity in continual crossover, let us consider this example in greater detail. The verbal text in question is a stanza by the Polish Romantic poet Cyprian Norwid that presents an image of a flaming hemp torch, violently flying apart as it burns; the stanza concludes: "Flaming, you know not if the flames bring freedom or death, consuming all that you most cherish; If only ashes will be left, and want, chaos and tempest shall engulf. . . . Or will the ashes hold the glory of a starlike diamond, the morning star of everlasting triumph." For Poles of Wajda's generation (who lived through the resubjugation of their nation by the Nazis and then by the Soviets after only two decades of freedom and independence), Norwid's stanza was taken as a metaphor for Poland's nineteenth-century struggles for liberation, rebellions that ended in martyrdom and futility, with the shining goal, independence, only an unrealized hope. The reading of these lines by the film's hero, Maciek, part of a brief dalliance with a pretty barmaid and having no bearing on his military-political mission, takes on immense signifying potential because of the film's visual imagery, within which it is set. Ultimately the meanings conveyed through more conventional use of film language are sharply juxtaposed against the essentially iconic meaning implied by the repetition of two sets of signs, one consisting of visual references to this stanza and the second consisting of images of the crucified Christ. Neither of these sets of images has anything to do with the film's plot in the conventional sense of that word. They are often in the background of shots or are sketched iconically rather than explicitly; only Norwid's embedded verbal poem points the viewer toward these visual icons and encourages their interpretation.

From the standpoint of its conventional cinematic codes, *Ashes and Diamonds* presents a sequence of actions that take place over a roughly fifteen-hour period and seemingly demonstrate the cynicism, the confusion, and often the cruelty of the anti-Communist Home Army forces that are attempting to counter Communist influence through terrorism and assassinations; the Communist Poles, returning from Russia with the Red Army to help set up a postwar government, are shown, in contrast, to be selfless, dedicated, and deeply humane. Such a message about the relative merits of Communists and anti-Communists would be entirely expected in a Polish film made in 1958, in a Communist state-run film industry where scripts were vetted in preproduction and completed films were subject to censorship. Building on the basic iconism always involved in cinema at the level of depiction of actions, the syntagmatic norms of classical film narration (quite applicable to socialist realist films) result in relatively clear and unambiguous interpretations of events, linked by a conventional editing system that produces spatial and temporal contiguities, a logical chain of causes and effects for the events, and explicit, verbally expressed character motivations as the primary "causes." These motivations are typically expressed in dialogue, a second conventional syntagmatic system that augments the film syntax. In combination these two systems promote a logical understanding of the narrative similar to aspects of the syntax of realist prose.

Let me briefly summarize the story as it is presented in the film's conventional narrative syntax. Two members of the anti-Communist Home Army attempt to assassinate a local Communist Party secretary, Szczuka, and his assistant, Podgorski, by ambushing their jeep as it passes a rural chapel, but instead they mistakenly attack a jeep carrying two cement plant workers, Gawlik and Smolarski. They kill both men, with Maciek shooting Gawlik in the back repeatedly as he attempts to take refuge in the chapel. The assassins flee, and moments later Szczuka arrives on the scene in another jeep. He gives a brave, patriotic, and implicitly pro-Communist speech to workers who have by now surrounded the dead bodies: "I'd be a bad communist if I tried to comfort you as if you were children. The end of the war doesn't mean the end of our fight . . . each one of us may be killed . . . any day. . . . Don't think I'm not grieved, because I know full well that these bullets were intended for me."[7] Monumental, low-angle shots are used to depict Szczuka, whereas Maciek had appeared to be a casual, crazed killer in the way he shot Gawlik repeatedly.

Maciek and Andrzej soon learn of their mistake, and Maciek books a room at the local hotel, the Monopol, waiting for another opportunity to carry out his mission. During the evening he flirts with the attractive barmaid, Krystyna; they make love in his room and then walk outside. Taking shelter from the rain in a bombed-out church, they come upon the verses from Norwid that I have cited and read them. Maciek regrets that he cannot pursue a love affair with Krystyna and live the normal life of a student; he hesitates in his plan, but when Andrzej appeals to his sense of honor, he resolves to carry out his mission. In the middle of the night, as Szczuka is going to see his son, who has just been arrested by the Polish security police (it turns out that Szczuka's son, who was raised by aristocratic relatives, is also in a Home Army unit), Maciek shoots and kills him. At dawn Maciek bids farewell to Krystyna in the hotel bar and prepares to hop a train out of the city, but at the railway station his behavior seems suspicious to security forces. He runs from them; they shoot at him, mortally wounding him. He escapes to a vast rubbish dump, where he dies, writhing in agony—"on the trash heap of history," as it were. His death seems to fulfill a curse uttered by Gawlik's fiancée when she first hears of her lover's murder; she cries out: "May they die a painful death." The death of the noble, brave Communist Szczuka is thus contrasted to the ignominious end of the anti-Communist assassin Maciek.

These are the meanings that a literally minded reader might get from the script, and presumably this was the way the film was understood by Communist censors when they approved its production. But the film's iconic signs suggest very different, even opposite, meanings. Images associated with fire are quite prominent even before Norwid's verses are read. When Maciek machine-guns Gawlik, not only do holes appear in his jacket, but these holes burst into flame. In the Monopol's bar Maciek lights a series of vodka glasses to commemorate his buddies who have died fighting in the Home Army's resistance against the Nazis. He lights two glasses for himself and for Andrzej as well, to the latter's dismay. Later, when Maciek twice runs into Szczuka casually in the hotel, the latter asks him for a light—and twice Maciek lights his cigarette. While in the church with Krystyna, Maciek accidentally comes upon the laid out bodies of his victims, Gawlik and Smolarski; votive candles burn on the altar above the bodies. When Maciek shoots Szczuka in the street, a burst of fireworks (people are celebrating the official end of World War II) seemingly erupts from his shoulder (the fireworks are some distance away, but in the composition of the shot it is almost as if a flaming torch grows from Szczuka's body).

The repeated occurrence of flames that either emanate from or are lit in commemoration of dead combatants in this ideological struggle make them *all*, Communists and anti-Communists alike, rhyme with the burning hemp torch in Norwid's poem. They are all victims of a terrible, tragic conflagration producing only "want, chaos and tempest." And what of the diamond in the poem (and, of course, in the film's title)? The hoped-for "morning star of everlasting triumph"? Krystyna is rhymed with images that suggest a diamond. In the smoky bar her blouse is the only patch of white in a series of shots. When Maciek recites the poem's final lines to her, she asks: "Who is the diamond?" He replies: "You are." When he comes to bid her farewell in the bar, minutes before he will die, she opens a transom and her image is bathed in light by the rising sun, so much so that she seems to be the source of the blinding light. What happens to this diamond? Maciek's death agony is intercut with shots of Krystyna, amid the smoke of the bar, being pulled into an off-key polonaise and then a lugubrious victory march by those opportunistic worthies of the town who are preparing to cooperate with the Communists who are coming to power. If Krystyna as the diamond is an icon for a free Poland, it is not to emerge from the smoke of post–World War II politics.

The many visual echoes of Norwid's poem in the film are augmented by the repeated appearance of crosses and of images of Christ in the background or the foreground of shots (these crucifixes and statues have nothing to do with the main action of the shot and none of the characters seems to notice them, nor are they commented on). The very first shot in the film is of the cross atop the small chapel near which Maciek and Andrzej lie in ambush (the camera pans down the church to reveal them). When we see Smolarski shot, lurching forward in his jeep, a wooden life-sized roadside Christ-on-the-cross occupies nearly half of the film frame in the immediate background. Moments later Gawlik's body, filled with bullets, rests against the chapel door, which now miraculously opens; he falls before a statue of a saint that stands behind the altar. In the scene immediately following Krystyna and Maciek's recitation of the Norwid verses, the couple walk in front of a large, inverted, partially burned crucifix looming in the foreground of the shot. Later, in the scenes of their deaths, both Szczuka and Maciek are visually disposed in such a way as to recall the crucified Christ. After he has been shot, Szczuka walks with arms outstretched toward Maciek and falls into his embrace (looking like Christ taken down from the cross). When

Maciek is mortally wounded, he hides briefly with his back against a T-shaped clothesline pole, his body covered by a sheet. He reaches around the sheet to touch his left side; a large bloody patch appears in the place where Christ was speared.

All these images suggest that the heroes, Maciek and Szczuka, and their surrogates (Gawlik and Smolarski) are all martyred Christs; whether Communists or anti-Communists, they die for Poland's eventual redemption. They are, at the same time, the burning hemp torch of Norwid's poem, to be destroyed in the name of an ideal that, in the film's visual answer to the verbal question in the poem, will not come as a result of their immolation. In 1958, when Wajda made the film, it was quite evident that no free and just Poland had emerged from the postwar struggles. *Ashes and Diamonds* would seem to confirm this in terms of an iconic web of images of universal conflagration and universal martyrdom, with no redemption. On the other hand, the film's conventional semiotic systems (in the sense of both the causal logic of classical narrative syntax and the explicit verbal texts included as dialogues) assert just the opposite—that Szczuka's work to establish a just and free Poland, understood as a Communist Poland, will ultimately bear fruit in spite of his heroic death, and that the violence carried out by Maciek represents a confused, misguided, and tragic effort to derail the inevitable progress toward a brighter future. Thus the meanings conveyed by the film's conventional and iconic sign systems, complexly embedded into each other in the flow of the text's signs, are not only different; they are very nearly opposite. This makes the film's "meaning" a complicated matter, indeterminate and fluctuating, because of the presence of two sign systems and the resultant messages, which cannot be combined in a logical way.

A more recent example of the intersecting nature of conventional and iconic sign structures can be found in Krzysztof Kieslowski's film trilogy *Three Colors: Blue, White, Red* (1993–94). Here stylistic modalities (the colors of objects within the frame) are used to imply a network of associations within the narratives of the three films, much as distinctive features in verbal language (the sounds that form rhymes) are used to produce an iconic web of associations in a poem. The films in Kieslowski's trilogy demonstrate Lotman's contention that marked stylistic features in cinema function in a manner similar to sound repetitions in verse. The film director used conventional signs (a verbal text) to assign meanings initially to the colors when he told interviewers that his film was inspired by the French flag and the motto of the French Revolution: "Blue, white, red: liberty, equality, fraternity. . . . Why not try to see . . . what our attitude to them is and how the three words liberty, equality and fraternity function today?—on a very human, intimate and personal plane and not a philosophical let alone a political or social one."[8]

All three films construct narratives in accordance with the conventional editing norms of classical cinema. However, the three colors of the title are foregrounded to a heightened degree within the film's shots so that in addition to the narrative of actions, *narration in the predicate*, there is a *narration in the nominative* (a narration that advances through the development of a nominal category, here a color, through its recurrences and alternations). As Lotman observes: "Narration can result from the joining of a series of shots showing different objects, or a series in which one object alters modalities" (*Semiotics of Cinema*, 59). Narration in the predicate is a matter of combining different things (once selected) into a chain of objects and actions that form a story. But in Kieslowski's trilogy the next sign in the text is *also* determined by the process of selecting one or another color.

In the trilogy's first film, *Blue*, an automobile accident causes the death of Julie de Courcy's world-famous composer husband, Patrice, and her nine-year-old daughter, Anna. To escape the pain of these deaths, Julie decides to abandon her own work as a composer (she is, it seems, the co-composer of her husband's new *Symphony for the Unification of Europe*), sell the family's country home, and move to a Paris apartment, where she plans to live, as much as possible, unconnected from other people (including her husband's collaborator, Olivier, who is in love with her), because she does not want to bear ever again the pain of the loss of loved ones. Quite coincidentally, against her best intentions, she becomes involved in the life of one of her neighbors, a call girl and stripper named Lucille. This connection, once again accidentally, leads to her discovery of the existence of her husband's mistress, Sandrine, to a reconciliation with her own grief and a reinvolvement in the world, and to her renewed capacity for love.

Kieslowski depresses the role of conscious character motivation in the film's narrative, however, through a deliberately foregrounded use of coincidence—thus depriving the text of what would be a major axis of coherence in the conventional system of narrative cinema. Julie's conscious motivations and deliberate actions are not what lead to the concluding events, which to a large extent appear at the end of the film in an unexpected and unmotivated (from the viewpoint of classical narrative cinema) way. Although the story tells us that life's events are unpredictable, arbitrary, mysterious, and perhaps absurd, a competing system of signs (the colors and the meanings that become associated with them through repetition) assert something quite different—that life unfolds in the context of certain immutable oppositions. As Kieslowski notes: "The colour is not decorative, it plays a dramaturgic role. The colour means something."[9]

As is often said of poetry, in *Blue, White, Red* we are invited to decode a message in a language we do not know. We are presented with signifiers and even with presumed "signifieds" (blue = liberty; white = equality; red = fraternity), but what kind of "liberty," what kind of "equality," what kind of "fraternity" is meant? These words are also, in their turn, only conventional signs, and the film redefines them through its images of events. Blue as an iconic sign gathers all the objects in the film and all the associated actions that are marked with the color blue. The meaning of blue cannot be reduced to a conventional sign in the film; instead it is a set of individual iconic signs formed into a larger composite icon.

As Julie prepares her home for sale, she refuses to accept from Olivier a blue folder containing some of her husband's letters and some photographs. She orders the "blue room" cleared of all furniture except for a mattress. But, seemingly inadvertently, a mobile made of blue glass beads is left hanging in the room. Julie is drawn to these beads and caresses them as if they were her loved ones. Thus, in its first marked occurrences, the color blue attaches to two nearly opposite semes: emptiness and isolation, on the one hand, and powerful connection to other human beings, on the other. When Julie moves to a Paris apartment to escape all contact with others, she nonetheless takes this precious blue mobile with her.

Another blue object that functions in a similar way is a blue foil lollypop wrapper, which had appeared in isolation, rippling in the window, in the film's second shot, where its motivation is entirely unclear. Only in the third shot do we see Julie's daughter, Anna, holding this blue foil wrapper out of the window of the moving car. Moments later the car will crash and she will die. Later in the film, when Julie accidentally comes across another such blue-foil-wrapped lollypop in her handbag, she devours it passionately, as if through some transubstantiation she could physically experience her daughter's touch again. Whereas the blues of the beaded mobile and the lollypop foil evoke memory, connection, and communion, the blues of the empty room and later of a swimming pool where Julie goes to swim and almost attempts suicide evoke isolation and oblivion. If this is liberty, it is a liberty Kieslowski causes us to reconsider in a more complicated way because of the complex of iconic imagery associated with it. Also when the color blue occurs in the film, it is accompanied on the soundtrack by strains of the *Symphony for the Unification of Europe,* which we come to believe was composed by Patrice and Julie together. Thus the color's meaning as communion is reinforced by the music even as, in the story, Julie attempts to disavow any connection with it and refuses to work on it (she throws it into a garbage truck's compactor).

The other two colors in the film trilogy, white and red, play a crucial role in the resolution of *Blue,* and their occurrences anticipate the meanings with which they will be associated in the subsequent two films, *White* and *Red.* White is the color of the hospital room where Julie first attempts suicide by swallowing a handful of white pills. Here white is linked to complete annihilation, death, but also to some absolute that may lie beyond death, which is suggested when the screen goes almost entirely white. White is also the predominant color of the sheet music for the symphony, which in heralding the unification of Europe suggests the creation of a utopian future. Thus, white appears both as an all-encompassing ideal and as nothingness (and these are precisely the semes that are developed through this color in the trilogy's second film). The color red becomes associated with anger, blood, sexual passion, and jealousy—and, conversely, with altruism and compassion. In a rage against the suffering she has had to bear, Julie hurls the white sheet music of the symphony into the garbage truck's red trash compactor. As she walks alongside a stone wall, she rubs her knuckles against it until they bleed. Julie is drawn into the life of her new neighbor Lucille, a life filled with anger and pain, all also heavily suffused with red: the red of the neon signs of nightclubs and strip joints. This is also a world of raw physical passion and sexual energy. But after Julie rouses herself to rescue Lucille in the middle of the night and immerses herself in this red world, her life begins to change. Red objects (previously entirely absent in the shots of her everyday life) now begin to appear with regularity: red flowers, a red coat, a red sign, a red car. In this world of increasing reds, Julie learns of the existence of her husband's mistress, Sandrine, and of her husband's child, whom Sandrine is bearing. In a remarkable denouement the color red marks her journey from jealousy and passion *(eros)* to compassion *(agape)*.

Space here does not allow for a full analysis of the ways that white and red appear in the trilogy's other two films, which I have provided elsewhere.[10] What is important about the highly complex use of these three primary colors in the films, however, is that they form an iconic representation of crucial forces in human life that cannot possibly be rendered in the syntax of conventional verbal language. We do not have a logical progression of signs leading to a unique meaning; we have only a spatio-temporal array of signifiers and actions associated with them, an *icon* of life. All three stories have resolutions in terms of their plots, but in fact these resolutions do not provide clear answers if they are taken alone. Only in conjunction with the films' iconic web do they take on meaning, but it is a meaning that is neither univalent nor completely comprehensible in purely verbal terms.

Beyond insisting on the creation of new meanings in artistic texts through the bipolar asymmetry of conventional and iconic semiosis, Lotman also insists on this asymmetry as the key to creative thought in the semiosphere, the universe of differing and evolving semiotic systems in a culture: "The structure of the semiosphere is asymmetrical. Asymmetry finds expression in the currents of internal translations with which the whole density of the semiosphere is permeated. . . . And since in the majority of cases the different languages of the semiosphere are semiotically asymmetrical, i.e., they do not have mutual semantic correspondences, then the whole semiosphere can be regarded as a generator of information" (*Universe of the Mind,* 127).

For Lotman the struggle to negotiate meaning within cultures, both in terms of evolution and of conflict between meanings "inside" and "outside" a culture's system, is often played out in terms of the dominance of conventional versus iconic sign systems. At the center of a culture he finds a predominance of conventions and norms, in a system possessing a metastructural self-description. Beyond the boundaries of the culture lie other systems and protosystems that can be apprehended only iconically, because their terms have no conventional translation in the language of the center. The creative collision of these different systems drives the evolution of culture (*Universe of the Mind,* 128–42).

Lotman's observations about the role of bipolar asymmetry and interdeterminacy in the functioning of the semiosphere provide a useful model for understanding the debates in film theory in the last quarter of the twentieth century. Although no film theory can be said to have provided a full description of conventions and norms that would have covered all film practice, a fusion of linguistic (Saussure), formalist (Russian formalists, Eisenstein), structuralist (Prague School, Lévi-Strauss), and the more recent semiotic approaches themselves, combined with the neo-formalist, cognitivist, and historical understandings advanced by David Bordwell among others, have approached a system possessing metastructural self-description.[11] A logical systematization of ideas about cinematic practices and techniques, audience reception, and diachronic development was in progress. While not indifferent to the possibility that psychoanalytic and ideological factors play a significant role in cinematic art, this neo-formalist/cognitivist approach did not privilege such factors over what it implicitly took to be more universal and more verifiable facts about human cognitive and semiotic proclivities. The new theoretical paradigms that emerged in the mid-1970s and which arguably dominated scholarly discussion and publication throughout much of the subsequent period insisted precisely on these subconscious or ideologically masked dimensions.

According to Lotman a relatively well-defined and codified semiotic system is eventually subject to incursions from other realms of the semiosphere, which provide the existing system with new codes and inevitably produce new meanings, because iconic elements of the new codes have no equivalent in the prevailing system; they are untranslatable and thus provide new information that could not have been generated in the established system alone. The psychoanalytic theories of Jacques Lacan and the neo-Marxist theories of Louis Althusser (both theories that pertain to all human subjectivity and culture and thus affect the semiosphere as a whole) were applied in many fields, but in the arts in particular, inasmuch as they focused attention on the shaping of human subjectivity by culture. The question of the nature of human subjectivity would clearly affect how we understand the creation of codes and the meanings they convey. In passing one might note that both Lacan's and Althusser's theories appealed to both conventional and iconic semiotic processes in their modeling of the subject and the world, as for example in Lacan's descriptions of the interactions between the imaginary, which provides the subject with iconic self-representations (as in the infant's so-called mirror stage), and the symbolic, which defines the subject in terms of the differences encoded in cultural systems, a process akin to conventional language. Althusser's theories absorbed and revised some of

Lacan's psychoanalytic approach to the subject and combined it with Marxist insights about the role of ideology as superstructure. Thus, in both types of models, culture defines and controls the subject through a complex interaction of iconic and symbolic codes.

When these broad theories were applied to cinema in particular, they yielded a variety of subtheories, all of which attempt to explain the interaction of two semiotic systems—the system of the subject (already in large degree constituted but always still in the process of being shaped) and the semiotic system perceived to reside in a particular film, a film genre, an entire approach to film art (such as classical Hollywood narrative film), or in the apparatus of cinema as a whole. The emerging approaches were diverse and mutually overlapping (poststructuralist, Frankfurt School, postmodernist, feminist, multiculturalist), and all contributed to the formation of what is now called cultural studies. Under their influence particular branches of film studies turned to questions of how notions about gender, class, race and ethnicity, and sexual orientation are encoded and/or resisted in filmic texts, and how such codes relate to the political and economic organization of the world and questions of power within it. Often what was presented as proof of the validity of a particular theory was its ability to provide a new interpretation of a film or a set of films. These procedures have been criticized by proponents of the cognitivist approach as circular and merely analogical (rather than causal), with films being interpreted in such a way as to provide instances of the master theories. Furthermore, it is argued, one should not rely heavily on psychoanalytic models of subconscious behavior when the predictive value of such models is still in question.[12] On the other hand, what has occurred in film theory over the last few decades fits Lotman's description of the semiosphere very well. As he often observed, the meaning of a text depends on the codes used to interpret it, and therefore works of art change in meaning with the semiotic codes of subsequent eras or different cultures. The new understandings, even if appreciated consciously only by those in possession of the new codes, doubtless constitute new information and information that the prior systems could not generate because it rests on new, complex iconic signs. Like the artistic text itself (whether a poem or a film), a semiotic system as a whole is a complex sign, internally coherent but, as a result of bipolar asymmetry, with its own inner contradictions and indeterminacies.

## Notes

1. Iurii Tynianov, *Problema stikhotvornogo iazyka: stat'i* (Moscow: Sov. pis., 1965), 71.

2. Iurii Tynianov, "On the Foundations of Cinema," in Herbert Eagle, ed. *Russian Formalist Film Theory* (Ann Arbor: Michigan Slavic Publications, 1981), 81–100.

3. Eisenstein's afterword to Kaufman's *Iaponskoe kino* (Moscow: Teakino-pechat', 1929) on Japanese cinema. The citation is from the better-known English translation, "The Cinematographic Principle and the Ideogram," in Sergei Eisenstein, *Film Form* (New York: Harcourt, Brace & World, 1949), 30–32.

4. Sergei Eisenstein, *The Film Sense* (New York: Harcourt, Brace & World, 1947), 105.

5. The works most relevant to our discussion are Christian Metz's *Essais sur la signification au cinéma* (Paris: Ed. Klincksieck, 1968) and *Langage et cinéma* (Paris: Larousse, 1971); Peter Wollen's *Signs and Meaning in the Cinema* (London: Secker & Warburg, 1969); and Umberto Eco's *Theory of Semiotics* (Bloomington: Indiana University Press, 1976).

6. Bazin's most influential writings can be found in his *What Is Cinema?* (Berkeley: University of California Press, 1967).

7. Andrzej Wajda, *The Wajda Trilogy: Ashes and Diamonds, Kanal, A Generation* (New York: Simon & Schuster, 1973), 170.

8. Krzysztof Kieslowski, *Kieslowski on Kieslowski* (London: Faber & Faber, 1993), 212.

9. Ibid., 222.

10. See Herbert Eagle, "Color in Kieslowski's Film Trilogy: *Blue, White, Red,*" *Periphery: Journal of Polish Affairs* 4–5 (1998–99): 138–45.

11. See, in particular, David Bordwell, *Narration in the Fiction Film* (Madison: University of Wisconsin Press, 1985); and David Bordwell, Janet Staiger, and Kristin Thompson, *The Classical Hollywood Cinema: Film Style and Mode of Production to 1960* (New York: Columbia University Press, 1985).

12. See David Bordwell, *Making Meaning: Inference and Rhetoric in the Interpretation of Cinema* (Cambridge, Mass.: Harvard University Press, 1989); and Noël Carroll, *Mystifying Movies: Fads and Fallacies in Contemporary Film Theory* (New York: Columbia University Press, 1988).

# Post-ing the Soviet Body as Tabula Phrasa and Spectacle

HELENA GOSCILO

The realm of culture is always the realm of symbolism.
Yuri Lotman, "Vvedenie"

The human body is always treated as an image of society, and . . .
there can be no natural way of considering the body that does
not involve at the same time a social dimension.
Mary Douglas, *Natural Symbols*

The body quickened through sexuality remains the object of
most intense interest for our culture.
Peter Brooks, *Body Work*

## Acculturation or Adulteration?
## Signs Stimulating Simulation

As the history of culture attests, few phenomena rival the body in
its extraordinary power to signify. Throughout centuries the body as
"'epistemophilic' project," to borrow Peter Brooks's handy term, has
engrossed anthropologists, doctors, psychoanalysts, artists, writers,
pornographers, advertisers, entrepreneurs, priests, lawyers, and police-
men.[1] Ceaselessly subjected to numerous modes of naturalization and
denaturalization, the body as (empirical) anatomical fact and (imaginative) cultural construction has functioned as the site of punishment and
adornment, as information center and obscure(d) focus of desire, as the
chief indispensable entity in rituals, and as perhaps the ultimate means of
self-expression. Unique in that it serves to integrate intensely individual

yet intensely collective levels of experience, the body defies final definition, exerts prodigious fascination, and stimulates impassioned but ever
inconclusive controversy.[2]

Whereas medicine anatomizes the body as a locus of experiment,
diagnosis, and verification—of evincive symptoms—art re/presents the
body as a mediated image of pleasurable contemplation, while pornography commodifies it as a fetishized object of (principally male) consumption.[3] Though sharing an assumption of the potential exteriority of
meaning—the primacy of visibility—these and countless other genres
and modes entertain divergent concepts of the body, concepts riddled
with paradoxes that have proliferated along with the scientific and technological advances of the last quarter-century.

Legal procedures long predicated on the body as irrefutable authentication of identity have tended to underestimate its capacity for masquerade as well as exposure. For instance, during the Napoleonic wars,
the writer Nadezhda Durova successfully passed herself off as a male of-
ficer in the tsarist army.[4] Her powers of impersonation pale beside those
of the Chinese transvestite opera singer, the subject of David Henry
Hwang's play (1988) and David Cronenberg's overwrought film *M But-
terfly* (1993), who, quite improbably, managed to conceal both "her" activities as a spy and her biological malehood from her French diplomat
lover of twenty years. More recently the revelation that the American
jazz musician Billy Tipton (1914–89) and the Spanish bullfighter Salva-
dor Sanchez—both married "family men"—were, in fact, women im-
pugns the notion of gender as the single body-specific characteristic that
is invariant from birth.[5] Such scenarios of protracted gender performance smack of lyrical fantasy today, when surgery actually enables sex
changes that discredit immemorial concepts of fixed gender identity.
Yet instances of subornative falsification corroborate an all too predictable corollary: given a broadly accepted bodily semiotics, nothing need
hamper the transmission of signs calculated to communicate desired
(but utterly inauthentic) messages. Novels such as Laclos's *Les Liaisons
dangereuses*, Stendhal's *Le Rouge et le noir*, and Lermontov's *Hero of Our
Time*, in fact, thematize and dramatize the untethered signs of Jean
Baudrillard's simulacra, which Soviet society adopted wholesale.

Bodily reconstruction in the form of reduction, enlargement, and
shape modification, as well as transplants, implants, and myriad forms
of plastic surgery, makes possible a fundamental physical transformation that in bygone eras relied on foot binding, neck stretching, head

shrinking, piercing, and earlobe elongation.[6] Extrapolating from contemporary experiments in genetic engineering, the plot of the futuristic
film *Gattaca* (1997) pivots precisely on an ability to manufacture an identity resistant to standard techniques of bodily verification (for instance,
fingerprinting) that vouchsafes "freedom from bodily determination."[7]
Whereas regulative institutions by and large continue to presuppose a
comparatively stable identity capturable through physical specifications
and documented in passports, driving licenses, and so forth, capitalist
markets expand chiefly through the effectiveness of campaigns exhort-
ing customers to alter their personae via an endless array of physical
metamorphoses: "Create a new you!"[8] Both, however, posit a continuity between a recognizable self and bodily appearance, anchored in the
body's tangibility, in its immanence, however illusory, elusive, and transient. As Elaine Scarry justly remarks: "Given any two phenomena, the
one that is more visible will receive more attention," and, doubting
Thomases might add, more credence.[9]

Despite the validity of some anthropologists' concern that "[t]he social body constrains the way the physical body is perceived," inasmuch
as bodies "are now used paradoxically to deny the natural and to 'embody' the contemporary homily that there is nothing outside of culture," anthropology as a discipline is still struggling to isolate the "natural" from the "social" and overwhelmingly emphasizes the latter over
the former.[10] Mary Douglas's legitimate conviction that there is "a continual exchange of meanings between the two kinds of bodily experience so that each reinforces the categories of the other" leads her to
conclude that this interaction renders the body "a highly restricted medium of expression."[11] Such a puzzling compressed syllogism verges on
a logical non sequitur, though one could tenably maintain that the modern world increasingly privileges the social over the natural.[12] Lotman's
fascinating commentary on guns implies as much, though in his model
the inextricability of the two both depends on *and* enables a malleable
and evolving body: "If one holds a modern gun and an old dueling pis-
tol, one is struck by how well the latter fits in the hand. One scarcely
feels the weight; it seems to be an extension of the body.[13] Objects of the
old everyday life [*byt*] were made by hand; this form was the result of
decades and sometimes even centuries of work, with the secrets of their
manufacture handed down from craftsman to craftsman. This process
not only produced the most appropriate form, but inevitably transformed the object into *the history of the object*, in memory of the gestures
connected with it. On the one hand, the object gave the human body

new possibilities, while on the other it placed man in tradition, i.e., both developing and limiting his individuality" ("Vvedenie," 12).[14] While coinciding with Douglas's idea of the symbiosis between nature and culture, Lotman's dynamic perspective recognizes the enrichment, as well as the restriction, resulting from that interplay.[15] My discussion of the post-Soviet body, a body emerging from seventy years of the centripetal drive that created the pseudo-unitary Soviet body politic, spotlights shifting modes of acculturation during a decade virtually unmatched for sociopolitical and psychological upheaval and, consequently, supremely vulnerable to centrifugal forces.

## Soviet Bodies: *E pluribus unum* versus *Ex uno plures*

The binarism that Lotman deems endemic to early, pre-Petrine Russian culture, manifested primarily as rivalry between the old *(starina)* versus the new *(novizna)* (Lotman and Uspenskii, "Binary Models," 33), likewise structured Soviet life and thought in a potentially endless series of imbricated, overdetermined dichotomies: public/private, left/right, East/West, xenophobic "we"/suspect "they" *(svoi/chuzhoi)*, loyalty/treachery, publicly professed/privately believed, and so forth. Within the context of a vigilantly monitored ideology, these pairs provided a convenient, ready-made repertoire of signs for conveying Sovietness (and its opposite). According to Baudrillard's morose scenario of substitutive semiosis, the monolithic, relentlessly reinforced equations capacitating this code enabled the Soviet population to simulate politically orthodox selves and attitudes through cynical mastery of signifiers wrenched free from signifieds.[16] Lotman's analysis of Khlestakovism as vulgarized mimicry captures the structure of, and enabling conditions for, such simulation. The conduct of a Khlestakov, Lotman contends, has no organic connection with the needs of individual personality. Instead, Khlestakov assumes a specific behavior (posture, set of gestures, phrases, and so forth) the way an actor dons a costume or executes a role. Such an enactment of a prescribed "self" depends on ready-made, recognizable models that a Khlestakov never generates but only uses. Imitable blueprints of this type originate in a society's solid entrenchment of sign systems—its semioticization *(znakovost')*—and the degree of alienation within that society determines the extent to which simulation becomes common praxis ("Concerning Khlestakov," 184). The Soviet era, and especially its Stalinist phase, maximized *znakovost'*, facilitating the

Figure 10.1. Keeping in ideological step. Ivan Shagin, *Sports Parade: Red Square, Moscow* (1932). Reproduced from Leah Bendavid-Val, *Propaganda and Dreams: Photographing the 1930s in the USSR and the US* (Zurich: Edition Stemmle, 1999), 82.

population's recourse to an unambiguous storehouse of signifiers. As during the Romantic period, on which Lotman focuses, the visible body unavoidably played a crucial role in the process of pseudosignification.

In general, officially sanctioned everyday Soviet life projected its citizens' bodies as the gray collective of mandated unanimity/uniformity satirized in E. Zamiatin's *We* (*My*, 1920): "The numbers walked in even ranks, four abreast, ecstatically stepping in time to the music — hundreds, thousands of numbers, in pale blue unifs . . . this mighty stream" (see fig. 10.1).[17] Since selfhood derived from a leveling paradigm, individualism constituted a psychological and political defect, to be extirpated via enforced social integration — the mandatory excision of the imagination in Zamiatin's *We* that would safeguard unobtrusive sameness. Though gigantic mass parades on Red Square permitted vivid color (appropriately, red), they showcased the impregnability of colorless Soviet consensus through a faultless choreography metamorphosing thousands of marching bodies into a single indivisible unit or "hyperbody" whose baroque excesses evoked, above all, Busby Berkeley musical extravaganzas (see fig. 10.2).[18] This modern feat of theatrical consolidation/synchronization resurrects the late-eighteenth-century

Figure 10.2. Mechanizing the human factor. A. Rodchenko, *The Wheel* (1936). Rodchenko and Stepanova Archive, Moscow. Reproduced from Dawn Ades et al., *Art and Power: Europe under the Dictators 1930–45* (London: Thames & Hudson, 1995), 216.

parade, beloved by Tsar Paul I, which, according to Lotman, likewise eliminated all individuality: "The parade . . . strictly regulated the conduct of each man, making him a silent cog in an enormous machine. It left no room at all for variation in the behavior of the individual. . . . [I]nitiative was transferred to the center, to the personality of the parade commander. From the time of Paul I, this was the Emperor" ("Theater and Theatricality," 154) and, for thirty years of Stalin's rule, the dictator's figure. Soviet bodies were uncompromisingly and consciously social, enlisted in the promotion of the country's self-advertised image of wholesome, industrious vigor springing from enlightened sociopolitical rectitude. Physical symmetry—of human "mannequins" guided by an incarnated political divinity (154)—thus ostensibly exteriorized consensus.

For the most part, Soviet cultural forms revived seventeenth-century utopianism by casting the body as a well-oiled, efficient machine, an impeccably functioning cog in the Stakhanovite labor complex. An analogous conception of the body dominated Soviet sports and their visual representation, with the smoothly operating mechanism of labor naturalized into a harmonious athletic organism modeled on the ancient Greek ideal. As Sergei Pavlov, head of the nation's Sports Committee from 1968, announced, "In our country, sport has come to occupy an important place . . . among the various means of Communist education of Soviet people, of their comprehensive harmonious development."[19] Numerous paintings by Aleksandr Deineka, the prolific pictorial chronicler of Soviet sporting life, depict in lyrical pastels athletes' healthy, streamlined bodies in motion, de-eroticized and idealized as an integral part of a bucolic landscape—the socialist Garden of Eden (see fig. 10.3).[20] These bodies attested the optimistic, productive energy harnessed to and equated with the Soviet way of life—one competitively superior to Western mores and morality, thus vindicated in every sporting victory. Tellingly yoking a teleology of labor and militarism, Politburo member Mikhail Kalinin acknowledged the nation's strategy of developing its citizens' athletic capabilities "so as to prepare them for work and defense *(oborona).*"[21] A British writer neatly summed up the ideological underpinnings of the Soviet state's investment in sports when he noted that Soviet sport was synonymous with "socialist morality." Athletes' individual achievements necessarily reflected and were subsumed by collective imperatives, their bodies disciplined to serve a higher historical purpose.[22] Members of sports teams who strove for personal glory

Figure 10.3. Blending with Nature's lyrical bounties in Soviet Arcadia. A. A. Deineka. *Razdol'e*. Reproduced from Sergei A. Luchushkin, *Sport v sovetskom izobrazitel'nom iskusstve* (Moscow: "Sovetskii khudozhnik," 1980), n.p.

manifestly violated the cornerstone principle of Soviet sports. Iurii Olesha's *Envy* (*Zavist'*, 1927) pointedly contrasts just such a (significantly, German) soccer player with the heroic Volodia Makarov, who aspires to become "a human machine": "As a player, Volodia was just about as different from Getzke as could be. Volodia was a sportsman; Getzke a professional. Volodia was interested above all in the whole game, in victory for his side. Getzke was there to display his individual art. He was an old, experienced player, very little concerned with the honor of his team. His personal success was what mattered. . . . Knowing that he could score against any team, he cared about nothing else. Because of this he could not be a truly great athlete."[23] Getzke embodies values likewise embraced by Skarlygin, the Dynamo center-forward in Abram Terts's *Trial Begins* (*Sud idet*, 1956/1960), driven exclusively by "the raging need to attain the goal. At any price—let it be death itself, or anything else. . . . All means are fair."[24] Both ego(t)ists transgress the socialist code, whereby in tournaments, matches, international competitions, and the Olympics, athletes' bodies ideally functioned as state property, publicly exemplifying the nation's collective robustness, discipline, and glory.[25]

The national pride invested in and impressed upon athletic bodies was supremely historical. That generalized historical imprinting also ensured that veterans were visibly honored through concrete insignia of their heroic readiness to expose their bodies to danger and death "for the sake of the nation." During public spectacles, especially those commemorating wars, decorated veterans traditionally displayed medals, orders, and ribbons that certified their contribution to the country's past and its survival. These metal symbols duplicated in anonymous miniature the stone and bronze statues of intrepid exemplars densely implanted throughout Russia's programmatically historicized landscape. Just as every small family took its cues from the Big Family (the Soviet state), so the average Soviet drew his inspiration (and earned his smaller recognition) from the epic exploits symbolized in the nation's oversized *bogatyr'* statuary.

Unobtrusiveness, usually coded by the word "decent" *(prilichnyi),* nonetheless characterized the authorized desideratum in Soviet deportment and general appearance. Ol'ga Vainshtein observes: "A particularly heightened awareness of individual differences in dress arose in reaction to the 'discipline' imposed by social dicta upon one's physical appearance. A unitary aesthetic derived from the ideology of collective 'leveling' codified public behavior, concepts of propriety, and thoroughly normative notions about beauty."[26] Readiness for individual bodily self-effacement split along gender lines, a discrepancy sanctioned by the Soviet presumption of womanhood as the secondary sex, prone to frivolity and material seduction. Men largely succumbed to the rule of sartorial conformity, presumably in a spirit of lofty indifference.[27] Women, however, resisted on the micro level, stubbornly chasing after a stylish scarf, an original belt, or an unusual piece of jewelry as distinctive marks in the mirror world of uniformity ironized in Larisa Zvezdochetova's painting *A Committee of Worried Citizens* (1983), which anthropomorphizes the focal concept of Walter Benjamin's essay "The Work of Art in the Age of Mechanical Reproduction" (1937) (see fig. 10.4). In the preadult sector of society, children's school uniforms, neatly beribboned pigtails for schoolgirls, and other instantly identifiable insignia of clean-cut underage civic responsibility underscored the tidy, earnest innocence of Pioneering and Komsomoling commonality. Clothes and grooming, in short, aspired to inconspicuous containment. Hair, in general—short for both sexes, but if long for women, then reassuringly controlled by styles that confined it into a bun, a braid, or a

Figure 10.4. Homo sovieticus, in the age of ideological reproduction, with citizenship confined to males. Larisa Zvezdochetova, *A Committee of Worried Citizens* (1983). Reproduced from David A. Ross, ed., *Between Spring and Summer: Soviet Conceptual Art in the Era of Late Communism* (Cambridge, Mass.: MIT Press, 1991), 47.

pleat—projected neatness and decorum *(prilichie)*, even when dyed shrieking red, egg-yolk yellow, or soot black owing to the primitiveness of domestic "beautification" products.[28] A body that stood out in a crowd by definition was a body that had to be laid low.

Given the absence of a pornography market, nightlife entertainment, and Western-style advertising, the Soviet body came chastely clothed. It appeared publicly naked only in bathhouses *(bani)*, for exposure of flesh elsewhere betrayed degeneracy, that is, Western values. Molded by "authoritative" pronouncements and images of an ideal disseminated through sundry publications, Soviet citizens' propriety was overseen by the nation's informal but stringent constabulary of public conduct—the ever-vigilant babushkas who chastised young women for truncated hemlines and bare heads in winter. The rare portrayal of nudity on screen or canvas inevitably metaphorized the (obligatorily) female form as the incarnation of a concept.[29] In films of the thirties, for instance, the lushly generous female body troped a primal force of nature, most commonly invoked in kolkhoz films and such screen classics by Aleksandr Dovzhenko as *Earth* (*Zemlia*, 1930). Alternatively, female nudity signaled a foreign, decadent sexuality in spy films that cast "loose" women (naked but of less prodigious proportions than Dovzhenko's earth-goddesses) and sexuality itself as the enemy's domain. Women's bodies as concrete objects of male desire remained outside the sphere of Soviet artistic representation.[30] Such paintings as Boris Kustodiev's *Russian Venus* (1925) and Arkadii Plastov's *Spring* (1953) (see fig. 10.5) likewise encoded the bared (over)ripe female body as nature's maternal bounty. Its association with the quintessentially Russian *bania* projected cleansed, de-eroticized nurture—the human equivalent of wholesome milk and bread, the latter depicted, for example, in Il'ia Mashkov's *Soviet Breads* (1936) as a metonymy for the nation's plenitude (see fig. 10.6).[31] The maternal body as a natural and national purveyor of life, like the cornucopia bursting with "the staff of life," reassured through a rhetoric of domestic re/production instead of arousing through the erotics of seduction. Indeed, the tradition of painted odalisques and their modern counterparts largely bypassed Soviet Russia, which generally avoided exhibiting the unclothed body in any form.[32] It is no coincidence that Vladimir Weisberg encountered accusations of pornography when he contributed two canvases to the celebrated exhibition of 1962 at the Manège, for one of them was a nude.[33]

Paradoxically, both nakedness and sui generis body semiotics thrived in at least one environment within the Soviet Union: the prisons and camps that, on the one hand, degraded the human body to its "most primitive state," yet, on the other hand, allowed inmates to elaborate an intricate semiotic system tattooed onto the body.[34] The practice of tattooing in the criminal milieu instantiated what Lotman calls "legitimized anti-behavior" ("Binary Models," 39), though one could conceivably label it an "illegitimate" revision of conventional social behavior, with its own rigorous stratification, "law," and rituals.[35] Literally and metaphorically stripped to its minimum, here the body functioned as a blank slate on which the incarcerated codified and imprinted the

Figure 10.5. Cleansed and desexed maternity as seasonal symbol. Arkadii Plastov, *Spring* (1953). Reproduced from *A. A. Plastov: zhivopis'* (Moscow: "Navyi Ermitazhodin," 2003), 70.

Figure 10.6. Plenitude, Soviet style. Il'ia Mashkov, *Soviet Breads* (1936). Reproduced from Helena Goscilo and Beth Holmgren, *Russia\*Women\*Culture* (Bloomington: Indiana University Press, 1996), 146.

principles governing their "inner" community. This phenomenon eerily played out the scenario of Franz Kafka's "In the Penal Colony" (1916), from which it diverged in several aspects, while sharing the central issue of semantically loaded body inscription. Whether Kafka's narrative cautions against "all our attempts to redeem the body for the signifying process, to make its naturalness into a cultural product," as Peter Brooks tentatively proposes, or, conversely, portrays "the process of enculturation as a torturous marking of the body," "totally imprinted by history" remains an open question.[36] In either reading, however, the prisoner's body in Kafka's tale is forcibly marked by totalitarian dictate, whereas for Soviet prisoners, who elected and, with considerable effort and ingenuity, secretly executed each painstaking (and painful) operation themselves, tattooing afforded the sole possible gesture of independence from their wardens and the Soviet system. Paradoxically, only the circle of initiates—the prisoners themselves—possessed the hermeneutical tools to interpret these legible (or, at least, constantly accessible and scrutinized) ambulatory texts, for the tattoos, whether consisting entirely of images or combining them with words, comprised a minority language within a larger, culturally dominant linguistic milieu that it excluded. Such anomalous circumstances turned outsiders—those outside The Law—into literal and figurative insiders who forged their own laws. This paradox seems to corroborate Aleksandr Solzhenitsyn's and Andrei Sinyavskii's contestable assertions, in *The First Circle (V kruge pervom)* and *A Voice from the Chorus (Golos iz khora)*, respectively, that under Soviet rule only prison offered a measure of liberty.[37] Whatever the validity of such a counterintuitive view, incarceration certainly distanced the citizen from the social convention of unobtrusive merging with the univocal multitudes.

Of all Soviet bodies, that of the Great Leader constituted the magnificent (and ever magnified) exception to the rule of anonymity and self-erasure. Whereas citizens' bodies were subject to homogenization, the Leader's underwent mythologization. Accordingly, while the population dissolved into a single united hyperbody, the singular body of the Leader hypertrophied and multiplied. It split into the king's two bodies as defined by Ernst Kantorowicz: the sublime, immaterial body of the Leader's symbolic function and the empirical, perishable envelope of his everyday inescapable self.[38] As a material entity Lenin was a short, small-eyed, balding man, plagued by atherosclerosis, migraines, and, toward the end, paralysis, dementia, and hallucinations—the long-suppressed image that inspired Aleksandr Sokurov's recent film *Taurus* (*Telets*, 2000). Lenin's successor was a stocky, swarthy, pockmarked Georgian, with a partly deformed left arm and, reportedly, a webbed left foot.[39] Conversion of both unprepossessing figures into the Leaders' sublime bodies necessitated representational techniques nowadays associated primarily with Hollywood celebrities.

Photographs, posters, and paintings either showed Lenin from a lengthening low-angle perspective or, more frequently, superimposed his amplified image on a background that metonymized Russia or the entire world (see fig. 10.7).[40] When not covered by the strategic peaked cap that allied him with the working masses, his bald head, in lateral or low-angle shots, conveyed brainpower, while his signature out-flung

Figure 10.7. The supreme ideological cleanser. Mikhail Cheremnykh and Viktor Deni, *Comrade Lenin Cleanses the Earth of the Unclean* (1920). Courtesy of Russian State Library.

Figure 10.8. Lord of all he surveys. Fedor Shurpin, *The Morning of Our Fatherland* (1948). Courtesy of Russian State Library.

arm pointed toward the radiant future. Identified with granite and steel—the materials used to reproduce his idealized image in the form of monuments, statues, and busts—Lenin owed the formidable dimensions of his Leader cult, especially in its posthumous phase, to Stalin, whose adopted name exploited the unsubtle connotations of steel imagery (to recast the ancient formula, "a steel-trap mind in a steel body").

Since the iconography of political supremacy mandates a total aesthetics to establish omnipotence, beyond the vicissitudes of space and time (see fig. 10.8), Stalin's sublime body became a meticulously orchestrated detemporalized product ("He is always with us") disseminated throughout the land.[41] Airbrushing smoothed his skin, flattering angle shots augmented his stature, a "paternal" pipe in his left hand masked his somatic deformity, and the military uniform encasing his body projected manly stoicism, the right hand tucked Napoleonically into his tunic.[42] Stalin's iconography gravitated skyward, increasingly elevating him above his surroundings. This gradual ascension, evident in such paintings as A. Gerasimov's *I. V. Stalin and K. E. Voroshilov in the Kremlin* (1938), culminated in the ingenious posters by Gustav Klutsis, where the Celestial Leader's body split further, to embrace not only his saluting cult Self but also the superman airplane bearing his name and hypnotizing all stunned spectators (*Long Live Our Happy Socialist Motherland*, 1935) (see fig. 10.9).[43]

As Slavoj Žižek, extending Claude Lefort's corrective to Kantorowicz's formulation, justly argues, the Leader's symbolic function "*redoubles his very body*," lending its transient form an ineffable aura.[44] Those habituated to the ubiquitous statues, portraits, and official appearances of Stalin as Leader eventually perceived the *man* as aureoled in a charismatic, superhuman glow that stimulated awed fascination with details of his everyday "private" life. As Father of the Big Family, Stalin adroitly exploited the domestic trope through films, paintings, and photographs that juxtaposed him with children, particularly beaming, pigtailed little girls as proleptic signs of the radiant future. While necessarily distanced from mortals through his divine omniscience, the mythological Stalin not only sacrificed his health "for the people" by ceaselessly toiling through the night but "went among them," true to the paradigm immortalized by the prototypical cult Leader, Jesus Christ. Thus the Stalinist cult of personality entailed not only a transubstantiation of the Leader but also a revolution in the vision of his worshipers; quite simply, they perceived both of his hypostases with transformed eyes.

The significance of the sublime political body for the Leader's material body expresses itself most clearly and emphatically in the preservation of the dead Leader's mortal remains as "an envelopment of the sublime Thing."[45] Boris Groys shrewdly notes that Lenin's mummified body is revered precisely because it evidences the irrevocable departure of the deceased as concrete individual from his body and from life, and "the only appeal that can be made to him is through the heirs who now stand upon his tomb."[46] In such slogans as "Lenin lived, lives, and will continue to live" and Maiakovskii's "Lenin is more alive than the living," the name Lenin signifies the sublime Thing, the deathless Idea subsequently inherited by Stalin, who created the mythological Father and whose own embalmed earthly body in 1953 lay beside the paternal relics in the mausoleum within the symbolic heart of the nation (see fig. 10.10). Contiguity affirmed continuity, then the ideological all. Eight years later, however, Lenin lost his filial bedfellow: Stalin's body was demoted, buried under the Kremlin ramparts, his name erased from the mausoleum's facade.[47] The vitality of the Idea, however, may be deduced from the impassioned post-Soviet debates about the appropriate permanent resting place for the historically divine remains. Recent battles over both

Figure 10.9. Stalin in the sky. Gustav Klutsis, *Long Live Our Happy Socialist Motherland* (1935). Courtesy of Russian State Library.

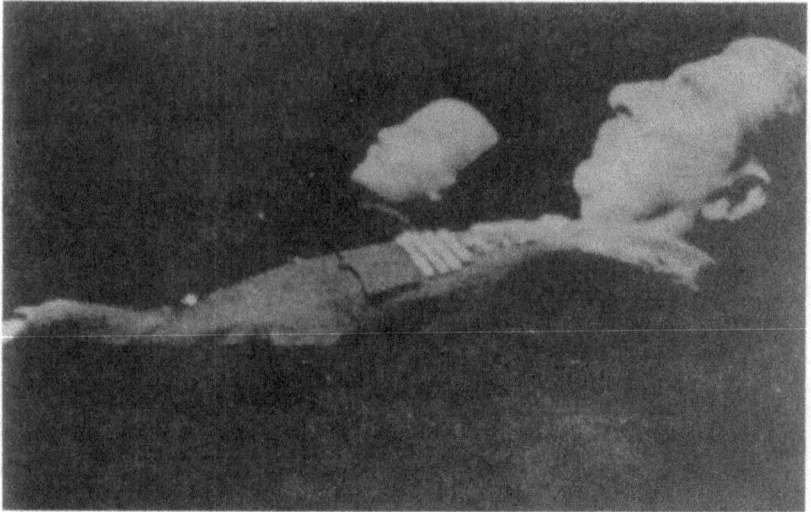

Figure 10.10. Mummified ideological bedfellows. Reproduced from Ilya Zbarsky and Samuel Hutchinson, *Lenin's Embalmers* (London: Harvill Press, 1998), 167.

Leaders' bodies attest the extraordinary power inherited cultural symbols wield over the imagination (Lotman, "Simvol v sisteme kul'tury," 8–9). The Leader's uniqueness as a summative condensation of the national ethos and its aspirations requires mythological as well as material "representation" for the indistinguishable masses that comprise the abstract concept of "the people"—a people in this case mysteriously bonded to the chemically sustained cultural sign of the Soviet prime cause.

## Bodily Divestment and Investment in the 1990s

Whereas Soviet body politics favored self-effacement and communality, de-Sovietization almost overnight transformed the Russian body into a site for individual self-expression or, more accurately, self-presentation.[48] Partly under Western influence, a new body culture and politics exploded in both capitals, overrunning virtually all walks of life, from strip joints targeting both genders (see fig. 10.11), to publications teeming with illustrated counsel about sexual pleasure, ads for health clubs, pornographic images, body art, self-installations, and performances (see figs. 10.12 and 10.13). Under acceleratedly altered conditions, the ideological

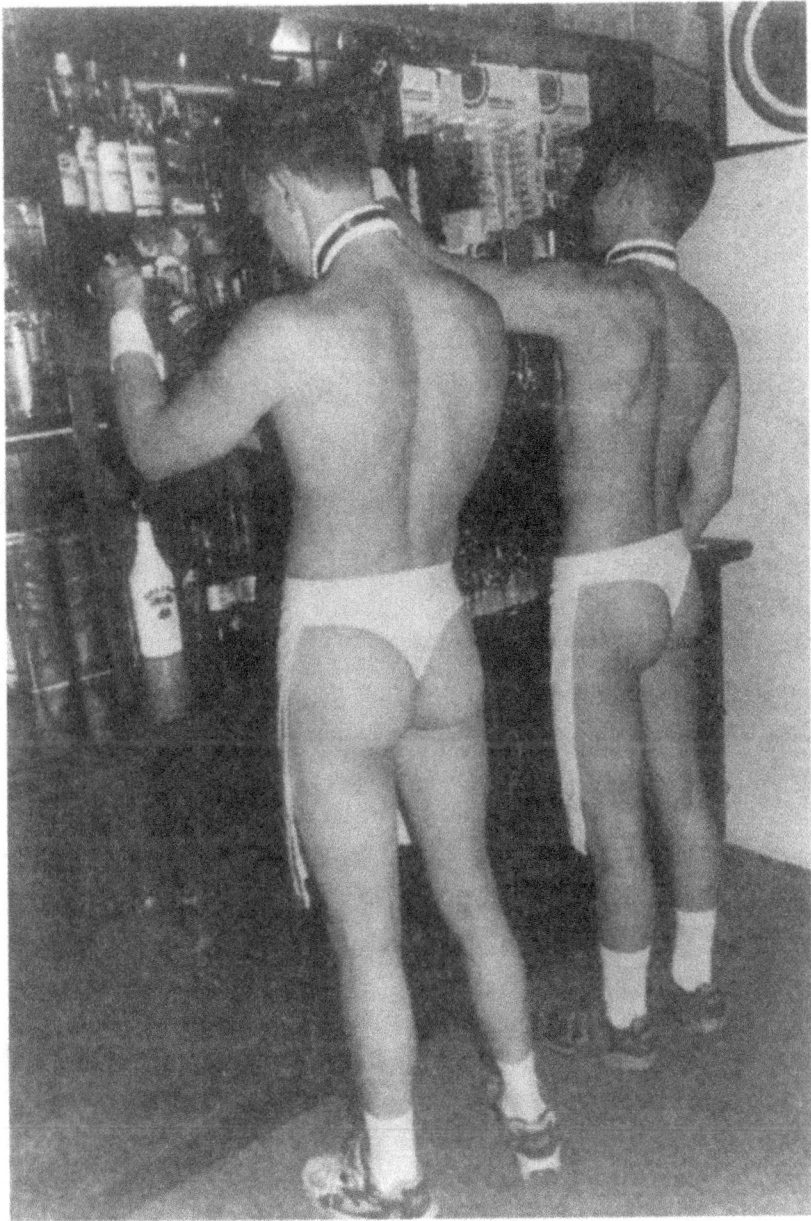

Figure 10.11. The chief attraction at a club for moneyed ladies' visual pleasure. Reproduced from *Argumenty i fakty* 32 (1997): 16.

Figure 10.12. The post-Soviet athletic body. Reproduced from *Andrei*, no. 6: 16.

Figure 10.13. Leisurely ladies of the world uniting? Reproduced from *Dzhentl'MAN* 2 (Summer 1995): 57.

body underwent radical commodification, as possibilities for body signification and merchandising seemed to multiply exponentially. Glossy
magazines and increased interaction with the West purveyed novel paradigms of desirability, even as trade in female flesh mushroomed into a
domestic and international billion-dollar industry.

The politics of unanimity had rendered the Soviet body a predictable semiotic center subject to minimal variation. By contrast, the influx
of Western cultural genres, whereby "the very advertisements whose
copy speaks of choice and self-determination visually legislate the ef-
facement of individual and cultural differences and circumscribe . . .
choices," disseminated a self-promoting illusion of diversity and freedom.[49] With the myth of an ascetic Soviet Eden shattered, post-Soviet
visions and dreams found incarnation in the pseudo-liberated, market-
friendly Russian body that clamored for attention. Though the private
body seemed restored to the citizenry, the new regime, rhetorically embracing a market economy, was invested in the public display of a body
imprinted with signs of a political reincarnation and a concomitant economic revolution (see fig. 10.14). Moreover, the promise of privacy, ironically, coincided with the post-Soviet passion for the dramatic gesture,
for the spectator-oriented theatricality that Lotman has isolated as one
of Romanticism's dominant features. To stand out, to impress, to stun,
to capture the limelight through the melodrama of the speaking body —
this goal united politicians, entertainers, and average citizens in a world
"reconstructed according to the laws of theatrical space in which things
become the sign of things" ("Theater and Theatricality," 141). "Stagi-
ness [took] command of life," for the transition to a dramatically new
era magnified people in their own eyes as "the dramatis personae of history," choosing their "type of behavior" (147, 149, 160). In such eras, as
Lotman notes, "[e]ventfulness, that is, the possibility that unexpected
phenomena and turns of events [will] happen, [becomes] the norm"
(160), and no one would dispute that eventfulness (economic and military disasters, loss of fortunes and elimination of entire industries overnight, the president's armed attack on the White House, repeated dismissal of the country's top administrators) reigned over the 1990s.

Above all, the post-Soviet body underwent rapid sexualization, the
prolonged national interdiction against the sexualized body both inten-
sifying its potency as a cultural sign and accounting for its indiscriminate, tireless ubiquity after the Soviet Union's dissolution.[50] The eccentric Liberal Democratic Party leader, Vladimir Zhirinovsky, author of

Figure 10.14. Luxury lesbians for male delectation. Reproduced from *Andrei*, no. 6: 16.

*The ABC of Sex* (*Azbuka seksa*, 2000) and self-proclaimed "sexual knight of all the girls in Russia," almost instantly grasped the potential of a newly permissible sexual discourse and, accordingly, supplemented his headline-seeking antics with political pronouncements steeped in hormoned rhetoric and mired in revelations of his personal libidinal adventures. In the flamboyant, lubricious style that quickly became his trademark, Zhirinovsky summed up the course of Soviet history by pronouncing Stalinists homosexuals, Khrushchev's era one of masturbation (or self-satisfaction), Brezhnev's epoch that of senile impotence, and the period under Gorbachev and Yeltsin a time of orgies and sexual confusion. As a solution to Russia's sociopolitical travails, Zhirinovsky advocated group sex (*Playboy*, 1995). Intriguing, above all, as a zoological case, Zhirinovsky instances, in extreme form, a widespread phenomenon that originally took the country by storm and in the last decade has settled into a familiar way of being.

The new body language belonged to the post-Soviet discovery of sexual discourse that in late 1997 brought the first Russian sex talk show, *About That* (*Pro eto*), hosted by Elena Khanga, on NTV late Saturday

Figure 10.15. Comprehensive, indiscriminate sexualization. Reproduced from *SPEED-Info* 3 (1997): cover.

night.[51] The show provided a forum for body-speak and public praxis, a theater for sexual speeches and spectacles: Khanga inveigled members of the TV studio audience into confessions (or boasts) about their sexual habits, preferences, and fantasies, as well as attitudes toward telephone sex lines, multiple partners, and the like. In the first broadcast, a "sex worker" elucidated the finer points of oral sex, simulated an orgasm, and warned wives to improve their performances in bed, lest they lose their spouses to mistresses or prostitutes.[52] Another session targeted sex after seventy, while a third elaborated on the perils and pleasures of sadomasochism, with an eager male volunteer energetically whipped by a black-leathered dominatrix.[53]

*About That*, which apparently draws mainly young male viewers, adheres to the format of its Western models. A more anomalous offering, with no counterpart in the West and peculiarly blighted by split signals, is the TV news show *The Naked Truth (Golaia pravda)*, whose shapely, coquettish newscaster resurrects the title's dead metaphor by literalizing it: She gradually strips down to her underwear or birthday suit (the irreducible essentials of the show's title) while reporting genuine, frequently disconcerting developments around the world. If Soviet body semiotics projected political probity through a quiescence that intimated bodily transcendence or indifference, during the 1990s glossies, films, literature, advertisements—in fact, every conceivable mode of cultural production—signaled the body's status as a determinedly post-Soviet entity through a thoroughly Westernized style of visual sexploitation (see fig. 10.15). The body became *the* universal signifier for a dizzying welter of signifieds, as well as a field of quasi- or incoherent signification—the last exemplified by *The Naked Truth*.

## The Cynosural Self: Trappings of the Look

Within Russia the Soviet era's "trend to blend" evaporated under the impact of the post-Soviet cynosural self. As images of affluent panache filled glossy magazines, money began talking, loudly and insistently, replacing the ethic of group-oriented, virtuous self-denial with a philosophy of self-indulgent self-beautification—a self on sale.[54] Advertisements for chic clothes, stylish accessories, famous brand cosmetics and perfume, and body shaping were supplemented by articles on vestmental semiotics (the history and significance of the tie, for instance), guidelines

for appropriate conduct and demeanor in restaurants, and other pedagogical counsel that helped the sufficiently wealthy Russian negotiate
the brave new world of physical refashioning (see fig. 10.16).[55] In a re-
gression to the nationwide schooling of the Petrine era, a post-Soviet society that for decades had actualized a "naturalized" semiotics now had
to learn the "rules and grammar" of a foreign (i.e., post-Soviet) language
that would supply "texts of behavior" ("Poetics of Everyday Behavior,"
68). Whereas ill-fitting, synthetic-knit suits, gaudy ties, and cardboard
shoes had rendered Soviets, including heads of state, instantly identifiable in any crowd, now politicians, businessmen, and the average urban
white-collar employee, all "dressed for success," became indistinguishable from other Europeans or Americans. In urban centers the unmis-
takable markers of the Soviet body vanished, and blending acquired a
new valency, now within the international arena. Paradoxically, the era
of proclaimed individualism produced a strong dose of leveled anonymity, for attraction to the theatrical gesture, to the arresting and "unique,"
stumbled against the limitations of available codes and accouterments.
In Lotmanian terms, aspiring Napoleons proved to be Khlestakovs.

As product advertising gradually became more differentiated and
magazines began catering to specific groups (e.g., *Medved'* to moneyed
macho men, *Ptiuch* to rock 'n' drug-friendly youth; see fig. 10.17), several
factors and factions—some predictable, others fascinating—emerged.
Age, gender, and financial status reconfigured social groupings made
legible through body signs or the Look. The soignée, designer image for
young women and the elegant business uniform of an imported three-
piece suit for men announced, along traditional Western lines, the aspiring entrepreneur. Spiked hairdos, shaved or Mohawked heads, body
piercing, tattoos, black leather, motorcycles, S and M paraphernalia—
the "outrageous" effect that largely mirrored Western anti-
aestheticism—signaled counterculture affiliations. Youth and beauty
became the dominant prerequisites for women seeking lucrative jobs in
fields with an international dimension: modeling, business, travel, entertainment, and so forth. In the absence of Western political correctness,
advertisements for the ("women only") position of translator, secretary,
and "assistant" in businesses specified good looks, long legs, and an age
of under twenty-five as necessary "professional qualifications." The
consequent obsession with the svelte, short-skirted female figure, impeccable grooming, and flawless packaging accounted for the sudden rash
of beauty salons, enterprises offering procedures to enhance appearance

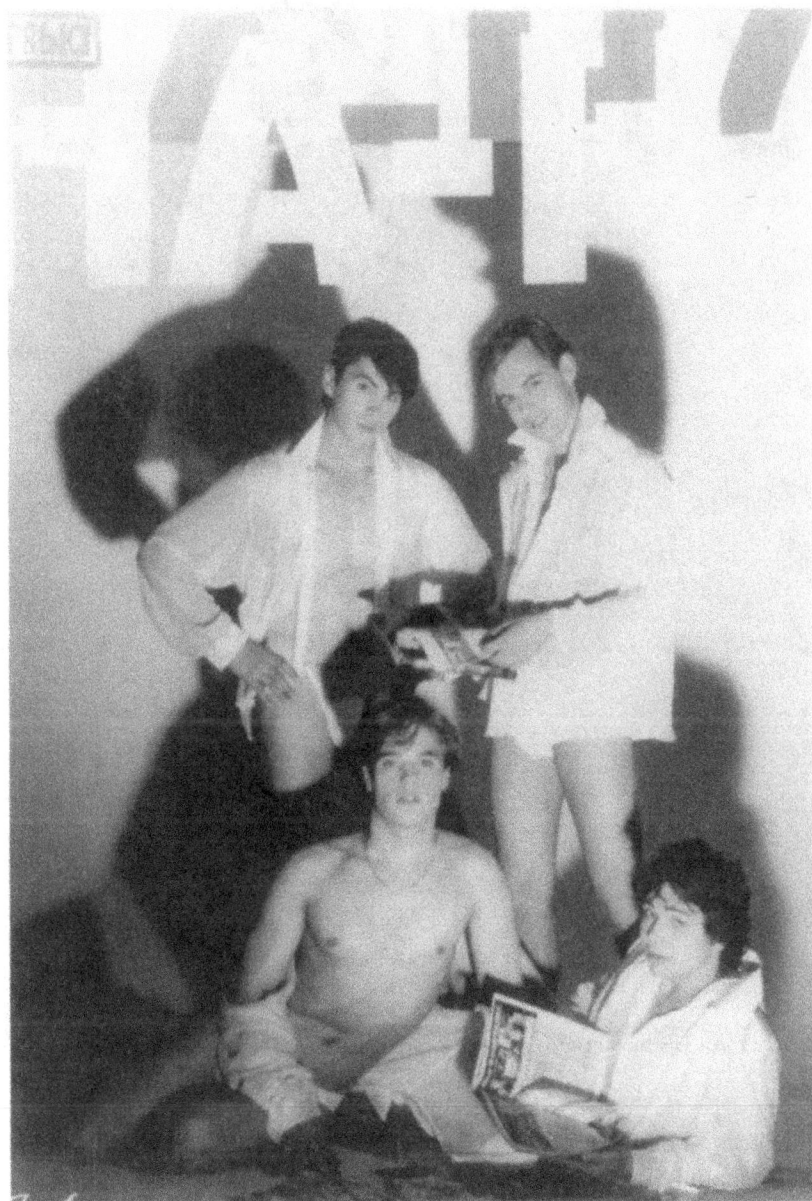

Figure 10.16. Chic, naughty boys—the soft rock group NA-NA. Reproduced from *Stas* 1 (June/July 1995): 28.

Figure 10.17. Democratic incoherence. Reproduced from *Ptiuch* 1 (1998): cover.

(including plastic surgery), and gyms emphasizing weight loss, fitness, and "shaping." Publications, TV, films, and contact with foreigners indefatigably trumpeted the benefits of a refurbished body aesthetic, and young Russians in particular answered that clarion call.

In the context of this comprehensive visual makeover, the quasi class of the New Russians attracted inordinate attention both in Russia and abroad not only for its fabulous wealth but also for the sui generis identity it projected through body semiotics. A highly specific amalgam of gesture, dress, and accessories made the New Russian an immediately recognizable being vulnerable to the reductive strategies of caricature that spawn *anekdoty* (jokes), a cultural genre invigorated in the 1990s precisely through cycles devoted to the New Russians. *Anekdoty*, films, and newspaper articles construed the New Russian as a grunting Neanderthal with more bucks than brains who resorted to caveman gestures as a substitute for speech. Distorting the Russian language beyond comprehensibility to anyone outside the in-group, the New Russian supposedly relied on two hand gestures that conveyed clan membership: the *koza* (goat), with the little finger of the hand extended, and *pal'tsy veerom* (fingers fanned out) (see fig. 10.18). This minimalist mode of communication evoked the Italian Mafia, and, indeed, the popular image of the New Russian drew on the criminal as his prototype. Especially in the early 1990s, the New Russian became synonymous with the "gangster style" in wardrobe and especially the flamboyant fashion designs of Versace, which, with the intensification of nationalism as the decade neared its close, yielded to those of Russia's own somewhat less extravagant Valentin Iudashkin.[56]

Though the New Russian favored opacity in his business practices, in the realm of cultural representation, transparency ruled his sartorial preferences. Devoid of taste as well as intelligence, this ambulatory apotheosis of tacky glitz paraded his newly acquired wealth on his body, a fatuous showcase for the material insignia of the *arriviste*.[57] Accordingly, jokes and cartoons portrayed him sporting a garish cranberry-colored jacket, Adidas sneakers, gold chains, gold Rolex or Cartier watch, and designer sunglasses, armed with a cellular telephone and flanked by Kalashnikov-toting bodyguard toughs.[58] Through this vulgar stylistic hash, the body of the New Russian unwittingly betrayed his epic philistinism, abetted by inconceivable wealth. The New Russian's sense of self derived from his acquisition of money, and, as Galina Grishena, a plastic-blonde New Russian wife, admitted, exhibiting one's perceived identity in hyperbolic form — wearing the maximum number of luxurious accessories — was intended to circumvent getting "lost in the crowd."[59] The New Russians' preemptive compulsion to "carry" their wealth and worth on their bodies as a guarantor of distinction resuscitated the bodily habits of an earlier, similarly moneyed class: the merchantry of the nineteenth century and especially the oversized merchant

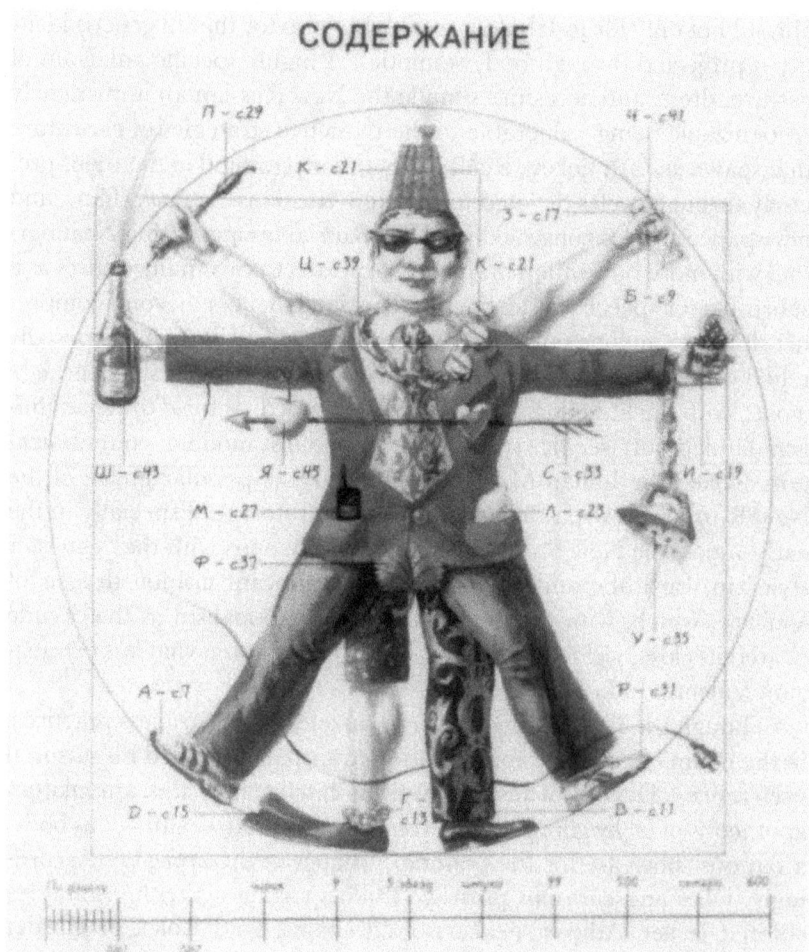

Figure 10.18. New Russians' sly self-irony. Reproduced from Katia Metelitsa and Viktoriia Fomina, *Novyi russkii bukvar'* (Moscow: Mir Novykh Russkikh, 1998), 5.

wives celebrated in Boris Kustodiev's colorful canvasses, their ample bodies—further broadened by ballooning skirts in expensive fabrics—peculiarly mirroring the tables weighed down by mountains of food and valuable possessions at which they usually presided. As in the case of the New Russians, the overdressed body of lush proportions amid signs of a materially centered existence displayed the values of triumphant entrepreneurship.

## Dermal Delights and Architectural Achievements

Whereas the New Russians personified excess transmitted through a familiar bodily sign system that registered lavish gains, the highly elaborated semiotics of body tattoos earlier practiced exclusively by prison inmates suffered losses. Quite simply, the criminal monopoly on tattoos ended with the post-Soviet vogue for ornamental tattooing: derivative playfulness replaced meaning. In the 1990s tattoos utterly devoid of any semiotic function, their selection dictated purely by personal taste, decorated shoulders, arms, necks, torsos, and, in extreme cases, more than half the body (see figs. 10.19 and 10.20). For the escalating number of aficionados of body piercing and S and M equipment, as well as for leathered skinheads, the hooliganish or subversive tattoo was assimilated into a framework of antimainstream body-speak; for countless "average" Russians, a tattoo represented a subgenre of body cosmetics, somewhat more risqué than the application of lipstick, with the notable difference of being "permanent."[60] While detractors consider the tattoo a lamentable vestige of primitivism, the worldwide appeal of the tattoo cult, its creation of a huge, lucrative market, and its inseparability from graphic design have recently legitimated the tattoo as a category of art.[61] The fashion for tattoos in Russia (more prevalent among men than women), when compared with America, England, and Holland, operates on a minuscule scale and remains on the margins of society, the victim and beneficiary of designification.

The marginalization of dermal decoration in both Soviet and post-Soviet times contrasts dramatically with the status of bodybuilding in Russia. Earlier, the potential to reconstruct one's physical envelope was confined primarily to two venues: (inter)national sports events and private or group-exclusive gyms. The first category boasted Herculean heroes who confirmed Soviets' might and maintained an officially monitored squeaky-clean image. The second category occupied a more ambiguous, though related, cultural space. In Liubertsy, a Moscow suburb notorious for its tough, lower-class, quasi-criminal element, young working-class males (Liubery) were addicted to outwardly projected masculinism, principally in the form of brawling and bodybuilding (see fig. 10.21). These neoproletarian, macho paladins pumped iron in clandestine, exclusionary dens, called *kachalki*, to inflate muscles for their stated vigilante mission of clearing Moscow's streets of "punks,

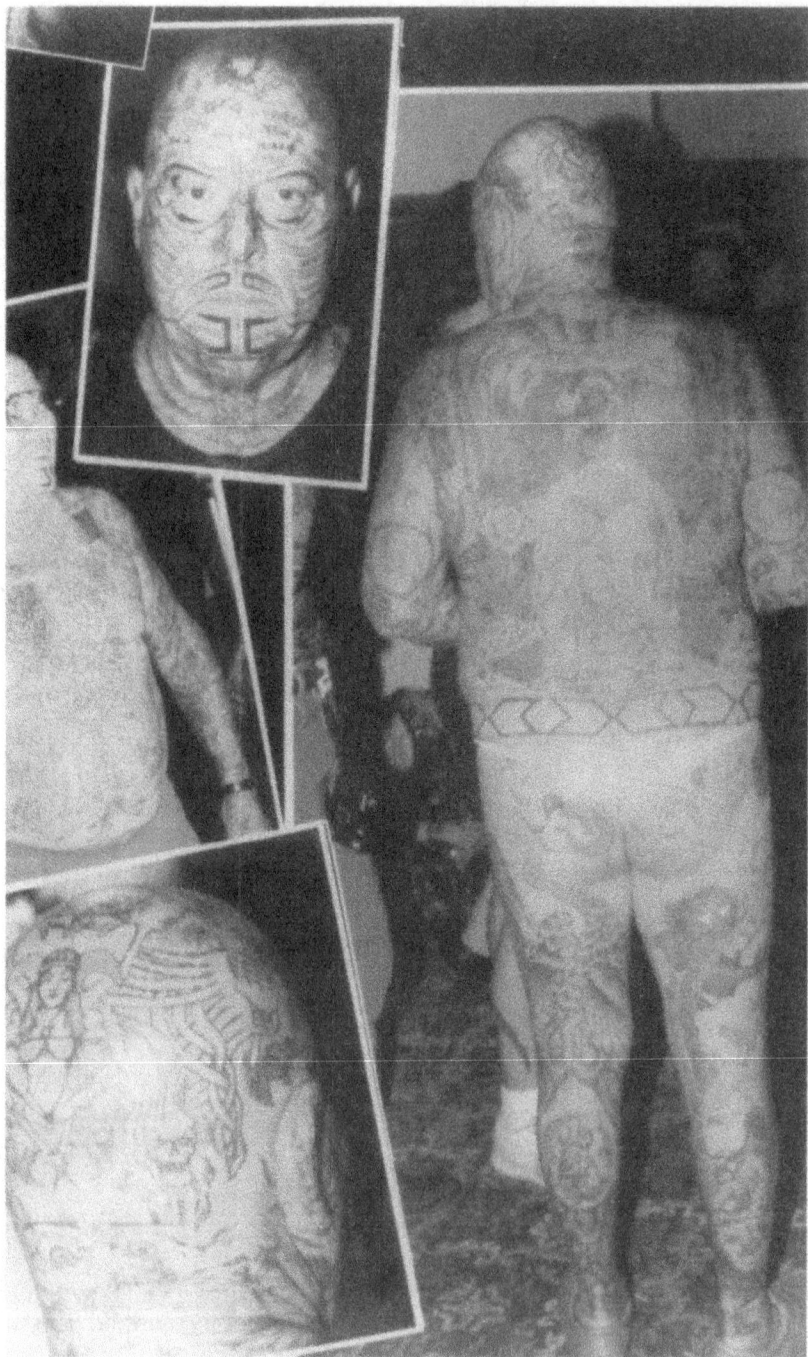

Figure 10.19. Bodily self-inscription, from one end to the other. Reproduced from *Supermen* 2 (1995): 27.

Figure 10.20. Tattoos, plus piercing. Reproduced from *Supermen* 2 (1995): 26–27.

Figure 10.21. A bodybuilder nicknamed "Jail," from Liubertsy. Reproduced from *A Day in the Life of the Soviet Union* (New York: Collins , 1987), 136–37.

hippies, and the like."[62] Liubery were the modern equivalent of ancient epic heroes *(bogatyri)*, who defended Russia's borders from unwelcome invaders. Perestroika's importation of Sylvester Stallone and Arnold Schwarzenegger as two icons of machismo (their bared, pneumatic torsos displayed on eye-catching posters in countless Moscow metro stations and along the city's streets) helped to disseminate and popularize the Liubery image as adapted to a stalwart post-Soviet domestic manhood. Indeed, the pop 'n' rock group Liube, debuting in 1989, successfully marketed its members as related to this brand of populist, anti-Western machismo by an attire that favored the retro working garb of the 1980s, exposing especially the muscled bulk of its lead singer, Nikolai Rastorguev, a former resident of Liubertsy. Yet interviews with Rastorguev, an earlier supporter of Yeltsin and a passionate fan of the Beatles, leave no doubt that adroit marketing of nostalgia, not political allegiances, dictated the group's Liubertsy image. In short, during the nineties the hyper-constructed male body as a *bogatyr'* ideal became delocalized, its proletarian provenance de-emphasized, and today, with the proliferation of bodybuilding magazines such as *Kul'tura tela*, featuring both foreign and Russian champions, that bulging, flexed body as sign sooner conveys masculine *style* than a national or class ideology.

## Gestural Genres

Not only everyday life but also various spheres of creativity placed the post-Soviet body in the spotlight, with recourse to the stratagem of historical revitalization. The St. Petersburg artist Bella Matveeva, for instance, not only fetishized the nude or semi-nude body by an obsessive recuperation of the decadent, aestheticized fin de siècle physique in her canvasses, but also incorporated live bodies into her mixed-media works, which juxtapose installation with canvas or bring to photographed life pre-scripted scenarios from bordellos of an earlier era (see fig. 10.22).[63] Tat'iana Antoshina reclaimed and revised Greek traditions by orchestrating implied visual narratives of balance, contemplation, or harmonious integration with nature, embodied in the naked male form, usually in recognizably classical postures. In their ironic photographic series titled *Satyricon*, Viktor Kuznetsov and Oleg Maslov, wearing crudely ostentatious makeup and little else and surrounded by exaggeratedly kitschy props, interpreted scenes from Petronius's famous novella (see fig. 10.23). In short, retrospectively inspired body performance, not representation, dominated art of the 1990s.[64]

The two performers most dramatically (and, often, ostentatiously) committed to personalized artistic bodily statements—the controversial Aleksandr Brenner and Oleg Kulik—have engaged in scandalous, outlandish acts to realize profoundly ideological projects. Brenner acquired international notoriety in 1997 for what seems a perverse retro reprisal of socialist realist principles: he protested the "capitalistic" elitism of museum art by spraying a green dollar sign on a Malevich painting housed in Amsterdam's Stedelijk Museum. Within Russia, however, his artistic reputation rests on his public nude appearances as an avowal of faith in "basic" (unclothed!) humanity and in the body's eloquent powers. Oleg Kulik, who in 1996 staged a performance titled "The Body Speaks Louder Than Words" at the Marat Gelman Gallery in Moscow, has flabbergasted audiences from New York to Italy by, quite literally, acting like an animal in public: naked and chained, he enacts doghood, crawling on all fours, eating dog food, growling, biting anyone in his vicinity, then being carted off to jail for unseemly canine behavior ("I Bite

Figure 10.22. Cover of Bella Matveeva's *Aesthetics of the Classical Bordello*. Reproduced from *Estetika klassicheskogo bordelia* (St. Petersburg: Izd-vo "Al'd," 1994).

Figure 10.23. Kuznetsov and Maslov's enactment of a scene from the *Satyricon*. Reproduced from *Creator* 5 (Spring 1997): 26–27.

America, and America Bites Me," 1997).[65] This sensationalist drama logically follows from Kulik's concept of "zoophreny"—"the relationship between man and animals, between culture and nature," in which the anthropocentrism of human society, lacking sympathy for other biological species, demeans and betrays the values of democracy. Kulik proposes a new Renaissance that acknowledges the equality of all biological species. He analogizes animals' modern circumstances with those of the Russian artist: the options of both reduce to biting or bootlicking, and Kulik favors the first on the grounds of authenticity.[66] His performances, therefore, metaphorically stage the artist's plight, while simultaneously urging trans-species egalitarianism (see fig. 10.24). The latter theme finds photographic articulation in his "catalog" titled *Deep into Russia* (1995, assembled with the participation of Vladimir Sorokin, a fellow apostle of body exploration), which exhibits the ever-naked Kulik in his signature doggie persona and in poses remarkable for their varying degrees of intimacy with animals. The formidable shock value of the visuals stems partly from Kulik's occasional ability to erase difference, whereby his own body is assimilated into the animal domain.

As Lotman persuasively argues, the assumption of roles through bodily semiotics rested at the core of eighteenth- and early-nineteenth-century theatricalization, in its most sustained and concentrated form attaining the status of impersonation and masquerade. In the contemporary art world, the most adept practitioner of these related genres is Vladimir Mamyshev (born 1969). Known in both capitals as Vladik Monroe, Mamyshev in 1989 launched his career as a drag queen by debuting at a "Woman's Art" exhibition dressed as Marilyn Monroe. His current notoriety and acclaim, however, date from his impersonatory photo exhibit titled Lives of Remarkable People (Moscow, 1995), which incontestably evidences Mamyshev's uncanny skill at metamorphosis into impeccable facsimiles of Lenin, Hitler, Napoleon, Count Dracula, Jesus Christ, Catherine the Great, Joan of Arc, and his signature persona of Marilyn Monroe (see fig. 10.25). Hailed as the best art show of the year, the exhibit produced multiple bodies that, though transient, were permanently captured via a camera lens—still credited as a tool of identity authentication. The chameleon Mamyshev calls his material transformations a "celebration" rooted in his audiences' eclectic collective unconsciousness.[67] A politically conservative gay with messianic delusions, he somewhat grotesquely embodies John Keats's notion of negative capability and, indeed, contends that his temporary duplication of a historical personage's body vouchsafes insight into that being's inner

Figure 10.24. Oleg Kulik and brother dogs. Reproduced from *Matador* 21 (July 1995): 45.

Figure 10.25. Vladik in his signature role of Marilyn Monroe. Reproduced from *Creator* 5 (Spring 1997): 18.

self, particularly into her or his behavioral motivations. Structurally the "external to internal" process of osmosis claimed by Mamyshev for his artistic mimicry parallels Lotman's notion of absorption within everyday life, in which (self-)conscious imitation leads to an assimilation that subsequently creates the impression of intrinsicality ("Poetics of Everyday Behavior," 68–69).[68] Whatever else Mamyshev's physical impostures achieve, they indubitably undermine the credibility of a visually validated stability of selfhood. While amply demonstrating the body's versatility, his unimpeachable impersonations discredit its function of corroborating a single, unassailable identity.

## The Leaders' Remains, or *Liebestod* Remnants of Bygone Days

Post-Soviet culture initially raced with arms outstretched to embrace Western "anti-bodies" and, in a widely publicized reflexive recoil, to clear its public spaces of the petrified bodies symbolizing Sovietdom. Like a betrayed lover, Russia relegated the toppled monuments of Lenin, Stalin, and Dzerzhinsky to the never-never land of oblivion and contemporary irrelevance. This *volte-face* instanced what Lotman defines as a facility for abruptly altering external behavior (here, symbolic landscape)—a developmental stage that replaces "organic evolution with 'costume changes'"—in an act of cultural amnesia ("Concerning Khlestakov," 183). Memory, or the return of history, however, inevitably proves recalcitrant, and never more so than during an era that experiences disillusionment with sudden, too swiftly adopted novelties.

Once its passionate but short-lived romance with Western alternatives cooled, Russia slid into a phase of nationalistic nostalgia that intensified the post-Soviet battle over two bodies inseparable from the socialist state: the mummified corpses of Lenin and Stalin.[69] These symbolic relics—the most expensive cosmetically treated bodies in the nation—proved the focus of impassioned polemics around a nexus of issues central to much of Lotman's scholarship: history, symbol, ritual, and everyday conduct. Russia's readiness to abandon the hammer and sickle for the two-headed eagle passed almost unnoticed, but the mere mention of removing Lenin's corpse from the mausoleum fueled passionate controversy, accusations of perceived opponents' denial of historical reality, and fears that segments of the population would respond violently to

Lenin's relocation and final burial. Indecisiveness regarding Lenin's bodily remains superbly captures not only Russia's current identity crisis but also the totem power of the ruler's symbolic body. Awareness of that power, no doubt, has prompted Vladimir Putin to launch a large-scale campaign of self-mythologization via the body: the Putin cult of personality emphasizes his credentials as a karate expert, as a trim, fast-moving man of action, quick on his physical as well as his mental toes.[70] Whereas Yeltsin's body bore the fleshly, visible signs of self-indulgent torpidity, Putin's slight figure conveys reassuring discipline and mobility. In one of his articles Lotman registers the persistent folk belief that "the body of the true tsar must bear the congenital 'tsar marks'" ("Concerning Khlestakov," 180), a remarkable confirmation of the primacy of bodily signs for the mystery of political and psychological "aura" as well as for legitimation.[71] While Putin's "marks" have yet to be revealed, until his agenda for Russia's future gains clarity and direction, he is wise to maintain the relics of the Soviet Source in its place of honor, for at some juncture it may prove expedient to claim ideological descent from, or to pay obeisance to, the once venerated body in the heart of Russia's capital.

## Notes

My warmest appreciation to Andreas Schönle for his thoughtful, enriching response to an early draft of this essay and to Seth (Sif) Graham for a profoundly informed dialogue with the text that pressed for greater rigor. As always, loving gratitude to Boženna Goscilo for her traditional role of intelligent critical reader and to Sasha Prokhorov for countless inspired suggestions that muscled my thoughts in exciting ways—not all of them, alas, reflected in the final form of this essay. To Susan Corbesero, affectionate thanks for specific points of information, as well as late-night vinous conversations stimulating intellectual energy. I am indebted to Russian and East European Studies at the University of Pittsburgh for the grant that underwrote the visuals accompanying this essay.

    1. Peter Brooks, *Body Work* (Cambridge, Mass.: Harvard University Press, 1993), 5.
    2. Regarding the body's integrative function, see Ted Polhemus, ed., *The Body Reader: Social Aspects of the Human Body* (New York: Pantheon Books, 1978), 150.
    3. Lotman contends that, in contrast to the "symbolizing consciousness," the "desymbolizing consciousness" operates by symptomatology, equating the writer with the medical diagnostician, much as Lermontov does in the foreword to *Hero of Our Time*. Lotman asserts: "that which for a symbolizing consciousness

is a symbol becomes a symptom for a desymbolizing one. . . . The desymboliz-ing nineteenth century saw in a given person or literary hero the representative of an idea, class, or group" ("Simvol v sisteme kul'tury," 193). This dual model of literary conception and perception parallels Roman Jakobson's binary of metaphoric and metonymic modes of representation.

4. Note, in this connection, Lotman's statement that "since women adopted trousers, their gait has changed, becoming more athletic, more 'mas-culine'" (*Besedy o russkoi kul'ture*, 11).

5. Anne Herrmann, "'Passing' Women, Performing Men," in *The Female Body: Figures, Styles, Speculations*, ed. Laurence Goldstein (Ann Arbor: University of Michigan Press, 1994), 178–79. Anglophone cinema during the 1980s was fas-cinated by cross-dressing in multiple forms, as witnessed by the release of *Tootsie* (1982), *Victor/Victoria* (1982), *Yentl* (1983), *Liquid Sky* (1983), and *Second Serve* (1986), and, in a tragic vein, *Boys Don't Cry* (1999). That series followed the much more radically subversive *Some Like It Hot* (1959) and preceded the excellently acted *Switch* (1991). None of these films, however, matches the bold satire on Stalinist "human engineering" by Sergei Livnev titled *Hammer and Sickle* (*Serp i molot*, 1994), in which a female kolkhoz worker is surgically transformed into a heroic urban male Stakhanovite as the incarnation of the Stalinist ideal. For an excel-lent analysis of this film, see Aleksandr Prokhorov, "'I Need Some Life-Assertive Character' or How to Die in the Most Inspiring Pose: Bodies in the Stalinist Museum of *Hammer and Sickle*," in *Studies in Slavic Culture*, vol. 1, ed. Helena Gos-cilo and Michael Brewer (Pittsburgh: University of Pittsburgh, 2000), 28–46.

6. See Frances E. Mascia-Lees and Patricia Sharpe, "Introduction: Soft-Tissue Modification and the Horror Within," in *Tattoo, Torture, Mutilation, and Adornment: The Denaturalization of the Body in Culture and Text*, ed. Frances E. Mascia-Lees and Patricia Sharpe (Albany: State University of New York Press, 1992), 1.

7. Susan Bordo, "'Material Girl': The Effacements of Postmodern Cul-ture," in *The Female Body: Figures, Styles, Speculations*, ed. Laurence Goldstein (Ann Arbor: University of Michigan Press, 1994), 106.

8. On the homogenizing and manipulative aspects of such campaigns, see the acerbic insights of Bordo's astute essay. The originality and breadth of pur-view of Bordo's publications on the body make them indispensable for any analysis of the topic. An earlier phase of the miraculous but attainable transub-stantiation of the embodied self marketed (via what now seem naive strategies) various slimming techniques and products, buttressed by "evidence" presented in success stories based on the "before and after" plot.

9. Elaine Scarry, *The Body in Pain: The Making and Unmaking of the World* (London: Oxford University Press, 1985), 12.

10. First quotation from Mary Douglas, *Natural Symbols* (New York: Pantheon Books, 1982), 65. Second quotation from Mascia-Lees and Sharpe, *Tattoo, Torture, Mutilation, and Adornment*, 166.

11. Douglas, *Natural Symbols*, 64.

12. The "natural," in fact, is often understood as something to be culturally produced – "naturalized"—as amply evidenced in the world of cosmetics and fashion.

13. David Cronenberg's *Videodrama* (1983) makes this point visually when the protagonist's hand actually transforms into a gun. (Thank you, Seth Graham, for drawing my attention to this parallel.)

14. Here I cite the unpublished translation of Lotman's article, "Vvedenie: Byt i kul'tura," by Benjamin Sutcliffe, amending it only to retain Lotman's emphasis in the original.

15. The ambiguous conclusion of Franz Kafka's complex story "In the Penal Colony" (1919) implies the body's resistance, or at least the limits of its susceptibility, to cultural imprinting.

16. Jean Beaudrillard, *Simulacra and Simulation*, trans. Sheila Faria Glaser (Ann Arbor: University of Michigan Press, 1994), 2. Needless to say, I am not making the ludicrously sweeping claim that no Soviet citizens participated in the country's sign system in good faith. My focus bypasses the question of genuineness in code enactment to examine, instead, the homogenized specifics of that code. For the cynical strain in Soviet culture during stagnation, see Alexei Yurchak, "The Cynical Reason of Late Socialism: Power, Pretense, and the *Anekdot*," *Public Culture* (1997) 9: 161–88.

17. Yevgeny Zamyatin, *We*, trans. Mirra Ginsburg (New York: Avon, 1999), 5.

18. Victor Turner has pointed out that black, white, and red are the colors recurring most frequently in ritual. Cited in C. R. Hallpike, "Social Hair," in *The Body Reader: Social Aspects of the Human Body*, ed. Ted Polhemus (New York: Pantheon, 1978), 134. Writing on symbols and their accretion of associations through history, Lotman observes: "It is precisely 'simple' symbols that form/ shape the symbolic nucleus of culture, and the degree to which a culture is saturated with them is precisely what allows one to judge/assess its symbolizing or desymbolizing orientation as a whole" ("Simvol v sisteme kul'tury," 193). In Russia, where the "beautiful/red corner" traditionally housed the icon, the specifics of the 1917 revolution and the civil war historically enriched red's primal evocation of passion and blood, freighting the symbol's "simplicity" with a wealth of Soviet-specific associations, while relying on its religious "traces." For Soviet citizens' behavior at parades, and the motivation behind it, see Yurchak, "Cynical Reason of Late Socialism." Tellingly, Lotman identifies the inspiration for the choreography of parades as the corps de ballet ("Theater and Theatricality," 154–55).

19. Sergei Luchishkin, ed., *Sport v sovetskom isobrazitel'nom iskusstve* (Moscow: "Sovetskii khudozhnik," 1980), no pagination.

20. Deineka observed that sport was "lyrical. It has a lot of optimism. It is

the start and essence of the heroic" ("[On] lirichen. V nem mnogo optimizma. B nem nachalo geroicheskogo"). See Luchishkin, *Sport v sovetskom isobrazitel'nom iskusstve.*

21. Luchishkin, *Sport v sovetskom isobrazitel'nom iskusstve.*

22. Among contrasting works, which ironically evoke sport as a metaphor for the trials of Soviet *byt*, see Georgii Daneliia's film *Osennii marafon* (1979) and Mikhail Zhvanetskii's satirical sketch "Vsia nasha zhizn' — sport" (1984).

23. Yuri Olesha, *Envy and Other Works*, trans. Andrew R. MacAndrew (New York: Anchor Books, Doubleday, 1967), 49, 109.

24. Abram Tertz, *The Trial Begins: On Socialist Realism*, trans. Max Hayward and George Dennis (New York: Vintage Books, Random House, 1960), 43–44.

25. For a compact overview of Soviet sport, see James Riordan, "Sport in Soviet Society: Fetish or Free Play?" *Home, School, and Leisure in the Soviet Union* (London: George Allen & Unwin, 1980), 215–38. For an analysis confined chiefly to the 1960s and usefully differentiating between "physical culture" and sports, see Irina Makoveeva, "Soviet Sports in the Sixties," unpublished manuscript. See also the recently published and excellent Mike O'Mahony, *Sport in the USSR: Physical Culture — Visual Culture* (London: Reaktion Books, 2006).

26. Olga Vainshtein, "Female Fashion, Soviet Style: Bodies of Ideology," in *Russia\*Women\*Culture*, ed. Helena Goscilo and Beth Holmgren (Bloomington: Indiana University Press, 1996), 66.

27. The exception to this rule was the young men influenced by Western style, the *stiliagi*, whose impact, of course, depended on their contrast to the overwhelming majority.

28. On the culture of hair, beauty salons, and availability of cosmetics during the Soviet period, see Nadezhda Azhgikhina and Helena Goscilo, "Getting under Their Skin: The Beauty Salon and Russian Women's Lives," in Goscilo and Holmgren, *Russia\*Women\*Culture*, 94–121. Long hair free from any "disciplining" strictures intimates a lack of amenability to social control and therefore remained outside Soviet permissibility. On the social symbolism of hair in general, see Hallpike, "Social Hair."

29. In that respect depiction of Soviet female nudity resembled the Western tradition of casting national causes in the form of (female) monuments. For an engaging, thoroughly documented survey of the latter, see Marina Warner, *Monuments and Maidens* (London: Vintage, 1995).

30. See Mikhail Iampol'skii, "V poiskakh utrachennogo naslazhdeniia," supplement to *Ogonek*, "Erotika v russkom kino" 5 (1990), video.

31. Darra Goldstein, "Domestic Porkbarreling in Nineteenth-Century Russia, or Who Holds the Keys to the Larder?" in Goscilo and Holmgren, *Russia\*Women\*Culture*, 146.

32. On the scarcity of nudes in Soviet art, see Mary Jane Rossabi, "Venus in the Looking Glass: Images of Venus and the Female Nude in

Twentieth-Century Russian Painting," unpublished manuscript. The small number of paintings showing female athletes in the process of undressing conveyed solid health, not eroticism, or, as in the case of A. Deineka's three naked women in *Playing Ball* (1932), the texture and monumentalism of the bodies transform flesh into an inorganic substance.

33. Igor Golomshtok and Alexander Glezer, *Soviet Art in Exile* (New York: Random House, 1977), 141.

34. Throughout I rely on the distinction between naked and nude formulated by Kenneth Clark and succinctly refined by John Berger, *Ways of Seeing* (London: BBC; Harmondsworth, UK: Penguin Books, 1977), 53–54. As Andrzej Jelski/Andzhei El'skii, *Tatuirovka* (Minsk: Met, 1997), 53–110, V. D. Kosulin, *Iskusstvo tatuirovki* (St. Petersburg: OOO "Zolotoi vek," ooo "Diamant," 2000), 187–206, and others have pointed out, the practice of prison tattooing has long been widespread throughout Europe.

35. For a summary of the long history of ritual tattooing among incarcerated criminals, which was surprisingly widespread, see Kosulin, *Iskusstvo tatuirovki*, 56–109.

36. First quotation from Brooks, *Body Work*, 286. Second quotation from Mascia-Lees and Sharpe, *Tattoo, Torture, Mutilation, and Adornment*, 146. Third quotation from Michel Foucault, *The History of Sexuality: An Introduction* (New York: Vintage, 1980), 148.

37. Both writers had political imprisonment in mind, whereas tattoos are the province of criminal prisoners. Yet the idea seems to obtain, if only partially, for both categories of incarceration.

38. See Ernst H. Kantorowicz, *The King's Two Bodies: A Study in Mediaeval Political Theology* (Princeton, N.J.: Princeton University Press, 1957).

39. Edvard Radzinsky, *Stalin*, trans. H. T. Willetts (New York: Doubleday, 1996), 30.

40. For a well-selected array of such images, see Victoria E. Bonnell, *Iconography of Power: Soviet Political Posters under Lenin and Stalin* (Berkeley: University of California Press, 1997), 169–79; for a comparable set of Staliniana, see pp. 180–85. The classic work on the Lenin cult in Soviet Russia remains Nina Tumarkin's monograph *Lenin Lives: The Lenin Cult in Soviet Russia* (Cambridge, Mass.: Harvard University Press, 1997).

41. On the orchestration of Stalin's official public image, see Bonnell, *Iconography of Power;* Evgenii Dobrenko, *Metafora vlasti: Literatura stalinskoi epokhi v istoricheskom osveshchenii* (Munich: Verlag Otto Sagner, 1993); Boris Groys, *The Total Art of Stalinism*, trans. Charles Rougle (Princeton, N.J.: Princeton University Press, 1992); and Helena Goscilo, *Dehexing Sex: Russian Womanhood during and after Glasnost* (Ann Arbor: University of Michigan Press, 1996), 160–63. Symptomatically, one of the late-perestroika films, by Tofik Shakhverdiev, was titled *Is Stalin with Us? (Stalin s nami? 1989).*

42. In his reminiscences, Lenin's embalmer, Ilya Zbarsky, comments on a colleague's surprise on first seeing Stalin's corpse at the mausoleum laboratory: "Stalin's face looked very different from the image used for propaganda purposes, for it was covered with pockmarks and liver spots, blemishes never seen by the public." Ilya Zbarsky and Samuel Hutchinson, *Lenin's Embalmers* (London: Harvill Press, 1998), 165-67.

43. The mythic dimensions of this cultist aviatory imagery were perceptively satirized by Vasilii Aksenov through a metamorphosis into the industrial-avian Stalin in *The Steel Bird* (*Stal'naia ptitsa*, 1970s).

44. Slavoj Žižek, *For They Know Not What They Do: Enjoyment as a Political Factor* (London: Verso, 1991), 255.

45. Ibid., 260.

46. Groys, *Total Art of Stalinism*, 67.

47. Zbarsky and Hutchinson, *Lenin's Embalmers*, 167.

48. For articles on diverse aspects of Russian culture related to the body, see Helena Goscilo, ed., *Studies in Twentieth-Century Literature: Russian Culture of the 1990s* 24, no. 1 (Winter 2000).

49. Bordo, "'Material Girl,'" 110.

50. For an examination of the body's signifying role in post-Soviet fiction, see Helena Goscilo, "Body Talk in Current Fiction: Speaking Parts and (W)holes," in *Russian Culture in Transition*, ed. Gregory Freidin, *Stanford Slavic Studies* 7 (1993): 145-77.

51. A fine discussion of the show within the larger post-Soviet context is offered by Eliot Borenstein, "*About That:* Deploying and Deploring Sex in Post-soviet Russia," *Studies in Twentieth Century Literature: Russian Culture of the 1990s*, ed. Helena Goscilo, 24, no. 1 (Winter 2000): 51-83.

52. Richard Beeston, "Russia's Black and Blonde Chat Show Host Scores Hit with Sex Fantasy TV," *The Times*, September 13, 1997.

53. David Carpenter, "Russians Warm Up to Racy Talk Show," Associated Press, November 21, 1997.

54. For an analysis of glossy magazines' role in this metamorphosis, see Helena Goscilo, "S(t)imulating Chic: The Aestheticization of Post-Soviet Russia," in *Essays in the Art and Theory of Translation*, ed. Lenore A. Grenoble and John M. Kopper (Lewiston, N.Y.: Edwin Mellen Press, 1997), 35-57.

55. Such items often were authored by scholarly experts in the pertinent field. For instance, Raisa Kirsanova, an outstanding scholar of costume and clothing, reportedly penned the pseudonymous item on ties.

56. For an intriguing profile of Iudashkin, see "Couturier," *Kul't lichnosti* (March/April 1999): 100-104.

57. My commentary focuses not on individual New Russians but on their image as constructed and reflected in articles, fiction, media, jokes, and films.

58. Russians refer to the jacket color as "raspberry" *(malinovyi)*.

59. Natasha Singer, "The New Russian Dressing," *Vogue* (1995): 352. The intelligentsia's resentful dismissal of the New Russians failed to take into account those representatives of the suddenly prosperous who possessed a marvelously ironic self-awareness, above all, Grigorii Bal'tser, the brains and energy behind the store-museum World of the New Russians *(Mir novykh russkikh)*. That emporium has immortalized the popular image of the New Russians in works of impeccable craftsmanship (Palekh boxes, Gzhel' figures, Zhostovo trays) that capture the New Russian version of capitalism, e.g., a "fairy-tale" depiction of leather-clad, sunglassed New Russians around a swimming pool, with a Mercedes Benz parked in the driveway of a huge, gaudy mansion.

60. Though tattoos may be removed, the procedure is painful, expensive, and time-consuming, which explains why this form of skin art tends to be considered long-term or permanent.

61. Kosulin, *Iskusstvo tatuirovki*, 138–49.

62. Hilary Pilkington, "'Good Girls in Trousers'—Codes of Masculinity and Femininity in Russian Culture," in *Gender Restructuring in Russian Studies*, ed. Marianne Liljeström, Eila Mäntysaari, and Arja Rosenholm (Tampere, Finland: University of Tampere, 1993), 177–78. Pilkington offers an insightful analysis of gendered images among the urban and provincial youth preceding and during perestroika.

63. Bella Matveeva and the majority of St. Petersburg artists belong to the city's Academist movement, spearheaded by Timur Novikov, which purports to salvage the values and aesthetics of classicism, while playing with gender-bending, "amoral" beautification, and noncommittal imitation of ancient models. The group, which boasts Novikov, Matveeva, Kuznetsov, and Maslov, among others, calls itself the New Academy of Fine Art. See "Russia's New Radicals: The New Academy: Concentrated Camp," *Creator* 5 (Spring 1997): 26–28.

64. Though much of this art on first glance seems to intersect with postmodernist trends, on closer inspection one sees that it allied itself with former historical assertions of absolutist power. The New Academism, similarly, advertised itself as a proponent of salvaged aesthetics ("ancient beauty"), but in fact flirted with fascist and sadistic paradigms.

65. On the Internet, Marat Gelman appears as Guelman, presumably to avoid Anglophones' mispronunciation of the initial letter in his surname (a soft, instead of a hard "g"). Jello carries associations no Real Man would court.

66. See http://www.smak.be/smak2000/expo/kulik/kule.html.

67. *Creator* 5 (Spring 1997): 20.

68. A dismaying development in post-Soviet Russia entails the traffic in women's bodies both internally and internationally, whereby women, either voluntarily or forcibly, join the indentured ranks of prostitutes. The dimensions, complexity, and implications of that topic preclude its examination in an article treating the post-Soviet body at large.

69. For a short period Georgian nationalists proposed having Stalin's remains exhumed and transported to Georgia. In Lenin's case, of course, the question concerns his removal from public view and his burial.

70. Whereas most Soviet leaders installed in Moscow's fascinating Wax Museum on Tverskaia wear "historical dress," Putin appears in a karate "kimono" that unavoidably implies his physical stamina and strength as well as the spiritual fortitude that underpins them.

71. In the eighth chapter of Pushkin's *Captain's Daughter* (1836), Pugachev in the bathhouse shows the tsar's signs on his chest: a two-headed eagle and his own image. The motif of body marks as signs of distinction frequently occurs in Russian fairy tales (e.g., the sun, the moon, and the stars on the bodies of the three brothers in "The Wicked Sisters"). Tellingly, the birthmark on Mikhail Gorbachev's forehead (often eliminated by image-sensitive photographers) impressed many Russians as the sign of the Antichrist, just as Anatoly Chubais's red hair evoked associations with the folkloric devil. The "most readerly nation" *(samyi chitaiushchii narod)*, after all, learned to read all legible signs susceptible to interpretation.

# NEGOTIATING
# THE EVERYDAY

# Eccentricity and Cultural Semiotics in Imperial Russia

## JULIE A. BUCKLER

Planets move all one and the same way in Orbs concentrick,
while Comets move all manner of ways in Orbs very excentrick.
Sir Isaac Newton, Opticks

With centric and eccentric scribbled o'er,
Cycle and epicycle, orb in orb.
John Milton, Paradise Lost

Eccentricities of genius.
Charles Dickens, Pickwick Papers

So would I bridle thy eccentric soul
In reason's sober orbit bid it roll.
Whitehead on Churchill

The eccentric is that which by consensus is unique. In spite of eccentricity's tendency to stand out, its natural and cultural manifestations nevertheless prove elusive objects of study. The opening chapter of *Eugene Onegin,* Alexander Pushkin's novel in verse, offers a vivid figure for eccentricity as ephemera, evoking the impressions of its narrator from his position on the street:

One splendid house is all alight,
Its countless lampions burning bright;

> While past its glassed-in windows flitter
> In quick succession silhouettes [*profili golov*]
> Of ladies and their modish pets [*modnykh chudakov*].[1]
>
> (stanza 27)

The concluding word, *chudakov,* translated as "pets" to form the second element of a rhyming pair, would be better rendered as "eccentrics," or, as Vladimir Nabokov phrases it, "[E]ccentric men of fashion, *hommes à la mode.*"[2] Trying to "read" eccentric behavior as a cultural text from the past is like looking through a window at shadows flitting by. Even the most energetic researcher can study historical eccentricities only at a muffled remove, divorced from their original cultural context.

The fashionable English-style dandy evoked by Pushkin was an eccentric type that caught on among the Russian aristocracy during the early nineteenth century. This new model for Russian gentlemen's self-presentation acquired cultural currency in sharp contrast to earlier behavioral norms imported from France. The English manner emphasized bold and direct expression rather than French subtlety and wit and asserted a style not previously associated with high society. This bit of cultural history illuminates the tension between the individual and contextual properties of eccentric behaviors. Eccentricities refer to their individual subject's peculiar and particular behavior but also manifest themselves in response to a specific historical context, such as aristocratic Russians' worship of French culture from the reign of Catherine the Great until the Napoleonic wars.

The English dandy cultivated a deliberately eccentric manner in the style of the convention-flouting Romantic hero. Yuri Lotman notes that the French model of comportment compelled members of society to submit themselves to general norms, whereas dandified English practices required their bearer to act strangely ("Roman A. S. Pushkina Evgenii Onegin," 124–25; see also "Russkii dendizm"). In other words, eccentric individualism itself became fashionable at this particular cultural moment. If eccentric behavior itself acquires a fashionable cachet, can such behavior still be considered eccentric?

The dandy is certainly not the sole example of eccentricity as a cultural trend in imperial Russia. Lotman examined eccentric behaviors produced by specific cultural circumstances in his article "Concerning Khlestakov," for example, documenting real-life counterparts to Nikolai Gogol's feckless literary antihero. This article articulates the connection between eccentricity and semiosis, with reference to Lotman's diverse body of work on cultural history, a hybrid discipline that examines unusual phenomena and provides unexpected perspectives on familiar features of the cultural landscape.[3] In fact, nineteenth-century cultural history was often written with reference to eccentrics and eccentricities, a Western trend that also reached Russia. Lotman's more contemporary work provides the basic tools for treating eccentricity as a cultural construct and demonstrates that eccentric behavior—that is, behavior that might seem to lie beyond the boundaries of a particular social context—can in fact be theorized as part of a larger cultural system. Lotman's frequent recourse to spatial metaphors provides an illuminating perspective on behavior that demonstratively places itself at the margins of cultural life, while his interest in historical contexts underscores the unstable and necessarily relative location of the eccentric as a cultural outpost.

## Etymological Eccentricities

Eccentricity (literally, "out of the center," from Greek, *ekkentros*) indicates a deviation from the norm. The opposite of eccentric is "concentric," an attribute of figures or trajectories that share a common center. The *Oxford Dictionary of English Etymology* stresses eccentricity's rejection of such a common center with definitions such as "not concentric" and "not central or referable to a centre." The *Oxford English Dictionary* makes eccentricity figurative, referring to an entity or action "regulated by no central control," a phenomenon that is "anomalous, proceeding by no known method, capricious." In astronomical terms (both Ptolemaic and Copernican), "eccentric" describes an orbit that is elliptical, parabolic, or hyperbolic, rather than circular. Eccentric behavior's divergent quality applies to social forms as well, since its rejection of norms is typically whimsical and unpredictable, rather than principled and political. Eccentricities do not seek to establish new norms, but they do challenge the notion of the normative. Perhaps it is more accurate to say that eccentricities create norms that apply to an individual.

Astronomical and behavioral conceptions of eccentricity converge in the German Romantic notion of the "eccentric path" *(exzentrische Bahn)*, a product of the late-eighteenth-century fascination with comets. These deviant bodies were seen as figures for the ambiguity and moral uncertainty of human life.[4] Eccentricity thus becomes paradoxically central in its application to all human subjects. The productive tension between eccentricity and the entity that defines eccentricity as such in relational terms (the sun, a specific cultural context) explains how it is possible that eccentricity can belong to the system from which it ostensibly departs.

The term *eccentric* complements its synonym *strange* (derived from *extraneus,* meaning "from the outside"). While eccentricity's defining gesture is a movement away from the cultural center, strangeness invades from the outside. Another synonym for eccentricity is *originality,* a word whose Latin root implies the meanings "source" *(origo)* and "rising" *(oriri).* In other words, like eccentricity, originality arises in relation to its own center. Behavior may thus be interpreted in spatial terms as an intrusion (strange), a departure (eccentric), or the appearance of an autonomous foreign body (original), all in relation to the interpreting subject's own cultural center. The notion of eccentricity should not be confused with Viktor Shklovsky's seminal concept of estrangement *(ostranenie),* according to which art challenges its audience to encounter once-familiar objects and experiences as if for the first time.[5] Eccentricity is *innovative,* meaning that it always departs from the familiar. Estrangement, in contrast, is *renovative,* giving new life to the familiar so that it *seems* to have come "from the outside."

The Russian word for an eccentric individual is *chudak,* related to *chudo* (marvel) and *chudovishche* (monster). Marvels and monsters cannot be explained in terms of known natural laws, and eccentric individuals correspondingly defy cultural norms. As Stephen Greenblatt notes, both Descartes and Spinoza believed that the wonder inspired by marvelous objects or beings "depends upon a suspension or failure of categories and is a kind of paralysis, a stilling of the normal associative restlessness of the mind. . . . The object that arouses wonder is so new that for a moment at least it is alone, unsystematized, an utterly detached object of rapt attention."[6] To be sure, Greenblatt's remarks are directed at travel literature and the discovery narratives of America. Eccentricity, as its etymology attests, nevertheless involves a similar suspension of semiotic codes and can in this respect be considered a form of armchair traveling. Like foreign wonders, local eccentricities help to fix the ever-shifting boundary between cultural inside and outside. (For this reason, the seemingly intuitive link between eccentricity and the "holy fool" figure [*iurodivy*] in the Russian cultural context is a specious one. Unlike the true eccentric, the "holy fool" represents an identifiable form of difference bearing a specific cultural function.)[7]

Eccentric behavior, then, is the exception that proves the rule—odd, uncodified individual practices that are nevertheless part of their host culture. Eccentric behavior in its violation of norms evokes the very process of semiosis, according to which elements come to acquire significance within a given cultural context. Lotman describes this process in connection with the spectrum of behavior exhibited by a fool, a sensible person, and a lunatic (*Kul'tura i vzryv*, 41–42). The fool's behavior is too predictable in its violations of appropriate conduct for specific situations, while the sensible person behaves in dull accordance with established norms. The lunatic is the most creative of the three because his behavior diverges from the expected in unexpected ways. Eccentricity and madness both exhibit "unmotivated innovation," the first stage in the journey from nonsemiotic existence to semiosis. It is no coincidence that eccentricity and madness are attributes of the cultural mythologies surrounding creative artists. The lunatic has been perceived differently from the eccentric, however, since Western and Russian societies imprison and repudiate madman, while reveling in the legendary antics of eccentrics.[8]

## Lotman and the Challenge of Cultural History

Studying eccentric behavior from a historical perspective is not unlike working with oral literature from the past, and the two projects present similar difficulties in identifying and using sources. Lotman himself reflected on the challenge of writing cultural history in a number of short, theoretical articles ("O metaiazyke tipologicheskikh opisanii kul'tury," "Pamiat' v kul'turologicheskom osveshchenii," and "Pamiat' kul'tury"). As Lotman observes, there exist two types of written materials useful for recovering oral literature, neither of them entirely satisfactory. The researcher can seek out forms of writing that are relatively close to oral genres (for example, collected anecdotes) or examine literary works inspired or influenced by oral literature from a specific, reconstructive perspective ("K funktsii ustnoi rechi v kul'turnom bytu," 430). The reverse translation from written to oral is problematic, however, in spite of the fact that written and oral forms use the same basic linguistic material. Oral speech allows for a greater number of ellipses and omissions because the speaker can make assumptions about what the addressee already knows. This elliptical quality to oral speech also derives from the "syncretism of behavior," which synthesizes gestures, expressions, visual and kinetic semiotics, and natural language ("Ustnaia rech' v istoriko-kul'turnoi perspektive," 186–87). As a consequence, oral forms provide both more and less information than written ones do. Written language can convert some of the nonlinguistic elements of oral speech into its own medium but cannot transmit a code for reconstructing the original oral form. Eccentric behavior, like oral literature, is performative and syncretic; it leaves no traces except for imperfect reflections in a textual medium. What solution does cultural semiotics offer to the problem of studying a nontextual form such as eccentric social behavior?

Cultural semiotics refers to the elaboration of a hierarchy of languages that express meaning through structural relations. Lotman's work posits a metalanguage based on spatial models for the description of culture, invoking the notions of figure, trajectory, and topology to describe cultural phenomena ("O metaiazyke tipologicheskikh opisanii kul'tury," 388–89). Lotman does not rely on Mikhail Bakhtin's well-known model of the "chronotope"—a characterization of genre in spatial and temporal terms—but rather makes use of a more mathematical and abstract conception of space. For Lotman cultural space refers to a grouping of related objects, which is to say, to the relationships described by these objects rather than to their individual properties ("Ot redaktsii," 3–4). The metaphorical use of space in Lotman's model, as he notes, allows mathematical and cultural realities to intersect meaningfully. The semiotician can thus demarcate eccentricities in relation to other behaviors within a given culture from the historical past.

The vagaries of cultural memory considerably complicate the process of reconstituting eccentric behaviors from shards of the past, however. Lotman characterizes culture as "collective intellect" and "collective memory" transmitting "texts" across time, often with significant alterations ("Pamiat' v kul'turologicheskom osveshchenii," 200). The "creative" part of cultural memory may forget or recall ("discover") elements from the past. Cultural memory is thus not simply a storehouse of information, since it subjects the past to a complex coding process for future recall in response to present circumstances, much as human memory does ("Pamiat' kul'tury," 194). Cultural history reflects the working of cultural memory, indeed of eccentricity itself, in its very particular and frequently opaque logic.

According to a recent study of Britain, France, and America, documented cases of notably eccentric individuals date from the middle of the sixteenth century and reach their peak during the last quarter of the eighteenth century.[9] "To be eccentric," write the authors, "is to be significantly different from everyone else, to be fundamentally at odds with customs and traditions permitted by a culture."[10] One way to approach historical eccentricities is as Lotman advocates, through a written subgenre that is close to oral literature, namely, biographical anecdotes about eccentric personages. In fact, a fad for such anthologies arose in England and America during the early nineteenth century. Anthologies represent an outgrowth of eighteenth-century museum culture, itself the result of the taxonomic practices in emergent natural sciences. These compendia generally offered biographical sketches of distinguished but distinctly peculiar individuals.[11] Such collections could also emphasize the freakish nature of their subjects, as in an 1869 anthology that provided accounts of a stone eater, a vain dwarf, a man who crucified himself, a person of surprising corpulence, and a "celebrated" Pig-Faced Lady, rendered monstrous by a beggar woman's curse visited on her pregnant mother.[12]

Even the titles of such anthologies make use of eccentricity's structural principle, spinning out whimsically lengthy strings that undermine the useful and practical functions of this paratext: *"The Eccentric Mirror: Reflecting a Faithful and Interesting Delineation of Male and Female Characters, Ancient and Modern, Who Have Been Particularly Distinguished by Extraordinary Qualifications, Talents, and Propensities, Natural or Acquired, Comprehending Singular Instances of Longevity, Conformation, Bulk, Stature, Powers of Mind and of Body, Wonderful Exploits, Adventures, Habits, Propensities, Enterprising Pursuits, &c., &c., &c. With a Faithful Narration of Every Instance of Singularity, Manifested in the Lives and Conduct of Characters Who Have Rendered Themselves Eminently Conspicuous by Their Eccentricities. Collected and Recollected, From the Most Authentic Sources by G. H. Wilson."*[13] These titles trumpet extraordinariness to such an extent that their wonders risk becoming monotonous. Furthermore, the insistence on authenticity conveyed by words such as *mirror, faithful,* and *sources* belies the affinity between eccentricity and art. The preceding title seems to promise an accurate reflection of its peculiar subject ("A Mirror of Eccentricity") but actually draws attention to the anthology's peculiar method of representation *(The Eccentric Mirror).*

During the latter part of the nineteenth century, Russians produced a few compendia of cultural eccentricities (discussed in the following section), but these publications represented literary anomalies rather than examples of an established subgenre. Realist literary sketches such as those in Nikolai Nekrasov's *Physiology of Petersburg* (1845) describe individuals who represented social groups ("types") rather than those who were unrepresentative of the cultural norm. Nekrasov's literary tradition of everyday naturalism lived on to the end of the tsarist era in works such as Anatolii Bakhtiarov's *Proletariat and Street Types of Petersburg: Everyday Sketches* (*Proletariat i ulichnye tipy Peterburga: Bytovye ocherki,* 1895), which might seem antithetical to the genre of eccentric compendia. Might there be less to distinguish between an eccentric individual and a "type" than at first appears to be the case? The nineteenth-century Russian literary critic Vissarion Belinsky believed that human individuals expressed the universal values of nationality, and that some could be seen as perfect incarnations of their nation or time.[14] By the same token, each nation represented an individuality that produced a unique national literature and national artists of genius. For Belinsky the typical merges with the particular in the precision and specificity of representation.

Individual eccentricities might also be considered representative of Russia's history as illustrated by Petr Viazemsky, who kept a series of notebooks covering the years 1813–78, filled with vivid anecdotes about individual Russians. He considered eccentric nonconformists to be the true makers of history.[15] In addition to eccentric behavior's historical significance for Russia, Viazemsky also acknowledged its literary potential: "If I knew how to write comedies or novels, I would treasure the legacy of our olden days; without bitterness, without pompous ranting, I would bring onto the stage certain eccentrics, living for their own pleasure, but . . . not harming anyone. Our old everyday life possessed its own dramatic personifications, its own movement, its own diverse colors."[16] Viazemsky proposed writing Russian cultural history in a literary-anecdotal manner that, in his view, best reflected Russia's historical situation.[17]

Russia seems an eccentric entity, as is so often asserted, in its confusing orientation toward both Eastern and Western cultural perspectives. According to this view, Russia also defines itself against both East and West as eccentrically neither. Studying social eccentricities against the anomalous background of Russian cultural history provides a challenging but productive perspective from which to observe a cultural system in motion.

## Burnashev's Chronicle of Cranks and Pyliaev's Wonderful Monsters

Russia came late to the genre of eccentric compendia, and two such works were published during the final quarter of the nineteenth century, after the fad had subsided in the West. This delay is not attributable to the time lag often characteristic of literary fashions imported to Russia. Rather these tributes to eccentricity manifest wistful nostalgia for a kind of Russian aristocracy of idiosyncrasy typical of the early nineteenth century. This nostalgia first appeared during the 1870s, a period characterized by inadequate social and political reforms, and grew alongside the repression and reactionary nationalism that followed.

Vladimir Burnashev is best known for his children's literature, in particular *Strolls with Children about St. Petersburg and Its Environs* (*Progulka s det'mi po Sankt-Peterburgu i ego okrestnostiam*, 1838), published under the pseudonym Viktor Bur'ianov. During the 1870s Burnashev turned to writing memoirs, frequently signing them "A Petersburg Old-Timer" *(Peterburgskii starozhil)*. He favored the genres of compendium and anecdote and created numerous anthologies of humorous, moralistic, and historical material, reviled by critics for their flagrant borrowing from other published sources. Burnashev's reputation as epigone and plagiarist makes all the more surprising the existence of his anomalous *Our Miracle-Workers: A Chronicle of Crankishness and Eccentricities of All Sorts* (*Nashi chudodei: Letopis' chudachestv i ekstsentrichnostei vsiakogo roda*, 1875), the first original anthology of eccentrics to appear in Russia, coyly attributed to the obviously pseudonymous Kas'ian Kas'ianov. As the author himself remarked, "Our literature is somehow careless toward Russians distinguished by their cranks and eccentricities. Western literature does not conduct itself in this way."[18]

Although the title of Burnashev's compendium seems to promise readers a wide selection of diverse eccentricities, the volume actually consists of five long literary sketches. Each piece describes an eccentric individual, among them Count Khvostov, the compulsive versifier *(metroman)*, and the merchant Egor Ganin, creator of a "caricature" garden that exhaustively replicated features of the imperial summer palace gardens in miniature. Burnashev writes Russian history more or less as advocated by Viazemskii, but his eccentric collection was but a prelude to a far more comprehensive effort produced at the end of the nineteenth century. Burnashev's eccentrics are rare exceptions whose exploits each merit an extended narrative. In contrast, Mikhail Pyliaev documented an entire landscape of eccentrics in anecdote, more truly casting eccentricity as Russia's native element.

Pyliaev's loosely structured *Remarkable Eccentrics and Originals (Zamechatel'nye chudaki i originaly*, 1898) presents Russian cultural history of the early nineteenth century through the lens of eccentricity. Pyliaev's attribute "remarkable" *(zamechatel'nye)* derives from the same linguistic root as the Russian guidebook term for "sights/sites of note" *(zamechatel'nosti)*, thus proposing his eccentrics as scheduled stops on an imaginary tour of old Petersburg and Moscow.[19] Eccentrics are distinguished not by character, morals, or views, but rather by strangeness of personal habits, way of life, external appearance, and whims. For example, Pyliaev describes a gentleman landowner whose estate featured a room "decorated in the Moorish style, in which the ceiling and walls were appointed with gold arabesques, radiant wreaths, and entire verse couplets from the poets of bygone times. And all of these cleverly plaited letters and wreaths were made from mice and rats' tails that had been cleaned, sorted, hardened, and covered with gilt."[20] The plaited tails exemplify the artistic powers of eccentricity, which can exert an enormous effort in the pursuit of its highly particular aesthetic vision.

Pyliaev claims that eccentric individuals are found infrequently among the lower classes, explaining, "With education, whimsy begins."[21] In fact, many of his eccentrics are members of the Russian elite — nobles, generals, and diplomats. Pyliaev's theory also accounts for the fact that so many upwardly mobile members of the *raznochinets* class affected eccentric mannerisms to cover their lack of social polish.[22] In this way peculiar social behavior could be construed as distinctive rather than inadequate.

Pyliaev possessed the requisite insider/outsider perspective for a true appreciation of eccentric behaviors. As a prodigious dilettante-scholar from a merchant family, Pyliaev was himself considered an eccentric — a quiet figure digging away in archives, booksellers' stalls, and the Petersburg Public Library. During the 1920s cultural historian P. N. Stolpianskii sharply criticized Pyliaev's practice of culling material from published memoirs, often without attribution and generally without footnotes.[23] In creating an entire volume devoted to eccentrics, Pyliaev nevertheless performed a service to Russian cultural history, selecting and framing his material to form an unprecedented picture of the past.

Pyliaev believes that eccentrics had been more numerous in the early nineteenth century, Russian life being more inconsistently regulated during that period than in the 1890s: "This phenomenon is understandable: whimsicality is the consequence of arbitrariness in life, and the more that arbitrariness rules in a disordered society, the more it gives rise to individual anomalies."[24] These remarks anticipate Lotman's reflections on the structural relationship between normative and transgressive practices within the contested semiotic sphere of imperial St. Petersburg during the early nineteenth century. St. Petersburg fulfilled two disparate functions simultaneously: as an economic center the city was home to a productive "semiotic polyglotism," while as the military capital St. Petersburg "demanded uniformity and strict conformity to a single semiotic system" (*Universe of the Mind,* 200–202). Pyliaev's rambling, nostalgic descriptions of Russian eccentrics celebrate the product of the cultural pole that Lotman characterizes as innovative "literary text," in its subversive relationship to controlling "metalanguage." Pyliaev's remarks also underscore the startling affinity between eccentricity and despotic "arbitrariness," neither subject to law or reason.

## Eccentric Spaces and Genres

St. Petersburg offers a fitting site for studying eccentric social practices, since the Russian imperial capital was unexpectedly constructed at the margins of an empire that was itself often described as a cultural oddity. As Lotman notes, "The eccentric city is situated 'at the edge' of the cultural space: on the seashore, at the mouth of a river" (*Universe of the Mind,* 192).[25] Eccentric structures tend toward "openness and contacts with other cultures," as opposed to "concentric" structures, given to "enclosure" and "separation" from surroundings that are considered hostile. Receptive to that which lies across the cultural borderline, eccentric behavior represents the native made foreign, and as such, eccentricities can make cultural boundaries seem less forbidding. Peter the Great's "transfer of the politico-administrative centre on to the *geographical* frontier was at the same time the transfer of the frontier to the *ideological* and *political* centre of the state" (141). In this sense the founding of St. Petersburg represents a shifting of the eccentric to a position of cultural legitimacy.

As Lotman makes clear, at the center of a given culture's semiosphere lie its most structurally organized languages, including its natural language. Eccentricities hover at the boundaries of a culture's "semiosphere" as examples of "transitional forms" that are part of any "language."[26] Eccentricities are excluded from a language's "grammatical self-description," since eccentric cultural practices are neither normative nor codified. These social forms do, however, belong to "the reality of semiosis," according to which a language represents "a cluster of semiotic spaces and their boundaries" (*Universe of the Mind*, 123–24). Viewing the semiosphere from the culture's periphery—which is, by definition, eccentric—further complicates this picture: "In the centre the metastructure is 'our' language, but on the periphery it is treated as 'someone else's' language unable adequately to reflect the semiotic reality beneath it. . . . [T]he relationship between semiotic practice and the norms imposed on it becomes ever more strained. Texts generated in accordance with these norms hang in the air, without any real semiotic context; while organic creations, born of the actual semiotic milieu, come into conflict with the artificial norms" (134). A semiosphere's inhabitants experience the center as neutral and the eccentric periphery as "brightly colored and marked" (141).[27] Yet Lotman's description suggests that peripheral formations are natural ("organic"), whereas the regulated center is rigid and artificial. Even if eccentricities are a phenomenon naturally occurring within cultural systems, however, there is no language to describe them, apart from elaborating what eccentricities are *not*.

Lotman proposes a definition of center and periphery that attributes a particular type of textual organization to each area. The central sphere of a culture resembles "an integrated structural whole," somewhat like a sentence. The periphery, in contrast, is like "a cumulative chain organized by the simple joining of structurally independent units." The center offers a "structural model of the world," while the periphery constitutes "a special archive of anomalies." A peripheral text thus "takes anomalies and exceptions as its plot elements" and creates a "picture of the world in which chance and disorder predominate" (*Universe of the Mind*, 162). Eccentric behavior displays no articulable logic in its combination of elements, instead manifesting its trademark aesthetics of whimsy.

Pyliaev writes, for example, of a general who adored "antiques" and collected items from all over Russia, among them a cane made from a horseradish root, a staff from dried burdock, and a metal poker bent into an arc by a strongman.[28] He owned a drum made from the skin of a robber punished by an Astrakhan chieftain and a portrait of a peasant whose wife had given birth to fifty-seven children. The general also took pride in a sculpture of a mouse made from apple seeds and in a huge pear submerged in a narrow-necked bottle of spirits. This pear had evidently been introduced into the bottle while still a bud attached to its tree and allowed to reach eccentric maturity there.

Like Lotman's characterization of the periphery as a simple linking of anomalous elements, no single object in the general's collection has ascertainable meaning as part of a whole, except perhaps as a portrait of an eccentric individual. That which is eccentric merits contemplation but thwarts any attempt to decipher its code. Pyliaev's own book-length collection of eccentricities takes the same form as the general's assemblage of strange objects. His lovingly detailed gallery of odd characters corresponds to Lotman's more abstract "archive of anomalies."

Must eccentric behavior entail chance and disorder from the point of view of its host culture? Can the eccentric be related in the form of narrative, as implied by Lotman's reference to "plot elements"? For Lotman plot involves the transgression of a cultural or semiotic boundary by a persona (*Structure of the Artistic Text*, 233); without this border crossing, there is no story. Such a definition of plot suggests that narrative transpires within the territory of eccentricity, in the peripheral area that lies close to a semiotic boundary. Lotman views eccentric behavior correspondingly as a transitory stage on the way to genuine plotted narrative. Theatrical-seeming behavior such as that exhibited by late-eighteenth-century Russian noblemen assimilating Western norms integrates itself within a new host culture by evolving from random creativity to role and finally to plot. Those behaviors initially regarded as merely eccentric may become more organized and consciously regulated ("Poetics of Everyday Behavior," 85–86, 94), but eccentric behavior must necessarily resist the assimilation that will lead inexorably to its death—that is eccentricity's own plot. The narrative of eccentricity is in this sense a mock-heroic one.

In treating eccentric practices from a literary perspective, it is helpful to review Lotman's structuralist characterization of stylistics and rhetoric. Stylistics makes it possible to express the same semantic content in different "registers," in each case drawing all signs from one particular register. In contrast, rhetoric relies for its effects on combining signs from different registers. Lotman distinguishes between the two "consciousnesses" as follows: "The stylistic effect is formed *within* a hierarchical subsystem. Stylistic consciousness, therefore, arises from hierarchical boundaries which it constitutes as an absolute, while the rhetorical consciousness arises from hierarchical boundaries which it constitutes as relative." In literary texts, however, "there can be a rhetorical attitude towards stylistics," since a "poetic stylistics" creates "a special semiotic space, within which a free choice of stylistic register is possible, this register no longer being automatically defined by the communicative situation" (*Universe of the Mind*, 51). A "poetic stylistics" implicitly evokes its corresponding violated norms to produce the requisite striking effect. Unlike rhetoric a "poetic stylistics" emphasizes the unorthodox combination of elements rather than the hortatory purpose for which the expected register is deemed inadequate.

Eccentric behaviors, like literary works, can blend stylistic registers in an unconventional manner. For example, Pyliaev describes a millionaire merchant who regularly invited passers-by from diverse social backgrounds to be his houseguests for the day, even offering a day's wages to poorer guests in exchange for their willingness to accept his invitation.[29] The merchant would lavish attention and dainties on his guests, gleefully disrupting the sociogeneric hierarchy. These gatherings were not analogous to masquerades, where any attendee might pretend to be well born. Instead, the millionaire merchant deliberately created an eccentric mix of strangers, all of whom he treated as close friends. His drawing room refracted the surrounding social reality, just as a work of literary art may challenge the expected hierarchy of stylistic registers.

## Collective Eccentricities

Particular eccentricities can acquire the status of stylistic registers rather than individual anomalies if these behaviors catch on as fashionable. Similarly, established stylistic registers may come to seem eccentric if the number of practitioners dwindles dramatically. Pyliaev describes the St. Petersburg streetscape of the early nineteenth century in terms of such cultural synchronicity as the overlapping of diverse stylistic principles:

> Fifty or sixty years ago, the street life of the capital still offered a great deal of freedom in terms of dress . . . a number of individuals from the

epoch of Catherine were still living, and they walked the streets adorned in stars, cloaks, and gold suits . . . ; one could also see old brigadiers in white-plumed hats. More than a few male aristocrats came to Nevsky Prospect carrying muffs and wearing red-heeled shoes, according to the court custom in the empress's time. . . . Fashionable young gents . . . opened their parasols against the palest rays of the sun. . . . A fashion for earrings bloomed particularly among the military men in the cavalry regiments. . . . Fifty years ago it was not considered strange for men to wear powder and rouge. . . . Military men laced themselves into corsets and raised their epaulets with shoulder pads.[30]

In contrast to the English-style dandy, who deliberately cultivated behaviors deemed peculiar within his own cultural-historical context, these gender-bending eccentrics seem odd only when *removed* from their context. For the Petersburg resident during the time of Tsar Nicholas I, vivid survivors from Catherine's era formed part of the general cultural picture, as did the modish younger generation. While Pyliaev's description attempts to convey a normative view of the streetscape in its own time, this passage also enacts the historical disintegration of an established register into its separate stylistic components. Like Lotman's work on cultural history, Pyliaev's descriptions render the cultural past legible as a stylistic register. These accounts do not artistically estrange the familiar but perform the complementary operation of making the strange into the familiar, recounting the exploits of eccentrics who belong to Russian cultural history.

If eccentricities represent individual behavior, what relation does eccentricity assume to the cultural collective? Lotman defines the relationship of individual to group behavior as follows: "Just as language norms are realized and simultaneously violated in thousands of idiolects, so group behavior is the sum total of the realization and violation of behavioral norms within the individual systems of innumerable group members. But 'incorrect' behavior that violates the behavioral norms of a given social group is by no means accidental. . . . Rules arise for violating rules and violations appear that are essential to norms. . . . A higher value may be assigned to following the norm. . . . Or a higher value may be assigned to the violation of the norm, leading to an emphasis on originality, oddity, eccentricity, playing the holy fool, and the devaluation of the norm through the ambivalent union of extremes" ("Decembrist in Daily Life," 96). Lotman characterizes the relationship between individual and group behavior as dialectical. Eccentricities come into being where the marginally normative overlaps with culturally sanctioned deviations from the social norm. In this way eccentricities exist as an integral part of the cultural system they only *seem* to defy.

In fact, eccentric phenomena often function as fixed features in a cultural landscape. The circular variety of eccentricity (that is, the elliptical rather than the parabolic trajectory) represents an *orbit*, meaning that—etymologically and figuratively speaking—eccentricity performs itself repeatedly, remaining identical to itself. Orbiting eccentricities are patterns extended over both time and space, strange behavior that is nevertheless consistent. In this sense eccentricity is predictable. Pyliaev tells of a count famous for passionate devotion to ice cream, which he "devoured in fearful quantities" even on his deathbed. "The dying man calmly ordered ten portions of ice cream brought to his bedroom in a silver mould and remarked, 'I have one more question: in the empyrean, will I be treated to ice cream?' Having finished his dessert, the count closed his eyes and crossed himself."[31] Here eccentricity offsets whimsy in becoming a monument to itself.

An individual eccentric orbit can come to resemble a work of art, as in the case of the *Kammerjunker* known to all as "Rococo." The gentleman's house was furnished with brocade, velvet, satin, gilt, marble, tapestries, statues, antique bronze, and Chinese porcelain, all spread haphazardly about "with such a lack of taste and in such disorder, that at first glance it seemed that all these valuable things had been transported there to be sold, as in a shop." When he was asked about "the expensive Chinese bronze mixed in with simple rustic clay peg-tops, irons, and oven prongs," or about "the splendid old paintings juxtaposed with daubing by peasant Raphaels," the gentleman replied that he aspired to the 'rococo.'"[32] The *Kammerjunker* associated the notion of rococo with a fanciful, asymmetrical, and elaborate combination of elements well beyond the French decorative style from the eighteenth century. This is perhaps an eccentric interpretation of the term and might better be rendered as "eclectic." Still, the gentleman's behavior was so predictably eccentric that the surrounding community canonized him in terms of his own idiosyncratic recourse to an established aesthetic category. Eccentricity may have staying power, but it has no identity of its own apart from the merely relational (out of the center).

Eccentricity can prolong its life by lagging *behind* fashion, as in the case of one Prince Kurakin: "In the time of Alexander I, when the emperor himself used only a single horse, and rich carriages had disappeared along with gold-laced liveries, . . . only Kurakin preserved the old Catherinian custom, riding in a gilt carriage with eight glass windows, tandem-harnessed, with a postilion and two lackeys, a footman on the back, two riders out in front, and two footmen running behind the carriage."[33] Defying the laws of time in such a public manner casts eccentric behavior as the guardian of a cultural text. Eccentricities thereby perform a public service.

Such were, similarly, those residents of the Petersburg Side who became ensnarled in impossible lawsuits. These unfortunates gathered at the ferry landing each morning, "weighed down by sheaves and scrolls of paper," as they prepared to cross the Neva River to reach the senate. One eccentric elderly man invariably carried a heavy birch log tenderly wrapped up. He was involved in a long-standing dispute over construction work for which he had never been paid, the client insisting that the logs had been cut too short. The now-elderly builder had preserved one such log and had attempted over the course of forty years to prove he was not at fault. Each day the ferry passengers politely asked the old man to tell his story, and he would oblige, never remembering that he had recounted his history many times before.[34] The passengers in this nested mininarrative sustain the old man's eccentricities by inciting repeated performances. The passengers' attention thereby acknowledges eccentricity as a shared cultural resource.

Eccentric behavior may represent the private inadvertently made public, thrilling its viewers. Alternatively eccentricities may be displayed in an overtly, even compulsively public manner, as in the case of Kolo-grivov, a Petersburg gentleman of high rank who would costume himself as an indigent Finn and sweep the public pavements, demanding alms from passing acquaintances and threatening them with his broom.[35] Other eccentrics behaved in a natural, unselfconscious way, among them the small gentleman of respectable appearance who frequented the Summer Garden, bowing to strollers.[36] This gentleman fancied himself a Kabardian prince secretly sent to Russia as an infant after an uprising in his native land. If tea or vodka were offered in company, he would stand and bow graciously to his hosts in keeping with court etiquette, which required the king's permission before refreshments could be served. He wrote to the royal families of Europe, soliciting their help in regaining his throne, but received no replies. Instead Petersburg residents sent him clothes and money in bundles purported to come from his loyal Kabardian subjects. Eccentricity's fragile beauty makes the host culture complicit in its survival, even as this culture strives to codify the exceptional—a logical and aesthetic impossibility.

Studying eccentricity sheds unexpected light on the structured, coded nature of the everyday as a semiotic system. As Lotman declares, "The further removed a society is in time, place, or culture, the more its everyday behavior becomes a well-defined object of scholarly attention. Most documents recording norms of everyday behavior have been written by or for foreigners, presupposing an observer external to the social unit." Lotman used the eccentric exception to prove the rule of the everyday, in describing the peculiar situation of the Russian nobility under Peter the Great. Struggling to adopt unfamiliar everyday norms from the West, the eighteenth-century Russian nobility treated the "natural" sphere of everyday life as formal and ritualized. Eighteenth-century Russian culture thus "patterned certain aspects of ordinary life on the norms and rules governing artistic texts and experienced them directly as aesthetic forms" ("Poetics of Everyday Behavior," 67–68). Because cultural communities perceive their everyday behavior as natural, they fail to perceive this behavior as social *form*. The eccentric constitutes a reverse image of the everyday, however, bringing these invisible structures into view.

Eccentricity, although always in the act of departing from the cultural center, nevertheless remains at home. Lotman's lessons in cultural history illustrate this principle, plotting eccentricity across time and space but situating it entirely within the province of a semiosphere that makes eccentric behavior both visible and meaningful. Rather than explaining away those colorful transitional forms of semiosis that flourish at the cultural margin, Lotman's systemic vision of culture reveals eccentricity as a vital common resource that moves a community to extend the reach of its norms.

### Notes

1 Alexander Pushkin, *Eugene Onegin*, trans. James E. Falen (Oxford: Oxford University Press, 1995), 16.

2. Alexander Pushkin, *Eugene Onegin*, trans. Vladimir Nabokov (Princeton, N.J.: Princeton University Press, 1975), 2:110.

3. For background on the development of this interdisciplinary pursuit, see H. Aram Veeser, "The New Historicism," in *The New Historicism Reader*, ed.

H. Aram Veeser (New York: Routledge, 1994). See also Stephen Greenblatt, "Towards a Poetics of Culture," in *The New Historicism*, ed. H. Aram Veeser (New York: Routledge, 1989).

4. Marshall Brown, "The Eccentric Path," *Journal of English and Germanic Philology* 77, no. 1 (January 1978): 108.

5. See "Art as Device" in Shklovsky's *Theory of Prose*, trans. Benjamin Sher (Elmwood Park, Ill.: Dalkey Archive Press, 1990), 6–14. My thanks to Amy Mandelker for helping me to clarify this distinction.

6. Stephen Greenblatt, *Marvelous Possessions: The Wonder of the New World* (Chicago: University of Chicago Press, 1991), 20.

7. Sources on the "holy fool" in Russian culture include Ingunn Lunde, ed., *The Holy Fool in Byzantium and Russia* (Bergen, Norway: University of Bergen, 1995); and Ewa M. Thompson, *Understanding Russia: The Holy Fool in Russian Culture* (Lanham, Md.: University Press of America, 1987).

8. In fact, a survey of eccentricity as a modern historical phenomenon asserts that in the past there may well have been confusion in differentiating the eccentric from the mentally ill of the middle and upper classes, who were often looked after at home. See David Joseph Weeks with Kate Ward, *Eccentrics: The Scientific Investigation* (London: Stirling University Press, 1988), 15–16, 23–26.

9. Ibid., 14.

10. Ibid., 17–18.

11. A small sampling of such compendia includes *Les fous célèbres* (Paris: B. Renault, 1835); William Russell, *Eccentric Personages* (New York: American News, 1866); *Biographical Sketches of Eccentric Characters* (Boston: N. H. Whitaker, 1832); Champfleury, *Les excentriques* (Paris: Michel Lévy frères, 1852); and Henry Wilson, *The Book of Wonderful Characters: Memoirs and Anecdotes of Remarkable and Eccentric Persons in All Ages and Countries* (London: J. C. Hotten, 1869). Compendia of eccentrics are also extremely well represented in Japan and China beginning in the late seventeenth century. For a description of this phenomenon in Japan of the Edo Period (1600–1868), see Shoichi Saeki, "Images of Eccentrics: East and West," in *Biography East and West: Selected Conference Papers*, ed. Carol Ramelb (Honolulu : College of Languages, Linguistics, and Literature, University of Hawaii and the East-West Center; distributed by University of Hawaii Press, 1989).

12. Henry Wilson and James Caulfield, *The Book of Wonderful Characters* (London: Reeves Turner, 1869).

13. (London: Printed for James Cundee, 1806–7). Yet another such title is *Eccentric Biography, or Memoirs of Remarkable Characters, Ancient and Modern: Including Potentates, Statesmen, Divines, Historians, Naval and Military Heroes, Philosophers, Lawyers, Impostors, Poets, Painters, Players, Dramatic Writers, Misers, &c. &c. &c. The Whole Alphabetically Arranged Forming a Pleasing Delineation of the Singularity, Whim, Folly, Caprice, &c. of the Human Mind* (Boston: B. & J. Homans, 1804).

14. For a summary of Belinsky's pronouncements on the subject, see the sections "Art and Individuality" and "Art and Nationality," in Victor Terras, *Belinskij and Russian Literary Criticism: The Heritage of Organic Aesthetics* (Madison: University of Wisconsin Press, 1974), 91–101.

15. Sally Kux, "Petr Andreevich Viazemsky: A Necessary Virtue," in *Russian Subjects: Empire, Nation, and the Culture of the Golden Age*, ed. Monika Greenleaf and Stephen Moeller-Sally (Evanston, Ill.: Northwestern University Press, 1998), 225.

16. L. Ia. Ginzburg, ed., *P. A. Viazemskii: Staraia zapisnaia knizhka* (Leningrad: Izdatel'stvo pisatelei v Leningrade, 1929), 270. Translation to English as per Sally Kux.

17. As Stephen Greenblatt declares, "If anecdotes are registers of the singularity of the contingent—associated . . . with the rim rather than the immobile and immobilizing center—they are at the same time recorded as *representative* anecdotes, that is, as significant in terms of a larger progress or pattern that is the proper subject of a history." See *Marvelous Possessions*, 3.

18. Vladimir Petrovich Burnashev, *Nashi chudodei: Letopis' chudachestv i ekstsentrichnostei vsiakogo roda* (St. Petersburg: Tip. V. Tushnova, 1875), 134.

19. Pyliaev is known for his books about Petersburg of the past: *Old Petersburg* (*Staryi Peterburg*, 1887) and *Forgotten Environs of St. Petersburg* (*Zabytye okrestnosti S-Peterburga*, 1889). In an obituary written for Pyliaev in 1899, Alexander Pleshcheev asserts that "[i]n his works, M. I. Pyliaev was always precise, and it is a mistake to assume that Pyliaev exaggerated in describing a particular eccentric or original. Pyliaev obtained his information from reliable sources and did not embellish facts with his own imagination." See "Pamiati M. I. Pyliaeva," *Istoricheskii vestnik*, no. 3 (1899): 966–75; also reprinted in *Staryi Peterburg* (Leningrad: Titul, 1990), iii–xi.

20. M. I. Pyliaev, *Zamechatel'nye chudaki i originaly* (St. Petersburg: A. S. Suvorin, 1898), 263.

21. Ibid., 1. Weeks and Ward similarly contend that eccentrics come mostly from the aristocracy, landed gentry, and upper middle classes (*Eccentrics*, 16). Their study invokes such well-known cultural models as eccentric millionaires, dotty elderly ladies who live in old family homes, absent-minded professors, mad scientists, and crazy inventors.

22. For a full elaboration of this theme, see Irina Paperno, *Chernyshevsky and the Age of Realism: A Study in the Semiotics of Behavior* (Stanford, Calif.: Stanford University Press, 1988).

23. P. N. Stolpianskii, "Bibliografiia Sankt-Piter-Burkha: Opisaniia i plany po ekzempliaram Publichnoi Biblioteki" (Leningrad, 1926), unpublished manuscript held in Reference Room, St. Petersburg State Public Library. See comments about Pyliaev's various publications.

24. Pyliaev, *Zamechatel'nye chudaki i originaly*, 2. Pyliaev's claim is similar to that of Wilson and Caulfield (*Book of Wonderful Characters*), who mourn the extent to which British people and places have become less and less distinguishable from one another. Wilson and Caulfield attribute this phenomenon to the influence of railroads, which eliminate local differences.

25. Note that Lotman's essay on Petersburg appears separately as "Simvolika Peterburga i problemy semiotiki goroda," in *Izbrannye stat'i*, vol. 1.

26. Lotman defines the semiosphere as "the semiotic space necessary for the existence and functioning of languages, not the sum total of different languages; in a sense the semiosphere has a prior existence and is in constant interaction with languages. In this respect a language is a function, a cluster of semiotic spaces and their boundaries, which, however clearly defined these are in the language's grammatical self-description, in the reality of semiosis are eroded and full of transitional forms" (*Universe of the Mind*, 123–24).

27. Lotman's conception of the periphery corresponds to characterizations of writing from the cultural margin, "from the boundaries of eccentricity—an eccentricity defined by the central culture's claim to universality." See Carlos Fuentes, "Central and Eccentric Writing," *American Review* 21 (1974): 85.

28. Pyliaev, *Zamechatel'nye chudaki i originaly*, 336–40.

29. Ibid., 82–85.

30. Ibid., 287–88.

31. Ibid., 88–89.

32. Ibid., 104–8.

33. Ibid., 159.

34. Ibid., 281–83.

35. Ibid., 166.

36. Ibid., 321–24.

# Writing in a Polluted Semiosphere

## *Everyday Life in Lotman, Foucault, and de Certeau*

### JONATHAN H. BOLTON

In 1983 Jan Zábrana copied into his diary a statement he had heard on the radio: "The sardines that are being imported to us from the Soviet Union are not sardines in the true sense of the word."[1] Zábrana did not normally pay much attention to sardine imports, but as a translator with an ear highly sensitized to the use and abuse of language, he followed linguistic imports closely. And as a Czech writer who had suffered considerably at the hands of Soviet-sponsored regimes, he seized on this apparently trivial comment as a sad and amusing emblem of all the artificial things that had made their way, under false names, to Czechoslovakia from the Soviet Union. This everyday moment, moving quickly from the trivial (the sardines) and random (a comment overheard on the radio) to a lightly subversive reinterpretation of a dominant discourse (the language of the state-controlled media in Czechoslovakia of the 1980s), captures many of the themes underlying the conception of everyday life in the work of Yuri Lotman.

Although Lotman did not seem interested in formulating a full-fledged theory of what everyday life is and does, he did work frequently with the idea, for example in his essays "The Poetics of Everyday Behavior in Eighteenth-Century Russian Culture" and "The Decembrist in Daily Life," as well as in his discussion of the semiosphere in *Universe of the Mind*. In what follows, I develop a Lotmanian conception of everyday life as a "boundary" zone in which our own practices and habits come into conflict with the codes and systems that a dominant discourse of the "center" seeks to impose on us—a zone, for example, where the word *sardines* no longer seems to fit the Soviet imports, tearing a tiny hole in the fabric of official codes. The everyday, for Lotman, is tied to the possibility of imagining alternatives to a dominant discourse (or the failure to do so), and I compare this aspect of Lotman's theories to analogous ideas in Michel Foucault and Michel de Certeau, hoping to reveal the theoretical power of Lotman's more flexible model of the everyday. Finally, I return to the diaries of Zábrana, interpreting them through a Lotmanian prism as a way of exploring the ambiguous poetics, the strengths and weaknesses, of a marginal position in everyday life at the boundary of a semiosphere.

## Versions of Everyday Life

Several of Lotman's key writings about everyday life center around the idea that the everyday is not "semiotized." It goes unnoticed precisely because it is so common, passing under the radar of our semiotic systems. In "Byt i kul'tura," the introduction to his *Besedy o russkoi kul'ture,* Lotman defines the Russian word *byt*—a capacious and ambiguous term that can refer, among other things, to the daily life and customs of a region, nation, or epoch: "*Byt* is the usual flow of life in its real and practical forms; *byt* is the things that surround us, our habits and everyday conduct. *Byt* surrounds us like air, and, like air, it is noticeable only when there is not enough, or when it is contaminated. We notice the peculiarities of someone else's *byt*, but our own *byt* is imperceptible—we tend to consider it as 'simply life,' the natural norm of practical existence. *Byt,* then, is always in the sphere of practice; it is, above all, the world of things" (10). Two elements of this definition stand out. One is the idea of routine: we don't notice our own daily life because it is so common, consisting of our "habits and everyday behavior" and the things that always surround us.[2] The second element is the idea of a "sphere of practice": the things making up *byt* tend to be perceived for their practical function, their use value, rather than for their symbolic meaning—just as bread, when eaten, "has a use and not a meaning" (6).

*Byt,* like bread, can *acquire* symbolic meanings and thereby enter into the semiotic sphere of "culture," but in and of itself it is practical and presemiotic. Thus, in "The Poetics of Everyday Behavior," Lotman divides our behavior into two categories: "ordinary, everyday, customary social behavior," which we perceive as "natural" and normal; and "ceremonial, ritual, nonpragmatic behavior" such as political ceremonies or religious rituals, which we "perceive as having an independent meaning." He continues: "People within a given culture learn the first type of conduct as they do their native language. They are directly immersed in it through direct use and do not notice when, where, and from whom they acquired it. . . . The second type of conduct is learned in the same way as a foreign language, with rules and grammar books. . . . The first type of behavior is acquired naturally, unconsciously. The second is acquired consciously, with the aid of a teacher, and its mastery is usually celebrated in a special rite of initiation" ("Poetics of Everyday Behavior," 68). Here again, one part of our lives is mastered in the course of things, absorbed through everyday use (and again, ideas of both repetition and practicality underlie this conception), while another part is learned, perceived as contrived or artificial. The everyday seems natural and "ours"; its semiotic and conventional character will be apparent only to a foreign observer—or when we are forced to adapt our own everyday behavior to an externally imposed pattern. Thus, when Peter the Great made the Russian nobility adapt "European" forms of dress and behavior, he turned the nobleman into "a foreigner in his own country," forced "to learn through unnatural methods what is usually acquired through direct experience in early childhood" (69).

The distinction between semiotic and nonsemiotic reality is one of Lotman's favored heuristic tools; it appears often in his large-scale "typologies" of different cultures and epochs—for example, when he describes medieval Russian culture as based on a division of all realities into the meaningful and the nonmeaningful, those that signify and those that just are.[3] But the semiotic/nonsemiotic distinction is a rather crude one that deserves interrogation, despite its considerable explanatory powers. For one thing, it seems dubious to draw such a stark distinction between the everyday and what we think of as conventional, foreign, or ritualized. In fact, we do learn some everyday behavior as we would learn a "foreign language"—the rules of driving, for example. Luckily, most of us are taught explicitly how to drive, rather than just "absorbing" the rules of the road from being "immersed in their usage." Here, then, is a case in which learned behavior can become everyday. Conversely, even as traffic laws become automatized, we are still aware of their conventional nature, as anyone waiting on a red light at a deserted late-night intersection knows. This simple example suggests that even codes we learn as "someone else's" can become as natural as the surrounding air for us, and conversely that even the most automatic or unnoticed behavior can seem conventional, under the right circumstances.

Indeed, Lotman seems aware of just this issue in "The Poetics of Everyday Behavior," where he suggests that Peter the Great's reforms forced the Russian nobility to become *explicitly* aware of its own daily life: "The area of subconscious, 'natural' behavior became a sphere in which teaching was needed. Instructions were issued regarding the norms of social behavior, since the entire previously existing structure had been rejected as incorrect and replaced by 'correct' European rules" (68–69). Lotman makes an analogous argument in "The Decembrist in Daily Life." First, he posits another version of the semiotic/nonsemiotic split, in which the European ideas and ideology of the nobility are set off from "the sphere of ordinary behavior—of everything related to everyday preoccupations, custom, the real conditions of estate management, and the real circumstances of the civil service." For Lotman, "the level of semiosis increased" as one moved up to the realm of ideas from the lowest, "purely practical stratum which, for the theorizing mind, was as good as nonexistent" ("Decembrist in Daily Life," 101). But, he continues, the Decembrists *rejected* this hierarchy, lending great importance to their own everyday behavior, such as their speech patterns and gestures. In other words, Lotman's Decembrists denied the very idea that everyday life is "natural" and prior to meaning: "[P]urely practical behavior . . . acquired a semiotic character, crossing over from a group of activities carrying no value to a group of actions interpreted . . . as 'noble' and 'dignified' or 'base,' 'boorish,' and 'vile'" (102). There could be no nonsemiotic sphere, since "neutral or nonsignifying acts did not exist" (107). Hence, the Decembrists' significance lies not only in their political program but also in their creative fashioning of a style of everyday behavior, which distinguished them just as surely as did their ideology.

Both of these articles are already far more subtle than the initial thesis that behavior can be divided into semiotic and nonsemiotic spheres.

They reveal that the line of division can be wavy and mobile, relativizing the whole idea of the everyday. They highlight our intuitive sense that what we take for granted, the routine and unnoticeable, can actually be a fragile construction; and they also indicate, unequivocally if obliquely, that everyday behavior is not a politically neutral concept. It can be altered by political fiat from above, as in Peter the Great's attempts to alter the customs and habits of his noble subjects, or it can acquire revolutionary valence, as in the unorthodox daily conduct of the Decembrists. What is missing in these articles is a more explicit theoretical construct that would allow us to examine the circulation of the everyday and the negotiations whereby the boundary of the everyday shifts back and forth—the mechanisms of change that alter our perceptions of what is imperceptible.[4] Such a theory emerges more clearly from Lotman's writings on the semiosphere.

## The Ragged Edges of the Semiosphere

This term, coined after Vernadsky's "biosphere" and Bakhtin's "logosphere," remains—like many fruitful concepts—a little vague.[5] In *Universe of the Mind,* Lotman defines it as "the semiotic space necessary for the existence and functioning of languages, not the sum total of different languages" (123). The semiosphere asks us to consider, not a particular language with its own well-developed grammar and self-description, but the way each language interacts with all the others around it: "In this respect a language is a function, a cluster of semiotic spaces and their boundaries, which, however clearly defined these are in the language's grammatical self-description, in the reality of semiosis are eroded and full of transitional forms" (123–24).

The interactions among languages can be seen as acts of *translation,* which is for Lotman a fundamental process of information generation, "a primary mechanism of consciousness. To express something in another language is a way of understanding it" (*Universe of the Mind,* 127). But translation is also a way of *changing* a message: as any translator knows, and as Lotman emphasizes, most translations generate new information. The original message is altered and augmented in being transmitted from one code to another. Thus translation is never a simple re-creation of an idea in a new code; it is never a transitive equation of identity. This irreversibility of translation helps account for the "erosion" and "transitional forms" at a language's boundaries. It also helps explain why the semiosphere is more than the sum of its parts, since the mutual translation among languages generates new information, not to mention entirely new languages. Indeed, one function of the semiosphere concept for Lotman is to explain how different languages can exist in continuous conflict and dialogue within a culture, along many different axes, forming an organic whole that never stops evolving. "As against the atomistic static approach we may regard the semiosphere as a *working mechanism* whose separate elements are in complex dynamic relationships. This mechanism on a vast scale functions to circulate information, preserve it and to produce new messages" (Lotman and Uspenskij, "Authors' Introduction," *Semiotics of Russian Culture*, xii).

As diverse and dynamic as the semiosphere is, however, it does follow a general pattern. Its very heterogeneity creates the need for some organization to counter this entropy, and so it tends to become organized as a "center" surrounded by a "periphery." The center is distinguished by a high level of self-description: "[T]he highest form and final act of a semiotic system's structural organization is when it describes itself" in "a necessary response to the threat of too much diversity within the semiosphere." This leads to more organization and stability, but also to a certain rigidity as the language "loses its inner reserves of indeterminacy" (*Universe of the Mind*, 128). For a time, this codified language will attempt to impose itself on the rest of the semiosphere: "Whether we have in mind language, politics or culture, the mechanism is the same: one part of the semiosphere . . . in the process of self-description creates its own grammar. . . . Then it strives to extend these norms over the whole semiosphere. A partial grammar of one cultural dialect becomes the metalanguage of description for culture as such" (128). Lotman gives examples such as the dialect of Florence becoming Italy's literary language during the Renaissance or the laws of Rome being imposed on the whole Roman Empire.

But this imposition also leads to friction, especially on the "periphery" of the semiosphere, where the grammar of the center may come into conflict with other languages, or with the "everyday reality of life" *(bytovaia real'nost')* from which some semiotic codes are derived (*Universe of the Mind*, 129). The periphery, of course, need not be a particular geographical location such as the border territory between two countries. Lotman defines it more broadly as the "boundary" between semiotic systems, where people feel a difference between first- and third-person forms, the space between "my (or our) world" and "their world." The periphery of the semiosphere can be defined as any place where the codified grammar of the center begins to fray, where it is felt as something foreign and imposed rather than "my own":

> In the centre the metastructure is "our" language, but on the periphery it is treated as "someone else's" language unable adequately to reflect the semiotic reality beneath it: it is like the grammar of a foreign language. As a result, in the centre of the cultural space, sections of the semiosphere aspiring to the level of self-description become rigidly organized and self-regulating. But at the same time they lose dynamism and having once exhausted their reserve of indeterminacy they became [sic] inflexible and incapable of further development. On the periphery . . . the relationship between semiotic practice and the norms imposed on it becomes ever more strained. Texts generated in accordance with these norms hang in the air, without any real semiotic context; while organic creations, born of the actual semiotic milieus, come into conflict with the artificial norms. This is the area of semiotic dynamism. This is the field of tension where new languages come into being. (134)

This intense semiotic activity at the boundary eventually gives rise to challenges to the hegemony of the center language. It "leads to an accelerated 'maturing' of the peripheral centres; metalanguages are born which in their turn claim to be universal metalanguages for the whole semiosphere" (135). The semiosphere, then, might be more accurately described as being organized around a number of competing centers— it is transected in all directions by "boundary" regions where codified systems are felt to be foreign, at odds with lived experience and "local" semiotic codes.

One way of understanding everyday life, on this model, would be as just such a boundary zone—not merely as nonsemiotic or presemiotic material, but as a world of *both* "practical functions" *and* ideas and meanings, a world in which we feel somehow at home. Or, to be more precise, we need not feel "at home" in our everyday life, but we must feel it is somehow "ours"—if only because it is familiar to us, thanks to repetition and routine, and embedded in our practical needs and daily activities. Given this sense of everyday life as "our" space, we can see why it is a realm of potential conflicts and contradictions with other codes imposed on us from the "center" of the semiosphere. Everyday life is one of the places the central code flexes its muscles, where it either extends its hegemony by describing diverse realities and coopting competing descriptions—or discovers the weakness of its own "eroded" and "transitional forms."

## Everyday Life as a Site of Power and Resistance

It may be useful to compare this semiospheric version of everyday life with two others, in order to bring out the theoretical power and subtlety of Lotman's model. Michel Foucault (in *Discipline and Punish*) and Michel de Certeau (in *The Practice of Everyday Life*) both give accounts of everyday life that can be seen as offering their own interpretations of the distinction between semiotic and nonsemiotic material. Both, however, remain ultimately rigid and one-sided: for Foucault everyday life is essentially vulnerable to external description, whereas for de Certeau, it is incapable of being captured in larger sign systems.

Foucault's *Discipline and Punish* looks at how, starting in the eighteenth century, European institutions such as schools, the army, hospitals, and prisons gradually began to exercise a kind of power—what Foucault calls "discipline"—that "fabricated" individuals largely in order to weave them more firmly into a web of control. Previously, power had been invested in the highly visible person of a monarch; now, says Foucault, it subtly shifted its location and spread invisibly throughout the entire social body, such that each person internalized a controller's gaze and became, in a sense, his or her own jailer. This last idea culminates in Foucault's famous discussion of Jeremy Bentham's plans for a "panopticon," a circular prison in which all the cells are exposed to a central guard tower. Whether this tower is occupied at any given moment is immaterial; prisoners know they *might* be observed at any time and thus are drawn into constant obedience. To escape punishment they must police themselves.

In an influential passage Foucault argues that power is not merely a restrictive or repressive force; it is also generative: "We must cease once and for all to describe the effects of power in negative terms: it 'excludes,' it 'represses,' it 'censors,' it 'abstracts,' it 'masks,' it 'conceals.' In fact, power produces; it produces reality; it produces domains of objects and rituals of truth."[6] Another thing power produces is individuals. Disciplinary institutions classify and describe so as to control; they differentiate people only in order to exploit their abilities and weaknesses more effectively. For example, rather than regarding all its workers as more or less interchangeable raw material, a factory might carefully survey their activities—through a foreman on the shop floor, for example—monitoring their abilities and placing them where they will be most productive. For Foucault, this collection of information, the documentation of people's tendencies and capabilities, is a crucial part of the "creation of the individual." Ultimately the workers are distinguished as particular "cases," not because anyone believes in the intrinsic worth or political capabilities of the individual, but because as individuals they are most easily manipulated and embedded in a larger system of production (or education, medicine, military discipline, and so on).

In contrast with a Lotmanian framework, Foucault does not focus on how the institutions may be changed by their own descriptive activity—how the extension of semiosis to "lower" levels tends to alter the very semiotic categories used for description. Foucault's famous thesis about power as a productive force has alerted us to how the exercise of power hides its own semiotic traces, as it were. But it also seems striking for its combination of naiveté and pessimism about the way semiotic codes are disseminated throughout a culture.

This pessimism is tied to a view of everyday life as a passive field waiting to be dominated by disciplinary structures. The lines of influence are all one-way. Thus it would only be a small step from the argument that discipline creates individuals to the argument that it also creates the everyday. Disciplinary institutions document and classify elements of daily life—"the dust of events, actions, behaviour, opinions," Foucault says, or (quoting Catherine II) the "things of every moment"—calling them into existence only to bring them more tightly under control. Even feedback from below—such as demands from French local notables or parish priests for the royal detention of their neighbors or enemies—served merely to interweave the king's absolute power with the more diffuse institutional disciplines at lower levels, "disciplining the non-disciplinary spaces."[7]

Especially striking, from the semiotic point of view, is Foucault's idea of a "threshold of description," which appears in his discussion of how forms of examination (medical, school, and so on) function in disciplinary terms to document and classify: "For a long time ordinary individuality—the everyday individuality of everybody—remained below the threshold of description. To be looked at, observed, described in detail, followed from day to day by an uninterrupted writing was a privilege. The chronicle of a man, the account of his life, his historiography, written as he lived out his life formed part of the rituals of his power. The disciplinary method reversed this relation, lowered the threshold of describable individuality and made of this description a means of control and a method of domination. . . . This turning of real lives into writing is no longer a procedure of heroization; it functions as a procedure of objectification and subjection."[8] Foucault describes here a "semiotization of everyday behavior" that, in some ways, evokes Lotman's idea of how the "center" discourse expands its norms over the whole semiosphere, even encompassing a reality that was previously "nonsemiotic." Peter the Great's attention to westernizing the dress and facial hair of his nobles could be seen simply as a way of bringing them more firmly under his control—disciplining a previously nondisciplinary space. But Foucault holds that "lowering" the threshold of description is a straightforward expansion of disciplinary power; he is not interested in how discipline must adapt itself "on the ground," since this ground does not even exist until disciplinary power endows it with meaning (with semioticity, we might say). For Lotman, on the other hand, everyday life, like any semiospheric "periphery," is a realm of already existing, competing codes—not simply a blank page waiting to be scripted. Accordingly, in "The Poetics of Everyday Behavior," Lotman shows how the explicit attention paid to everyday life by the Russian nobility created a *range* of behavioral strategies and styles: "Thus, after the first step—the semiotization of everyday behavior—there followed a second: the creation of styles within the framework of everyday norms" (74). These styles reflected the influence of already existing codes such as church ritual, common or "folk" behavior, geographical and social norms, and poetic or theatrical models.

Lotman's model of the semiosphere reveals Foucault's pessimism to be not only depressing but also semiotically incoherent. Lotman's careful attention to meaning-*generating* mechanisms in *Universe of the Mind* suggests just how difficult it is to throw a net of power over any complex reality; nets of power are nets of meaning, and they will always settle onto the contours of the reality they are trying to contain, themselves becoming misshapen or tangled in the process. Because translation is not a relation of identity, it becomes almost impossible, in Lotman's world, for any sophisticated code to reproduce itself perfectly in a new sphere of behavior.[9] This is another way of saying that we all inhabit some boundary or other of the semiosphere; no matter how few codes we have to work with in understanding the world or describing ourselves, we can always juxtapose conflicting descriptions of reality and examine the new meanings that result. What Foucault calls the "panopticisms of every day," then, need not reinforce each other but can give rise to conflicting interpretations as they seek to control ever more details of our daily lives.[10]

A more optimistic, but equally unsatisfactory, view comes from Michel de Certeau, whose *Practice of Everyday Life* responds explicitly to Foucault. Where Foucault sees power as seeping down into the tiniest details of everyday life, de Certeau emphasizes the way in which people "consume" the larger systems that attempt to manipulate them. Consumption changes what is consumed, just as translation changes what is translated. For example, de Certeau suggests that even though mass media and marketing tend to impose a uniform view of the world on us, we still perceive them in the context of our own lives and have some room for maneuver to make of them what we will: "If it is true that the grid of 'discipline' is everywhere becoming clearer and more extensive, it is all the more urgent to discover . . . what popular procedures (also 'miniscule' and quotidian) manipulate the mechanisms of discipline and conform to them only in order to evade them. . . . The goal is not to make clearer how the violence of order is transmuted into a disciplinary technology, but rather to bring to light the clandestine forms taken by the dispersed, tactical, and makeshift creativity of groups or individuals already caught in the nets of 'discipline.'" A dominant discourse, then, will always be "caught in the trap of its assimilation by a jungle of procedures rendered invisible to the conqueror."[11] These procedures are the everyday practices by which power is instantiated but simultaneously modified and eroded. If Foucault suggests that we participate in our own subjection, Certeau argues that we cannot be subjected without our participation, and hence we retain some control.

Thus, if Foucault sees the shop floor as one place where individuals were described and organized so as to maximize production, de Certeau famously emphasizes the practice of *la perruque*, "the wig"—the French term for personal work done on the job, using time and materials filched from one's employer: "La perruque may be as simple a matter as a secretary's writing a love letter on 'company time' or as complex as a cabinetmaker's 'borrowing' a lathe to make a piece of furniture for his living room. . . . In the very place where the machine he must serve reigns supreme, he cunningly takes pleasure in finding a way to create gratuitous products whose sole purpose is to signify his own capabilities."[12] In some ways de Certeau's emphasis on the "consumption" of power, on how it must adapt to the messy realities of everyday life, recalls Lotman's discussion of the semiosphere. In both writers we find an account of how a dominant discourse "loses touch" with everyday reality, fraying at the edges as it tries to encompass ever new details. But there are differences. De Certeau's comment that a worker engaging in *la perruque* "create[s] gratuitous products whose sole purpose is to signify his own capabilities," is, in its way, as gratuitous a semiotic oversimplification as Foucault's idea that the signification of daily life is wholly determined by disciplinary structures. Of course, *la perruque* will signify many different things, depending on one's point of view—depending on where one stands in the semiosphere.

But the issue of the signification of everyday practices becomes even more problematic in de Certeau. He distinguishes between two types of practice, strategies and tactics. *Strategies* are the tools of "a subject with will and power (a business, an army, a city, a scientific institution)"; they rely on a Cartesian delimitation between ourselves and the outside world, an appropriation of space as one's own, "an effort to delimit one's own place in a world bewitched by the invisible powers of the Other." Strategies attempt to fix objects and direct change; they are "panoptic," turning "foreign forces into objects that can be observed and measured." *Tactics,* on the other hand, are mobile, unpredictable, "an art of the weak" that presupposes no place of one's own. "The space of a tactic is the space of the other. Thus it must play on and with a terrain imposed on it and organized by the law of a foreign power." Rather than changing the face of this terrain, an art of tactics strikes suddenly and then moves on: "What it wins it cannot keep. This [art of being] nowhere gives a tactic mobility, to be sure, but a mobility that must accept the chance offerings of the moment, and seize on the wing the possibilities that offer themselves at any given moment."[13]

If, for Lotman, everyday life is where the question of what is "mine" and what is "foreign" becomes explicit and acute, de Certeau tries to take the "mine" out of this equation altogether. Opposition, for him, is a practice that leaves no traces, excluded by its very logic from the economy of observation and documentation on which power structures rely. The very notion of a unified identity, in his framework, evokes and depends on the strategic and the manipulative; everyday practices are better suited to a fragmentary, protean subject, a subject that is always on the move and possesses nothing it can call its "own."

What is missing here, however, is a sense of the subject as its own set of codes, constantly translating and transposing itself in interactions with external structures without ever completely losing itself in the process. The de Certeauian semiosphere, we might say, would preserve the idea of a rigid, highly codified dominant discourse in the center as well as the creative generation of new information at the "periphery" of everyday life, while attempting to dispense with the idea of a "boundary" zone where two consistent and structured languages conflict and cooperate—where the language of the center is translated into the language of the self, and vice versa. Instead, de Certeau envisions sudden and inexplicable guerrilla strikes by unidentified opponents of the dominant discourse—opponents who will remain unidentified because they have no "identity," the whole idea of identity being a strategic and hegemonic construct. It comes as no surprise, then, to see de Certeau reinterpret the "us-them" distinction, when he discusses Wittgenstein's investigations of ordinary language. Wittgenstein, as an Austrian in England and a wealthy bourgeois living the life of an ascetic, "sees the metaphors of *foreign* analytical procedures *inside* the very language that circumscribes them." For de Certeau, he thus puts himself in a position "which consists in being a foreigner *at home*, a 'savage' lost in the midst of ordinary culture, lost in the complexity of the common agreement and what goes without saying. And since one does not 'leave' this language, since one cannot find another place from which to interpret it, since there are therefore no separate groups of false interpretations and true interpretations, but only illusory interpretations, since in short there is no *way out*, the fact remains that we are *foreigners* on the inside—*but there is no outside*."[14] These formulations pose a striking contrast to Lotman's remarks on the Russian nobility under Peter, who felt like "foreigners in their own country." Rather than theorizing this position as a kind of essentialized lostness—for de Certeau, a metaphysical desideratum—Lotman shows how it leads to the search for *new* models of behavior based on games, theater, and literature. These "interpretations" may be "illusory," but some of them will still feel more "ours" or more "theirs," more "natural" or more "foreign." Lotman's research program is not only much more interesting than de Certeau's, pushing us as it does to explore all the illusory interpretations that we struggle to make our own;

it is also more semiotically coherent. De Certeau wants to invoke an us-them distinction without the "us," but in doing so, he overlooks the myriad ways in which our sense of who we are is shaped by, and shapes, the laws, codes, and systems surrounding us.

Foucault and de Certeau, we might say, both offer a "semiosphere without translation." In Foucault, the "target" language of the everyday is missing; the extension of discipline does not generate new meanings but simply re-creates the existing power of disciplinary structures. For de Certeau, the "source language" of the everyday self is absent; its interventions into dominant discourses cannot be lasting because it does not itself represent a stable perspective. It should be clear that I find Lotman's semiosphere more helpful in exploring the complicated negotiations that constitute everyday life as a set of activities mediating between our sense of who we are and our embeddedness in larger codes that seem external, yet not entirely irrelevant, to our own identities. In what follows, I examine one such set of negotiations, applying Lotman's model to Zábrana's diaries. A Czech poet and translator, Zábrana was in many ways an archetypal "boundary" figure who exhibited all the strengths and weaknesses of this ambiguous position in the semiosphere of the repressive Czechoslovak regime of the 1970s and 1980s. His example not only reveals the force of Lotman's model but also, in turn, suggests ways in which it might be modified.

## A Life In-Between: Jan Zábrana as a Boundary Figure

At first glance, Jan Zábrana hardly seems a likely candidate for a "boundary" figure. Much of his life and writing were predicated on absolute hatred of all things Communist. As he wrote in his diary in 1978: "One of the most important conclusions I drew—for myself—from the fifties can be expressed in four words: *Don't answer their questions.* Because they are *their* questions, not mine. . . . The most important thing is *not to have the slightest good will toward them. Not a shadow of any kind of good will, of the willingness to compromise, to try to get along, to communicate with them de facto in any way.* . . . Seek possibilities for contact, establish contact? Never. It's *them* we're talking about."[15] There are no ragged edges here. Zábrana's consistent use of the pronoun *they* to refer to the Communists sets up the clear distinction between first and third person that, for Lotman, generally signals one's presence firmly *inside* a semiotic code, rather than on its periphery. An implacable hatred, insisting on an impermeable boundary between himself and "them," runs throughout Zábrana's diaries.

This is no surprise. Zábrana had ample reason to hate the government that came to power in February 1948. His parents were both arrested in the first years of the Communist regime; his mother was sentenced to eighteen years in prison, his father to ten. The family's property was confiscated, and Zábrana was denied admission to college because of his "absolutely insufficient political qualifications for study."[16] During the early 1950s he worked in a trolley-bus factory and then an enamel works, visiting his parents in prison on the weekends. In 1954 he began to support himself as a freelance translator, although he often saw this work as a pale substitute for writing his own poetry—he would publish only three collections during his life, all in the relatively liberal late 1960s.

The Soviet invasion of Czechoslovakia in 1968 dealt another major blow to Zábrana. Some of his dearest friends emigrated, contributing to an increasing feeling of isolation. Publishers refused to publish several of his translations, and Zábrana's promising poetic career was cut short. After 1969 he would not publish a single poem of his own. The 1970s and 1980s were thus years of hard work that he felt were taking him away from his true vocation, poetry; years of loneliness, in which he lost contact with many friends, and both his parents died; and years of sickness: in 1976, after suffering from excessive thirst, kidney difficulties, skin problems, and bad vision, he recognized his symptoms while reading James Dickey's poem "Diabetes."[17] Feelings of despair, isolation, and hopelessness dominate the diaries he kept from January 12, 1970, until his death in 1984, and their fragmentary nature—most of the entries are only a few sentences long—reflect his demanding work schedule.

Thus, it is not surprising that after the posthumous publication of Zábrana's diaries in 1992, Czech critics tended to characterize him primarily as an uncompromising foe of the government. In the 1998 *Dictionary of Czech Writers after 1945*, for example, the diaries are seen as presenting "a person standing in internal opposition to the Communist regime, a person deeply embittered by both private and public affairs, but also possessing firm aesthetic, moral, and political standpoints."[18] Ultimately, however, we must qualify this view of a well-defined identity grounded firmly on a personal code of honor and hatred—not so as to doubt Zábrana's anti-Communist antipathies, but rather to gain a deeper understanding of his complex, and vastly interesting, position in Czech literature.

In fact, the "boundary" moments in Zábrana's life are far more numerous than his uncompromising rejection of the Communists might suggest. As a writer he was notably protean, experimenting with numerous genres and styles. Not only did he write poetry, essays, and detective novels, but the fragmentary entries of his diaries comprise a vast compendium of genres: aphorisms, anecdotes, nonsense rhymes, short essays, testimonies, overheard speech, prayers and antiprayers, memories, diatribes, character sketches, jokes, and so on. They are evidence of a mind that was never satisfied with a single way of thinking, constantly viewing ideas through multiple prisms. To this myriad literary activity we must add Zábrana's work as a translator, an archetypal boundary position that Zábrana managed to intensify even further—first, by his choice of languages to translate, Russian and English, bridging the poles of the bipolar Cold War world; and second, by his choice of genres, ranging from the detective novels of Ed McBain to Conrad's *Heart of Darkness* and the gnomic poetry of Osip Mandel'shtam.

Furthermore, if Zábrana's politics were uncompromisingly anti-Communist—a stance reflected in his absolute refusal to publish his own poetry after 1968—his position in Czech culture was more complicated. As much as he suffered during the 1970s and 1980s and regarded the government with an absolutely sincere mixture of scorn, hatred, and condescending irony, Zábrana never moved into open opposition. There were good reasons for this. In part it was because he saw many of the dissidents as barely reformed Communists who had suffered, in 1968, from criminally naive illusions about how far the Soviets would tolerate reform; but his reticence can also be traced to the fact that he played a role, albeit a minor one, in the very official structures he criticized.[19] Zábrana translated for the same publishing houses he reviled for their censorship and suppression of opposition writers. In a typical diary entry he laments having been awarded a translation prize, saying he would accept it only because "[i]n a police state, refusing a prize you've been given means immediate repression. . . . And so I'll accept . . . in the interests of personal safety. . . . A feeling of despair."[20]

In entries such as this, he reflects on his boundary position as one of compromise and despair. But this is not always the case. Consider another entry from 1975, in which he writes: "A well-translated detective novel is—in the element of language—more than a badly translated

Pushkin."[21] And as we'll discuss later, he saw his choices of which authors to translate, especially from Russian, as exerting a barely perceptible but, over the years, sizeable influence on the Czech understanding of Russian literature. Moments such as these counterbalance the entry quoted earlier, about not answering "their" questions. They suggest that Zábrana's complicated position—between Russian and American culture, high and low literature, hatred of the regime and dependence on it—far from being barren ground, was fertile soil for a creative engagement with the forces he so mightily despised.

## Writing in a Polluted Semiosphere

Much of this engagement plays itself out in what we might call a "linguistic" everyday. Over and against the drab grayness of socialist reality, language is a source of endless fascination for Zábrana, and he carefully monitors the way words are used in conversations, newspapers, radio broadcasts, and literature. Overall he paints a panorama of linguistic everyday life focused on informal, colloquial, and unofficial usage. This panorama provides an antidote to some of the prevailing contemporary visions of Communist discourse, which saw the "official language" of newspapers, radio, and politicians as an inflexible structure forcing any recalcitrant reality into the straitjacket of its rigid ideological schema.[22] Zábrana, it is true, seems sometimes to second this notion of official language as sterile and impervious to outside influences: "The speech of politicians = speech wearing a condom."[23] But more often he follows the *circulation* of language throughout official and unofficial settings, tracking especially the boundary zones where words cross from one to the other; and this circulation, he feels, cannot be directed from above. Over and over, Zábrana notes moments of linguistic "crossover"—moments where a transient use of language fixes a funny, bizarre, or thought-provoking translation from one linguistic realm, or realm of experience, to another.

  Zábrana records, for example, phrases or scraps of conversation overheard in the street, citations from radio broadcasts and the newspaper, typographical errors discovered as he corrects proofs of his translations, translation mistakes that change the meaning of the original in an amusing way, and the strange metamorphoses and evolutions of words that take place in half-awake states or in dreams. These moments belong to everyday life, both because they occur daily—examples appear on nearly every page of the diaries, and it is significant that Zábrana often notes the time and date he heard them, as if to fix them in their original context—as well as because they are trivial and banal, tied to common experiences such as listening to the radio or walking in the street. We can understand these moments of found speech, in Lotmanian terms, as instances of translation taking place at the boundaries of different codes.

Often words appropriate to one context are transplanted, resulting in a witticism or an amusing linguistic disorientation:

> *A child is a little monkey made of snake tails.* . . . (A beautiful contamination from a grandmother's account—on the radio—of how she baby-sits her children's kids.)[24]

> "The whites *cut down* the bison and it was all over for the Indians." Another patient said that; maybe he thinks the bison were some kind of tree . . . I don't know. I don't want to ask.[25]

Such examples reveal amusing misunderstandings, as in the grandmother's contortion of the children's rhyme "Snakes and snails and puppy dogs' tails, that's what little boys are made of." But this mechanism can carry a political meaning as well, especially when it undermines the established phrases and "ready-made" language common in the official state media. Many of Zábrana's "overheard" passages thus involve contaminations from the state radio and newspapers. The point of some is an unintended connotation, as in the newspaper heading "Tomorrow to the Urns"—in Zábrana's characteristic gallows humor, the urns into which ballots are thrown are conflated with those holding the ashes of the dead, and the headline ends up meaning more than that there will be an election tomorrow.[26] At other times Zábrana records an unintended metaphor: "'The operation was performed on Samson the bullock on the occasion of the visit of the Soviet delegation. He received a polyurethane heart.' (from the radio)."[27] This sentence is already somewhat ridiculous thanks to the juxtaposition that begins it: *bý ček Samson,* or "little bull Samson." But more pointedly, the idea of receiving a plastic heart in honor of a Soviet delegation surely resonated with Zábrana, just as the ersatz sardines did.

In these examples a statement unwittingly awakens an alternative interpretive matrix that gives it another meaning. At other times Zábrana draws attention to the *meaninglessness* of phrases—"'The nutritional value of nutrients is still not fully appreciated' (From a lecture on the radio)"—or absurdly bureaucratic language—"'We were losing a considerable percentage of meat because cannibalism was raging among the pigs. We eliminated its causes, by means of which the growth of animal production rose sharply' (radio news, 7:55 p.m.)." One of his favorite pastimes is finding official statements that—through some minor change, often a typographical error or a misspoken word on the radio— turn out to be surprisingly close to absolutely different formulations: "'A communiqué in which the *úsporná* attempt to justify the deployment of new missiles in Europe was obvious' (misspoken on the radio)." *Úsporná* means "frugal"; the announcer meant to say *úporná*, "stubborn." Or again: "Beautiful typo in the paper today (*Free Word*, June 9, 1982): 'After a week in Portugal, the Brazilian players moved to Seville, where their *fašounci* greeted them with songs and dances in a samba rhythm.'"[28] A juxtaposition of the letters *n* and *š* changes *fanoušci*, "fans," into *fašounci*, which can only be a diminutive form of the insult *fašoun*, "fascist."

These examples exhibit the kinds of "eroded and transitional forms" that break down the "center" language—here, Communist discourse— at the edges of the semiosphere. The central discourse is always open to unexpected interpretations that might be occasioned by its own clumsiness, a minor typographical error, a slip of the tongue, or any of the myriad distortions that tend to result when we use a language that is not fully adapted to all the demands made on it. These unexpected interpretations need not be consciously injected into the system by an oppositional agent; they are rather a natural result of the mixing of codes— what we might call, adapting a New Historicist trope, "the circulation of weakness" within the semiosphere. These errors should be semiotically trivial; from the "center's" point of view, they don't even exist, because they have no meaning in the code of official language. For Zábrana, however, they leap into significance by demonstrating the fragility of all constructions of meaning, their vulnerability to chance deformations; this is why the random mistakes of everyday language are so important for Zábrana, acquiring meaning precisely because they are random.

In his more optimistic moments, however, Zábrana did conceive of an organized and *intentional* opposition, acting on the center from the periphery—in particular, he thought about how his translations might affect Czech language and literature on a larger scale. Earlier I cited his remark that a well-translated detective novel does more for a language than a badly translated Pushkin, and in another entry, with a rare absence of modesty, he claims—with some justification—to have single-handedly transformed the Czechs' view of Russian literature, replacing "their" Ostrovskiis and Gladkovs with Osip Mandel'shtam, Isaak Babel', Andrei Platonov, and other writers Zábrana loved, in part, because they were on the margins of the official Soviet literary canon: "The contours of a *completely repainted picture* are only now becoming visible, after almost thirty years of work; like it or not, sometimes unwittingly, without realizing it, they're forced to accept *these authors*, they're surrounded by them, while *their idols* have turned into paper tigers and, although they haven't been struck from the official lists, are faded and dull. . . . I don't know what I'll still manage to get done, but I hope that the contours of all this work, which had a definite purpose and aimed at a definite goal, will become even clearer in the future."[29] This remarkable entry is reminiscent of Lotman's account of the transfer of cultural values across a boundary—here, not just the boundary between Czech and Russian language, but between the official Soviet canon of writers and the "unofficial" pantheon. It shows that Zábrana was aware of the interactions between competing codes within the semiosphere—to use Lotman's terms—and saw these codes as sometimes oppressive, but always mutable, unstable, in a word, translatable. Zábrana realized that significant change could filter from a boundary region into the rest of the semiosphere; when he writes, in the same entry, "you have to work *on the side, from below, from the side*," he is expressing not a sense of marginalization but rather a sense of what a "marginal" figure can achieve.

This is not to say that Zábrana's boundary position doesn't raise issues of its own. Lotman's writings on the semiosphere tend to portray the boundary as a zone of creative ferment, but that need not always be the case. As we saw in the case of the award Zábrana was afraid to refuse, he could despair at the thought of his own *complicity* in official structures; as is only natural, he was sometimes unwilling or unable to distinguish between participating in official codes and creatively reworking them.

Thus, translation—that elemental unit of creativity for Lotman—was not always a creative act for Zábrana. At times he opposes it to true creative endeavor and turns it into an emblem of slavery: "I was translating a stupid Russian story (Soviet, actually) until three a.m. last night, for the anthology *First Loves* for the People's Publishing House. I can't just abandon it, because without that publisher I couldn't survive as a freelance translator. When I realized that, as a result of the defeat in February 1948, I was sitting thirty-five years later at three a.m. at night in front of a piece of paper, patching together some slavish crap that I'd really just like to throw out the window, I had a feeling of total despair, I wanted to cry." Elsewhere he calls translation the "room for maidservants" in the house of literature: "[A]ll my life I was a good maidservant."[30] Translation becomes symptomatic of his own lack of freedom and symbolic of his own failure.

We can see a similar tension between the poetics of closed and open systems in Zábrana's conception of *citation*. In a Lotmanian framework citation should be another creative boundary moment, in which two codes come into contact and transform each other. And in the 1960s, indeed, the citation was a crucial part of Zábrana's poetics in his three published collections. Many of his poems were complicated games, interweaving unacknowledged quotations from banned authors with lines from English, American, and Russian poets—sometimes from his own translations of them. At times in his diaries, he follows the journeys of a phrase or image from one poet to another, fascinated by how "poets take words from poets as they read one another."[31]

But in the 1980s this intricate web of intertextual references is brushed away and replaced by a simpler model: plagiarism. Zábrana stoically records in a series of diary entries how Miroslav Florian and Ivan Skála, two of the regime's most assiduous poetic careerists, are consistently plagiarizing unusual images and rhymes from his published translations and his poetry of the 1960s. Where Zábrana had written, for example, "Even the sun came out that day . . . *in print!*," Florian some years later came up with: "It's Thursday, the sun has come out in a new edition."[32] And in his translation of Osip Mandel'shtam's "Decembrist," Zábrana used a rhyme that wasn't in the original—*Lorelei* and *ráj* (paradise)—which then showed up eight months later in a poem by Ivan Skála.[33]

It is interesting to note that these "borrowings" are generally not direct copies of the original; under other circumstances some of them, at least—for example "the sun came out in a new edition"—might have qualified as legitimate intertextual allusions rather than outright plagiarism. Zábrana himself had had no qualms, say, about smuggling a line from Viktor Shklovskii's *Zoo* into one of his sonnets in 1968—nor should he have.[34] The difference here, of course, is that Zábrana was being "cited" at a time when he couldn't publish his own poetry: "In other words," he writes after recording one of Florian's "petty thefts," "it's not enough that we've silenced poets like Zábrana and forbid them from publishing; now, in addition, we're going to rob them and serially plagiarize them."[35]

Two points can be made here. First, Zábrana's anger is, of course, perfectly legitimate. It is conditioned, however, not on the borrowing per se, but on the fact that Florian and Skála could publish their own poetry, while Zábrana could not. In Lotmanian terms he had been banned from freely circulating his own linguistic innovations. This situation poignantly underscores the weakness of Zábrana's position on the borderline of Czech letters—the vulnerability of his attempts to bring new meanings into Czech. Second, it seems worth noting that Zábrana is working here with a somewhat different conception of the circulation of language—of the semiosphere, we might say—than he uses in speaking of poets he respects. Especially interesting is his sense of the *sterility* of poetic language, even his own. The "recycling" of his phrases and images does not represent, for example, a step forward in the language of Czech poetry. It is rather a violation of the closed world of his own published poetry. This poetry becomes for him vulnerable, a closed game reserve roamed by unwelcome poachers, and he becomes resigned to the fact that he cannot defend it. When the new rhyme *ráj-Lorelei* is sent out into the world and stolen by the kind of regime poet Zábrana hated, there is nothing he can do except watch and record, "without commentary and without anger," as he writes in another entry.[36] It is as if the verse were no longer his; once it has been incorporated into the language of published literature, it ceases to be a creative act and becomes instead an element of the dead, unimaginative official language Zábrana hated.

These examples remind us that *both* circulation and restriction are inherent in the model of the semiosphere. We might say that some semiospheres are more open than others or, extending the ecological metaphor, that all semiospheres suffer from various degrees of "pollution" that inhibits the free flow of information. The idea of a polluted semiosphere preserves the idea of the circulation of information among competing codes but alludes as well to the limitations on the free flow of information that are, after all, implicit in Lotman's "center-periphery" model. Without going so far as to embrace Foucault's worldview, where the center code simply imposes itself unchanged on everyday life, we should remember that dominant codes have, to varying degrees, the ability to enforce themselves even where they are seen as foreign and unwanted. Thus, if Amy Mandelker rightly observes that we can see the semiosphere as "nurturing dialogic relations within itself," we must also be aware of ways in which it orchestrates, limits, and even censors such dialogue, offering a limited repertoire of codes to work with and privileging center codes at the expense of peripheral ones.[37]

The overall picture of everyday life that emerges from Lotman is one of a realm of circulation, translations, and contradictions. It is the place where our sense of who we are, potentially, comes into conflict with the "center" discourses that shape the semiosphere in its various manifestations. Everyday life is thus neither a site of resistance, as in Certeau, nor one of intensified manipulation, as in Foucault. It is potentially both and essentially neither. Lotman helps us see everyday life as a realm of organized creativity, a place where we can shape ourselves—but only in concert or conflict with the larger codes that also make up our identities. The case of Zábrana gives us one version of how this shaping might look—an example that should keep us from romanticizing the marginal and everyday as a realm of privileged freedom, while nevertheless reminding us of the unusual kinds of power exercised from the edges.

## Notes

1. Jan Zábrana, *Celý život* [All my life], 2 vols. (Prague: Torst, 1992), 984. All translations are my own unless otherwise noted.

2. The word I translate here as "everyday" is *kazhdodnevnoe,* a less ambiguous term than *byt*. In general Lotman tends to use *byt* (as well as the adjective *bytovoi*) and other terms such as *kazhdodnevnyi, povsednevnyi* ("Dekabrist v povsednevnoi zhizni," "The Decembrist in Everyday Life"), and *prakticheskii* more or less interchangeably, as all referring to the same "sphere" of life.

3. For example, "[t]he Medieval cultural consciousness divided the world into two groups, sharply opposed to each other by the sign of significance/insignificance [*po priznaku znachimosti/neznachimosti*]. Phenomena *having a meaning* fell into one group, and those belonging to practical life into the other; it was as if they didn't exist" (Lotman, "Problema znaka," 402).

4. I use the words *circulation* and *negotiation,* with their New Historicist echoes, intentionally. The New Historicist methodology of working from the peripheries of cultures to their centers—usually by beginning a study with an anecdote, a detail of everyday life that exposes unexpected strains in the dominant discourse of a culture—finds its analog in Lotman's discussion of how a dominant discourse can lose touch with reality at the margins of the semiosphere and how information circulates among various codes. Conversely, some

of Stephen Greenblatt's formulations are markedly semiotic, as when he speaks of "an intensified willingness to read all of the textual traces of the past with the attention traditionally conferred only on literary texts." See Stephen Greenblatt, introduction to *Learning to Curse* (New York: Routledge, 1990), 14, as well as Andreas Schönle's essay in this volume.

5. Amy Mandelker, "Logosphere and Semiosphere: Bakhtin, Russian Organicism, and the Semiotics of Culture," in *Bakhtin in Contexts: Across the Disciplines,* ed. Amy Mandelker (Evanston, Ill.: Northwestern University Press, 1995), 181.

6. Michel Foucault, *Discipline and Punish: The Birth of the Prison,* trans. Alan Sheridan (New York: Vintage, 1979), 194.

7. Ibid., 213, 215.

8. Ibid., 191–92.

9. "Although Lotman doesn't abandon the concept of culture, in his later period he concentrates more on characterizing its internal dynamism than on questions of its typology; he is instead interested in everything that interferes with the application of any kind of general law, type, or model. . . . The establishment of universalistic ideas that would somehow delimit and limit things beforehand is immediately perceived as misleading and is disrupted soon thereafter." Vladimír Macura, "Lotmanova 'jiná' dekonstrukce," *Tvar* 6, no. 1 (1995): 10.

10. Foucault, *Discipline and Punish,* 223.

11. Michel de Certeau, *The Practice of Everyday Life,* trans. Steven Rendall (Berkeley: University of California Press, 1984), xiv–xv, 32.

12. Ibid., 25.

13. Ibid., 36, 37.

14. Ibid., 13–14.

15. Zábrana, *Celý život,* 613.

16. Details about Zábrana's life are most accessible in the chronology assembled by his widow, Marie Zábranová, and Jiří Trávníček. See Jan Zábrana, *Jistota nejhoršího: Výbor z básnické pozůstalosti* [Certainty of the worst: A selection of unpublished poetry], ed. Jiří Trávníček (Prague: Československý spisovatel, 1991), 111–47, 119.

17. Zábrana, *Celý život,* 310.

18. Bohumil Svozil, "Jan Zábrana," *Slovník českých spisovatelů od roku 1945* [Dictionary of Czech writers after 1945], ed. Ústav pro českou literaturu Akademie věd české republiky, vol. 2 (Prague: Brána, 1995 and 1998), 686.

19. Regarding his disillusionment with many of the dissidents, Zábrana wrote in 1972: "Their worries were foreign to me. The worries of people who have hope. It was the same in 1968" (Zábrana, *Celý život,* 228).

20. Ibid., 476.

21. Ibid., 415.

22. For a statement of this view, see the analyses of the Communist press by Petr Fidelius, *Řeč komunistické moci* [The language of Communist power] (Prague: Triáda, 1998). Vladimír Macura, inspired by Lotman and working with a more flexible view of official language, nevertheless comes to similar conclusions about its imperviousness to reality in his masterful study *Šťastný věk: Symboly, emblémy a mýty, 1948–1989* [The happy age: Symbols, emblems, and myths, 1948–1989] (Prague: Pražská imaginace, 1992).

23. Zábrana, *Celý život*, 510.

24. Ibid., 963.

25. Ibid., 1087.

26. Ibid., 671.

27. Ibid., 845.

28. Ibid., 1051, 557, 775, 943.

29. Ibid., 927–28.

30. Ibid., 996, 478.

31. Ibid., 1036.

32. Ibid., 708.

33. Zábrana, *Celý život*, 1018. For further examples, see Zábrana, *Celý život*, 781 and 857.

34. The poem "Žárlení" (Jealousy) ends with the lines *Být krutý v lásce je snadné. / Stačí nemilovat* ("In love it is easy to be cruel. / It is enough not to love"), a citation (italicized but not otherwise acknowledged) from letter 4 of Shklovskii's epistolary memoir. See Jan Zábrana, *Stránky z deníku* [Pages from a diary] (Prague: Československý spisovatel, 1968), 61.

35. Zábrana, *Celý život*, 781.

36. Ibid., 922.

37. Mandelker, "Logosphere and Semiosphere," 185.

# Afterword

*Lotman without Tears*

WILLIAM MILLS TODD III

*Habent sua fata libelli.* So do theories, especially the twentieth-century Russian ones that escaped the linguistic and political borders of the Soviet Union. The formalists of the early Soviet period, repressed under Stalin but already losing some of their methodological edge as they branched out into the sociology of literature and literary history in the 1920s, were reborn in European and American literary theory with a series of translations and scholarly discussions in the 1950s through the 1970s.[1] Roman Jakobson's emigration to the United States and his long, productive life (second decade of the twentieth century to 1982), mastery of foreign languages, and ability to make productive alliances with younger scholars certainly facilitated this survival and rebirth, as did the arrival of formalism in an Anglo-American academy with its own "intrinsic" approach to literature, the New Criticism. Mikhail Bakhtin's path to an English-reading public has been more tortuous, as is well documented in the outstanding critical studies by Katerina Clark, Caryl Emerson, Michael Holquist, Gary Saul Morson, and others.[2] But a career challenged by exile, serious illness, and the hostility of the Soviet establishment found a destiny abroad as fortunate as the native one was disastrous. Almost as soon as his texts could be printed in Russia, Caryl Emerson and others provided outstanding English translations, often more readable than the Russian originals, which—especially the early and late works—had not been polished for publication. Bakhtin's celebration of the carnivalesque were greeted by irreverent English and American scholars of the 1960s and early 1970s. Critics anxious to move beyond formalized narratology welcomed Bakhtin's sociolinguistic studies of novelistic discourse in the 1980s. The disputed attribution to Bakhtin of works by Valentin Voloshinov and Pavel Medvedev lent Bakhtin useful credentials (on Marxian and Freudian discourse) for the early years in the development of cultural studies. When cultural theory in the later 1980s and the 1990s labored under the relentless gaze of Foucault's disciplinary order or drifted amid deconstruction's infinite deferrals of meaning, a fresh supply of Bakhtinian publications offered agency, answerability, outsidedness, and unfinalizability.

The Tartu-Moscow school of semiotics and Yuri Lotman in particular have not endured and enjoyed such extremes. Lotman was able to make a career at Tartu University, which—however remote from Moscow and Leningrad—had long been Russia's most European place of study; he was able to work with brilliant students and colleagues, many of whom have contributed significantly to Soviet, post-Soviet, and overseas scholarship. In forty years he published works of intellectual history, literary scholarship, criticism, and cultural theory, which—however small their print runs—found an elite readership. Long distant from the two capitals, he became a popular television figure toward the end of his life with his *Conversations about Russian Culture*. In the United States, however, he has not found a place on fashion's reading table. To be sure, a number of his works have been translated, and these translations are amply cited in this volume. Unlike the work of the formalists and of Bakhtin, however, they have generally come at the wrong time to be as productive in English-language scholarship as, this volume convincingly argues, they deserve to be. The English translation of Lotman's intricate, many-leveled *Structure of the Artistic Text* (1970) appeared only in 1977; its framing of conceptualization in terms of information theory could only seem technicist in a critical milieu increasingly taken with French poststructuralism and German *Rezeptionsästhetik*. Only its innovative discussion of eventfulness, cited by Julie Buckler in this volume, gained widespread attention. Tartu-Moscow studies of myth reached the West only when scholars there felt that they had gone beyond the Anglo-American variant of myth analysis in Northrop Frye's *Anatomy of Criticism*. Lotman's dazzlingly binary studies in the typology of cultures encountered readers taken with Clifford Geertz's "thick description" and sharply opposed to essentializing theories. Nor did it help that Lotman had conducted his principal "field work" in a milieu, time, and place—the educated gentry of late-eighteenth- and early-nineteenth-century Russia—far removed from the presentist concerns of English and American cultural studies or from the Shakespearean Renaissance of American cultural poetics. In *Mythologies* (1957) Roland Barthes could offer a bold anticolonialist analysis of a Franco-African soldier saluting the French flag; the mind boggles at the thought of Lotman doing something similar with a Chechen soldier in Soviet uniform.[3] The political level of Lotman's semiotics remained virtual. Soviet readers were wont to interpret Lotman's analyses of the Pushkin period as Aesopian fables about their present, a venerable Russian custom, but this could not, needless to say, enter into public discussion during the "epoch of stagnation," although it would have provided an interesting instance for his theories about text and context.

As Lotman's son has recently noted, his father avoided polemics with competing theoreticians, and at least during the 1950s–1970s, many were unfamiliar to him and his school or could not be cited in Soviet publications.[4] One can only imagine how much performance studies would have gained from witnessing Lotman's treatment of theatricality in dialogue with Erving Goffman's *Presentation of Self in Everyday Life*, or the cultural anthropology of the Tartu-Moscow school playing off the work of Western anthropologists such as Victor Turner, Clifford Geertz, Mary Douglas, or James Clifford. Lotman himself did not initiate such dialogues, and his Western readers, primarily Slavists, did not conduct them for him.

This volume is a welcome exception. Not uncritical of Lotman, its authors—none of them directly a student of Lotman and none personally close to him—project an intricate image of the scholar as Dantesque teacher-exile (Bethea), antidote to Western positivism (Urban), Stoic sage (Zorin), and underground man (Schönle). All credit him with unusual vitality and curiosity as they chart his progress from intellectual historian to deductive Saussurean structuralist to subtle empirical observer of historical gradations, levels of culture, varieties of communication.

Like his favorite literary subjects, Pushkin and Karamzin, he emerges as a figure capable not only of principled retreat but also of change and maturation.

The customary outpouring of tributes and nostalgic memoirs—the author is quite alive in Russian culture—marked Lotman's passing. The conferences and summer schools of the Tartu-Moscow semioticians and the group's publications had created an inner circle anxious to perpetuate the carnivalesque atmosphere that had, for many, been the incubator of their scholarly lives. But a decade later, the time for grieving has passed, and the Soviet world in which Lotman lived and worked becomes ever more remote from the Russian present. The old Tartu University publications, with their tiny print runs (typically under one thousand copies), shabby newsprint, and blurred, faint ink, have yielded to legible, well-distributed editions. A more accessible language—less scientistic, less jargonistic—marks the publications of Lotman's last years, especially the *Conversations about Russian Culture*. It has become appropriate to test Lotman's legacy by setting it against alternative theories and by extending it to different social sciences and to new cultural spheres, ones Lotman himself had not thoroughly surveyed.

The contributors to this volume do just this, giving us Lotman without tears or sentimentality. They give Lotman's argumentation, especially in his unfinished *Culture and Explosion,* the benefit of the doubt. The elliptic but provocative concepts of Lotman's writing about the semiosphere may be a bit vague, but they become fruitfully so, as Jonathan Bolton observes, as he turns Lotman's late writing on the inner dynamics of culture into an instrument for the study of everyday life, comparing it incisively with conceptualizations by Michel Foucault and Michel de Certeau before turning to an instance from contemporary Czech literature, an area outside Lotman's own expertise.

Such encounters and extensions, advertised in the volume's title, abound in its individual essays. Written by scholars a generation or two younger than Lotman, they address the theoretical and research concerns of contemporary cultural studies, not the past of Tartu-Moscow semiotics. When they revisit Lotman's earlier texts, it is to contrast them with new texts or, as in Caryl Emerson's creative essay, to repair them with new terms and ternary awareness from the later work. When they confront Lotman's work with that of other thinkers, it is with older ones who have been recycled to join in our current discussions (e.g., Gramsci, Florenskii, Buber) or with ones still very much active (Geertz, Kristeva,

Greenblatt, Baudrillard) or recently so (Bourdieu). Their research agendas—Iranian and American politics, contemporary Russian and Czech politics, sexuality and the body—are distant from Lotman's own, but his concepts and awareness yield invariably illuminating results.

The human sciences, unlike the natural sciences, revisit theories of the past, and vital ones that address enduring problems, such as self and society, prove particularly resilient. Twentieth-century appropriations of Freud are a fine example. Stripped of his outdated medical underpinnings, Freud has entered hermeneutics, narrative theory, reception theory, cultural studies, and widely divergent schools of psychoanalysis, long after his fellow physicians have turned elsewhere. This volume demonstrates that Lotman's work can have a similar vitality, once taken from its early contexts and placed in new ones. At its best—and even in its earlier stages—his work exhibits an awareness of polysemousness, polyperspectivalism, and variable formalization. This awareness makes it a subtle instrument—at worst a heuristic—for interrogating the arts, culture, politics, and society. Inevitably a new generation will raise new questions, perhaps turning to aesthetics or perhaps seeking greater formalization than cultural studies now offers. The essays here suggest that Lotman's thinking may have a place, too, in these possible future agendas.

*Notes*

1. Victor Erlich, *Russian Formalism: History, Doctrine,* 3rd. ed. (New Haven, Conn.: Yale University Press, 1981). First published in 1955, this work continues to offer the most comprehensive overview.

2. Katerina Clark and Michael Holquist, *Mikhail Bakhtin* (Cambridge, Mass.: Harvard University Press, 1984); Gary Saul Morson and Caryl Emerson, *Mikhail Bakhtin: Creation of a Prosaics* (Stanford, Calif.: Stanford University Press, 1990); Caryl Emerson, *The First Hundred Years of Mikhail Bakhtin* (Princeton, N.J.: Princeton University Press, 1997).

3. Roland Barthes, *Mythologies* (New York: Hill & Wang, 1972), 116–17.

4. Mikhail Lotman, "Semiotika kul'tury v tartusko-moskovskoi semioticheskoi shkole," in Iu. M. Lotman, *Istoriia i tipologiia russkoi kul'tury* (St. Petersburg: Iskusstvo-SPB, 2002), 6.

BIBLIOGRAPHY

CONTRIBUTORS

INDEX

# BIBLIOGRAPHY

## Cited Works by Lotman

Lotman, Ju. M. "'Agreement' and 'Self-Giving' as Archetypal Models of Culture." 1981. In Lotman and Uspenskij, *Semiotics of Russian Culture*, 125–40.

Lotman, Iu. M. *Aleksandr Sergeevich Pushkin.* 1983. In Lotman, *Pushkin*, 21–184.

Lotman, Yuri. *Analysis of the Poetic Text.* 1972. Ann Arbor: Ardis, 1976.

Lotman, Iu. M. "A. N. Radishchev v bor'be s obshchestvenno-politicheskimi vozzreniami i dvorianskoi estetikoi Karamzina." PhD diss., Leningradskii Gos. Universitet, 1951.

———. "Asimmetriia i dialog." 1983. In Lotman, *Semiosfera*, 590–602.

———. *Besedy o russkoi kul'ture: Byt i traditsii russkogo dvorianstva (XVIII–nachalo XIX veka).* St. Petersburg: Iskusstvo-SPB, 1994.

Lotman, Iurii M. "Concerning Khlestakov." 1975. In Lotman, Ginsburg, and Uspenskii, *Semiotics of Russian Cultural History*, 150–87.

———. "The Decembrist in Daily Life (Everyday Behavior as a Historical-Psychological Category)." 1975. In Lotman, Ginsburg, and Uspenskii, *Semiotics of Russian Cultural History*, 95–149.

Lotman, Iu. M. "'Dogovor' i 'vruchenie sebia' kak arkhetipicheskie modeli kul'tury." 1981. In Lotman, *Izbrannye stat'i*, vol. 3, 345–55.

———. "Evoliutsiia mirovozzrenia Karamzina (1783–1803)." 1957. In Lotman, *Karamzin*, 312–48.

———. "Ideinaia struktura *Kapitanskoi dochki*." 1970. In Lotman, *Pushkin*, 212–27.

———. "Ideinaia struktura poemy Pushkina 'Andzhelo.'" 1973. In Lotman, *Pushkin*, 237–52.

———. *Izbrannye stat'i.* 3 vols. Tallinn: Aleksandra, 1992–93.

———. "Iz kommentariev k *Puteshestviiu iz Peterburga v Moskvu.*" In Lotman, *Izbrannye stat'i*, vol. 2, 124–33.

———. "Kanonicheskoe iskusstvo kak informatsionnyi paradoks." 1973. In Lotman, *Izbrannye stat'i*, vol. 1., 243–47.

———. *Karamzin.* St. Petersburg: Iskusstvo-SPB, 1997.

———. "K funktsii ustnoi rechi v kul'turnom bytu pushkinskoi epokhi." 1979. In Lotman, *Izbrannye stat'i*, vol. 3, 430–38.

——. "Kul'tura i organizm." Unpublished manuscript.

——. *Kul'tura i vzryv.* Moscow: Gnozis, Publishing Group "Progress," 1992.

——. "Kul'tura kak kollektivnyi intellekt i problemy iskusstvennogo razuma." 1977. In Lotman, *Semiosfera,* 557–67.

——. "Liudi i znaki." 1969. In Lotman, *Semiosfera,* 5–10.

——. "Mozg—tekst—kul'tura—iskusstvennyi intellekt." 1981. In Lotman, *Semiosfera,* 580–89.

——. "O metaiazyke tipologicheskikh opisanii kul'tury." 1968. In Lotman, *Izbrannye stat'i.,* vol. 1, 386–406.

——. "O prirode iskusstva." 1990. In Koshelev, *Iu. M. Lotman i tartusko-moskovskaia semioticheskaia shkola,* 432–38.

——. "O soderzhanii i strukture poniatiia 'khudozhestvennaia literatura.'" 1973. In Lotman, *Izbrannye stat'i,* vol. 1, 203–15.

——. "Ot redaktsii: K probleme prostranstvennoi semiotiki." *Uchenye zapiski Tartuskogo gos. universiteta,* no. 720 (1986) : 3–6. *Trudy po znakovym sistemam* 19: Semiotika prostranstva i prostranstvo semiotiki.

——. "Pamiat' kul'tury." In *Iazyk, Nauka, Filosofiia,* edited by R. I. Pavilionis, 193–204. Vilnius: Akademiia nauk litovskoi SSR, 1986.

——. "Pamiat' v kul'turologicheskom osveshchenii." 1985. In Lotman, *Izbrannye stat'i,* vol. 1, 200–202.

——. *Pis'ma: 1940–1993.* Edited by Boris Egorov. Moscow: Iazyki russkoi kul'tury, 1997.

Lotman, Iurii M. "The Poetics of Everyday Behavior in Eighteenth-Century Russian Culture." 1977. In Lotman, Ginsburg, and Uspenskii, *Semiotics of Russian Cultural History,* 67–94.

Lotman, Iu. M. "Problema znaka i znakovoi sistemy i tipologiia russkoi kul'tury XI–XIX vekov." 1970. In Lotman, *Semiosfera,* 400–417.

——. *Pushkin.* St. Petersburg: Iskusstvo-SPB, 1995.

——. "Pushkin: Ocherk tvorchestva." 1989. In Lotman, *Pushkin,* 187–211.

——. "Pushkin pritiagivaet nas, kak sama zhizn'." 1993. In Koshelev, *Iu. M. Lotman i tartusko-moskovskaia semioticheskaia shkola,* 439–41.

——. "Puti razvitia russkoi prozy 1800–1820-kh gg." 1961. In Lotman, *Karamzin,* 349–417.

——. "Russkii dendizm." In Lotman, *Besedy o russkoi kul'ture,* 123–35.

——. *Semiosfera.* St. Petersburg: Iskusstvo-SPB, 2000.

Lotman, Jurij. *Semiotics of Cinema.* 1973. Translated by Mark E. Suino. Michigan Slavic Contributions, no. 5. Ann Arbor: Department of Slavic Languages and Literature, University of Michigan, 1976.

Lotman, Iurii. "Simvol v sisteme kul'tury." 1987. In Lotman, *Izbrannye stat'i,* vol. 1, 191–99.

——. *Stat'i po tipologii kul'tury.* 1970. In Lotman, *Semiosfera,* 391–459.

Lotman, Jurij. *The Structure of the Artistic Text.* 1970. Translated by Ronald

Vroon. Michigan Slavic Contributions, no. 7. Ann Arbor: Department of Slavic Languages and Literature, University of Michigan, 1977.

Lotman, Iu. M. "Tekst i poliglotism kul'tury." In Lotman, *Izbrannye stat'i*, vol. 1, 142–47.

Lotman, Ju. M. "The Theater and Theatricality as Components of Early Nineteenth-Century Culture." 1973. In Lotman and Uspenskij, *Semiotics of Russian Culture*, 141–64.

Lotman, Iurii. "Theses on the Semiotic Study of Cultures." In *The Tell-Tale Sign: A Survey of Semiotics*, edited by Thomas A. Sebeok, 57–93. Lisse: Peter de Ridder, 1978.

Lotman, Yuri. *Universe of the Mind: A Semiotic Theory of Culture*. Translated by Ann Shukman. Bloomington: Indiana University Press, 1990.

Lotman, Iu. M. "Ustnaia rech' v istoriko-kul'turnoi perspektive." 1978. In Lotman, *Izbrannye stat'i*, vol. 1, 184–90.

———. "Vvedenie: Byt i kul'tura." In Lotman, *Beseda o russkoi kul'ture*, 5–16.

———. "Vospominaniia." In Egorov, *Zhizn' i tvorchestvo Iu. M. Lotmana*, 271–354.

———. "Zhenskii mir." In Lotman, *Besedy o russkoi kul'ture*, 46–74.

———. "Zhenskoe obrazovanie v XVIII–nachale XIX veka." In Lotman, *Besedy o russkoi kul'ture*, 75–88.

Lotman, Iurii M., Lidiia Ia. Ginsburg, and Boris A. Uspenskii. *The Semiotics of Russian Cultural History*. Edited by Alexander D. Nakhimovsky and Alice Stone Nakhimovsky. Ithaca, N.Y.: Cornell University Press, 1985.

Lotman, Iurii M., and Boris A. Uspenskii. "Binary Models in the Dynamics of Russian Culture (to the End of the Eighteenth Century)." 1977. In Lotman, Ginsburg, and Uspenskii, *Semiotics of Russian Cultural History*, 30–66.

Lotman, Iurii, and Iurii Tsiv'ian. *Dialog s ekranom*. Tallinn: Aleksandra, 1994.

Lotman, Ju. M., and B. A. Uspenskij. Authors' introduction. 1984. In Lotman and Uspenskij, *Semiotics of Russian Culture*, ix–xiv.

———. *The Semiotics of Russian Culture*. Edited by Ann Shukman. Michigan Slavic Contributions, no. 11. Ann Arbor: Department of Slavic Languages and Literatures, University of Michigan, 1984.

## Works on Lotman

Alexandrov, Vladimir E. "Biology, Semiosis, and Cultural Difference in Lotman's Semiosphere." *Comparative Literature* 52 (2000): 339–62.

———. "Drugost': Germenevticheskie ukazateli i granitsy interpretatsii." *Voprosy literatury* 6 (2002): 78–102.

Andrews, Edna. *Conversations with Lotman: The Implications of Cultural Semiotics in Language, Literature, and Cognition*. Toronto: University of Toronto Press, 2003.

———. "Lotman's Communication Act and Semiosis." *Semiotica: Journal of the International Association for Semiotic Studies* 126, nos. 1–4 (1999): 1–15.

————. "Text and Culture: Continuous Discontinuity in Lotman and Zamia-tin." *Russian, Croatian and Serbian, Czech and Slovak, Polish Literature* 49, no. 4 (2001): 347–69.

Baevskii, V. S. "Iu. M. Lotman—issledovatel' Pushkina." *Izvestiia Akademii Nauk: Seriia Literatury i Iazyka* 61, no. 6 (2002): 49–56.

Baran, Henryk. "Retseptsiia moskovsko-tartuskoi shkoly v SShA i Velikobritanii." In Nekliudov, *Moskovsko-tartuskaia semioticheskaia shkola*, 246–75.

Bethea, David. "Bakhtinian Prosaics versus Lotmanian 'Poetic Thinking': The Code and Its Relation to Literary Biography." *Slavic and East European Journal* 41, no. 1 (1997): 1–15.

Blaim, Artur. "Lotman in the West: An Ambiguous Complaint." In *Neo-Formalist Papers*, edited by Joe Andrew and Robert Reid, 329–37. Amsterdam: Rodopi, 1998.

Champagne, Roland A. "A Grammar of the Languages of Culture: Literary Theory and Jury M. Lotman's Semiotics." *New Literary History* 9, no. 2 (1978): 205–10.

Crowe, N. J. "Jurij Lotman and the Re-Presentation of Eighteenth-Century Russian Literature." *Russian, Croatian and Serbian, Czech and Slovak, Polish Literature* 36, no. 3 (1994): 277–84.

Eagle, Herbert. "The Semiotics of the Cinema: Lotman and Metz." *Disposition: Revista Hispanica de Semiotica Literaria* 1 (1976): 303–13.

Eco, Umberto. Introduction to *Universe of the Mind*, by Yuri M. Lotman, vii–xiii. Bloomington: Indiana University Press, 1990.

Egorov, B. F. "Iurmikh i Zara." *Zvezda* 2 (2002): 137–42.

————. *Zhizn' i tvorchestvo Iu. M. Lotmana*. Moscow: Novoe literaturnoe obozrenie, 1999.

Gasparov, M. L. "Lotman i marksizm." *Novoe literaturnoe obozrenie* 19 (1993): 7–13.

Grzybek, P. "Bakhtinskaia semiotika i moskovsko-tartuskaia shkola." In *Lotmanovskii sbornik*, 240–59.

Kiseleva, L. N. "Iu. M. Lotman: Ot istorii literatury k semiotike kul'tury (o granitsakh lotmanovskoi semiosfery)." *Studia Russica Helsingiensia et Tartuensia* 6 (1998): 9–21.

————. "Materialy k bibliografii trudov professora Iu. M. Lotmana." In *Sbornik statei k 70-letiiu prof. Iu. M. Lotmana*, 514–65. Tartu: Tartuskii universitet, 1992.

————. "Spisok trudov Iu. M. Lotmana." In Lotman, *Izbrannye stat'i*, vol. 3, 441–82.

Knabe, G. S. "Znak, Istina, Krug (Iu. M. Lotman i problema postmoderna)." In *Lotmanovskii sbornik*, 266–78.

Koshelev, A. D., ed. *Iu. M. Lotman i tartusko-moskovskaia semioticheskaia shkola*. Moscow: Gnozis, 1994.

Kristeva, Julia. "On Yuri Lotman." *PMLA* 109, no. 3 (1994): 375–84.

Kvan, Kim Su. *Osnovnye aspekty tvorcheskoi evoliutsii Iu. M. Lotmana.* Moscow: Novoe literaturnoe obozrenie, 2003.

*Lotmanovskii sbornik.* Vol. 1. Moscow: Its-Garant, 1995.

Mandelker, Amy. "Semiotizing the Sphere: Organicist Theory in Lotman, Bakhtin and Vernadsky." *PMLA* 109, no. 3 (1994): 385–96.

Nekliudov, S. Iu., ed. *Moskovsko-tartuskaia semioticheskaia shkola: Istoriia, vospominaniia, razmyshleniia.* Moscow: Iazyki russkoi kul'tury, 1998.

O'Toole, Michael. "Russian Literary Theory: From the Formalists to Lotman." In *The Routledge Companion to Russian Literature,* edited by Neil Cornwell, 163–73. London: Routledge, 2001.

Pliukhanova, Mariia. "Iurii Lotman on Old Russian Literature and the Eighteenth Century." *Slavonic and East European Review* 72, no. 4 (1994): 60–68.

Reid, Allan. "Who Is Lotman and Why Is Bakhtin Saying Those Nasty Things about Him." *Discours social/Social discourse* 2 (Spring–Summer 1990): 311–24.

Segré, Cesare. "Culture et texte dans la pensée de Iurij M. Lotman." In *Semiosis: Semiotics and the History of Culture,* edited by Morris Halle et al., 3–15. Ann Arbor: Michigan Slavic Publications, 1984.

Seyffert, P. *Soviet Literary Structuralism: Background, Debate, Issues.* Columbus, Ohio: Slavica, 1985.

Shukman, Ann. "The Dialectic of a Semiotician." In *The Sign: Semiotics around the World,* edited by Richard Bailey, L. Matejka, and P. Steiner, 194–206. Ann Arbor: Michigan Slavic Publications, 1978.

———. *Literature and Semiotics: A Study of the Writings of Yu. M. Lotman.* Amsterdam: North-Holland, 1977.

———. "Semiotics of Culture and the Influence of M. M. Bakhtin." In *Issues in Slavic Literary and Cultural Theory,* edited by Karl Eimermacher, Peter Grzybek, and Georg Witte, 193–207. Bochum: Brockmeyer, 1989.

Todd, William Mills, III. "Moscow-Tartu School." In *Routledge Encyclopedia of Philosophy,* edited by Edward Craig, vol. 6, 583–88. London: Routledge, 1998.

Uspenskii, B. A. "Progulki s Lotmanom i vtorichnoe modelirovanie." In *Lotmanovskii sbornik,* 99–127.

Vetik, Raivo. "The Platonism of J. Lotman." *Semiotica: Journal of the International Association for Semiotic Studies* 99, nos. 1–2 (1994): 67–79.

Winner, Irene Portis. "Some Comments upon Lotman's Concepts of Semiotics of Culture: Implications for the Study of Ethnic Culture Texts." In *Semiosis: Semiotics and the History of Culture,* edited by Morris Halle et al., 28–36. Ann Arbor: Michigan Slavic Publications, 1984.

Zenkin, S. "Boi s ten'iu Lotmana Zametki o teorii, 1." *Novoe literaturnoe obozrenie* 53 (2002): 340–47.

Zylko, Boguslaw. "Culture and Semiotics: Notes on Lotman's Conception of Culture." *New Literary History* 32, no. 2 (2001): 391–408.

# CONTRIBUTORS

KATHRYN BABAYAN is an associate professor of Iranian history and culture at the University of Michigan. She specializes in the cultural and social histories of Safavid Iran. She is the author of *Mystics, Monarchs and Messiahs: Cultural Landscapes of Early Modern Iran* (Cambridge: Harvard Middle Eastern Monographs, 2003) and a coauthor of *Slaves of the Shah: New Elites of Safavid Iran*, with Sussan Babaie, Ina Baghdiantz-McCabe, and Massumeh Farhad (London: I. B. Tauris, 2004). Her most recent scholarship on female friendships will appear in *Islamicate Sexualities Studies: Translations across Temporal and Geographical Zones of Desire*, coedited with Afsaneh Najmabadi (Cambridge: Harvard Middle Eastern Monographs, forthcoming).

DAVID BETHEA is the Vilas Research Professor of Slavic Languages at the University of Wisconsin–Madison and professor of Russian studies at the University of Oxford. He is the author or editor of various studies of classical and modern Russian literature, including books on Pushkin, Khodasevich, Brodsky, and the effect on literary form of Russian apocalyptic thinking. His research interests center on Russian poetry, cultural mythology, Russian philosophy and religious thought, and literary biography. At present he is working with Sergei Davydov on a "creative biography" of Pushkin.

JONATHAN H. BOLTON is an assistant professor of Slavic languages and literatures at Harvard University, where he works on Czech and Central European literature of the nineteenth and twentieth centuries. He is currently finishing a book on Czech modernism entitled *Prague between Two Empires: Literary Culture in Interwar Czechoslovakia*.

JULIE A. BUCKLER is professor of Slavic languages and literatures at Harvard University. She works on literature, the arts, and urban culture in imperial Russia. She is the author of *The Literary Lorgnette: Attending Opera in Imperial Russia* (Stanford University Press, 2000) and *Mapping St. Petersburg: Imperial Text and Cityshape* (Princeton University Press, 2005). Her current project is titled *Russian Imperial Masterworks and Their Post-Histories.*

HERBERT EAGLE teaches Russian and East European film and literature at the University of Michigan. He is the editor of *Russian Formalist Film Theory* (1981) and coeditor of the recently republished *Words in Revolution: Russian Futurist Manifestoes, 1912–28* (2005), as well as the author of over forty articles and book chapters, including "Verse as a Semiotic System: Tynjanov, Jakobson, Mukarovsky, Lotman Extended" (1981), "Little Vera's Indexicality and the End of Socialist Realism" (1990), "Color in Kieslowski's Film Trilogy: Blue, White, Red" (1998/99), and "Visual Patterning, Vertical Montage, and Ideological Protest: Eisenstein's Stylistic Legacy to East European Filmmakers" (2001).

CARYL EMERSON is A. Watson Armour III University Professor of Slavic Languages and Literatures at Princeton University, where she chairs the Slavic Department with a co-appointment in comparative literature. She publishes on Pushkin, Tolstoy, Dostoevsky, Russian literary criticism (especially Mikhail Bakhtin), and Russian opera and vocal music.

HELENA GOSCILO, professor of Slavic at the University of Pittsburgh, writes primarily on gender and culture in Russia. The twenty-odd volumes that she has authored or (coedited) include *Dehexing Sex: Russian Womanhood during and after Glasnost* (1996), *Russian Culture in the 1990s* (2000), *Politicizing Magic: An Anthology of Russian and Soviet Fairy Tales* (with M. Balina and M. Lipovetsky, 2005), and *Gender and National Identity in Twentieth Century Russian Culture* (with Andrea Lanoux, 2006). Among her current projects are *Encyclopedia of Contemporary Russian Culture* (with T. Smorodinskaya and K. Evans-Romaine, Routledge 2006), *Poles Apart: Women in Modern Polish Culture* (with Beth Holmgren, *Indiana Slavic Studies* issue, 2006), and *Fade from Red: Screening the Ex-Enemy during the Nineties* (with B. M. Goscilo), which analyzes celluloid images of former Cold War antagonists in American and Russian film of the last fifteen years.

AMY MANDELKER is associate professor of comparative literature at the Graduate Center of the City University of New York. She is the author of books and articles on Russian and European literature and literary theory.

ANDREAS SCHÖNLE is professor of Russian studies at Queen Mary, University of London. He is the author of *Authenticity and Fiction in the Russian Literary Journey* (Harvard University Press, 2000). He just completed a monograph on the politics of landscape design in Russia called *The Ruler in the Garden* and a collective interdisciplinary volume entitled *Ruins of Modernity*. He is currently writing a book on the meaning of ruins in Russian culture.

JEREMY SHINE teaches at the Brandeis-Hillel Day School in San Francisco. He is a Ph.D. candidate in political science at the University of Michigan and his research is on Jewish self-identification in the former Soviet Union.

MAREK STEEDMAN is assistant professor of political science at the University of Southern Mississippi, where he teaches political theory and Southern politics. He is currently at work on a project examining conceptions of race and labor in the post-bellum U.S. South.

WILLIAM MILLS TODD III is Harvard College Professor and Harry Tuchman Levin Professor of Literature at Harvard University. He has written *The Familiar Letter as a Literary Genre in the Age of Pushkin, Fiction and Society in the Age of Pushkin*, and articles on literary theory, sociology of literature, and nineteenth-century Russian literature. He is currently writing a book on the serialization of the novel.

MICHAEL URBAN is professor of politics at the University of California, Santa Cruz, where he teaches courses focusing on politics, culture, and language. His published works include *Russia Gets the Blues: Music, Culture and Community in Unsettled Times* (Cornell University Press, 2004) and *The Rebirth of Politics in Russia* (Cambridge University Press, 1997).

ANDREI ZORIN is professor of Russian, University of Oxford. He is the author of *Kormia dvuglavogo orla* [Feeding the Two-headed Eagle: Russian Literature and State Ideology in Russia in the Last Third of the Eighteenth and First Third of the Nineteenth Centuries] (Novoe Literaturnoe Obozrenie, 2001; 2nd ed. 2004) and of more than one hundred articles on Russian literature and culture.

# INDEX

363

www.ingramcontent.com/pod-product-compliance
Lightning Source LLC
Chambersburg PA
CBHW060324100426
42812CB00003B/876